Intelligence Power in Practice

Series Editors: Richard J. Aldrich, Rory Cormac, Michael S. Goodman, Hugh Wilford and Daniela Richterova

This series explores the full spectrum of spying and secret warfare in a globalised world.

Intelligence has changed. Secret service is no longer just about spying or passively watching a target. Espionage chiefs now command secret armies and legions of cyber warriors who can quietly shape international relations itself. Intelligence actively supports diplomacy, peacekeeping and warfare: the entire spectrum of security activities. As traditional inter-state wars become more costly, covert action, black propaganda and other forms of secret interventionism become more important. This ranges from proxy warfare to covert action; from targeted killing to disruption activity. Meanwhile, surveillance permeates communications to the point where many feel there is little privacy. Intelligence, and the accelerating technology that surrounds it, has never been more important for the citizen and the state.

Titles in the *Intelligence, Surveillance and Secret Warfare* series include:

Published:
The Arab World and Western Intelligence: Analysing the Middle East, 1956–1981
Dina Rezk

The Twilight of the British Empire: British Intelligence and Counter-Subversion in the Middle East, 1948–63
Chikara Hashimoto

Chile, the CIA and the Cold War: A Transatlantic Perspective
James Lockhart

The Clandestine Lives of Colonel David Smiley: Code Name 'Grin'
Clive Jones

The Problem of Secret Intelligence
Kjetil Anders Hatlebrekke

Outsourcing US Intelligence: Private Contractors and Government Accountability
Damien Van Puyvelde

The CIA and the Pursuit of Security: History, Documents and Contexts
Huw Dylan, David Gioe and Michael S. Goodman

Cognitive Bias in Intelligence Analysis: Testing the Analysis of Competing Hypotheses Method
Martha Whitesmith

Defector: Revelations of Renegade Intelligence Officers, 1924–1954
Kevin Riehle

Intelligence Power in Practice
Michael Herman with David Schaefer

Forthcoming:
The Snowden Era on Screen: Signals Intelligence and Digital Surveillance
James Smith

Intelligence, Security and the State: Reviewing the British Intelligence Community in the Twentieth Century
Christopher Murphy and Dan Lomas

Estimative Intelligence in European Foreign Policymaking: Learning Lessons from an Era of Surprise
Christoph Meyer, Michael S. Goodman, Aviva Guttmann, Nikki Ikani and Eva Michaels

British Security Intelligence in Singapore: Counter-Subversion for Southeast Asia, 1939–1963
Alexander Nicholas Shaw

The President's Kill List: Assassination and US Foreign Policy since the Cold War
Luca Trenta

https://edinburghuniversitypress.com/series-intelligence-surveillance-and-secret-warfare.html

Intelligence Power in Practice

Michael Herman with
David Schaefer

EDINBURGH
University Press

Edinburgh University Press is one of the leading
university presses in the UK. We publish academic
books and journals in our selected subject areas across
the humanities and social sciences, combining cutting-
edge scholarship with high editorial and production
values to produce academic works of lasting
importance. For more information visit our website:
edinburghuniversitypress.com

Edinburgh University Press Ltd
The Tun – Holyrood Road
12(2f) Jackson's Entry
Edinburgh EH8 8PJ

Typeset in 11/13 Adobe Sabon by
IDSUK (Dataconnection) Ltd

A CIP record for this book is available from the
British Library

ISBN 978 1 4744 9954 5 (hardback)
ISBN 978 1 4744 9956 9 (webready PDF)
ISBN 978 1 4744 9957 6 (epub)

Contents

Foreword

Coincidentally with my appointment as Cabinet Secretary in 1987, Michael Herman retired from GCHQ and took up a research fellowship at Nuffield College Oxford.

This marked a transition from Michael's active involvement in intelligence work – in addition to his career at GCHQ he had served in the Cabinet Office as Secretary of the Joint Intelligence Committee and in the Defence Intelligence Staff – to academic research into the organisation and use of intelligence. A product of this research was his highly praised book *Intelligence Power in Peace and War* and he has subsequently authored many other papers on aspects of intelligence, some of which are published in this book for the first time.

Michael was also the founding director of the Oxford Intelligence Group, which brought together practitioners and academics to discuss intelligence matters. My post as Cabinet Secretary carried with it at that time the chairmanship of the Permanent Secretaries' Committee on the Intelligence Services and responsibility as Accounting Officer for Government Expenditure on the Secret Vote. In that role I attended and benefited from several events organised by Michael and the Oxford Intelligence Group.

After I retired from the Cabinet Office in 1998 my next involvement with Michael was when he gave very valuable evidence to the Review of Intelligence on Weapons of Mass Destruction, which I chaired in 2004 following the apparent failure of British intelligence on Iraqi WMD in the lead-up to the Second Gulf War. Michael had published his recommendations for the future of the British system of intelligence in 1997 and this was a key issue in our review. Michael's evidence on the role of assessment and the constitution and functioning of the Joint Intelligence Committee played a key part in our review's recommendations, particularly on the development of appropriate training. A transcript of his oral evidence to the committee is published for the first time in this volume.

Michael's career at GCHQ and his subsequent interests have concentrated on the organisation and management of the use of intelligence rather than on the technicalities of collection and decryption. As my 2004 review showed, intelligence, however good, is only as valuable as the way in which it is used. Misuse of it can be disastrously damaging, as illustrated by Stalin's rejection of the intelligence on the build-up to the German invasion of Russia and Freyberg's scepticism about the intelligence he received before the German invasion of Crete in the Second World War.

It is generally acknowledged that the British machinery of the Joint Intelligence Committee and the supporting joint assessment staffs have served the country well over the years. Yet these institutions are not enough by themselves. The assessment and use of intelligence needs the right balance between expertise and experience, and between objectivity and policy awareness; and this balance needs to be recalibrated all the time. It also requires involvement of the right people with the right training and adequate periods in office.

Intelligence has become increasingly important over recent years as the means for collecting it has grown exponentially. It is now generally recognised that future wars, even more than previous wars, will be wars of intelligence – intelligence about the strengths of potential enemies and about their vulnerabilities. It is no good having weapons so accurate that they can land on a postage stamp without knowing which postage stamps to hit and making the right judgements about them. It is also essential to know and understand enough about the mindset of potential enemies to be able to forecast how they are likely to act and react.

As I have reread the papers by Michael Herman in this book, I have been reminded of the crucial importance of the machinery for assessing and making decisions based on intelligence. These papers are a very valuable resource for anyone thinking or teaching about these issues or anyone organising the government machinery for dealing with them.

The Rt Hon. The Lord Butler of Brockwell

Preface

This book is the product of a lifetime spent practising and studying the art of intelligence. It should be read as a final contribution to scholarship by Michael Herman, who died in February 2021 at the age of 91. Michael is perhaps best known as the author of *Intelligence Power in Peace and War*, a landmark study that condensed a wealth of experience and knowledge into what arguably remains – more than a quarter of a century later – the most comprehensive account of intelligence and government in the modern world. This was followed by other publications on secret organisations and history, which confirmed Michael's place as the pre-eminent intelligence professional cum academic. When I first met Michael several years ago, I was therefore surprised to learn that he planned to write yet another book in his late eighties. As he explained to me, his earlier writings were necessarily limited by security obligations, with certain things left unsaid. The steady release of intelligence archives and the commissioning of authorised and official histories in the years since offered him a chance to revisit some issues. There was now greater scope for him to add a few personal impressions to the historical record, elaborating on his view of intelligence as a distinctive form of power exercised by governments.

The result is this collection of essays, which draws together Michael's most substantive writings with some new historical research and reflections from his professional life. These are all shaped by two 'operational' experiences of intelligence amid the high stakes of the Cold War: Michael's career-long focus at GCHQ with tracking and understanding its main target, the Soviet Union; and his engagement with the Joint Intelligence Committee (JIC) as its Secretary from 1972–5, which led to a lifelong interest in the committee and the peculiar service it provides to government. Even the more recent commentaries are grounded in Michael's appreciation of British intelligence as it developed after 1945. In that sense, this book embodies the 'British school' of intelligence studies, a field centred on historical perspective and inquiry, which considered Michael to be its leading figure.

In selecting the chapters Michael and I sought to examine the practice of British intelligence, particularly the form and shape it developed under the competitive pressure of the Cold War. My hope is that this offers a balanced view on intelligence power in action, reflecting insights from the front lines of collection and the centre of government in Whitehall. We had some regret that we could not cover another significant aspect of Michael's career – his involvement in the UK–US intelligence relationship – but this features in the background of many chapters, and we have drawn on relevant scholarship where possible. While perhaps incomplete, Michael saw the result as a 'clearing of the decks' in his late age. He hoped it would be of interest on those terms, and hopefully prompt a younger generation of historians to investigate some issues in more depth than we do here.

Michael originally approached me to provide some research and writing assistance with one chapter, but this developed into a wider partnership, as I drafted and edited sections of text, and advised Michael on some of his newer material. The only part of this book that remained unfinished at the time of Michael's death was this preface. We had disagreed about what to include. Michael characteristically shied away from the suggestion to include more personal reminiscences or elaborate on his life story; he preferred a simple, brief explanation of chapters. His view was that anything more than this would be an indulgence, and risked distracting from ideas in this collection which were informed by conversations with the many unnamed colleagues from his long career. I think it is fair to say that Michael's impressive body of scholarship – more than a dozen articles and books published after his retirement from GCHQ – suggests he was being unduly modest about the value of his own contribution.

While respecting Michael's wishes, I do want to mention one feature of his personality that will not be apparent to the reader. Michael had a rare kind of intellectual humility for someone of his vast learning and experience. Behind the towering reputation was a generosity of spirit that made him such a warmly regarded presence at academic forums. Even at an advanced age he displayed an almost-youthful enthusiasm for the work of others, and this did much to encourage younger researchers, such as myself, who would otherwise feel intimidated in his presence. He was a true gentleman and role model who inspired many in his small acts of kindness as much as in his pioneering writings. It was thus a great joy to work with him on this project, and I am consoled that he knew it was going to be published before he died. As I was tasked with one final edit of the collection after Michael's death, any errors of fact or omissions are my responsibility and mine alone.

The book is divided into four sections. The first section includes an interview Michael conducted with Mark Phythian from the *Intelligence and National Security* journal, which covers the broad outlines of his career: how he joined GCHQ, and migrated into academia later in life. This is followed by a historical study which explores the transition in Britain from the absolute secrecy of intelligence in the post-war years to greater democratic scrutiny by the time of his retirement, spurred by the revelations of Enigma and other codebreaking exploits. There are also two republished articles: one on GCHQ's controversial de-unionisation episode, which forced an unprecedented degree of public exposure on his employer; and a second on the ethical challenges of intelligence after the end of the Cold War, as Michael grappled with the new demands on secret agencies operating in a globalised world.

The second section of this book concentrates on Cold War intelligence. Two republished chapters constitute Michael's attempt to answer a question which lingered for many professionals of his generation: amid the various successes and setbacks for espionage what, if anything, was the wider effect on the history of the Cold War? These are followed by four chapters which detail various aspects of the 'intelligence war' which Michael experienced first-hand. These deal with the unique experience of GCHQ in Western intelligence, the national system which developed to guide and allocate British intelligence resources, the post-war craft of radio interception which predominated in the early years of Cold War signals intelligence, and the evolving needs and unresolved challenges which led to the construction of Teufelsberg, a listening station in West Berlin, which remains to this day as a symbol of the intelligence war between East and West.

The third section addresses the organisational issues which Michael explored later in life as an academic. It begins with his republished studies of the 1945 proposals for an intelligence machine in peacetime Britain, and the British intelligence community in the aftermath of the Cold War. Both chapters demonstrate Michael's long-standing concern with analytical professionalism in Britain's decentralised intelligence community. The need for more specialised training to enhance national assessment was made forcefully in his testimony to the Butler inquiry in 2004, which is declassified for the first time in this book. Michael's evidence to this inquiry is followed by a republished article of his examining Butler's report. The final chapter in this section offers a reflection on Britain's assessment machinery ten years after the Butler reforms, and notes with concern the challenge of continually nurturing expertise in the centre of government.

The fourth and final section explores the neglected role of personality in intelligence history. Issues of personnel – recruitment, training and management – are a recurring theme in this book; Michael wanted to stress the influence of individual personality on the performance of British intelligence. Two republished papers discuss the role of 'flair' in GCHQ's recruitment, and the civil service professionalism which he encountered during his time as JIC Secretary in the Cabinet Office. These are followed by three chapters which offer a portrait of the JIC members in the 1970s when Michael was its Secretary, the Directors of GCHQ in the first half of his career, and the contribution of his GCHQ colleague, Harry Burke, to understanding the Able Archer war scare of 1983. A final, revised study recounts the influence of Mike MccGwire, one of Michael's early friends at GCHQ, who left an outstanding impression on British naval intelligence, and to whom Michael wanted to pay tribute.

We were assisted by a number of people in assembling this collection, and I would like to record our thanks to Michael's friends and associates who helped him in the last years of his life. Unfortunately, Michael had only begun to compile a list of names but I know that he was particularly grateful to Steve Dawes,

Gwilym Hughes and Peter Hennessy. The late Ralph Erskine helped to expand our study of the history of wartime codebreaking, with expert precision and detailed notes. Lord Butler of Brockwell provided a most generous foreword for which we are deeply appreciative. Elliott Finn at Taylor & Francis kindly supported us in securing permission to republish some of Michael's earlier works. Ersev Ersoy at EUP was an enthusiastic recipient of the book proposal and, together with Sarah Foyle, Joannah Duncan and Geraldine Lyons, she guided me through the editorial process after Michael passed away. Richard Aldrich was a source of considerate and generous support, who was always happy to offer his assistance and feedback. Mike Goodman was, as usual, a wonderful source of advice: it was Mike's idea to connect me with Michael as the idea for this book first took shape. Together Richard and Mike helped to shepherd the manuscript to press.

The final name on Michael's list is that of his wife, Ann, who offered him loving support and sensible counsel for so many decades. I should like to extend my own gratitude to Ann for her kindness these last few years. Together with Michael she provided my wife Jasmina and I with generous hospitality in the early days of this project. Her encouragement also helped me to finish this book after the sad news of Michael's death. I would also like to mention the wonderful support I received from Jasmina. Along with Ann, she bore with great patience the working routine Michael and I established: regular, not-so-productive 'business' meetings over lunch, and a long, meandering correspondence about draft chapters where I took the opportunity to question him at length about intelligence history. That Michael and I managed to produce a book in the end is largely because it was a collective effort between our two families.

Finally, I would like to record my appreciation for Michael as a co-author, mentor and friend in the twilight of his extraordinary life. It is with great pride and fond memories that I dedicate this book to his legacy.

David Schaefer
June 2021

PART I

Secrecy and Liberal Society

I   Profiles in Intelligence: An Interview with Michael Herman[1]

[2017]

Michael Herman is a pioneer of the academic study of intelligence. His career spans the worlds of intelligence and academia in the United Kingdom, and has done much to bring the two closer together. Born in 1929, Michael was educated at Scarborough High School before securing a scholarship to read Modern History at Queen's College Oxford, in 1946. His studies there were interrupted by two years' National Service between 1947 and 1949, when Michael served in the Intelligence Corps in Egypt. He then returned to Oxford to complete his studies and was awarded a first class degree. In 1952 he joined the Government Communications Headquarters (GCHQ) based in Cheltenham, where he was to remain in a succession of roles until 1987, a period that also included secondments to the Cabinet Office, as Secretary of the Joint Intelligence Committee, and to the Defence Intelligence Staff.

On his retirement from GCHQ in 1987, Michael moved to Nuffield College Oxford, initially as a Gwilym Gibbon Research Fellow, and it was here that he began to work on what would become his landmark study of intelligence organisations, roles and effects, *Intelligence Power in Peace and War*. This was published by Cambridge University Press and the Royal Institute of International Affairs in 1996. On publication, Professor Christopher Andrew called it: 'the best overview of the nature and role of intelligence that I have read. It is surely destined to become a standard work.' This was a prescient comment, as *Intelligence Power* quickly established itself as a key reference point for all those seeking to study the nature, roles and impact of intelligence as a state function, influencing a whole generation of academics drawn to its study.

Michael has continued to publish regularly and promote the study of intelligence ever since. He was the founding Director of the Oxford Intelligence Group, which provided a valuable space in which to discuss intelligence and played a role in bringing together practitioners and academics. His recommendations for the future of the British system of intelligence appeared in 1997 as a Centre for Defence Studies publication and elsewhere. He gave evidence to the Butler review of intelligence into weapons of mass destruction in the wake of the 2003 invasion of Iraq which influenced the review group's recommendations around improving professional intelligence standards and training. A collection of his academic articles was published as *Intelligence Services in the Information Age: Theory and Practice* by Frank Cass in 2001. More recently he has co-edited and contributed to a special issue of *Intelligence and National Security*, subsequently published as a book, *Intelligence in the Cold War: What Difference Did It Make?* This collection posed key questions about the role of intelligence in the conflict that had dominated Michael's career in intelligence and reflected his deep interest in intelligence history and firm belief that theory needs to be grounded in thorough historical research.

Apart from his lengthy associateship at Nuffield, he has been an Honorary Departmental Fellow in the Department of International Politics at Aberystwyth University and a Senior Associate Fellow of St Antony's College Oxford, and he has had other professional relationships elsewhere at home and abroad. In 2005, Michael was made an Honorary Doctor of Letters by the University of Nottingham and in June 2016 he received the Lifetime Achievement Award from the International Association for Intelligence Education.

What follows is the edited transcript of an interview conducted with Michael Herman at Nuffield College Oxford on 10 March 2016.

MARK PHYTHIAN: Your book, *Intelligence Power in Peace and War*, is a landmark work in the study of intelligence. Can I begin by asking you how and why you came to write it?

MICHAEL HERMAN: When I finished reading history here in Oxford in 1952 I was torn between trying to be an academic and going into the Civil Service. Then GCHQ offered a job interview via my tutor, John Prestwich, a medieval historian who had been a distinguished member of wartime Bletchley Park. GCHQ were starting to recruit cadets as 'managerial types' rather than potential technical experts, and Prestwich suggested that I should apply. This innovation in GCHQ's recruitment may have owed something to (Sir) Eric Jones who became its Director in 1952. He had originally left school at fifteen and established his own company in the wool trade, and was very much a managerially inclined, non-specialist leader. So two of us were recruited as the new, and controversial, 'managerial types'. We had an unhappy first year; the other chap left, I realised that I did not have Sigint's professional talents, and I was all set to come back to Oxford at the end of my first year. However, I was given a more interesting job, and had started playing for the office rugby team, and I decided to stay. So there was an element of accident about it, but I had a thoroughly enjoyable career and have no regrets about it. Among the interesting jobs I did was to be Secretary of the Joint Intelligence Committee (JIC) in the Cabinet Office in London in 1972–5; and a few years later I was put in charge of our Soviet and Warsaw Pact Division, running nearly 1,000 people in Cheltenham and half our collection resources worldwide, and with all the American and other foreign contacts this entailed: the sort of job you dream about. I did it for five years, and other jobs afterwards. But from my Cabinet Office tour I had got interested in the intelligence community as a whole and the big questions about it, and had developed a hankering to think and write about it academically, and this became my retirement.

MARK PHYTHIAN: During the period when you were rising up the ranks at GCHQ was there an intelligence literature that you could draw on?

MICHAEL HERMAN: No, we didn't read books. For most of the time there was little serious intelligence literature. The first volume of Hinsley's official history of intelligence in the Second World

War was published in 1979[2] and others followed soon afterwards, but these were late in the day as far as I was concerned, and the prevailing attitude anyway was that intelligence books were dangerous and discouraged. The institutional wisdom of past experience was passed down inside the organisation, so we learned something about wartime Bletchley and its successes. But for most of my time there was no serious literature and no particular reason for looking for it.

MARK PHYTHIAN: It wasn't encouraged?

MICHAEL HERMAN: On the whole, not. The highly classified wartime histories were of course available, but locked away in cupboards: and who could spend his working hours delving into past history? When I was running the Soviet effort I tried to get people to read more of the published Western literature about Soviet military forces, but even this was not altogether straightforward when, until 1983, GCHQ was still supposed to be doing something quite different. Part of the culture of secrecy in any case is that the office is something that you leave behind when you go home.

MARK PHYTHIAN: What you did after retirement from GCHQ was a radical departure at the time. It certainly wasn't the norm to make this transition from practitioner to academic commentator, so you were a trailblazer in a way?

MICHAEL HERMAN: Yes, I was, and I was a fortunate trailblazer, because the senior members of GCHQ who had to deal with my academic plans had all worked for me and were personal friends, and they did all they could to let me do what I wanted. It was all carefully documented in an agreement with the Cabinet Office that I would submit everything for official clearance, and a result was that what I wrote had to be academic stuff with very little personal element. Having been involved at times in discouraging potential intelligence authors I was familiar with the official sensitivities, so there were few problems about clearance for what I submitted. But I was lucky: all those involved could have been much more difficult, particularly since Mrs Thatcher through the 1980s was taking a strong line against all intelligence publications.

MARK PHYTHIAN: So you have now left GCHQ and you are working on what will become *Intelligence Power in Peace and War* from 1987 onwards. At this point is there a literature out there that you draw on that inspires you, because one of the notable things about the book is the way in which you combine literatures on military history, strategic studies, international relations and public administration. What were the key things that influenced you at the time?

MICHAEL HERMAN: There was certainly good intelligence history.[3] Chris Andrew was already publishing;[4] the Hinsley official histories were becoming available; R. V. Jones had produced his account of wartime technical intelligence.[5] What is now the academic London Study Group was meeting from around 1982 or 1983. (I remember that while still working I wanted to go to one of their first conferences, and met with a quite passionate appeal from my security colleague not to let the side down by going.) On intelligence's political science and international relations aspects there was less available, but there were the American books of the 1970s and 1980s on warning failure and World War II deception, based on the much earlier study of Pearl Harbor[6] and fuelled of course by the Cold War's constant worry of warning failure of a Soviet attack.

MARK PHYTHIAN: I guess that in the US there would have been an emerging literature on oversight and accountability, but that would have been outside your focus?

MICHAEL HERMAN: Yes. Loch Johnson was already producing his studies of American intelligence's legality and accountability,[7] but I consciously decided to avoid such issues. There was no guarantee that I would get approval for publishing anything, and adding these to the issues discussed would increase the hazards. They were also not as prominent as they became later: the British community had not acquired its full legal status, and as a country we had not yet acquired the American fixation with problems of legality and oversight. With hindsight it was a major omission from the book, but perhaps I was really not sufficiently interested. My interests were (perhaps still are) those of a large-scale production manager who worries about making his product as accurate and useful as possible, and not those of a liberal lawyer.

MARK PHYTHIAN: So, the production of the book, from moving to Oxford and beginning to think about it, to actually publishing the book, was a period of eight or nine years?

MICHAEL HERMAN: Yes. I was worried for a long time that as an academic, or quasi-academic, I ought to be producing theory and didn't seem to be doing so. I now think of the book as a thoughtful textbook, but that originally seemed too prosaic. But it took shape eventually, helped by invitations to talk about intelligence in Oxford and elsewhere. The fact that I was based on Nuffield College for most of this work was also fortunate. For my first year the college gave me a fellowship originally created for civil servants in mid-career – far removed from my situation – and it was subsequently generous with an associate membership. I also had a later spell running seminars at St Antony's which developed into the Oxford Intelligence Group that still continues at Nuffield. Apart from anything else the Nuffield connection in the early days acted as an indication of respectability, at a time when any insider trying to write about intelligence would be suspected of being a whistleblower. The book itself was also positively backed by Chatham House, through Admiral Jim Eberle,[8] whom I had met in my GCHQ days and was running it in his retirement, and his deputy John Roper.[9] In their support for the book they were keen on convening an invited Chatham House study group to comment on draft chapters as they were written. The idea was put to the Foreign Office for comment – a reminder of the period's sensitivities – and encountered objections, and eventually John Roper accepted the condition that no current or retired intelligence practitioners would be invited. So it was an odd body for its purpose, made up substantially of former diplomats who had been users of intelligence but not producers. In practice it was useful to have the drafts picked over in this way by the great and the good, particularly by the brilliant but acerbic Reginald Hibbert.[10] I had hitherto thought that I was reasonably adept with bureaucratic prose and intelligence reports, but his comments made me decide I needed to develop a new style of writing.

MARK PHYTHIAN: The book was published in 1996 and it appeared in the midst of the post-Cold War debate about the future of intelligence and whether or not there should be a peace dividend that extended to intelligence. So the intelligence landscape has changed an awful lot from 1996 to the present day. How would you characterise the nature and extent of the changes to intelligence, as either a function or a set of practices, between then and now?

MICHAEL HERMAN: One major change has of course been the major technical source of material on the internet, which didn't exist in my day. More important, perhaps, have been the changes in targets, above all the priority for counterterrorism and its targets of individual *people* and not *things*. It must be so different from our old concentration on Soviet military forces and their weapons. I suppose the other big change since the 1990–1 Iraqi War has been the extensive support for active military operations: intelligence for war rather than peace. I guess that this, like counterterrorism, has had a much bigger tactical component than was usual in my day, when field units were mainly reporting back to the centre and the effects on decisions were at the London level. What the Russians were doing was rarely of immediate tactical concern, but contributed to the strategic picture of Soviet intentions and capabilities. Post-1990 support for military operations must involve more devolution towards the front line, and the same must be true of counterterrorist support to the police. Yet central government gets involved in tactical decisions as well as strategic ones, so the whole thing has to be a carefully orchestrated balance between the field and the centre. The other difference, of course, is the huge change in intelligence's legal situation and public *persona*, which were so different in my experience. Ministerial approval for some things was then taken seriously – as seriously as it is taken now – but for our attitudes to it I treasure a colleague's description of it in counterterrorism as 'the procedures designed to turn our sprint into a hurdle race'.

MARK PHYTHIAN: And from a foreign intelligence perspective, boundaries were much clearer in the Cold War era, whereas boundaries are much more indistinct and permeable post-Cold War?

MICHAEL HERMAN: I guess so. Of course not everything was part of the Cold War, and there was competition from very different targets. I recall our problem in the Cabinet Office when Sir Leonard Hooper arrived as Intelligence Coordinator and in revising the JIC's annual guidance sought to specify whether the highest priority target was the huge Soviet Union or the relatively tiny IRA. He eventually put them as equal priority. It is the sort of question that still interests me: what are these intelligence formalities designed to achieve and what difference do they actually make?

MARK PHYTHIAN: One other transformation involves the *extent* to which intelligence is truly global now, whereas big states invested in it heavily during the Cold War, but not everyone did in any large way.

MICHAEL HERMAN: Yes, every country now has a security organisation of some kind and I imagine that for many of them the prime requirement is to keep the regime in power. Even if this is not the case the primacy of counterterrorism must have changed the shape of national intelligence everywhere, including the balance inside it. Until recently almost all our JIC chairmen were Foreign Office or ex-Foreign Office officials, but the last two have come from elsewhere. In this same period two former Directors General of the Security Service have recently been rewarded in retirement with promotion to the House of Lords, a sign of the part of modern intelligence that most counts.

MARK PHYTHIAN: And in many ways the 11 September 2001 terrorist attacks are the pivot. You published an article on these in the following year, which posed the question '11 September:

Legitimizing Intelligence?' How far, in retrospect, do you think it did and in what ways, and why was there a need to legitimise intelligence? The title seemed to suggest that in 2001 there was a question of legitimacy, which may have been the post-Cold War debate about whether that scale of operation was necessary?

MICHAEL HERMAN: I think I assumed that 9/11 would eliminate the debate about intelligence methods and individual liberty: at bottom, perhaps, a debate whether this particular counterterrorist campaign is war or policing. As you'd expect I tend to think of it as a variant of war, but I am critical of the international lawyers who have failed to develop proper concepts for this sort of conflict. It must worry intelligence's current practitioners. In my experience the job takes on a different hue when people feel they are saving lives. This applied to the national effort against the IRA, and also to our GCHQ involvement in the Falklands War, when the full-time effort involved was relatively small in numbers but somehow transformed the whole department with the psychology of war and not peace. It must be difficult for people nowadays to have a constant eye on what the lawyers will allow them to do. This leads me to add that I would like someone to do a follow-up to my comments in *Intelligence Power* on the effects of secrecy on people and organisations: what's special about secret organisations and the people in them? Some years ago, the CIA commissioned an anthropologist to study this,[11] but otherwise it has not been looked at in any detail, and I would like to see it properly tackled.

MARK PHYTHIAN: And what's the answer?

MICHAEL HERMAN: The answer I suggested in the book was that secrecy makes for high morale. Even in my time people at GCHQ felt a sense of difference, of being secret and somehow 'special'. In fact it was dealing largely with peace and not war, but in the background there was always the risk of the nuclear war which we felt we were there to prevent. GCHQ tried hard to behave as a normal government department, but most people did not embrace the image of the conventional civil servant and preferred to think that they were 'different' (as indeed they were). A downside was of course that the idea of 'difference' could produce unrealistically high expectations which could turn into powerful disappointments if they were not realised amid the normal rough-and-tumble of organisational management: some of the reactions to GCHQ's de-unionisation in 1984 probably fell into this category.

MARK PHYTHIAN: Thinking about national systems in terms of concentric circles, as you do in *Intelligence Power in Peace and War*, seems to me to still offer a very good way of approaching comparative analysis. Could you explain that idea and how the detail of the different circles might look today?

MICHAEL HERMAN: I was baffled for a long time about how one should write about types of organisations in academic terms, when the individual examples are so variable in form, effectiveness and everything else. I read bits of Weber about 'ideal types' and dabbled in other organisational writers, but the idea of the three concentric circles was the only way I could find of describing what I was doing. But what I wrote was still very UK–US centred. I hope for example that someone will soon come up with a competing concept of European 'continental intelligence'; and this might only be a start for developing other cultural and regional models.

MARK PHYTHIAN: There has been considerable discussion of the European Union as an intelligence actor. In your view, what are the possibilities and limitations regarding an EU intelligence role? Is this something we should welcome?

MICHAEL HERMAN: Sigint has certainly produced the exclusivity of the Five Eyes alliance. World War II was fought by a multinational alliance but intelligence remained a UK–US prerogative, substantially because of the Bletchley dimension, as in the exclusion of the exiled French and Polish governments from all its output. In the Cold War, the Soviet espionage threat produced the similar barrier in NATO between the top-drawer, CANUKUS intelligence product and all the lower-category material; and much of this seems to have continued afterwards. At the top level I am disappointed that there hasn't been a NATO JIC or something of the kind. It is strange that the Americans, Canadians and Australians contribute to some JIC assessments and attend appropriate parts of the meetings, and yet France, Germany, also Japan – the big powers – are almost totally excluded. Though I understand the practical reasons, it's a pity that a European forum of some kind hasn't emerged – in response to the Ukrainian situation, for example.

MARK PHYTHIAN: One of your key areas of interest has been the role of intelligence in the Cold War. You have highlighted one easily overlooked intelligence contribution to a peaceful outcome – the way in which intelligence provided reassurance. Would you say this was ultimately the most important contribution of intelligence in the Cold War?

MICHAEL HERMAN: I think it was important. The psychology of the Cold War on both sides was so fertile for exaggeration that anything that brought the threat assessments towards reality was helpful. In two chapters in our recent Cold War book[12] I argued that Western intelligence reassured its governments that the feared Soviet attack was not about to be launched, but that it also scared the Soviet leadership by the intrusive collection methods it employed to get this intelligence before the American satellite photography became available.

MARK PHYTHIAN: Western intelligence assessments of Soviet military strength came to be quite accurate as the Cold War evolved.

MICHAEL HERMAN: Yes, and even in the earlier days they could have been worse. It is often written that the West was virtually blind through the 1950s, yet even then it did well in reconstructing the complete Soviet order of battle. One wonders what conclusions governments would have reached about the threat if these estimates had not been available. Nevertheless, the sources at that time were still mainly inferential, non-textual ones that lacked the insights that come from access to documents, messages and conversations. From the non-textual sources it was concluded that the peacetime Soviet army was made up of 170 divisions, without realising for a long time that most of them were skeleton formations to be manned on mobilisation. I argued in *Intelligence Power* that most intelligence sources can be divided into textual and non-textual ones, with the former tending to be the richer; and at this stage of the Cold War the non-textual ones predominated. Subsequently of course the whole picture was enriched when the American imagery became available and the targets for the first time could be seen and measured, and the data played against what was known from the other sources. Intelligence on the Soviet forces acquired a depth and confidence that it had not had previously.

MARK PHYTHIAN: At the same time, the question of Soviet intentions remained quite opaque. Was this a serious shortcoming or was it unrealistic to expect intelligence to be able to deliver on this?

MICHAEL HERMAN: It certainly was a serious shortcoming that there was never a clear answer to the question posed at the beginning of an early JIC report:[13] 'What is Russia trying to do?' But did the tightly drawn, conspiratorial Soviet regime ever define its long-term objectives realistically, beyond survival? Does any government? Yet the Soviet system wrote things down, and a top-level defector or access to central documents, or a combination of both, would have provided better access than intelligence obtained. It was its bad luck that it never managed this kind of access, but against the power of Soviet secrecy this was hardly a culpable failure. Intelligence was guessing like everyone else, and deducing Soviet intentions from the scale of its capabilities; though I suspect that a particular weakness of the Whitehall system was that those who were writing the Soviet estimates did not have full access to the Western action being taken against the USSR, principally by the Americans: the intrusive intelligence flights, the penetrations of territorial waters, the maritime cable-tapping, the extensive information warfare, and of course the conclusion drawn from them of Western motives. If assessments are seeing things through the target's eyes, those writing them need all the information it draws on, and those doing the job in Whitehall probably lacked some of it.

MARK PHYTHIAN: You have also posed the key question relating to intelligence and the Cold War: 'what difference did it make?' How would you answer this question now?

MICHAEL HERMAN: Ducking the question slightly, you need studies of comparative Cold War psychology on both sides, which I don't think exist. We thought the Cold War was all-pervading to an extent that is forgotten now, because the war never happened and we now think there was not much sustained risk of it. Yet war breaks out in the unexpected circumstances, and I suggest that intelligence in this period made the West's actions more rational, less error-prone than they might have been. I have no idea whether Soviet intelligence worked in any comparable way within the regime of which it was such an integral part. Those are my answers, but the historians need to work properly at the questions.

MARK PHYTHIAN: And there were, of course, individual episodes in the Cold War where the role of intelligence, particularly in some cases British intelligence, may have been crucial. Len Scott's piece on Able Archer '83[14] highlights one, for example.

MICHAEL HERMAN: My friend Harry Burke had been my deputy in GCHQ's Soviet Division and chief Soviet expert; I much respected his expertise and had worked for two or three years to get him made my deputy. After the appearance of the Nicoll Report on the JIC's warning failures[15] and the experience of the Falklands War, Sir Antony Duff as Intelligence Coordinator got Harry drafted to the Committee's Assessments Staff in 1982 to boost its warning performance, and it was really he who subsequently discovered the Able Archer scare of November 1983. Oleg Gordievsky had told London of the KGB's intelligence alert, but it was Harry who looked at the technical intelligence reports of the time and noticed signs of a Soviet military alert, though spotty ones. He had to fight to get his conclusion through a sceptical JIC, but the Committee's eventual report on it had its effect on UK and US governments' attitudes.

MARK PHYTHIAN: You gave evidence to the Butler Review[16] established in the wake of the 2003 invasion of Iraq and controversy over the case for war, particularly in relation to weapons of mass destruction. What would you say are the key lessons of the Iraq episode for intelligence collectors, analysts and managers, and for politicians?

MICHAEL HERMAN: This was the only time I seriously went public. It was in a *Panorama* programme about it. Judging whether Saddam had operational WMD in 2002–3 was exactly the same as deciding in 1959–61 whether the West was then threatened with operational Soviet missiles. I was asked to give evidence to the Butler Committee,[17] and I suggested to them that they should not worry about the JIC itself but concentrate on the subsidiary Current Intelligence Groups where the judgements are formulated; and I recommended some training for this top level of assessment. This was taken seriously and some serious training has been introduced. But I also pointed out that the aim of creating the Assessments Staff in 1968 had been to make assessment more 'professional', and this had not happened: the main weight has been borne instead by secondments from policy departments. Altering this situation needs changes in the careers and status of the analysts in the Defence Intelligence Staff and the creation of a bigger analyst class, and on these little has happened. So we have the oddity that the product of our highly professional intelligence community still depends substantially for its assessment for top government on policy officials seconded for single intelligence tours.

MARK PHYTHIAN: What would you say are the key areas where we still need to improve our knowledge and understanding of intelligence? What are the most important gaps that scholars should be looking to fill?

MICHAEL HERMAN: There are so many avenues for exploration, but I'll limit myself to two of them. One is to make intelligence studies properly worldwide, to understand for example how it is that the British and Chinese have very different intelligence organisations in their different settings, yet both are felt to have an activity in common. The other is to develop links with other parts of public administration, particularly with studies of governments' other knowledge systems. I am struck for example by the parallels in the evolution and organisation of intelligence and government statistics, and I hope people will develop comparisons of this kind.

MARK PHYTHIAN: Thank you very much for your time.

Notes

1. Originally published as Phythian, M. 'Profiles in intelligence: an interview with Michael Herman', *Intelligence and National Security* 32, no. 1, 2017: 1–8, reprinted by permission of Taylor & Francis Ltd: http://www.tandfonline.com. An accompanying introduction by Loch Johnson is available on the journal website at: https://www.tandfonline.com/doi/abs/10.1080/02684527.2016.1199528
2. Hinsley, F. H with E. E. Thomas, C. F. G. Ransom and R. C. Knight, *British Intelligence in the Second World War: Its Influence on Strategy and Operations. Volume 1* (London: HMSO, 1979).
3. *Intelligence and National Security* first appeared in 1986, co-edited by Christopher Andrew and Michael Handel.
4. For example, Andrew, C. and D. Dilks (eds), *The Missing Dimension: Governments and Intelligence Communities in the Twentieth Century* (London: Macmillan, 1984); Andrew, C., *Secret Service: The Making of the British Intelligence Community* (London: William Heinemann, 1985).
5. Jones, R. V., *Most Secret War: British Scientific Intelligence 1939–1945* (London: Hamish Hamilton, 1978).
6. Wohlstetter, R., *Pearl Harbor: Warning and Surprise* (Stanford, CA: Stanford University Press, 1962).
7. For example, Johnson, L., *A Season of Inquiry: The Senate Intelligence Investigation* (Lexington: University of Kentucky Press, 1985).
8. Admiral Sir James Eberle, GCMG (1927–2018), formerly Commander-in-Chief Fleet and Commander-in-Chief Home Command.
9. Lord Roper of Thorney Island (1935–2016) was a Labour Party MP from 1970 who defected to the newly formed Social Democratic

Party in 1981, serving as a SDP MP and the party's Chief Whip until 1983. After leaving the House of Commons he took up a senior staff role at the Royal Institute of International Affairs (Chatham House) in 1984. He was created a life peer in 2000.

10. Sir Reginald Hibbert (1922–2002) served in the Special Operations Executive during the Second World War before joining the Foreign Service where he held numerous posts, culminating in his appointment as Ambassador to France. After retiring, in 1982 he became director of the Ditchley Park Foundation. His notable lecture on 'Intelligence and Policy', given in Oxford in 1989, was published in *Intelligence and National Security* 5, no. 1, 1990: 110–28.

11. Johnson, R., *Analytic Culture in the US Intelligence Community* (Washington, DC: Center for the Study of Intelligence, 2005).

12. Herman, M. and G. Hughes (eds), *Intelligence in the Cold War: What Difference did it Make?* (Abingdon: Routledge, 2013).

13. *Russian Interests, Intentions and Capabilities*, JIC(48)9(O)Final, 23 July 1948, London: India Office Library and Records, L/WS/1/1173 (now in the British Library), first paragraph of Annex I, the summary.

14. Scott, L., 'Intelligence and the Risk of Nuclear War: Able Archer-83 Revisited', *Intelligence and National Security* 26, no. 6, 2011: 759–77. Reprinted in Herman and Hughes (eds), *Intelligence in the Cold War*.

15. See Goodman, M., 'Avoiding Surprise: The Nicoll Report and Intelligence Analysis', in R. Dover and M. Goodman (eds), *Learning from the Secret Past: Cases in British Intelligence History* (Washington, DC: Georgetown University Press, 2011), pp. 265–92.

16. *Review of Intelligence on Weapons of Mass Destruction: Report of a Committee of Privy Counsellors* (London: The Stationery Office, 2004).

17. See Chapter 13 in this collection, 'Evidence to Butler'.

Michael Herman: A Select Bibliography

1989. 'Intelligence and the Assessment of Military Capabilities: Reasonable Sufficiency or the Worst Case?', *Intelligence and National Security* 4, no. 4: 765–99.

1991. 'Intelligence and Policy: A Comment', *Intelligence and National Security* 6, no. 1: 229–39.

1992. 'Intelligence Warning of the Occupation of the Falklands: Some Organisational Issues', in Alex Danchev (ed.), *International Perspectives on the Falklands Conflict* (London: Macmillan), pp. 153–64.

1995. 'Assessment Machinery: British and American Models', *Intelligence and National Security* 10, no. 4: 13–33.

1996. *Intelligence Power in Peace and War* (Cambridge: Cambridge University Press/Royal Institute of International Affairs).

1997. *British Intelligence Towards the Millennium: Issues and Opportunities*, Centre for Defence Studies Paper No. 38 (London: Brassey's for the Centre for Defence Studies).

1997. 'Up from the Country: Cabinet Office Impressions 1972–75', *Contemporary British History* 11, no. 1: 83–97.

1998. 'Cold War Naval Intelligence', in Ken Booth (ed.), *Statecraft and Security: The Cold War and Beyond* (Cambridge: Cambridge University Press), pp. 93–8.

1998. 'Diplomacy and Intelligence', *Diplomacy and Statecraft* 9, no. 2: 1–22.

1999. 'Intelligence Services and Ethics in the New Millennium', *Irish Studies in International Affairs* 10: 249–65.

2001. *Intelligence Services in the Information Age: Theory and Practice* (London: Frank Cass).

2001. 'Modern Intelligence Services; Have They a Place in Ethical Foreign Policies?', in Harold Shukman (ed.), *Agents for Change: Intelligence Services in the Twenty-First Century* (London: St Ermin's Press), pp. 287–311.

2001. *The Role of the British Joint Intelligence Committee: An Historical Perspective*. In Lars Christian Jenssen (ed.), *Proceedings of the XXVI International Colloquium of Military History on Intelligence after World War II*, August 2000 (Oslo: Norwegian Institute for Defence Studies), pp. 25–39.

2002. '11 September: Legitimizing Intelligence?', *International Relations* 16, no. 2: 227–41.

2003. 'Counter-terrorism, Information Technology and Intelligence Change', *Intelligence and National Security* 18, no. 4: 40–58.

2003. 'Intelligence Doctrine for International Peace Support', in Ben de Jong, Wies Platje and Robert David Steele (eds), *Peacekeeping Intelligence: Emerging Concepts for the Future* (Oakton, VA: OSS International Press), pp. 157–70.

2003. 'Intelligence's Future: Learning from the Past', *Journal of Intelligence History* 3, no. 2: 1–8.

2003. 'Threat Assessments and the Legitimation of Policy?', *Intelligence and National Security* 18, no. 3: 174–8.

2004. 'Ethics and Intelligence after September 2001', *Intelligence and National Security* 19, no. 2: 342–358.

2004. 'Intelligence and the Iraqi Threat: British Joint Intelligence after Butler', *RUSI Journal* 149, no. 4 August: 18–24.

2007. '"The Customer is King": Intelligence Requirements in Britain', in Loch K. Johnson (ed.), *Strategic Intelligence, Volume 2: The Intelligence Cycle* (Westport, CT: Praeger Security International), pp. 165–80.

2011. 'Intelligence as Threats and Reassurance', *Intelligence and National Security* 26, no. 6: 791–817.

2011. 'The Post-War Organization of Intelligence: The January 1945 Report to the Joint Intelligence Committee on "The Intelligence Machine"', in Robert Dover and Michael S. Goodman (eds), *Learning from the Secret Past: Cases in British Intelligence History* (Washington, DC: Georgetown University Press), pp. 11–42.

2011. 'What Difference Did It Make?', *Intelligence and National Security* 26, no. 6: 886–901.

2013. 'Intelligence in the Cold War: Did it Matter?', in Carlos Collado Seidel (Festschrift for Wolfgang Krieger) (ed.), *Geheimdienste, Diplomatie Und Krieg: Das Raderwerk Der Internationalen Beziehungen* (Berlin: Lit Verlag), pp. 55–69.

2013. Co-edited with Gwilym Hughes. *Intelligence in the Cold War: What Difference Did It Make?* (Abingdon: Routledge). (Originally published as a special issue of *Intelligence and National Security* 26, no. 6, 2011.)

2 The Rush to Transparency: Releasing Wartime Codebreaking Secrets

Intelligence's modern legitimacy owes a lot to its increased openness: it is no longer a sealed Black Chamber permanently closed to public gaze. British initiatives have contributed substantially to this openness, particularly through three decisions in 1969–74 and their implementation in the rest of the decade. All were related to the Second World War successes at Bletchley Park in decrypting German messages enciphered in the 'Enigma' machine and other sophisticated enemy ciphers.[1] The first decision, proposed in 1969 and taken in 1971, was to commission an official history that drew on these successes and became the multi-volume *British Intelligence in the Second World War*,[2] known as the 'Hinsley histories' after Sir Harry Hinsley, their editor and principal author.[3] The second decision, in 1974, was to acquiesce in the publication of the first British book-length account of the Enigma success, written by Group Captain Winterbotham and published as *The Ultra Secret*.[4] The third decision, also in 1974, was for the wholesale release of these decrypted messages and intelligence reports based on them, with relatively few exceptions. For convenience they are all described here as 'decrypts' or 'archives'.

Since then successive British governments have followed the Hinsley model, of commissioning independent scholars and providing full access to the archives, for other official intelligence histories: of the Security Service (2009), the Secret Intelligence Service (SIS) (2010), the Joint Intelligence Committee (JIC) (first volume 2014), and the Government Communication Headquarters (GCHQ) (2020). Australia has published official histories of its Security Service counterpart.[5] A similar formula has been adopted for intelligence histories in Germany, the Netherlands,

Norway and Denmark.[6] Even a six-volume official history of Russian intelligence appeared between 1999 and 2006.[7] As for the availability of intelligence archives, Britain's release of Enigma decrypts was followed by other pre-1945 intelligence records, a process which is now almost complete except for those of the SIS. Some British post-1945 documents have also become available, and more files are likely to be released following the publication of GCHQ's history. Elsewhere in Europe there have been extensive and important documentary releases on the Soviet-dominated intelligence organisations of the former Warsaw Pact countries, and some releases elsewhere, though the overall position on archival releases was assessed in 2015 as 'a rather haphazard process, if it exists at all'.[8] There is no comprehensive American programme of official histories on quite the British model, but historians have been assisted in many other ways. The CIA has released documents in great quantity: it was said in 2012 that by then it had made some four million declassified documents available at the US National Archives.[9] NSA's Center for Cryptologic History has published numerous accounts of that agency's history, including a (much redacted) complete account of the Cold War.[10] Official histories and documentary releases have become marks of accountable intelligence in a substantial part of the world, with the British as pace-setters from the 1970s onwards.[11]

This historical openness has encouraged academic interest in intelligence everywhere. Students of international diplomacy and military studies now recognise the role of intelligence power, particularly in the study of war and violence, and the inherent conflict between ease of communication and the need to make it secure. As put by John Ferris on the land battles of the Second War, 'Only a traitor used radio, only a fool did not. Without radio there was no certainty of command. With it there was no guarantee of secrecy.'[12] As another illustration of modern interest, Sir Hew Strachan's volume on the opening year of the Great War contains sixty-nine entries on 'intelligence' in the index.[13] All this has followed the British moves to openness discussed here.

Yet these pioneering British actions were mainly reactions to pressures and events, reversals of established policy, more complete than when they began: an unintended rush to transparency.

This chapter discusses how it happened. It sets out the background in the official British histories of the two World Wars; discusses the influence of Bletchley's codebreaking on the wider intelligence secrecy of the Cold War; and describes how the subsequent moves to openness took place. Richard Aldrich, Christopher Moran and Brett Lintott have already written on this subject and argued that the Hinsley histories were (in Lintott's words) 'a means through which the state could regain control of the public narrative about the secret services'.[14] I draw on them for details, as I do for an unpublished lecture by Lord Hennessy;[15] but I add my own recollections from my time as Secretary of the JIC from 1972–5.[16] The assessments of policies and individuals are my own in collaboration with David Schaefer.

First War Official Histories

Histories have long been produced under government patronage. English accounts of this kind date back to the sixteenth and early seventeenth centuries: the *Anglia Historia* was published in 1534 and a Historiographer Royal was appointed in 1660. Chinese dynasties had their official histories, many between the seventh and fifteenth centuries. Modern equivalents began in continental Europe in the second half of the nineteenth century as histories of wars or usually, to be precise, their own sides' part in them. Official British studies of the Boer War were already underway when a historical section of the Committee of Imperial Defence was created in 1906 to take them over, with four published volumes the result.[17] In August 1915 the Cabinet authorised preparations for an Official History of the First World War 'to provide a popular and authoritative account for the general reader; for the purpose of professional reference and education'; and (in the Cabinet Secretary's words) 'to provide an antidote to the usual unofficial histories'.[18] The work began in 1919 and recorded Britain's industrial-scale war on an almost industrial scale itself: including peripheral operations such as those in Northern Russia in 1919–20, it eventually ran to eighty-seven volumes, the last published in 1987.[19] Despite this scale, its treatment reflected the interests of the time, with an emphasis on land battles rather than grand strategy, supporting arms or the home front; in modern parlance, accounts of 'ops' rather than total war.[20] There were indeed some volumes on supporting arms – one on transportation on the Western front, twelve on military medicine worldwide and one on the veterinary services – but not many. The Boer War history was proportionately more generous to such functions, with a fourth volume of seven factual appendices on such subjects as ordnance, post office and remounts.

Despite this military concentration the First War series did extend to some civilian studies, but these were subsidiary parts of the main enterprise, often produced mainly for future war planning and in some cases not publicly available.[21] Lord Franks remembered that reading the official history of the Ministry of Munitions in the First War was his initiation to the Ministry of Supply in the Second.[22] The editor of the whole series, Brigadier-General Edmonds, was in post almost from beginning to end, and had little stimulus from academics to broaden his approach. There was no right of public access to official records before the Public Records Act of 1958 and the fifty-year rule it established.[23]

So it is not surprising that intelligence in the official series had light treatment. In his final volume Edmonds made a tantalising reference in 'the great lessons of 1914–18' to 'the wonderful success in the field of the Intelligence Branch of the General Staff [that] has been mentioned from time to time';[24] but it was never discussed explicitly. His military volumes quote the appreciations of enemy strengths and intentions that underlay command decisions, but usually without identifying them as intelligence inputs, and without discussion of sources, methods, strengths and weaknesses. (An exception was the treatment of codebreaking in the naval volumes, discussed below.) Intelligence was kept at arm's length, and the reader had to work out its contribution and look elsewhere for how it was accomplished. The result could still be serious history: in recent years the place of still-sensitive sources obliged Lawrence Freedman to give intelligence a similar treatment in parts of his official history of the Falklands War.[25] But readers of the First War military histories probably now find them rather two-dimensional compared to their modern equivalents.[26]

No doubt this reticence owed something to intelligence's traditional aura of secrecy. Edmonds occupied intelligence-related military posts from 1899 onwards and was associated with the creation of the Secret Service Bureau in 1909, and this experience may have strengthened the inclination towards caution over intelligence history.[27] But an equally important influence was probably intelligence's status at the time as not a particularly significant military arm. Thoughtful officers respected Clausewitz's dismissive dictum that 'Many intelligence reports in war are contradictory; even more are false and most are uncertain . . . most intelligence is false, and the effect of fear is to multiply lies and inaccuracies'.[28] By 1914 intelligence had indeed become a recognised staff function, but in the British case it was still seen as the 'field intelligence' of colonial warfare with reconnaissance on horseback as the main means of information-gathering. The Boer War history asserted that intelligence's 'only certain means of obtaining information' was through 'keen-eyed men on good horses'.[29] The 1914–18 war revolutionised the situation, with systematic POW interrogation, air photography, Sigint and above all the intelligence staffs' all-source analysis of all these reports: intelligence became for the first time a matter of professional study.[30] But this had only limited influence on post-war thinking, perhaps because most of those involved retired to civilian life. Field Marshal Wavell was an intellectual soldier and subsequently sought to make good use of intelligence in the first years of the Second War, but in his prestigious Cambridge lectures on 'Generals and Generalship' in 1939 he made no reference to it.[31]

To this cautious treatment of intelligence there was a limited exception for naval codebreaking, particularly the official accounts of its part in the Battle of Jutland.[32] The first official volume described the Admiralty's codebreaking centre, Room 40, and its acquisition of a German codebook, and the subsequent Jutland volume was explicit that the Admiralty decrypted a proportion of German radio messages. Later editions went further, and eventually (in 1940) included pasted inserts and an appendix with a complete list of the decrypts that should have been signalled to the C-in-C Fleet.[33] These references were prompted in the 1920s by the post-Jutland controversies, particularly Churchill's revelations in *The World Crisis* (appearing from 1923 onwards) that 'without the cryptographers' department there would have been no Battle of Jutland. But for that department, the whole course of the naval war would have been different.'[34] It has been suggested incidentally that this publicity for the weakness of the German naval codes helped to persuade post-war German authorities to move to the electro-mechanical Enigma, whose widespread use in the Second War ironically became a disastrous weakness.[35] But these intelligence details in the official First War histories were exceptional. The three-volume Room 40 history written by its participants gave a full account of naval Sigint, but it was not available to the public until the present century.[3]

Second War Intelligence History

With this naval exception there was little post-war publicity for First War intelligence. There was an official scare over a lecture in 1927 by the one-time head of Room 40, and a book about it was published in 1932.[37] In another episode the novelist Compton Mackenzie was prosecuted and fined after publishing accounts in 1931 and 1932 of his war in what became the SIS, and there were other less spectacular publications;[38] but First War intelligence as a whole had little publicity, a situation that continued under the Second War's censorship. There is no indication that intelligence was considered as a subject when that war's official history series was first commissioned in April 1945.[39] The volumes as they eventually appeared – 148 in all – were more numerous but also more comprehensive than those on the First War. The twenty-nine campaign histories still predominated, but they were accompanied by seven volumes on grand strategy, a separate series on wartime diplomacy, a much fuller treatment of the home front, and histories on military specialisations and supporting arms, including three army volumes on 'special weapons', seven in an RAF series on 'signals', and other subjects. In 1945 Bletchley followed its Room 40 predecessor by embarking on its own classified wartime history.[40] Given intelligence's special importance in the war, a separate volume on it might well have been considered in other circumstances as one of the supporting arms.

But any thoughts of an official wartime intelligence history must have been stifled by the special sensitivity of wartime Sigint, and the intensity with which this was protected afterwards. On the day after the European War ended Bletchley's staff were notified that their wartime obligation of secrecy was to continue for life, and this was followed by a directive that Bletchley's 'Special Intelligence' was to be kept completely secret, with no time limit. ('Special Intelligence' was used to refer to high-grade decrypts and the resulting analysis through most of the war: Ultra, the services' own shorthand for this term, was still officially a classified codeword used in its second half).[41] Secrecy covered the fact and value of codebreaking successes as well as the organisation and techniques that made them possible: it was 'imperative that the fact that such intelligence was available should NEVER be disclosed'.[42] A political rationale was added, that the Axis powers had to recognise their defeat by force of arms and should not receive non-military excuses, as had been offered by Germany after 1918.[43] Official historians were given Special Intelligence briefings and instructed to exclude this material from everything they wrote, and the edict had a wider effect than originally specified.[44] The ban on including Special Intelligence became a blackout on most wartime Sigint, not just the cryptanalytic product, and the same reaction followed any suggestion of private writing. Secrecy about all wartime intelligence became dominated by the protection of Ultra, and merged with the concealment of GCHQ's post-war functions and the other agencies. The result was to establish and reinforce a general government policy of 'no comment' on intelligence of any kind, past or present.

Ultra was subsequently joined in this position by the Second War's big deception secret, also without qualification or time limit. This was Double Cross, the nickname of the committee that ran the successful UK–US strategic deception operations which at their highest point persuaded Hitler to withhold twenty-two of his divisions from the Normandy battles in 1944 to meet the (fictional) landing of twenty-five non-existent American divisions suggested for the Pas de Calais. Double Cross was to be treated as a secret on a par with Ultra, partly (as with Ultra) to prevent it being used as an excuse for German defeat, but also to conceal the identities of the double agents involved as well as the support it received from codebreaking. Ultra was part (though only a part) of the deception secret, and as one big wartime secret it became entwined with the other. For both secrets the force of secrecy was conveyed by the mood of 'NEVER' revealing them, and its popular label of being 'carried to the grave'.[45] The same force was held to apply to its support from the Official Secrets Act, later described by Cabinet Secretary Sir Burke Trend (later Lord Trend)[46] as 'a tremendous sanction at the back of everything you say and do', though in reality the sanction turned out to be much less usable.[47] All this was reinforced by the Cold War's nature as substantially an intelligence war. Protection of its special secrets gained the force of dogma, with any relaxation seen as a slippery slope to source betrayal.

This official view was maintained at a time when the nation was seeing the contradictory process by which, in Moran's words, 'the British press, during the Cold War, promoted the public's "right to know" and rolled back the frontiers of government secrecy'.[48] But in the press disclosures and ministerial revelations of the first half of the Cold War intelligence did not loom large. The official historians excluded Ultra as they had been directed.[49] In his official naval histories Captain Roskill with his intelligence background touched on the role of radio direction-finding in the Atlantic battles, the British captures of cryptographic material from German weather ships, and the German breaking of British naval codes; and on this last point he hinted that 'The reader should not, of course, assume that we British were meanwhile idle in achieving the opposite purpose.'[50] But he stuck to the rule about avoiding specific Special Intelligence, if not its wider interpretation.[51] Private authors were on the whole successfully restrained; Churchill was persuaded to have the successive drafts of his memoirs vetted; caches of wartime intelligence documents were reclaimed from other retired hands;[52] RAF Marshal Lord Slessor was by no means alone when he wrote in 1974 that for twenty years he had tried to get the ban on Ultra lifted, but failed and had observed the rulings.[53] Intelligence was not yet a popular subject, and military historians as a body remained incurious or discreet. In his best-seller history in 1952 Chester Wilmot described the successful deception over the Normandy invasion but did not mention the 'turned' German agents or the code-breaking support, though he may have been aware of both.[54]

This protection of Ultra had American collaboration, and the academic reticence or lack of curiosity over intelligence applied equally in American studies of the Pacific War. The breaking of Japanese diplomatic ciphers had been revealed in the post-war congressional investigations into Pearl Harbor and was discussed in Roberta Wohlstetter's important 1962 study of the Japanese attack,[55] but it was the best part of a decade before her work was followed up on any scale. The vulnerability of German communications was also briefly raised in these hearings, after the leak of a confidential letter from General George Marshall referring to American codebreaking efforts against Germany with British assistance, which was published in *Time* magazine.[56] Nonetheless the lack of specific details meant that the story was not taken up by others, and at a formal level British intelligence remained insulated from public curiosity for a surprisingly long time. As late as the mid-1970s the JIC still had no official post-war existence; SIS had no official recognition at all; GCHQ was recognised but with a misleading declared role until 1983; the armed forces still could not include their substantial Sigint activities in recruiting literature. GCHQ had a scare when two Oxford undergraduates wrote in a student magazine in 1958 about their radio interception of Soviet targets as conscripts in the navy, but such publicity was rare.[57] The threat to the Double Cross secret was more specific from the determined establishment figure of Sir John Masterman – Oxford's former Vice-Chancellor and Provost of Worcester College – but was successfully contained until later.[58] In a related area – the interrogation of German POWs in the London 'cage' – the officer in charge was successfully dissuaded from publishing his account in the early 1950s.[59] For the first half of the Cold War, intelligence as a whole, and Sigint in particular, was hidden from the public gaze.

By the 1960s, however, the media's appetite for intelligence was being stimulated by a succession of Cold War spy cases: John Vassall, the civil servant recruited by Soviet intelligence; the Soviet Portland spy ring; George Blake's prosecution as a Soviet spy in the SIS, and his escape from prison five years later; a Soviet intelligence officer's appearance in the Profumo affair; Kim Philby's exposure as a Soviet agent, followed by his autobiography from Moscow, its selection by the Book Society in England and the Book of the Month in America, and the other publications it inspired.[60] On legal aspects of intelligence there was the public controversy in 1967 over the peacetime interception of cables, one result of which was to draw attention to the precise D Notice procedure for providing government advice on handling sensitive subjects.[61] The voluntary nature of this procedure, quite distinct from proceeding under the Official Secrets Act, was a background influence in much of what followed. Inevitably this developing interest in Cold War intelligence encouraged questions in parallel about its wartime history, with the blanket 'NEVER' approach to secrecy coming under increasing strain. This also had a direct cause: the government's own legislation in 1967 had reduced the statutory withholding of official archives from fifty to thirty years, and the Public Records Office (PRO, now the National Archives) was expected to release wartime records by the early 1970s. Intelligence agencies' own records could continue to be exempted, but this would not automatically apply to their reports in the Ministry of Defence (MoD) archives, formerly those of the three separate armed services. This and similar issues were first put to the JIC in March 1966,[62] and in late 1968 the Committee recommended the exemption of the agencies' own records and most of their reports in the MoD, including the decrypts of Axis communications. On this the appropriate Lord Chancellor's action for withholding was subsequently taken.[63] This did not completely end the JIC's concern, as there were fears that withholding complete categories of MoD's intelligence files would still provoke curiosity. The Committee therefore spent time at the end of the decade devising a plan to unobtrusively release a 'trickle' of selected Ultra documents.[64] This idea eventually came to nothing, but the new thirty-year rule meant that those responsible for protecting intelligence had to consider issues of archives and publications for the first time, and how to keep the two in balance.

Despite these challenges, intelligence records were of less direct concern at this stage than the pressure developing outside government for historical accounts of Ultra while those able to write them could still do so. Computers were changing the face of cryptography: could the breaking of the German electro-mechanical machines before 1945 still be a worthwhile secret? Their exploitation had been a national triumph which should be recorded and made known, particularly after intelligence's bad post-war publicity about Soviet penetrations. Those advocating publication were a mixture of former Bletchley insiders and wartime customers, some keen to write about it themselves, and professional writers (in the US as well as the UK) who had got wind of the story and sought to use it. In no sense were they a mass movement of public opinion but their arguments were increasingly persuasive, and underlying them was the liberal assumption that secrecy in peacetime needed substantial justification. As put by Sir Michael Howard, an author of one Hinsley volume, in a letter to Masterman, 'it seems to me *ipso facto* desirable that chronicles of the past should be as complete and accurate as human endeavour can make them';[65] especially, he might have added, for a national triumph.

This pressure increased from the mid-1960s onwards. Masterman was part of it, though he was concerned only with Double Cross and had begun much earlier than others. He helped to run the wartime deception operations and in 1945 had written an account of them as his last military activity before returning to Oxford to teach history. He kept a copy, and as early as 1954–5 had raised the idea of publication with his former pupil, Dick White,[66] by then head of the Security Service. After his retirement in 1961 Masterman wrote that 'some might say that it [the publication of the story] had become an obsession'.[67] His autobiography records exchanges over the next decade with White (by then head of SIS), and a selection of Ministers and top civil servants, some of them his former Oxford pupils.[68] All were being asked to authorise his use of what was technically still an official document, and doubly secret because it detailed success in deception and codebreaking. These officials managed to put Masterman off through the 1960s, but by the end of the decade he was losing patience and contacted American publishers, though he did not immediately act with them.[69]

Ultra's secrecy did not have such a determined individual critic, but a list circulated in Whitehall in 1970 illustrated the growing challenge, citing twenty-six published and unpublished works of sensitivity.[70] Coincidentally the whole interest in Sigint was fuelled during these years, and well beyond, by the scholarship of David Kahn, an American journalist-historian whose best-selling history of codebreaking appeared as *The Codebreakers* in the US and UK in 1967. It was warmly received and remains the standard work.

Its implications for Ultra were first discussed by the JIC in June 1966 and intermittently thereafter.[71] At that stage US authorities were leaned on to persuade Kahn to remove his few references to Bletchley,[72] and in the first edition Kahn wrote relatively little about Ultra,[73] though the book was still advertised in 1968 in the UK as containing 'some sensational revelations which will draw attention to notable gaps in the official histories'.[74] Quite apart from its revelations, the book encouraged codebreaking as a respectable subject of historical research, and no longer a geekish speciality.[75] The BBC planned a television series based on it in 1970 and initially refused to have the script vetted, though it eventually climbed down after a top-level approach and accepted some changes, including abandoning a live interview with the author.[76] Kahn knew more about Ultra when he produced a popular edition of the book in 1973, though by that time Sir Leonard Hooper, Director of GCHQ from 1965, had met him in London while he was at St Antony's College Oxford in 1972–4.[77] From Hooper's influence this edition still had more in it about German codebreaking and American Pacific successes than about Bletchley, though it indicated the scale of the British effort and its reading of U-boats' traffic.[78] With the growing interest in Bletchley and Ultra, the meeting with Kahn had been by no means Hooper's only intervention, and he had other successes in persuading potential authors to delay publication or publish less.[79] His characteristic energy, persuasiveness and close transatlantic relationships were substantial assets in holding the line of non-publication.

Nevertheless the wartime revelations were already accumulating when two new publications appeared close to each other in 1968 and moved Ultra's exposure to a new level. The first was a critique of Philby's autobiography, written by Hugh Trevor-Roper, Oxford's Regius Professor of History, and published in an April 1968 periodical and in a short book immediately afterwards.[80] In a wide-ranging discussion of British intelligence, Trevor-Roper was brief but explicit about 'the breaking of the "Enigma" machine' – probably the first public reference to its German name – and his judgement that of the 'great intelligence triumphs of the war . . . almost all of them were made practical by the work at GC & CS [Bletchley]'.[81] Since he also mentioned 'the highly successful deception programme' controlled by MI5, he managed to blow both the big wartime secrets in one go. As a response to Philby's autobiography the piece had been solicited from within government, and no immediate action was taken over the indiscretions, though they were apparently remembered the following year when Hooper wrote that Trevor-Roper would be unsuitable as an author of the Official History.[82]

The other important publication was by Donald McLachlan, editor of *The Sunday Telegraph* until 1966, who had spent most of the war in the Admiralty's Naval Intelligence Division (NID) and after retirement began an account of its wartime work. For this he sought access to classified monographs by Admiral Godfrey, NID's Director for the first half of the war, and official clearance to describe Ultra. These requests appeared on the JIC agenda in the summer of 1966 and McLachlan's work remained there regularly until the next year.[83] He was eventually given access to Godfrey's official memoirs and NID monographs,[84] and in the book he acknowledged naval support from 'at least two hundred NID friends'.[85] His friends and advisers included Vice-Admiral Sir Norman Denning, a leading member of the wartime NID and eventually senior member of the Defence Intelligence Staff until 1965,[86] and there were Whitehall grumbles that the navy was giving McLachlan favoured treatment.[87] Explicit revelations about Ultra remained nevertheless a sticking point with GCHQ, which removed some passages from the proofs late in the day and kept them in its custody.[88] Despite this, when the book appeared as *Room 39: Naval Intelligence in Action 1939–45* it still included a full chapter on 'The Wireless War'[89] as well as references to the German successes against British codes, the naval operations to capture German cryptographic material, and the role of British direction finding and traffic analysis.[90] McLachlan was following Roskill's example in sailing close to the wind over Ultra without being explicit,[91] though he may have got rather the better of GCHQ in what he managed to publish with his unofficial naval encouragement.[92] The book was a success, and Peter Calvocoressi of wartime Bletchley may not have been alone in enquiring even before it appeared whether he could now write about Ultra.[93] McLachlan's book was in fact an admirable outline of wartime naval intelligence as a whole minus Bletchley, and its combination with Trevor-Roper's explicit revelations may have helped to persuade officials in early 1969 to move from an out-and-out defence of Ultra to a more discreet way of handling the story.

The Official Intelligence History

For this they also had the stimulus from outside government for an official history. In September 1968 McLachlan reviewed Trevor-Roper's piece on Philby and, having just had details of Ultra removed from his own book, he used the professor's indiscretions as an excuse for revealing that 'We learn that the signals of the German intelligence service were decoded in great volume ... Codebreakers at Bletchley mattered far more than SIS.' He concluded that 'I can see no reason why a volume of the official history of the war entitled "intelligence" should not be begun next week, with the Regius Professor as editor-in-chief and many distinguished dons, late of MI5 and MI6, to help him.'[94]

On 1 February the following year – four months after this suggestion and just before the first official moves – McLachlan sent Trend a copy of *Room 39* and wrote that 'it is my considered opinion that a full and valuable history of intelligence during the war could be written on this kind of semi-official basis while the participants are still alive'. It was not a job he wanted, but it would be possible to assemble 'a small group of first-class historians who were in the work and could make a safe as well as a good job of it. Without it, the existing official histories incorporated some gross deceptions of the public and posterity.'[95] Trend replied with cautious interest, writing that 'although I think I can see certain potentially serious snags and difficulties here, I will turn the idea over in my mind'.[96]

His Bletchley experience made Hinsley also weigh in for an official history. In the previous year he had written a favourable review of McLachlan's book and guardedly commented that it revealed enough of the secret world of codes and ciphers 'to show readers that they are highly secret because they were crucially important'.[97] Early in 1969, just before McLachlan wrote to Trend,

Hinsley wrote to Denning saying that he had heard about the idea of an official history from McLachlan and another.[98] He suggested a panel of authors, and put himself forward as one, citing his time in Bletchley and his professional background there, which in 1945 had included writing the internal naval history. He also specified his terms: 'I should be reluctant merely to provide an outside author with my reminiscences.'[99] Apparently, it was some time before Denning passed this letter to the Cabinet Office, though this did not prevent Hinsley's eventual appointment as editor-in-chief.[100] No doubt the idea of a history was already a talking point among other wartime insiders, within government and outside it. But McLachlan was the first to go public about it, and then proposed it to Trend, and there seems no reason not to credit him as its main progenitor with support from Hinsley.

This was not quite the end of McLachlan's appearance on the JIC's agenda. In 1970 it discussed his proposal for a book on intelligence's general relationship with policy and action, and his request for assistance with aspects of the wartime history.[101] The idea caused alarm, and in a report to Trend the JIC pronounced that 'The book proposed by McLachlan is obviously undesirable in so far as it again draws unwanted public attention to intelligence matters on which it is Her Majesty's Government's policy not to comment.'[102] The book was never written: McLachlan and his wife were killed in a car crash in the following January. Had he lived it might have been a notable contribution to what became a central issue in academic intelligence studies as it subsequently developed.

That then was the background in the winter of 1968–9 when officials moved away from the purely passive defence of Ultra to exploring limited and inconspicuous releases in some form. At this stage, they were already considering a controlled trickle of archival releases that would indicate Ultra's existence without revealing its scale and importance.[103] A senior GCHQ official had written that although 'No knowledge would suit GCHQ best', so many potential writers were in the wings that 'it would be wise to take a lead and arrange at a time and in circumstances for release that would cause it to make the least impact worldwide'.[104] The following year Hooper as GCHQ's Director still believed that a 'limited and controlled release policy was likely to be less damaging than a complete withholding of records'.[105] Trend had recommended to the Prime Minister in early 1969 that 'we should spread releases over a period so as to generate the minimum public interest', and it was briefly seen as an alternative to commissioning an official history.[106] But the idea was eventually abandoned in the autumn of 1970 after Heath's critical response as Prime Minister to all proposals for intelligence openness,[107] plus an MoD report shortly afterwards that it had very few Ultra documents in its records to be released in this way.[108] This turned out to be quite wrong, but by then Whitehall's attention had been taken by the idea of an official history for stemming the flow of Ultra-related publications, with archival releases put to one side for the moment.[109]

Inside Whitehall the immediate stimulus for the Official History was a minute by Denning, who after retirement from the navy had become secretary of the D Notice Committee in MoD, and in this role acted as link-man with authors as well as the media.[110] He wrote on 11 February 1969 to Sir James Dunnett, his Permanent Secretary, about the growing problem of actual and prospective intelligence authors.[111] Dunnett sent the minute to Trend, who convened a meeting for 26 February of agency heads and other JIC members, including Sir Dick White who had moved to the new post of Intelligence Coordinator the previous year. The meeting was set up specifically to discuss the desirability of an intelligence history to counterbalance unofficial accounts and provide leverage for containing them, and it recorded support for the idea and invited White to develop it,[112] though later files suggest that the intelligence community's support was less than wholehearted.[113] My predecessor as JIC Secretary, Brian Stewart, had recently arrived in post and his recollection to me of one of the meetings was that 'The whole tenor of the discussion was negative', though a positive recommendation emerged from the centre.[114] White reported to Trend a few months later that in the FCO (Foreign and Commonwealth Office) and MoD 'the difficulties in the way are clearly considerable'.[115] But in convening the meeting Trend had probably already decided to press for the history, no doubt after speaking to Dunnett, White and perhaps Hooper.[116]

It was not Trend's first involvement in a project of this kind: he was already a supporter of official histories. From the Treasury in his earlier days he had helped to launch an account of operations in France of the Special Operations Executive (SOE), the wartime organisation established in 1940 to 'set Europe ablaze'.[117] The book was begun by the historian M. R. D. Foot in the early 1960s, formally commissioned in 1964, and published in 1966 as *SOE in France*. It was a considerable success, but its citing of participants' names produced expensive libel threats and action which the government settled out of court.[118] Trend was by then the Cabinet Secretary, responsible ultimately for the Historical Section, and – an enthusiast for the secret world – he had wanted more SOE histories. But a section of Whitehall opinion remained entrenched against any repetition,[119] and when attention turned to the intelligence history SOE was put on the shelf.[120] Nevertheless Foot's book was cited by Trend as a useful precedent for an intelligence publication. A practical result of Foot's bruising experience was Hinsley's policy of omitting all personal names, the feature that produced the criticism of his history that it was 'written by a committee, about committees, for committees'.[121]

But the history itself was still an ambitious project. Despite what was said about countering private publications there was complete uncertainty about how it was to handle Ultra itself. The academic world also had little experience of assessing intelligence on the scale of what became Hinsley's ambitious title: *British Intelligence in the Second World War: Its Influence on Strategy and Operations* (though it excluded the Far East). Hinsley pointed out in his first preface that 'we venture to point out the novel and exceptional character of our work. No considered account of the relationship between intelligence and strategic and operational decisions has hitherto been possible [. . .] .'[122] It was a high wire experiment for academics as well as for government.

To return to the bureaucratic details: after Trend's meeting White produced a lengthy report in June 1969 which was taken by the JIC and Chiefs of Staff, and Trend put the project to the Prime Minister (Wilson) on 29 July and received tentative approval subject to consultation with Ministers and Opposition.[123] The military Chiefs of Staff were unenthusiastic and grumbled about what they saw as a hasty submission to Ministers.[124] There was then some delay before Wilson wrote to Heath as Leader of the Opposition, who in turn consulted two former Prime Ministers (Macmillan and Eden) who both followed him in being critical.[125] After the general election and change of government in June 1970 Trend tried again in November with Heath, now Prime Minister, and failed,[126] and a meeting on 19 February 1971 with Trend, White and senior Ministers was needed to finally persuade him.[127]

Heath's doubts had some justification, given the uncertainty of what was being proposed, but their effect was to delay the project by the best part of fifteen months. When the history was eventually commissioned it was forecast as two main volumes, plus another on security and counterintelligence, and a fourth on strategic deception. It was to take two years, costing £10,000 for each of the authors:[128] a considerable underestimate. Excluding the specialist volumes, Hinsley's history ran nominally to three volumes, really four, since volume three had two parts, the second over 1,000 pages.[129] As originally put in White's paper, the purpose included meeting the claims of history by filling the gaps in the existing official histories and preserving proper knowledge of Bletchley's wartime contributions, even if only for officials.[130] If the history, or a version of it, were published it would also de-sensationalise public accounts and pre-empt or at least correct private authors: an 'accurate but controlled' official history would be better than leaving the field to inaccurate private recollections.[131] Restoring intelligence's public reputation may have also been in officials' minds, but was not part of the submission. In finally putting the idea to Heath, Trend cited the basic 1945 case for complete secrecy, though toned down: 'in the worst case this [a full history] could lead to a review by some countries of the security measures employed against us'.[132] He therefore suggested a full-scale history was out of the question and proposed instead a 'limited' version which might be 'synoptic and illustrative', perhaps with the Ultra evidence disguised as 'communications intelligence' or 'special sources'. A bowdlerised version of an unpublished official history, or an 'illustrative' account of selected episodes, could be used as a historical training aid.[133] He laid weight on a distinction between 'how' and 'what': between 'how' intelligence produced its reports and 'what' effect these had on commanders' decisions. The history's emphasis was to be on the second and not the first, dealing with Ultra in this way without revealing much about it.

This formula now appears geared to overcoming Heath's scepticism, with only limited resemblance to what was eventually published about Bletchley's codebreaking. Trend had originally put it to Wilson in 1969 that the history would be written in the hope if not the expectation of publication and this had been repeated to Heath, but the approval eventually reported back to the JIC was for a 'classified limited official history', of which 'publication was not at present contemplated'.[134] As such it got underway in late 1971, with Hinsley as the most experienced historian gradually assuming responsibility as editor-in-chief of the series, except for the volume on strategic deception. One guesses that his brief was to write proper history in some form whatever the eventual decision about publication; though in this he must have been much aided in 1974 when Winterbotham's book changed the situation so completely.

Private Writers: Masterman and Winterbotham

While the proposal for the history was being refashioned to meet Heath's scepticism, reports of sensitive publications continued and Masterman's moves for publication came to their climax. His previous refusals had been accompanied by encouragement about the future: in a letter from the Cabinet Office in March 1969 White wrote that neither he nor Martin Furnival Jones (the Security Service's Director General)[135] would raise security objections to publication.[136] But Masterman was finally turned down by the Home Secretary (Callaghan) in April 1970, and he picked up his negotiations in the United States.[137] He wrote later that 'I did not think the government would prosecute me or that if they did they would secure a conviction.'[138] When his intention became known, Furnival Jones took a strong line and wrote that 'I consider your action is disgraceful and have no doubt that my opinion would be shared by many with whom you worked during the war.'[139] White on the other hand commented in a draft note for Trend that Masterman's determination was 'an indication of the strength of feeling outside official circles on the subject of our present security policies'.[140] The Prime Minister was informed, and the Attorney

General and Home and Foreign Secretaries (among Masterman's former pupils) became involved. The Attorney General saw no prospect of a successful prosecution after White's letter had affirmed there were no security objections, and in summer 1971 the government caved in. Masterman accepted some deletions to the text, mainly references to Ultra, and the book was published in February 1972, with royalties split between him and the government. It sold well in English (45,000 hardback copies and 200,000 in paper) and there were agreements for translations into German, Italian, Portuguese and Swedish.[141] Other publications on wartime deception followed. Despite the government's deletions, a discerning reader could find hints about the codebreaking support, and the eventual identification of some double agents may also have been made slightly easier; but there was no obvious damage and it is difficult now to see why government took so long to compromise with the author except for the dogma of 'never reveal'. In calling the bluff of Heath's government Masterman had exposed the Official Secrets Act of the day as a blunt weapon and laid the ground for the more comprehensive revelations of Winterbotham.

Group Captain F. W. Winterbotham had been a Royal Flying Corps pilot in the First War and a member of SIS for ten years before the Second War, when he had a wartime role of organising and supervising the distribution of Ultra reports to recipients from Churchill downwards, as well as checking that they were used without compromising the sources. Bletchley records show, incidentally, that this involved him in devising the 1945 edict for their post-war protection.[142] This role came from what were still the SIS Chief's formal responsibilities for the secure distribution and use of Sigint reports, and they were indeed important features of Bletchley's success. It now seems from the SIS's official history that Winterbotham was also involved in other wartime SIS business of substance.[143] He was appointed CBE in 1943, but his Sigint role never made him one of Bletchley's key insiders.

After some post-war years with British Overseas Airways Corporation and the Colonial Development Corporation he retired to a smallholding in Devon on his SIS pension, said later to be £90 annually, and in 1969 he published an unsensational account of his pre-war contacts with Nazi leaders and others in Germany.[144]

This did not specify his SIS affiliation and was accepted by Whitehall, apparently after he removed three chapters at Denning's request: perhaps an early attempt to breach the Bletchley secret.[145] His controversial book in 1974, *The Ultra Secret*, was an account of wartime Bletchley and Enigma, and the distribution of intelligence, with his recollections of the highlights of decrypted army and air messages (though less of the naval material), and less reliable memories of the use made of them, notably his erroneous claim that Coventry was left undefended from the German air attack in 1940 to safeguard Ultra's secrecy, a story that remained in circulation for many years. The book was composed from memory, some way from a comprehensive and reliable history, but it became a best-seller as the first popular account of Bletchley's achievements, and transformed Ultra's whole position. How then was this allowed to happen?

In an autobiography produced later Winterbotham claimed that he was visited in 1972 by an unnamed journalist who was planning to write about Ultra. The visitor was actually Anthony Cave Brown, British though by then based in the United States, whose capricious intentions became an influence on Winterbotham's plans and London's reactions.[146] The autobiography claims that the visit led Winterbotham to contact Denning about writing about Ultra himself, and then to a London meeting at which he was accepted as a suitable person to do it. On his account he then bought a tape recorder and dictated this first version of the book.[147]

The archives give a different story. There is no official record of a London meeting that encouraged Winterbotham to write his account, and his later recollections confused some key dates.[148] In November 1971 he was already writing the book and wrote to Masterman to enquire about the Abwehr's use of ciphers.[149] He submitted his manuscript to Denning in autumn 1972 under the D Notice procedure for seeking government advice on sensitive subjects,[150] and it was considered at JIC meetings from late October onwards. As a result he met Denning on 14 December 1972 in company with his successor-designate as the D Notice Secretary, Rear-Admiral Kenneth Farnhill, and Hooper, still Director of GCHQ. At the meeting Hooper repeated the official refusal over publication but offered the consolation that the embargo would not last much longer. He also told him that the text contained important inaccuracies, though it could possibly be examined for correction. After approval from the Prime Minister (Heath), the official reply from Farnhill on 26 January 1973 was that 'the publication of your material would for some time to come cause serious injury to national security', and it qualified for D Notice protection, though Whitehall would tell him when the situation changed and then consider correcting his text.[151] Winterbotham agreed to hold off publication and safeguard his draft, on the understanding that he would be told when the objections lapsed, and his accuracy checked.[152] He sought again to get the checks done at that stage, but Whitehall pushed this firmly into the future, and on 15 April 1973 Winterbotham accepted that 'Yes, of course I shall be quite willing to wait until the time arrives to do the rewriting.'[153]

At the JIC it had been noted that although there was 'a continuing need to retain Winterbotham's goodwill if publication was to be avoided', written confirmation was needed of his agreement not to publish, *inter alia* 'in view of other publications which might be imminent . . .'. The rest of that sentence has been excised from the released record, but it may have been connected with Cave Brown's intended publication in the United States.[154] The JIC's concern had been reinforced by a request from Trend to check any commitment to Winterbotham with the Attorney General,[155] and the minutes also recorded an important observation that although 'the technical reasons against publication would probably be removed in a few years' time, it did not necessarily follow that HMG would then wish to facilitate publication of Winterbotham's book'.[156] Nevertheless the Committee could think that Winterbotham had been dissuaded for the time being and would cooperate in the future, while he for his part could feel that Hooper had given his intention some official recognition, perhaps not unlike the limited assistance previously given to McLachlan.

In the event things moved far quicker than expected, and Winterbotham tried again less than a year later, with a changed approach and a completely different outcome. The available records of the correspondence are limited but it seems from these that a revised manuscript and request for D Notice clearance were put to Farnhill in early 1974, not it seems by Winterbotham personally but by the London publishers Weidenfeld and Nicolson.[157] Hooper was by then Intelligence Coordinator in the Cabinet Office and had been succeeded at GCHQ by 'Bill' (later Sir Arthur) Bonsall. Compared with the previous year this exchange was more formal and limited, with no suggestion of a meeting nor of having the text (officially) corrected. The JIC's recommendation was not referred to the Prime Minister (still Heath) before the general election in late February 1974, nor apparently to his successor (Wilson) who is only recorded as being informed on 8 April of Farnhill's response after it had already been made.[158]

In this there was a complete change in the official view about the book. I recall that Hooper personally drafted the JIC's conclusion that its damage to current intelligence 'must now be considered hypothetical' and did not warrant D Notice action to prevent its publication.[159] (I recall that Hooper showed me his draft and I was tempted to suggest replacing 'hypothetical' with better wording but did not.) In his official reply to Winterbotham, drafted by the JIC, Farnhill maintained

> It is my opinion that, although there are objections to it [the book] on grounds of security, they are not sufficient to warrant my advising you that publication would contravene 'D' Notices. You will appreciate that I am competent only to advise on the application of the 'D' Notices and the opinion I have expressed does not in any way express official endorsement of the manuscript itself or of your intention to publish it.[160]

Winterbotham and his publishers took this as acquiescence, and *The Ultra Secret* appeared promptly on both sides of the Atlantic. Extracts were first serialised in the UK in two successive issues of *The Sunday Telegraph* from late July 1974 and the book followed in October.

Coincidentally the JIC had been warned that an important book about the CIA was to be published in the United States that summer with extracts in the British press, and in that context it had made preparations for the questions that might arise from Winterbotham's account.[161] But I recall that there was still some surprise over the claims of the Sunday headlines and the enthusiasm of the reaction. Journalists wrote of the secret intelligence which had won the war, and Kahn in a measured review in the United States called it 'the greatest secret of World War II after the atomic bomb'.[162] Moran comments that 'press reviews forecasted wholesale revision of the history of the Second World War, with some journalists excitedly proposing that Ultra alone had won it'.[163] A hundred thousand hardback copies were sold by Christmas,[164] and according to Winterbotham his book was subsequently translated into every major language except Chinese.[165] Other potential writers demanded to have the new position clarified. It was the complete end of NEVER revealing Bletchley's secrets.

For Winterbotham himself there were mixed results. He became affluent: he records that, after he and his family had managed retirement with few extras, 'Suddenly, there were new motorcars, both for us and our grown-up daughter, there were horses, and holidays abroad. There was joy and untold happiness.'[166] But to the intelligence community he became the villain of the day, condemned for betraying national secrets for money. When asked privately what Winterbotham was expected to do after receiving Farnhill's letter, Bonsall – normally the most restrained of men – replied with uncharacteristic heat that as a professional intelligence officer he should have refrained from publication after being told of the continued security objections.[167] Many judgements were in stronger terms. The fact of his pre-war SIS service probably encouraged the view that he was a professional letting the side down, in a similar vein to Peter Wright of subsequent *Spycatcher* fame: an intelligence veteran with a meagre pension who welcomed book royalties to finance retirement.[168]

There was also widespread surprise that government had allowed this to happen. Sir Clive Loehnis, GCHQ's Director before Hooper, wrote that he was 'maddened' by the revelations: 'words failed me when I read the Winterbotham saga'.[169] The NSA's greatly respected Deputy Director Louis Tordella concluded in a lengthy classified review that

> . . . successful cryptanalysts of the ENIGMA in the 1940s as set forth in the book gives an accurate measure of competence not hitherto

available in unclassified literature. Extrapolation from that information in the light of the power of modern, very powerful computers may well cause several lucrative targets to have second thoughts about their present systems and to take remedial measures. I do not believe the book should have been published ... Further revelations can only make steeper and rockier the road today's cryptanalysts are walking.[170]

Even the wartime insiders who had argued for revealing Bletchley's secrets were distressed that it had happened in such an apparently haphazard way, in an account that was incomplete and sometimes wrong, and without any official explanation. Those hoping to write themselves felt unfairly beaten by an unexpected outsider. The many others who were equally bound by Bletchley's secrecy were left uncertain about their continued obligations. It was clumsy administration, below Whitehall's normal Rolls Royce standards. So what produced this speedy reversal of the line taken only a year previously?

GCHQ's Change of View

For GCHQ's revised assessment, that Winterbotham's draft was unlikely to cause substantial direct damage, a specific reason was quoted by David Kahn in his review of the book:

> It seems that after World War II, Britain gathered up many of the tens of thousands of Enigmas as she could find and later sold them to some of the emerging nations. Presumably if the UK could read Enigma messages in 1940, she could do so in 1950. Only recently have these countries replaced their Enigmas with new cryptosystems.[171]

Kahn was given this story when Hooper met him in July 1974,[172] and it has subsequently been quoted elsewhere.[173] On its veracity, Hooper would be better informed than anyone else. Emerging nations, like many others, had acquired machines of Enigma's type, and perhaps some actual Enigmas; surplus Enigmas were known to be used by East German authorities in the early 1950s.[174] But by the

45

1970s the obsolescence of these electro-mechanical machines was common knowledge. It is hard to believe that, in the fifteen months between Winterbotham's two applications, wartime Enigmas used by Third World targets had been scrapped on a sufficient scale, and with significant effect on GCHQ's operations, to be more than a minor contribution to its major change of view. The example of the Enigmas was quoted by Hooper when he was persuading Kahn to publish less, not more, and there could have been some exaggeration in a good cause after a good lunch. Professor Ferris's history of GCHQ maintains that the story of Enigmas 'deliberately flogged' in the post-war years was false.[175] There is also no reference to the Third World machines in the (admittedly incomplete) JIC papers referring to the new GCHQ assessment.

Another minor – but perhaps more likely – contribution to GCHQ's new view may have been the change in the head of cryptanalysis who made the assessment. Hugh Alexander, one of Bletchley's and GCHQ's leading figures, had retired in 1971 after twenty-one years in the post,[176] and his successor was notably open-minded. He may well have reached a new conclusion from the evidence in 1974 even if he had gone along with the received view the previous year.[177] An internal GCHQ minute to Bonsall later that year described revised cryptanalytic thinking about Ultra security, of a kind that had the new cryptanalytic head's fresh thinking about it.[178]

But despite these possible influences, GCHQ's change of view was based on new published revelations. These were in the memoir published in Paris in early 1973 – just after Whitehall's refusal of Winterbotham's first application – by Gustave Bertrand, the former military intelligence officer who had at one time commanded the French Sigint organisation,[179] and who incidentally was the French officer who delivered a Polish replica of the Enigma machine to London on 16 August 1939.[180] His book centred on the breaking of Enigma and drew on his own professional experience of it, supported by little-known works published earlier in France and Poland.[181] It was the first accessible account of the pre-war Polish attack on the machine, the related French progress, and the UK's involvement from summer 1939 onwards, plus brief accounts of the subsequent British (and French) successes.

It was not translated into English, did not attract any English-speaking comment at the time of publication, and had little public impact.[182] Nevertheless it is clear that GCHQ and NSA assessed that Bertrand's book would alert foreign security authorities, and that little could be done about it.[183] Brigadier John Tiltman, Britain's lifelong cryptanalyst, wrote in a classified NSA journal the following year that it 'was decisive in discussions between Deputy Director NSA [Tordella] and Director GCHQ on the matter of whether to attempt to restrain Winterbotham and his publisher'.[184] He elaborated in a later interview that 'we tried to get legal action taken against him [Winterbotham] under the Official Secrets Act, which was defeated because we were advised that we would never get a case through to him unless we could prove he was doing damage to our security now'.[185] Bonsall himself was adamant in old age that GCHQ's changed judgement resulted from Bertrand's publication. From his experience with the cable interception controversy in 1967 he was well aware of the limitations of the D Notice system and the difficulties of using the Official Secrets Act – it was not until 1989 that its sanctions available specifically against intelligence practitioners were strengthened[186] – and he mused that as GCHQ's Director after Bertrand's revelations he was 'probably seeking a soft landing'.[187] I am surprised that quite so much weight was placed on these relatively inconspicuous disclosures, but Bonsall was definite in what he said. He still deplored the revelations, but it was characteristic of his good sense to be convinced that, whatever the result, a legal action against Winterbotham would do more harm than good. Though incomplete, the declassified JIC files also point to the influence of Bertrands's disclosures.[188] There is little doubt that, although the Committee as a whole still disapproved of publication, it accepted GCHQ's advice not to take action against Winterbotham because of Bertrand's publication.

What is less clear from the documentation is why the JIC also changed its tactics in dealing with Winterbotham at a personal level. After his submission of his revised manuscript through his publishers, there was apparently no further official attempt at any direct persuasion. The Official History was underway to restrain private writers, but there is no record of the JIC's trying to use it to influence Winterbotham, or to delay him by having his manuscript corrected. Chris Moran has suggested that the threat of Cave Brown's publication in the United States led Whitehall to help Winterbotham deliberately to get his book produced first,[189] as indeed it was: Cave Brown's *Bodyguard of Lies* did not appear until the following year (1975), and was then more about Double Cross than Ultra.[190] Whitehall certainly assisted Winterbotham to the extent of not threatening legal action against him, but why would it do this to help him to beat his US-based competitor in this unwelcome whistleblowing? I have no memory of this as an official objective; I had delegated much of the work on intelligence publications to John Morrison and have surprisingly few recollections of it (but he concurred with this view before his death in June 2018).

Most of the relevant official documents are still withheld, but some light on the JIC's tactics comes from a 1992 article on publishing intelligence memoirs, including Winterbotham's, by Robin Denniston, a publisher with intelligence connections: his father was Bletchley's operational head until 1942.[191] His account of Winterbotham's first draft in 1972–3 fits what appears in the released files, including the story of the Enigma machines sold to Third World countries and Winterbotham's agreement 'not to go ahead until Hooper had given him the green light'.[192] But Denniston continues that Winterbotham was then 'justifiably rattled' by hearing that Cave Brown's publication was 'looming on the horizon' in the United States, and accordingly followed Masterman's example and sold his book's world rights to an American firm, Harper and Row, who were also handling Cave Brown. No date is quoted. A later Cabinet Office brief explained that Winterbotham 'was initially deterred from publishing . . . but the appearance of two books caused him to return to the charge'.[193] According to Denniston, his London publishers (Weidenfeld and Nicolson) were also shown Winterbotham's draft and signed an agreement with him after securing the British rights from Harper and Row. Winterbotham's autobiography is consistent with this account and puts it that 'the race was on [with Cave Brown] to get the proper version out first'.[194] Weidenfeld and Nicolson's editor addressed the original draft and later 'took it apart' to produce a fresh version, with the concentration on Ultra that made the book the success it was. In Denniston's words the editor made it 'not a masterpiece but a corking good short read'.[195]

His account gives some dates. The British publisher's editor made her first recommendation on 23 May 1973 so had received the original text before then. (Winterbotham's letter assuring Farnhill of his willingness to wait for the official view to change, and his promise to safeguard his draft, was dated 15 April that same year).[196] The editor wrote again to the publishers on 2 August, and on 6 August the author signed the contract.[197] The editor then revised the text in 'only a few months', and the manuscript was submitted to Farnhill on 15 January 1974 and received what Denniston describes as the *nolle prosequi* in Farnhill's letter of 1 April, after which publication went ahead.[198] Until the publishers sent the manuscript to Farnhill, Winterbotham had sought to keep Whitehall in the dark about the publishing agreements and revision of the text, but unsuccessfully. The author Nigel West has revealed that Britain's SIS 'was aware of every stage of the production process' of the book through a contact in the London publishers and, despite being 'especially anxious', was nevertheless party to the decision 'not to place any legal obstacle in his [Winterbotham's] path'.[199]

There is also some confirmation from the few official files that have been released. The partially redacted conclusions of a JIC meeting on 21 March 1974 record that Bertrand's publication had 'weakened the arguments previously used with Winterbotham'; that 'he [Winterbotham] and his publishers were determined to publish and further approaches to him were unlikely to succeed'; and that government action against him was unlikely to succeed and in any event would bring bad publicity.[200] The existence of an 'intending United States publisher' was also mentioned,[201] and a later summary of events also recorded that Winterbotham had been 'prepared to have his book published abroad if HMG had continued to be intransigent'.[202] The Committee's first and presumably most important finding has been completely redacted from the released minutes of that meeting, but it may have been that Winterbotham had been double-dealing by contacting publishers and was no longer persuadable. Arguably he was still playing partly by the rules in having his revised manuscript submitted for D Notice clearance, but in releasing it to publishers he had presumably broken his undertaking to safeguard it: Winterbotham had undertaken to provide safe custody for the manuscript, and officials would have presumably learned from the SIS informant that the revised version had been sent to publishers in the UK and the US. The bearing of Cave Brown's American plans on the JIC's attitude is also not clear. Nevertheless the decision not to renew contact with Winterbotham made a distinctive contribution to what followed. By giving up any chance of influencing him and his publication, the JIC unintentionally opened the way for the summer and autumn of 1974 to be a period of more intense interest and decisions for more extensive Enigma revelations than expected.

I suggest that an understanding of this 'hands off' attitude to Winterbotham needs to take into account the political and economic background of the time, the personal positions of top officials, and the change of government in late February. For Britain the winter of 1973–4 and months that followed was a period of international and domestic crisis: the Yom Kippur War from 6 October 1973 onwards; the consequent US–Soviet alert and stresses in UK–US relations; the worldwide explosion in oil prices; the British miners' industrial action; the government's response of a national three-day week, the voluntary speed limit and preparations for petrol rationing; IRA bombs in London either side of Christmas; the general election at the end of February on 'who runs the country?' and the fall of Heath's government that followed. The relevant chapter in Heath's biography has the stark title 'Hurricane'.[203] It was a tense and uncomfortable period, encapsulated in memories of winter afternoons and evenings when the Intelligence Coordinator, JIC Secretary and the Secretariat in their Whitehall offices observed government decree and tried to work by candlelight.[204] There was a feeling of emergency and slimming-down to essentials. As put in the previous year by the JIC Chairman (Sir Geoffrey Arthur of the FCO) in a quite different context: 'The trouble with you intelligence people is that you think you are not part of politics, but you are.'[205] The JIC in 1973–4 was certainly not insulated from the strains of the day.

The top officials were as influenced as anyone and had also changed since Winterbotham's previous application. Sir Geoffrey Arthur became the JIC's Chairman in spring 1973 in combination with his senior FCO position and, though very able, had not wanted the job and brought a disorderly and verbose style to its meetings. Over 1973–4 he was deeply involved not only in the overseas crises but also in Irish and other issues under his FCO hat, and in his time the JIC's discussions were not at their most economical.[206] More significant, however, was Trend's retirement as Cabinet Secretary in October 1973, with Sir John Hunt (later Lord Hunt) succeeding him just as the crises began. Hunt was a former JIC Secretary, but he did not have Trend's empathy with intelligence and inclination to go an extra mile on its behalf, and the events also emphasised his quality as a hard realist. He did not refer Winterbotham's application to Heath and his ministers before the election.[207] Wilson himself then came into office in a strained political position, with no overall majority, the pressure for an autumn election, and a secrecy issue already looming over cabinet revelations in the Crossman diaries.[208] Most of all, Wilson himself had just published his own book about his previous administration, despite earlier advice from Trend, and was in a weak position for action against Winterbotham and might well have declined to take it.[209] Hunt had to establish his standing with the new government and, though I have no recollection, he may have let it be known to Hooper that an entanglement with Winterbotham was to be avoided.

The official most directly concerned was Hooper who was also new in post, having become full-time Intelligence Coordinator in autumn 1973 following his part-time predecessors.[210] With his unrivalled experience and high reputation he was well fitted to lead over Winterbotham, in alliance with Bonsall at GCHQ. But as a workaholic accustomed to worldwide responsibilities he did not enjoy his advisory role as Coordinator, was not close to Hunt, and was less confident in his new role than he appeared. Over Winterbotham's first application he had gone out on a limb in encouraging him for the future, and in allowing the official correction of the draft's errors to be considered as a possibility,[211] and he may have then felt personally injured and angry over Winterbotham's undeclared agreements with publishers and determined not to deal with him again.

Having been the JIC's main weapon for persuading potential Ultra authors to delay, he had now defused himself. I recall commenting at the time that he was now 'damned if he was going to give lunch to another aspiring author'.[212]

Combined with these attitudes was the change in government after the election, from a party instinctively inclined to support intelligence to one with less supportive instincts. In their different positions both Hooper and Hunt were working their passages with new masters, in conditions that put a special premium on avoiding embarrassment for the Wilson government in the spring–summer of 1974. The decision over Winterbotham's publication was essentially based on GCHQ's revised technical assessment, but these personal and political factors came together to make officials forego any last-minute attempt to persuade Winterbotham to still stay silent. There was little chance of succeeding, but an unexpected result was for 1974 to see the enthusiastic public reaction. Intelligence as a whole had never had such good publicity.

Bigger Consequences

The immediate consequence of the government's reply to Winterbotham was an adjustment of the policy for public comments on intelligence matters. After the JIC discussions in March 1974, Hooper began a review of Ultra policy and he proposed some modest relaxations in late June,[213] which Wilson as Prime Minister approved on 8 July.[214] These focused on acknowledging the existence of the Official History if it was judged necessary to dissuade other private authors or publishing firms. This was recommended only if Winterbotham's book stoked enough interest and in response to media enquiries, but it had strong backing from Bonsall at GCHQ, who thought it would be possible to publish some of Hinsley's first draft without much trouble.[215] An official statement on the history was resisted by others, and Hooper deferred this and the question of archival releases until the history was complete. In the meantime, all departmental and agency files regarding wartime intelligence were to continue being withheld. The other concession was to permit Hinsley and his co-authors to disclose the existence of the Official History in the course of their work if they were asked by wartime veterans.[216] In recommending the new guidelines to the Prime Minister, Hunt observed the 'JIC doubt if the book itself will provoke great interest though (partly because of its many inaccuracies) it could provoke reviews and comment leading to further revelations'.[217] It seems clear that officials did not reckon quite how successfully the publisher's editor had turned Winterbotham's manuscript into the 'corking good short read' that Denniston described, or how warmly the public would react to the story of Bletchley's spectacular wartime triumphs after all the post-war misfortunes and crises of 1973–4. Officials had perhaps become too close to it to realise what a great story it actually was, and how much effect it could have when splashed in *The Sunday Telegraph* extracts in late July when political news had slackened.

It is not clear how far these late July publications would have affected the JIC's cautious changes since they were followed almost immediately by another, completely unforeseen blow.[218] *The Sunday Telegraph* was contacted by a reader in early September who had seen documents marked 'Top Secret Ultra' in the batch of wartime files released to the PRO from 1972 and asked for confirmation that these were the subject of Winterbotham's story. The letter found its way to John Morrison in the JIC Secretariat who had recently come from the Defence Intelligence Staff after previously reading history at Glasgow University, where he had been taught to check his sources. He took a bus to the PRO (then still in Central London) to see the evidence himself, and returned with alarming news: a treasure trove of decrypted German Air Force and some Army Enigma messages had been erroneously released and were available to the general public.[219] He reported with understatement that they 'revealed a good deal about wartime intelligence sources'[220] and that some had already been accessed by readers.[221] An investigation revealed 230 files containing Ultra decrypts and other sensitive material, alongside more than 2,000 wartime files deposited by intelligence units and staffs of service commands, which the MoD should have withheld from the PRO.[222]

The Committee's immediate reaction was to remove the offending records, but rumours about the PRO discovery were picked up by at least one informed observer.[223] When added to Winterbotham's revelations and the public interest it pushed the JIC to a radical decision in late October which it would not otherwise have taken: the Committee recommended not only that this released material be returned to public view, but also that all the other German armed forces' Enigma messages – army, navy and air force – in the MoD files should be examined with a view to their eventual release as well.[224] For this, a new distinction was drawn between 'really sensitive' documents, which gave technical details of codebreaking, other Sigint techniques or operations, or people, and the great majority of service intelligence records which did not. The sensitive items would still be withheld along with the internal files of the intelligence agencies, but all the others in MoD archives would be released. Subsequently it was decided that gaps in these MoD records would be filled by releases from GCHQ.

The planned release of the translations and reports derived from this material was the biggest single move to intelligence openness since 1945, and perhaps since. From the available records it seems the JIC was worried about more publicity over the PRO mishap,[225] and the attitude of former insiders seeking to publish accounts of Bletchley who would find themselves denied access to files that had been made available to others.[226] Returning these files and including the rest of the wartime service intelligence records would establish coherence in release policy; and at least for GCHQ the details about Enigma contained in this material were less sensitive than other wartime achievements that had yet to be revealed.[227] The main hesitation to the new policy in the JIC came on 10 October from the Chairman (Arthur) when he unexpectedly questioned what was being proposed, and cited Soviet efforts to monitor the archives as an additional reason for caution.[228] The surprising intervention was consistent with his chairmanship, but also reflected the FCO's wariness about the sensitivity of any intelligence disclosures. The Committee held several meetings on the issue, the minutes of which are still partially withheld, but in correspondence the following year Hooper referred to a protracted debate of which, in his words, 'certain aspects aroused more heat at JIC than I have seen for some time'.[229] Nevertheless as Coordinator he had proposed the radical policy of wholesale

Enigma releases, in a move that must have had full support from Bonsall, and was endorsed by the Committee despite some misgivings.[230] Hunt put the proposal for this change to Wilson who approved it on 18 November 1974.[231]

Although withholding 'really sensitive' files, the effect of this change was to put large quantities of Enigma-derived intelligence into the public domain. An indication of its bulk is given by the monthly figures of raw Enigma decrypts for the three German services, which rose from 39,000 at the beginning of 1943 to about 90,000 from the end of that year.[232] It was in a sense a return to the earlier, abandoned idea of selective Enigma releases, but this policy was on a totally different scale: releasing a mass of intelligence to satisfy public interest rather than small quantities designed not be noticed. Bonsall also pushed at the JIC for a public notification for Bletchley's veterans about their revised security obligations but was strangely cut short by Arthur (to an extent concealed in the minutes).[233] Perhaps Arthur was reluctant to offer any more excuse for publicity, in the face of what must have seemed like a sudden and escalating momentum for openness by the end of 1974.

Implementation took time, but Hooper (up to his retirement in spring 1978) and Bonsall made effective arrangements for the systematic release of service intelligence records. Enigma decrypts began to arrive at the PRO in 1977 and over time these would expand to include decrypted messages of non-military users of Enigma such as the Abwehr (foreign intelligence) the SD (security service), German diplomatic traffic, other messages of enemy countries and neutrals, and eventually Bletchley's own archives.[234] In the immediate years following Winterbotham's revelations the public appetite for intelligence history was also met by a rush of private publications. *The Ultra Secret* had many reviews, some correcting errors,[235] and other accounts soon followed, with Beesly (1977), Lewin (1978), Bennett (1979), and Calvocoressi (1980) all publishing works of quality.[236] R. V. Jones's account of wartime scientific and intelligence (1978) dealt with Ultra's contribution, but put it valuably into perspective with other sources.[237] An outline of the cryptanalytic successes against Enigma was also included in the first volume of Hinsley's history (1979) though this was expanded in later volumes.[238]

Thanks to Winterbotham this attention was all focused on Enigma, but officials also had to reckon with another part of Ultra codenamed 'Fish', which denoted the German High Command's cipher systems for teleprinter traffic carrying top-level messages, such as Hitler's orders to his senior Army commanders.[239] Bletchley's priority within this target was given to the Lorenz SZ 40/42 machines codenamed 'Tunny', and from these a total of 13,508 messages were broken from November 1942 onwards when the counts apparently started.[240] Initially this decryption was by hand methods, but these were augmented with the construction of the experimental Heath Robinson machine, and its more powerful successor, Colossus.[241] Developed to attack Tunny, Colossus became operational (in its Mark II version) just in time for the Western Allies' invasion of France and the subsequent campaign, about which Hinsley wrote of the 'enormous benefit to the Allies for the light it [Tunny] threw on German intentions, dispositions and resources', and its use 'with a view to achieving the maximum effect at the cost of the minimum expenditure of Allied resources and lives'.[242] The quality of this top-level information made Tunny at least as valuable as Enigma's greater quantity and topicality at the lower command levels where it was principally used.[243]

Later generations of telecipher machines were still in use by some GCHQ targets in the 1970s,[244] and the Fish decrypts were not included in the releases sanctioned in 1974 nor mentioned in the resulting publications.[245] Winterbotham made a single vague reference to computers in his confused description of Bletchley codebreaking,[246] and Kahn's book review named Colossus as an electronic computer but did not elaborate.[247] Calvocoressi mentioned the German teleprinter system but wrote that he knew nothing about it.[248] Nevertheless Fish haphazardly followed Enigma into openness over time, partly through academic pressure for Colossus to be recognised as the world's first digital computer, initially from Professor Brian Randell,[249] with support from Kahn and others keen to advertise Britain's contribution to modern science. Randell met Hooper and GCHQ's chief scientist in 1975 and was dissuaded for a time,[250] but the close association among computer specialists made him more difficult to restrain:

Randell had been alerted to Bletchley's achievements when Jack Good, a veteran of Bletchley and post-war GCHQ, mentioned Colossus's hardware at an academic conference in America in 1970, though Good's memory of some details was wrong; this was followed by a contribution from another Bletchley expert, Donald Michie, a few years later.[251] An uneasy compromise was brokered between Randell and the JIC when photos of Colossus were displayed at the PRO with a brief description and technical details[252] but with no indication of its intelligence function.[253] The various snippets about Fish were then collected in 1977 in a BBC documentary series, *The Secret War*, hosted by R. V. Jones with further input from Randell.[254] This offered a fuller description of Colossus and explicitly connected it with codebreaking, although the documentary identified the wrong telecipher machine as its target.[255] The file on the impact of the BBC series is still withheld.[256]

Despite this seepage the general Fish secret was officially maintained[257] until a brief reference was included in Hinsley's second volume (1981), followed by a more detailed account in part 1 of the third volume (1984).[258] These seem to have been effectively the official announcements of Bletchley's success against Fish, roughly one decade after Winterbotham first revealed the breaking of Enigma. It seems that Fish decrypts began trickling into PRO releases later that decade but were never announced, with the large-scale declassification of materials only recorded from 1996.[259] Quite unlike Enigma, the small amount of Fish material which was released never gained much attention beyond a few expert researchers. Perhaps the public interest in wartime codebreaking had become sated, or more probably Fish was deliberately handled unobtrusively, as had been the official intention for a 'trickle' of Enigma releases briefly considered in the 1960s.

This low profile did not apply to the other important decision of the decade: to publish the first volume of the Official History and to do so in its complete form, not one of the bowdlerised versions formerly envisaged. It may now seem that after Winterbotham's publication and the subsequent archive releases this was inevitable, yet it was in fact considerably delayed within the intelligence community and then threatened by a politician's last-minute obstruction. These were the final episodes of the decade's rush to openness and can conclude the substance of this chapter.

The History's Publication

The work on the Official History had not been publicly avowed when its future was reviewed in 1974 after the Winterbotham and Enigma decisions. While GCHQ had favoured announcing it, the problem of safeguarding the identities of agents and their handlers after Masterman's publication then made its mark, particularly for the security and deception volumes where individuals featured more prominently. SIS's concern over identities had already been registered in White's early consultations about the history in 1969,[260] and was reinforced when it was discovered that they were a significant element of the 'really sensitive' files discovered in the PRO in 1974.[261] Hooper speculated a year later that it might be necessary to publish the security and deception histories, and perhaps the other volumes, as 'short synoptic volumes' to meet these concerns,[262] and it was not until November 1977 that the Official History project was formally disclosed.[263] By then the draft of volume I had been completed for some time (in 1975), and when its publication was discussed Sir Maurice Oldfield, Chief of SIS, put the case against it. His professional conviction was that recruitment and handling of agents depended on a reputation for effective and perpetual secrecy for these sources, which would be jeopardised by publishing works of intelligence history.[264] Even without the issue of personal identities, revealing SIS's wartime activities would invite questions about its peacetime role, a concern strongly shared by the FCO. Hooper favoured publication, and argued that excising all the references desired by SIS would rule out the whole project.[265] Oldfield – like Hooper a former postgraduate historian[266] – replied that 'at the risk of being considered obscurantist I would prefer this than [sic] any action which could compromise our present position'.[267] After a meeting of those concerned on 21 July 1977 Hunt advised the Prime Minister (by then Callaghan) to agree in principle to publish the History's first volume, subject to careful sanitisation arranged by the authors.[268]

Callaghan accepted subject to Ministerial views, but the Foreign Secretary (Owen) with his responsibility for SIS urged further consideration of Oldfield's case.[269] This was dismissed by the Prime Minister: 'everyone knows its [SIS's] existence – we can surely resist any disclosures about activities, as we do now in the case of MI5'.[270] Owen was worried but yielded, though SIS was offered an opportunity to conduct its own review of Hinsley's text for sensitive material.[271]

Surprisingly this was not the end of the problems. As the history covered the period of the wartime coalition, Callaghan followed Wilson's practice in 1969 and wrote in July 1978 to the Conservative and Liberal leaders about its publication.[272] The Liberal agreed, but Mrs Thatcher did not. After becoming Conservative leader in 1975 she received intelligence briefings including one from SIS and had become (and remained) an enthusiastic supporter.[273] Accordingly, she sent a suitably combative response apparently off her own bat. Why take a decision about this first volume while others were incomplete? Why admit anything if not obliged to do so? Characteristically she took the offensive and asked how and why knowledge of the Official History had been leaked. More to the point, she also asked what would happen if she declined to agree to publication.[274]

This produced an official scurry for precedents, of which none could be found: official histories had never previously become matters of party dispute.[275] Hunt met Mrs Thatcher on 28 July 1978 in her room in Parliament and explained how people had been consulted over the History, though (perhaps tactfully) he did not remind her of the Parliamentary announcements already made about it. He outlined the History's background including the original decision under Heath, but Mrs Thatcher was adamant that it should never have been started and she did not want to be involved with it. Hunt put the key question: if publication went ahead, would she criticise the decision? She replied that she would remain silent.[276] For Hunt this was mission accomplished, and he received the go-ahead for publication from Callaghan on 31 July.

After becoming Prime Minister in 1979, Mrs Thatcher was still in a position to limit the history's effect. Hinsley's first volume was already in publication, and she did not seek to block volumes two and three (the latter in two parts) that followed in 1981, 1984 and

1988. She had more scope with the two specialised volumes, on security plus counterintelligence and strategic deception, in which human sources gave more reason for SIS's concerns.[277] These were completed in 1978 and 1980, but, citing the sensitivity of spy cases in the media – she had announced Blunt's past as a Soviet agent – Mrs Thatcher blocked the publication of both volumes for some years. She finally changed her mind in 1985, in response to enquiries from Trend and her Cabinet Secretary,[278] but by the time these were sanitised and published in 1990 she had left office.[279] Sir Michael Howard, author of the deception volume, observed that by then the elderly wartime participants had already leaked all of his book's revelations, but he chalked up his involvement in the project to experience.[280]

Despite these relaxations Mrs Thatcher's period in office signalled some reversion to secrecy as the preferred policy on intelligence issues that came to her notice. Under her influence GCHQ began to act more strictly over the 1974 distinction between 'really sensitive' details (effectively the details of codebreaking) and releasable content. Gordon Welchman was one of Bletchley's leading figures and had become an American citizen after the war, and in 1982 he published a more extensive account of Bletchley and its Enigma techniques, for which he was deprived of his security clearance with his then American employer.[281] Three years later he submitted an amplifying article for publication in the UK and received D Notice clearance for it, immediately followed by a strong rebuke from GCHQ's Director criticising his 'direct damage to security'. He died soon afterwards. The article was published early the following year with the related correspondence, including a defence of Welchman's publication by a distinguished Bletchley colleague.[282]

Mrs Thatcher's attitude had certainly rubbed off on this episode of intelligence openness.[283] But except for delaying the remaining volumes of the Official History the general effect under her government was to tighten secrecy on topical intelligence issues instead of history, and even here there was considerable progress. The important legislation for communications interception was established in 1985, followed by the Security Service's legal standing in 1989, while intelligence's greatest publicity – at the heart of politics and issues of public interest, overtaking Bletchley's wartime success – came under Mrs Thatcher's de-unionisation of GCHQ in 1984. The principle of historical transparency had been more or less established at the end of the 1970s, and democracy had by then moved on to more immediate matters.

Reflections

This account has described the move from the virtually complete protection of wartime Sigint up to the late 1960s to a relative openness by the end of 1970s. Its episodes hang together in a quite dramatic and unplanned fashion. The formal commissioning of the Official History in 1971 prepared the community for modifications to complete secrecy, though no one knew what form these would take. Winterbotham's publication then triggered a rushed policy change, with the wholesale Enigma releases that followed after the surprise discovery of PRO files. These in turn were followed by the extension of release to Fish and other intelligence material over time. Winterbotham's book and the released archives for their part encouraged Whitehall to publish Hinsley's history in the unexpurgated historical form that made it such a success. Without the combined impetus of all these events the first volume of the history might not have been completed before Mrs Thatcher became Prime Minister in 1979, and its publication might have been long delayed. But this did not happen, and the arrangements for wartime openness were substantially complete by the time she took office. The settlement with Masterman also made a significant contribution at the beginning of this process, but its effect on official policy remained relatively small. The commissioning of the Official History, Winterbotham's book, the massive releases of decrypted enemy messages, and later the history's full publication – all unplanned – were the main parts of this process and key to establishing intelligence history as an acceptable bridge between secrecy and openness. Of its significance, Richard Aldrich has concluded that 'Official history, although bringing its own difficulties, offers government a middle way and an opportunity of making a positive response to the problems of policing the past';[284] and the same applies to documentary releases. Peter Hennessy wrote enthusiastically in 2005 of the prospects for 'a mixed economy of intelligence history', combining Official History with private writing and access to archives.[285]

So what should now be thought of post-war Britain's management of the Ultra secret? The original prescription of 'NEVER' releasing it does not seem surprising. Britain in 1945 was exhausted and impoverished, and already had intimations of the Cold War and risk of armed conflict with the USSR. Government policy needed all the help intelligence could provide. Bletchley had demonstrated the potential for the machine-aided exploitation of targets' ciphers, and there seemed a possibility of exploiting Soviet ciphers on that scale if necessary. The developing Cold War was to become substantially an intelligence war. If real conflict had occurred, intelligence might have been be a war-winning capability, or at least a war-surviving one. In such circumstances the edict of perpetual secrecy was understandable.

But historians can ask what this secrecy achieved. It is now accepted that wartime Ultra was betrayed through Soviet human sources during the Second War and soon thereafter, and was an influence in the high standards of Soviet communications security as long as the Cold War lasted. This Soviet knowledge was recognised as a factor in the JIC review of Ultra's protection in 1968, and in this respect the defensive British effort to keep the secret from the Cold War adversary was a failure almost before it started.[286] But the post-war UK and US Sigint efforts had many non-Soviet targets, and it is reasonable to assume that some work on them benefited from wartime codebreaking methods as long as Ultra's history was kept secret.

Should it therefore have been defended longer? Some things might indeed have been done differently. The Official History was intended to deter aspiring authors but palpably failed to stop Winterbotham, perhaps partly through the fifteen months' delay in commissioning the project after Heath's critical reaction. The JIC could have followed up its early idea of releasing Enigma messages in an unspectacular trickle, though this would have been unlikely to stop Winterbotham, and there is no guarantee that it would have worked anyway. The Committee might also have deflected attention from cryptanalysis by giving more emphasis to Bletchley's exploitation of captured German crypto material, particularly for naval Enigma, building on the outline already sketched by McLachlan,[287] but a deliberate deception of this kind would have had its own problems. Those responsible would have been torn between slanting them to minimise Ultra's significance and the temptation to let the full triumph emerge, and it is not surprising that in the circumstances of 1973–4 officials settled for extensive revelation.

On the other judgements by the JIC, the emphasis placed on Bertrand's memoir is still surprising, and Winterbotham might have been handled differently. Fish was subsequently handled unobtrusively, but by then the Ultra secret had already had its day. These and other relevant decisions were all unplanned, reactive to events and influenced by personal and political factors. Civil servants and intelligence officers were as human in their reactions as everyone else. The Committee's minutes do not record much discussion of long-term considerations. With hindsight it was a weakness that a plan was not prepared in advance for a series of Ultra releases when the appropriate time arrived, but this would have needed considerable effort to overcome the agencies' instinctive opposition.[288] There was – perhaps still is – a strong conviction behind the GCHQ statement that 'no knowledge would suit GCHQ best'.[289]

But whatever their limitations the decisions taken were of great significance. They established, effectively and for the first time, that the secrecy of high-grade wartime codebreaking would no longer be protected as a matter of principle. Historical secrecy had to be defended when necessary on a case-by-case basis; they were no longer driven by the professional instinct for secrecy. Damage assessment was to be the criterion for intelligence history, and was thereby set on its way to become the test for protecting current methods. I wrote a long time ago that 'real secrets must in practice be surrounded by a wider glacis of secrecy if they are to be successfully defended',[290] and the depth and nature of the glacis are still constantly debated. Even for intelligence history the problems of protecting individuals' identities – touched on in this paper, but at that time mostly subsidiary – remain of concern, and other problems of transparency remain. But the automatic protection of intelligence secrets is essentially no longer acceptable as dogma. Whatever criticisms can be made of the details, the JIC's decisions aligned British intelligence with what became the tide of liberal Western standards, and indeed substantially contributed to this change.

This result can be debated, although not here; though one unexpected product of openness with intelligence history should be noted in passing. The Ultra revelations of the 1970s embedded Bletchley into the British national memory, with practical results. In the intense political struggle from 1984 onwards over Mrs Thatcher's banning of national trade unions in GCHQ, it was common ground for all the parties that the importance of the work was not in question. Largely through the Bletchley example, intelligence was accepted by then as a necessary government service, to an extent that would not have been found under the earlier secretive position of the post-war years.[291] Incidentally, the publicity over de-unionisation also boosted GCHQ's recruitment applications.[292]

Where then does credit for this openness lie? Bonsall was no enthusiast but was determined to protect GCHQ from a damaging public battle with Winterbotham, and worked for efficient releases once committed to them. Hooper was a consistent influence: initially defending the Ultra secret while recognising that it could not last for ever, then leading over Winterbotham, and subsequently (with Bonsall) releasing archives and securing the Official History's publication. The History underpinned the whole openness process, and credit is due to McLachlan who first suggested it. But the key success was getting the project running when politicians (particularly Heath) were unenthusiastic and had no apparent reward of press and public interest, or political kudos. Leadership came from officials, and more from the Cabinet Office than the agencies. Hooper led there from autumn 1973 though he had not been the History's early proponent. A significant part had been played by White as Intelligence Coordinator: he produced the original study in 1969, took a main role in getting Heath's approval, and returned in retirement to chair the History's Steering Group. Michael Howard subsequently wrote that 'I had the impression that he [White] was the driving force behind the whole project . . . [his] determination and enthusiasm were quite remarkable.'[293]

On the other hand I am inclined to identify Trend's initial determination and authority as the main force, with White as his supporter and implementer.[294] Trend was a patriot with a special enthusiasm for intelligence, and he was more conscious than most of the obligation to history, particularly for a national triumph. On intelligence he had earlier persuaded the Prime Minister to create the Economic JIC and the Assessments Staff in 1968. Malcolm Mackintosh who became the staff's longest serving member commented later that Trend's attitude to anything was 'Can we do it better?'[295] Over the putative SOE histories Aldrich has described his attitude as 'important, positive and benign',[296] and this was his relationship with all intelligence on his watch, no more so than over the Official History. On this he called the original meeting, refashioned the proposal to get eventual approval, and oversaw its launch. Without his determination it would never have got started. He was, uniquely, both Cabinet Secretary and intelligence enthusiast, but he also respected a greater good: that liberal democracy needs objective history, not secrecy and myth.

Notes

1. Including particularly the Lorenz SZ 40/42, codenamed 'Tunny', one of the German telecipher machines which were collectively known at Bletchley as the 'Fish' ciphers to distinguish them from Enigma. Another Fish machine was the Siemens & Halske T52, codenamed 'Sturgeon', but its traffic was not broken as regularly as Tunny, which supplied most of Bletchley's Fish decrypts.
2. Hinsley, F. H. and E. E. Thomas, C. F. G. Ransom, R. C. Knight, C. A. G. Simkins, *British Intelligence in the Second World War*, 4 vols (London: HMSO, 1979–93); and Howard, M. E., *British Intelligence in the Second World War: Strategic Deception, Vol. 5* (London: HMSO, 1990).
3. Sir Harry Hinsley, 1918–98. St John's College Cambridge (wartime Bletchley Park); Master 1979–89; University Vice-Chancellor, 1981–3; knighted in 1985.

4. Winterbotham, F. W., *The Ultra Secret* (London: Weidenfeld and Nicolson, 1974). I have followed official practice in using the code-word Ultra as shorthand for the product of these codebreaking achievements.

5. Horner, D. and J. Blaxland and R. Crawley, *The Official History of ASIO*, 3 vols (Sydney: Allen & Unwin, 2014–17).

6. de Jong, B., 'Official Intelligence Histories. Is there a Problem?', *Leidschrift* 30, no. 3, 2015: 83–97. An earlier official history, published in English, was Riste, O., *The Norwegian Intelligence Service 1945–1970* (London: Cass, 1999).

7. de Jong, 'Official Intelligence Histories', pp. 90–5.

8. Ibid., p. 97.

9. Quoted by Aldrich, R. J. and J. Kasuko, 'Escaping from American intelligence: Culture, Ethnocentrism and the Anglosphere', *International Affairs* 88, no. 5, 2012: 1018, fn. 51.

10. See for example Johnson T. R., *American Cryptology during the Cold War, 1945–1989*, 4 vols (Washington DC: Centre for Cryptologic History, 1995) and related histories of the NSA and the US Army's Signal Security Agency available at: https://www.nsa.gov/news-features/declassified-documents/cryptologic-histories/

11. British authors of these later histories now prefer to call them 'authorised', to indicate their independence. The term has been used elsewhere for privately commissioned biographies of individuals. The Hinsley histories were originally described as 'official' and I have kept this description here. For a discussion of the usage, see Murphy, C., 'The Origins of SOE in France', *Historical Journal*, 46, no. 4, 2003: 935–52. The Cabinet Secretary (Trend) explained to the Prime Minister in 1965 that the published history of the SOE in France was a companion to the official histories, not an official history proper, since 'it had not been written by a team of historians . . . or subjected to the full process of departmental scrutiny' (Murphy, 'The Origins of SOE in France', p. 936, fn. 3). This now seems a fine distinction, indeed an unconvincing one.

12. Ferris, J., 'The British Army, Signals and Security in the Desert Campaign, 1940–42', in M. Handel (ed.), *Intelligence and Military Operations* (London: Routledge, 1990), p. 256.

13. Strachan, H., *The First World War: Volume 1: To Arms* (Oxford: Oxford University Press, 2001).

14. Aldrich, R. J., 'Policing the Past: Official History, Secrecy and British Intelligence since 1945', *English Historical Review*, 119, no. 483, 2004: 922–53; Moran, C., *Classified: Secrecy and the State in Modern Britain* (Cambridge: Cambridge University Press, 2013); Lintott,

B. E., 'Dudley Clarke's Official History of Military Deception, 1944–1945', *Intelligence and National Security*, 32, no. 1, 2017: 55.

15. Hennessy, P., 'The Last Customer: British Intelligence and the British Historian', Hinsley Memorial Lecture, St John's College Cambridge, 24 October 2005. Unpublished, quoted with author's permission.

16. Strictly speaking there were then two committees. The main JIC was the JIC(A) and there was a short-lived JIC(B) for economic subjects, subsequently renamed the Overseas Economic Intelligence Committee. After the JIC(B) title was discontinued in 1974, the JIC(A) reverted to its old title and it is used here throughout.

17. Maurice, J. F. and M. H. Grant, *History of the War in South Africa, 1899–1902*, 4 vols (London: Hurst and Blackett, 1906–10). For more on the origins of the Official Histories see the Cabinet Office, 'The UK Government's Official History Programme', accessed on 30 December 2020 at: https://webarchive.nationalarchives.gov. uk/20080205143007/http://www.cabinetoffice.gov.uk/publication-scheme/published_information/1/officialhistory.aspx

18. Cited in Green, A., *Writing the Great War: Sir James Edmonds and the Official Histories, 1915–1948* (London: Frank Cass, 2003), p. 6.

19. The 1987 volume – *The Occupation of the Rhineland 1914–1918* – was produced as a confidential document in 1944.

20. Thirty-eight out of the total 87 volumes were single-service studies of ground campaigns. In an early controversy about one of the draft Gallipoli volumes the committee controlling the history ruled that 'the military histories were to deal only with operations'. See Green, *Writing the Great War*, p. 98.

21. A volume on the blockade of the Central Powers was produced as a confidential document in 1937 and made publicly available in 1961.

22. Danchev, A., *Oliver Franks: Founding Father* (Oxford: Clarendon Press, 1993), pp. 40–1.

23. I recall asking in 1952 about doing postgraduate research on the 1914–18 war and being dissuaded by the future author of the first official volume on Second World War strategy, on the grounds that I would have no access to official records.

24. Edmonds, J. E. and R. Maxwell-Hyslop, *Military Operations: France and Belgium 1918, The Advance to Victory, Vol. 5* (London: HMSO, 1947), p. 611.

25. Freedman, L., *The Official History of the Falklands Campaign*, 2 vols (London: Routledge, 2005).

26. Compare for example with Strachan's *The First Wold War* and its substantial sections on national attitudes, financing the war, industrial mobilisation and the ideas of 1914.

27. Green, *Writing the Great War,* p. 27.
28. von Clausewitz, C., *On War,* ed. M. E. Howard and P. Paret (Princeton, NJ: Princeton University Press, 1976), p. 117.
29. Maurice and Grant, *History of the War in South Africa, Vol. 4,* p. 392.
30. I owe this understanding to Beech, J., *Haig's Intelligence: GHQ and the German Army, 1916–1918* (Cambridge: Cambridge University Press, 2013).
31. Wavell, A. P., *Generals and Generalship; The Lees Knowles Lectures Delivered at Trinity College, Cambridge in 1939* (London: Penguin Books, 1941).
32. Corbett, J. S., *History of the Great War: Naval Operations, Vols 1–3* (London: Longmans, Green and Co, 1923 onwards); Newbolt, H. J., *History of the Great War: Naval Operations, Vols 4–5* (London: Longmans, Green and Co, 1931).
33. Corbett, *History of the Great War, Vol. 3,* 2nd edition (1940). The list of decrypted Jutland signals is in the 1938–40 edition of volume 3, appendix J, p. 442.
34. Churchill, W. S., *The World Crisis: 1916–1918, Vol. 3, Part 1* (London: Thornton Butterworth, 1927), p. 188. His first volume also described the capture of the Baltic German codebook, as well as cryptanalytic recoveries, and direction finding and analysis; see Churchill, W. S., *The World Crisis: 1911–1914, Vol. 1* (London: Thornton Butterworth, 1923), pp. 460–3. Churchill's brushes with authority are described in Moran, *Classified,* pp. 57–9.
35. Kahn, D., *Seizing the Enigma: The Race to Break the German U-Boat Codes, 1939–1943* (London: Souvenir Press, 1992), pp. 38–41. This refers to Churchill's revelations in volume 1 of *The World Crisis,* which was translated into German in 1924.
36. Clarke, W. F. and F. Birch, *A Contribution to the History of German Naval Warfare 1914–1918,* 3 vols. These volumes can be found at the UK National Archives (TNA), HW 7/1 through HW 7/4. Unless otherwise stated, all archival series – CAB, DEFE, HW, PREM, PRO – hereafter refer to TNA records.
37. The lecture was by Sir James Ewing. The book was Hoy, H. C., *40 O.B., or How the War was Won* (London: Hutchinson, 1932).
38. Moran, *Classified,* pp. 63–9; Jeffrey, K., *MI6: The History of the Secret Intelligence Service, 1909–1949* (London: Bloomsbury, 2010), pp. 236–44.
39. Cabinet Office, 'The UK Government's Official History Programme'.
40. With substantial contributions from Frank Birch, an author of the First World War history of Room 40, who later became head of

Bletchley's Naval Section for part of the Second World War. A copy is available as HW 41/1 through 43/3.

41. Special Order by Sir Edward Travis, 7 May 1945, HW 3/29, quoted in Aldrich, 'Policing the Past', p. 927.

42. JIC(47) 81st meeting (0), 'Use of Special Intelligence by Official Historians', Confidential Annex, 21 November 1947, CAB 103/288.

43. Ibid. See also Kahn, D., 'How the Allies Suppressed the Second Greatest Secret of World War II', *The Journal of Military History*, 74, no. 4, 2010: 1229–41.

44. LSIB Meetings Summary No. 13, 18 July 1945, WO 208/5126. See also Aldrich, 'Policing the Past', fn. 10 and fn. 21.

45. JIC(45) 223 (0), 'General Directive for Safeguarding Intelligence Sources in Compiling Official Histories', draft memo in Annex, 20 July 1945, CAB 103/288; JIC(48) 14 (0), 11 February 1948, CAB 103/288.

46. Burke Frederick St John Trend, 1914–87. Cabinet Secretary, 1963–73; Rector of Lincoln College, Oxford, 1973–83; knighted in 1962; Life Peer (Baron Trend) in 1974.

47. Moran, *Classified*, p. 9. Trend quoted in Franks, O. S., *Departmental Committee on Section 20 of the Official Secrets Acts 1911* (London: HSMO, 1972), Cmnd 5104, Vol. 3, p. 320.

48. Moran, *Classified*, p. 95.

49. The historians of the bomber offensive drew considerably from the results of the photographic reconnaissance that was their main input for targeting, but steered clear of Ultra, which was not supplied directly to RAF Bomber Command. See Webster, C. K. and N. Frankland, *The Strategic Air Offensive against Germany, 1939–1945*, 4 vols (London: HMSO, 1961).

50. Roskill, S. W., *The War at Sea, 1939–1945: The Period of Balance, Vol. 2* (London: HMSO, 1956), p. 208. The relevant section reads: 'It was not until May 1943 that the discomfiture of the skilled German cypher-breakers was made complete and final. The reader should not, of course, assume that we British were meanwhile idle in achieving the opposite purpose.'

51. See also Roskill, S. W., *The Secret Capture* (London: Collins, 1959).

52. Reynolds, D., 'The Ultra Secret and Churchill's War Memoirs', *Intelligence and National Security*, 20, no. 2, 2005: 209–24.

53. Foreword to Winterbotham, *The Ultra Secret*, p. xii.

54. Wilmot, C., *The Struggle for Europe* (London: Collins, 1952), pp. 199–201, 332, 334. For the suggestion that Wilmot may have been aware of intelligence details, see Aldrich, 'Policing the Past', fn. 16.

55. Wohlstetter, R., *Pearl Harbor: Warning and Decision* (Stanford, CA: Stanford University Press, 1962).
56. 'Secret Lost', *Time*, vol. XLVI, no. 25, 17 December 1945.
57. The article (unsigned) was published as 'Frontier Incidents – Exposure', *The Isis Magazine*, 26 February 1958, p. 12. There is a brief account in Carpenter, H., *That was Satire, That Was* (London: Phoenix, 2002). The Lord Chief Justice took their court case in person and, despite his reputation as a hanging judge, awarded light sentences of three months' imprisonment, and specified that the undergraduates should not be exposed to criminal influences (personal recollection).
58. Described in Aldrich, 'Policing the Past', pp. 929–31.
59. Fry, H., *The London Cage: The Secret History of Britain's World War II Interrogation Centre* (New Haven, CT, and London: Yale University Press, 2017), pp. 1–4.
60. Philby, K., *My Silent War* (New York: Grove Press, 1968). Three books about Philby, and a fourth on its way, were mentioned in Trevor-Roper, H. R., 'The Philby Affair', *Encounter*, 30, no. 4, 1968: 3–26.
61. Wilkinson, N., *Secrecy and the Media: The Official History of the United Kingdom's D Notice System* (London and New York: Routledge, 2009), chapters 39–43.
62. JIC(66) 10th meeting, 'Disposal of Departmental Records', Confidential Annex, 10 March 1966, CAB 159/45.
63. Griffiths (GCHQ) to Stewart (Secretary JIC), 10 March 1969, CAB 163/134.
64. JIC(A) (69) 23rd meeting, 'The Release of Historical Intelligence Records', Confidential Annex, 12 June 1969, CAB 163/133.
65. Masterman, J. C., *On the Chariot Wheel: An Autobiography* (London and New York: Oxford University Press, 1975), p. 357.
66. Sir Dick White, 1906–93. Director General of Security Service, 1953–6; Chief of the Secret Intelligence Service, 1956–68; Intelligence Coordinator, 1967–73; knighted in 1955.
67. Masterman, *On the Chariot Wheel*, p. 350. His battle with the authorities is described in chapters 32 and 33.
68. Michael Howard quotes Sir Alec Douglas Home, Foreign Secretary (1970–4) recalling his shock at the idea of prosecuting Masterman, distinguished as sportsman as well as academic: 'I squashed that pretty quickly, I can tell you. Lock up the best amateur spin bowler in England? They must have been out of their minds.' See Howard, M., *Reflections on Strategic Deception* (Austin, TX: The Harry Ransom Humanities Research Center, 1994), p. 7.

70

69. Masterman to Harmer, 25 March 1969, WOR/PRO 10/1/128/2, Masterman papers, Worcester College, Oxford.
70. These were intelligence-related publications which had implications for the pressure on the D Notice system. The list had some rather strange inclusions. Copy enclosed in Stewart (Secretary JIC) to Fyffe (MoD), 9 December 1970, CAB 163/256.
71. The first reference can be found in JIC(66) 23rd meeting, 2 June 1966, CAB 159/45. It appeared regularly throughout that year and intermittently in 1967. See for example JIC(67) 16th meeting, 13 April 1967, CAB 159/47.
72. Hooper to Richards (Secretary JIC), 13 October 1966, CAB 163/66. See also CAB 301/424, and *Brigadier John Tiltman: A Giant Among Cryptanalysts* (Fort Meade: Center for Cryptologic History, 2007) p. 60.
73. E-mail to author 21 April 2003 from David Kahn. This edition described the seizure of cryptographic material in early June 1944 from the captured German submarine U-505, it followed it with, 'The Allies now read U-boat operational traffic. For they had, more than a year before the theft, succeeded in solving the difficult U-boat systems and – in one of the finest cryptanalytic achievements of the war – managed to read the intercepts on a current basis.' See Kahn, D., *The Codebreakers: The Story of Secret Writing* (New York: Macmillan, 1967), p. 506. In a more recent publication, Kahn states that the capture enabled the Allies to read the additionally enciphered positions in the German messages; see Kahn, D., *Seizing the Enigma* (New York: Barnes and Noble, 1991), p. 264. Hinsley attributed much less value to the capture in *British Intelligence in the Second World War: Vol. 3, Part 2*, p. 852.
74. On the back cover of my copy of McLachlan, D., *Room 39: Naval Intelligence in Action 1939–45* (London: Weidenfeld & Nicolson, 1968). It is also advertised there as 'the first full treatment of the history of codes and cyphers – concentrating on their all-important use in World War II'.
75. Assessing the impact of *The Codebreakers*, Hooper minuted that '. . . reviews of this book provided in themselves additional material on the importance of Sigint in war and specifically of the British Sigint effort'. See 'Published material on the organisation of Intelligence in WWII', enclosed in Hooper to White, 27 May 1969, CAB 163/134. This referred to a book review by an American veteran of Bletchley: Friendly, A., 'Secrets of Code-Breaking', *The Washington Post*, 5 December 1967. A copy of Friendly's book review can be found in CAB 163/230.

76. JIC(A)(70) 34th meeting, Confidential Annex, 3 September 1970; CAB 185/4; JIC(A)(70) 41st meeting, Confidential Annex, 22 October 1970, ibid.

77. Kahn, D., 'How I Discovered World War II's Greatest Spy', *Cryptologia*, 34, no. 1, 2009: 16.

78. Kahn, D., *The Codebreakers: The Story of Secret Writing* (London: Sphere, 1973), pp. 263–5, 268–71, 340. See also 'Published material on the organisation of intelligence in WWII', enclosed in Hooper to White, 27 May 1969, CAB 163/134.

79. A list prepared by Hooper suggests that authors influenced included David Irving and Malcolm Muggeridge; see 'Published material on the organisation of intelligence in WWII', enclosed in Hooper to White, 27 May 1969, CAB 163/134. This included The Hon. Ewen Montagu, CBE, 1901–85; Judge Advocate of the Fleet, 1945–73; lawyer and author of *The Man Who Never Was* (1954). JIC records show Hooper accompanied the Attorney General to a 1971 meeting with Montagu and persuaded him to delay another book he planned on deception; see JIC(A)(72) 26th meeting, Confidential Annex, 13 July 1971, CAB 185/10. Bletchley veteran Gordon Welchman also recalls meeting Hooper in 1972 and being asked to delay his memoir; see Welchman, G., 'Ultra Revisited: A Tale of Two Contributors', *Intelligence and National Security*, 32, no. 2, 2017: 249.

80. Trevor-Roper, H., *The Philby Affair: Espionage, Treason, and Secret Services* (London: Kimber, 1968).

81. Trevor-Roper, 'The Philby Affair', p. 18. He added further details about codebreaking success against German intelligence in the book version: '. . . all Abwehr hand-cyphers were read by the British from the beginning of 1940 and machine-cyphers – which were clearly thought to be invulnerable – from 1942' (*The Philby Affair*, p. 116).

82. Hooper to Millward, 2 October 1969, 'Histories, Records Etc.', copy to White, CAB 163/155. Hooper's minute also cited the equally distinguished historian Jack Plumb who had worked at Bletchley on German naval ciphers. No reasons are given.

83. McLachlan had asked particularly about advice on the JIC post-1943 when his own knowledge of the Committee lapsed. Trend to Burrows (Chairman JIC), 23 July 1966, CAB 163/66.

84. Forward to PUS (RN), 27 September 1967, DEFE 24/153. McLachlan's signature can apparently be seen on some Bletchley documents in this period (private information).

85. McLachlan, *Room 39*, p. xvi.

86. Vice-Admiral Sir Norman Egbert Denning, 1904–79. Director of Naval Intelligence, 1960–4; Deputy Chief of Staff for Intelligence, 1964–5; Secretary of Services, Press and Broadcasting ('D Notice') Committee, 1967–72; knighted in 1963.

87. McIndoe to Burrows (JIC), 'Naval intelligence during the War', 22 June 1966, CAB 163/66. Trend was also concerned about McLachlan's access, at one point reminding the JIC Chairman that 'I would be opposed, in principle, to giving him any detailed information about the existence, composition or functioning of any part of the intelligence community's machinery'; see Trend to Burrows (JIC), 23 July 1966, CAB 163/66.

88. Hooper to Richards (Secretary JIC), 13 October 1966, CAB 163/133.

89. McLachlan, *Room 39*, chapter 4.

90. McLachlan included the deliberate 'pinches of cipher material' in chapter 12. His statement that from the planned seizure of a small German weather ship 'A valuable haul of documents was made which was to have a decisive and lasting effect on the conduct of the Battle of the Atlantic' could hardly have been clearer; see McLachlan, *Room 39*, pp. 272–3.

91. For example, 'They [German naval authorities] were loath to believe that the British – or the Americans – had at any time broken into their signals traffic on any serious scale. They retained confidence in the Enigma machine . . . and took great pains with their changes of ciphers. Thus it was that the NID, from March 1942 to early 1943, knew nothing from this source about the Atlantic U-boats.' McLachlan, *Room 39*, p. 89.

92. One GCHQ official warned that 'We need to bear in mind all along that MacLachlan's general strategy is one of "grandmother's steps" i.e. to move from one position to another further forward without being noticed.' Evans (GCHQ) to Morgan (FO), 30 December 1966, DEFE 24/392.

93. Calvocoressi to Evans (GCHQ), 12 September 1967, CAB 163/133; Millward (GCHQ) to White, 27 October 1969, ibid. Calvocoressi's account was later published as *Top Secret Ultra* (London: Cassell, 1980).

94. McLachlan, D., 'Intimate Enemies', *The Listener*, 26 September 1968. A copy of this review can be found in CAB 103/709.

95. McLachlan to Trend, 1 February 1969, CAB 103/703.

96. Trend to McLachlan, 10 February 1969, CAB 103/703.

97. Hinsley, F. H., 'Taboo or Not Taboo?' *The Observer*, 12 May 1968.

98. Hinsley to Denning, 17 January 1969, CAB 163/133. Hinsley's other source was Robin Denniston, whose father was head of Bletchley for the first half of the war; see Denniston, R., *Thirty Secret Years: A. G. Denniston's Work in Signals Intelligence, 1914–1944* (Clifton-upon-Teme: Polperro Heritage Press, 2007). Hinsley had been author of part of Bletchley's classified wartime history compiled by Frank Birch, later edited by John Jackson and published as *The Official History of British Signals Intelligence: 1914–1945, Vols 1–2* (Milton Keynes: Military Press, 2004–8).

99. Ibid. (Hinsley to Denning).

100. Denning forwarded Hinsley's letter to GCHQ, but not the Cabinet Office; see Millward (GCHQ) to White, 27 October 1969, CAB 163/133.

101. McLachlan had first raised this idea with his friend, Denning; see Denning to McLachlan, 24 April 1969, CAB 163/134.

102. JIC (A)(70) 51st meeting, 23 November 1970, CAB 186/6.

103. A JIC working party reviewed the policy of intelligence records over 1967–8; see JIC(68) 46 (Final), 'The Release of SIGINT Records', 13 November 1968, PREM 13/3252.

104. Millward (GCHQ) to Richards (JIC Secretary), 25 July 1968, CAB 163/156.

105. Draft memorandum by Hooper, 'Release of World War II Intelligence Records', enclosed in Hooper to Stewart (JIC Secretary), 29 July 1969, CAB 163/156.

106. Trend to Wilson (PM), 'The Release of SIGINT Records', 25 March 1969, PREM 13/3252.

107. Gregson to Norbury, 16 November 1970, DEFE 23/107; Note by Cornish, 'Transfer to Public Record Office of World War II Papers with Intelligence Implications', 30 November 1970, CAB 163/255.

108. The JIC recorded that '. . . the MoD review had disclosed only a relatively small number of papers which had intelligence references. It should be possible to clear those during the next twelve months . . .' – a judgement which turned out to be mistaken. See JIC(A)(70) 47th meeting, Confidential Annex, 3 December 1970, CAB 185/4.

109. 'The Release of Departmental Records with Intelligence Implications', enclosed in Stewart (JIC) to Norbury (CAB), 29 January 1971, CAB 103/703; 'Record of a Meeting', 19 February 1971, ibid.

110. On Denning's press connections see Moran, *Classified*, pp. 312–13.

111. Two of these 'perhaps less scrupulous authors' cited by Denning were David Irving and Patrick Seale. Attached to Denning's minute

was a list of intelligence-related publications written since 1945, an odd mix of memoir, professional history and speculative journalism. Copy enclosed in Denning to Dunnett, 11 February 1969, DEFE 23/107.

112. 'Intelligence Activities, 1939–1945: Note of a Meeting held in Sir Burke Trend's Room', 26 February 1969, DEFE 24/656.

113. See the various concerns raised by officials in 'Record of a Meeting Held by the Intelligence Coordinator on 12th March 1969', DEFE 24/656.

114. (Undated private letter, possibly 2003.) However he was not recorded among those present at Trend's original meeting; perhaps it was a later one.

115. White to Trend, 13 May 1969, CAB 163/134.

116. Stewart's recollections of the time (private letter).

117. Aldrich, 'Policing the Past', pp. 923–4.

118. £10,000 for pay-offs and £40,000 for other expenses; see Aldrich, 'Policing the Past', p. 939.

119. Ibid. I remember hearing 'never again' from the Cabinet Historical Section.

120. The record of a meeting between Trend, White and Hooper mentions that '[i]t would not be desirable to repeat the experience of SOE in France'; see 'Release of Records: Note of a Meeting in Sir Burke Trend's Room', 1 October 1969, CAB 103/703.

121. Attributed to Sir Maurice Oldfield, Chief of SIS, in Deacon, R., 'C': A Biography of Sir Maurice Oldfield, Head of MI6 (London: Futura, 1985), p. 217. This condition was relaxed in later volumes, which included some names.

122. Hinsley et al., British Intelligence in the Second World War, Vol. 1, p. vii (introduction).

123. Trend to Wilson (PM), 29 July 1969, CAB 103/703; Halls to Trend, 1 August 1969, ibid.; Gregson to Lloyd Jones, 29 October 1969, ibid.

124. Fyffe to Elworthy (CDS), 6 October 1969, DEFE 23/107; Dunnett to Maguire, 18 November 1970, ibid.

125. Wilson to Heath, 16 March 1970, DEFE 23/107; Heath to Wilson, 17 April 1970, ibid.

126. Trend to Heath (PM), 'Official History of Intelligence in the Second World War', 10 November 1970, CAB 163/255; Gregson to Norbury, 16 November 1970, DEFE 23/107.

127. 'Record of a Meeting Held at 10 Downing Street', 19 February 1971, CAB 163/255.

128. At this stage the suggested authors were Calvocoressi (volume 1), Hinsley (volume 2), Anthony Simkins (volume 3) and Peter Fleming (volume 4). 'Note for the Record', 22 April 1971, CAB 163/255. See also the memorandum prepared by White and Stewart for Trend, 'The Intelligence History', 15 April 1971, CAB 163/255.

129. Hennessy, 'The Last Customer' (unpublished). See also Trend to Heath (PM), 'Official History of Intelligence in the Second World War', 10 November 1970, CAB 103/703.

130. 'Proposal for an Official History of British Intelligence Activities in World War II', 14 July 1969, CAB 163/255.

131. Trend to Heath (PM), 'Official History of Intelligence in the Second World War', 10 November 1970, CAB 103/703.

132. 'Proposal for an Official History of British Intelligence Activities in World War II', 14 July 1969, CAB 163/255.

133. Ibid. See also Trend's discussion of the report in 'Proposed Official History of Intelligence During the Second World War', 23 July 1969, CAB 163/155.

134. Trend to Wilson (PM), 29 July 1969, CAB 163/133; JIC(A)(71) 14th meeting, Confidential Annex, 1 April 1971, CAB 185/6.

135. Sir Martin Furnival Jones, 1912–97. Director General of the Security Service, 1965–72; knighted in 1967.

136. White to Masterman, 29 April 1969, WOR/PRO 10/1/128/2, Masterman papers, Worcester College, Oxford.

137. Masterman, *On the Chariot Wheel*, p. 356.

138. Ibid., p. 354.

139. Quoted in Harrison, E. D. R., 'J.C. Masterman and the Security Service, 1940–72', *Intelligence and National Security*, 24, no. 6, 2009: 802.

140. White to Trend (draft), 13 May 1969, CAB 163/134.

141. Winks, R., *Cloak and Gown: Scholars in America's Secret War* (London: Collins, 1987), p. 296.

142. For examples at TNA, see HW 14/131 and HW 49/7.

143. See the eleven index entries in Jeffrey, *MI6*, p. 840.

144. Winterbotham, F. W., *Secret and Personal* (London: Kimber, 1969). This biographical account was later expanded and republished as *The Ultra Spy: An Autobiography* (London: Papermac, 1989–91).

145. Winterbotham to Masterman, 1 November 1971, WOR/PRO 10/1/130, Masterman papers, Worcester College, Oxford.

146. Anthony Cave Brown, 1929–2006; British-American journalist, writer and historian.

147. Winterbotham, *The Ultra Spy*, pp. 245–6.

148. 'Frederick William Winterbotham', Oral History Interview, 19 February 1984, Imperial War Museum. Reel 34 discusses his decision to publish *The Ultra Secret*, but in this he recalls meeting with his publisher (Denniston) in early 1974 and writing the book in the following months, rather than in 1973 as the record indicates.
149. Winterbotham to Masterman, 12 November 1971, WOR/PRO 10/1/130, Masterman papers, Worcester College, Oxford. For his part, Masterman notified Dick White of the request who responded that Winterbotham's book '. . . fills me with foreboding'; see White to Masterman, 18 November 1971, ibid.
150. Brearley to Stowe, 8 July 1975, PREM 16/670.
151. Farnhill to Winterbotham, 26 January 1973, enclosed in INT 37 (73) 3, 'Publications: Winterbotham', Annex, 26 February 1973, CAB 190/53. A later Cabinet Office minute confirmed that 'When Winterbotham first sought official clearance for the work in in late 1972 Mr Heath approved an approach to Winterbotham which successfully deterred him until last year [1974] when the issue arose again.' See Brearley to Stowe, 8 July 1975, PREM 16/670.
152. Winterbotham to Farnhill, 2 February 1973, enclosed in INT 37 (73) 3, 'Publications: Winterbotham', Annex, 26 February 1973, CAB 190/53.
153. Winterbotham to Farnhill, 15 April 1973, enclosed in INT 37 (73) 12, 'Publications: Winterbotham', Annex, 22 May 1973, CAB 190/53.
154. JIC(A)(73) 2nd meeting, Confidential Annex, 11 January 1973, CAB 185/12. Cave Brown planned to come to London in late January to discuss his manuscript and Ultra. The visit was subsequently called off, and the JIC was told that the manuscript would not be ready until later that year. See INT 37 (73) 9, 'Book by Cave Brown', Annex, 9 March 1973, CAB 190/53.
155. Trend to Rawlinson, 18 January 1973, enclosed in INT 37 (73) 8, 'Book by Winterbotham', Annex, 26 February 1973, CAB 190/53.
156. JIC(A)(73) 2nd meeting, Confidential Annex, 11 January 1973, CAB 185/12.
157. Hunt to Wilson, 'Marchetti and Marks and Winterbotham', 8 April 1974, PREM 16/670. No date is quoted for Farnhill's letter.
158. Ibid. The original file is retained, but a copy of Hunt's minute includes Wilson's signature and his response as 'Noted'.
159. Ibid.
160. Extract of Farnhill's letter cited in 'The Official History of Intelligence in World War II and Related Subjects', enclosed in Hooper

to White, 7 November 1975, CAB 103/726. This brief is unsigned but was probably written by John Morrison.

161. The book in question was Marchetti, V. and J. D. Marks, *The CIA and the Cult of Intelligence* (New York: Knopf, 1974).

162. Kahn, D., 'Enigma unwrapped', *The New York Times*, 29 December 1974. A copy of this review can be found in CAB 190/84.

163. Moran, *Classified*, p. 278.

164. Denniston, R., 'Three Kinds of Hero: Publishing the Memoirs of Secret Intelligence People', *Intelligence and National Security*, 7, no. 2, 1992: 119.

165. Winterbotham, *The Ultra Spy*, p. 245.

166. Ibid., p. 246.

167. Conversation with author in the Cabinet Office at the time.

168. In the words of Brigadier John Tiltman, 'I would have also said to Winterbotham, "You are a regular officer . . . We'd like you to know that your colleagues regard your actions as being dishonourable."' See 'Interview with Brigadier Tiltman', 13 December 1978, NSA Oral History 06-78, p. 33. This is part of the declassified NSA's Oral History series, accessed on 29 June 2017 at: https://www.nsa.gov/news-features/declassified-documents/oral-history-interviews/

169. Loehnis to Beesly, 6 November 1975, Christ Church Cambridge, quoted in Moran, *Classified*, p. 279.

170. Tordella, L. W., 'Book Review of The Ultra Secret by F. W. Winterbotham', *Studies in Intelligence*, 19, no. 3, 1975: 47. This article was released by the CIA Historical Review Program, and was accessed on 29 June 1017 at: https://www.cia.gov/library/center-for-the-study-of-intelligence/kent-csi/vol19no3/pdf/v19i3a05p.pdf

171. Kahn, 'Enigma unwrapped'.

172. Kahn repeated this story in a lecture in Christ Church Oxford, 5 September 2002. While Kahn cited the sale of Enigmas in his review of Winterbotham's book, his correspondence at the time referred only to a discussion with Hooper about 'Enigma-type machines'. See Kahn to Denning, 19 July 1974, DEN 2/7, Denning papers, National Maritime Museum, Greenwich.

173. Aldrich, 'Policing the Past', p. 932; also Hennessy, 'The Last Customer' (unpublished).

174. Kvetkas, W. T., 'The Last Days of the Enigma', *Cryptologic Almanac 50th Anniversary Series*, March–April 2002. Accessed on 29 June 2017 at: https://www.nsa.gov/Portals/70/documents/news-features/declassified-documents/crypto-almanac-50th/The_Last_Days_of_the_Enigma.pdf

175. Ferris, J., *Behind the Enigma: The Authorised History of GCHQ, Britain's Secret Cyber-Intelligence Agency* (London: Bloomsbury, 2020), p. 271.

176. Denham, H., 'In Memoriam: Conel Hugh O'Donel Alexander', *Cryptologic Spectrum*, 4, no. 3, 1974: 31. Accessed on 29 June 2017 at: https://www.nsa.gov/Portals/70/documents/news-features/declassified-documents/cryptologic-spectrum/in_memoriam.pdf

177. I recall that on some security issue – perhaps this one – he minuted internally that GCHQ would be best served by a professional reputation for operational incompetence: not the management's received view, or likely to become one.

178. Commenting on the need to safeguard knowledge about breaking Fish devices in late 1974, a senior GCHQ official (not one of the cryptanalysts) minuted '. . . I find H [Cryptanalysis Division] now inclining to the view that the details of machines and techniques, and the similarities between WWII and present-day machines, will not be worked out by his main adversaries and are not all that important: that what counts is the general sense of unease about machine cyphers, which to some extent may already have been generated.' See Goodall to Bonsall, 4 December 1974, CAB 163/230.

179. Bertrand, G., *Enigma; ou, La plus grand énigme de la guerre, 1939–1945* (Paris: Librarie Plon, 1973).

180. Hinsley et al., *British Intelligence in the Second World War: Vol. 3, Part 2*, p. 950.

181. For earlier, fragmentary recollections of this story by Polish and French officials see Kozaczuk, W., *Bitwa o Tajemnice. Sluzby wywiadowcze Polski I Rzeszy Niemieckiej, 1922–1939* (Warsaw: Ksiazka I Wiedza, 1967); and Garder, M., *La Guerre Secrète des Services Spéciaux français* (Paris: Librairie Plon, 1967). I am grateful to Ralph Erskine for these references, and for earlier hints in books by David Irving and Malcolm Muggeridge, and American authors (on the Pacific War) Roberta Wohlstetter and Samuel Eliot Morison.

182. A group of Polish veterans at the Sikorski Institute in London nonetheless set about producing their own history to correct what they saw as Bertrand's misrepresentation of the Polish contribution. See (unsigned) minute to Goodall (GCHQ), 3 May 1974, HW 25/16.

183. A classified book review for the NSA concluded that Bertrand's book was 'interesting and indiscreet. The English version, with Kahn's introduction, should be a collector's item. It will also hurt.' See 'Book Review: The Cryptologists Who (Briefly) Went Back Into the Cold', 15 May 1974, HW 25/16.

184. Tiltman, J. H., 'Winterbotham's "The Ultra Secret": A Personal Comment', *NSA Cryptolog*, 2, no. 12, 1975: 1. This article was declassified on 10 November 2012. Since 1964 Tiltman in retirement had been consulting for the National Security Agency in Washington but the article would be agreed with GCHQ.

185. 'Interview with Brigadier Tiltman', p. 33.

186. The strengthened sanctions were included in the *Official Secrets Act 1989*, c.6. Available at: http://www.legislation.gov.uk/ukpga/1989/6/contents

187. Conversation with Bonsall some years before his death in 2014.

188. 'The Official History of Intelligence in World War II and Related Subjects', enclosed in Hooper to White, 7 November 1975, CAB 103/726; JIC(A)(74) 12th meeting, 'Books on Intelligence: Book by Winterbotham', Confidential Annex, 21 March 1974, CAB 185/15.

189. Moran, *Classified*, pp. 277–8.

190. A further version of Cave Brown's influence was provided later in published American correspondence about his book, in an assertion that 'it was Cave Brown who persuaded Winterbotham to write his memoirs, helped him to do so, provided some of the material and arranged for a publisher'. See MacDonald, C. B., 'Lie Fishing', *The New York Review of Books*, 1 April 1976. The writer was the Deputy Chief Historian of the US Army and was defending Cave Brown's book after a critical review by Trevor-Roper. There is no other evidence to this effect. Cave Brown was a powerful figure whose intended publication seems to have made repeated waves on both sides of the Atlantic but, at least on Ultra, had less effect when it eventually appeared.

191. Denniston, 'Three Kinds of Hero'.

192. Ibid., p. 118. Denniston cites a letter said to be in the files at Weidenfeld and Nicolson.

193. This summary was prepared, probably by Morrison, for Hooper to send to White. See 'The Official History of Intelligence in World War II and Related Subjects', enclosed in Hooper to White, 7 November 1975, CAB 103/726. One of the books was Bertrand's. The other was said in the brief to have been Masterman's, though this was published before Winterbotham's first application.

194. Winterbotham, *The Ultra Spy*, p. 245.

195. Denniston, 'Three Kinds of Hero', p. 119.

196. Winterbotham to Farnhill, 15 April 1973, enclosed in INT 37 (73) 12, 'Publications: Winterbotham', Annex, 22 May 1973, CAB 190/53.

197. Denniston, 'Three Kinds of Hero', p. 119.
198. Ibid. The editor was Venetia Pollock.
199. West, N., *Historical Dictionary of British Intelligence* (Oxford: Scarecrow Press, 2005), p. 584.
200. JIC(A)(74) 12th meeting, 'Books on Intelligence: Book by Winterbotham', Confidential Annex, 21 March 1974, CAB 185/15.
201. Ibid.
202. 'The Official History of Intelligence in World War II and Related Subjects', enclosed in Hooper to White, 7 November 1975, CAB 103/726.
203. Ziegler, P., *Edward Heath, the Authorised Biography* (London: HarperCollins, 2010), chapter 19, recounts the spectacular collapse under strain of his Head of the Home Civil Service and closest adviser, Sir William Armstrong; see pp. 423–4.
204. Those on 'essential work' had exemption from the national policy of no office lighting. Under Percy (later Sir Percy) Cradock the Assessments Staff on the other side of the corridor had declared themselves essential and switched on.
205. Conversation with him over the American gesture of cutting off intelligence supplies to the UK in August 1973.
206. It should be recorded that along with Arthur's unusual style of chairmanship he was kind and considerate to work for. See Chapter 18 in this collection, 'The Joint Intelligence Committee 1972–5'.
207. Hooper to Hunt, 4 December 1974, PREM 16/670.
208. Crossman, R., *The Diaries of a Cabinet Minister*, 3 vols (London: Hamilton and Cape, 1975–7).
209. On the political situation, see Ziegler, *Edward Heath*, chapter 20. For Wilson's book and the Crossman diaries see Moran, *Classified*, pp. 241–3, 239–40.
210. Brian Stewart, JIC Secretary 1969–72, told me subsequently that White was initially operating full time but had been persuaded by him to become part time (private letter to author). White's successor Sir Peter Wilkinson succeeded him part time over 1972–3 but suffered from ill-heath and was hardly a player.
211. Winterbotham to Farnhill, 2 February 1973, enclosed in INT 37 (73) 3, 'Publications: Winterbotham', Annex, 26 February 1973, CAB 190/53.
212. Personal recollection of author, perhaps of a conversation with John Morrison.
213. INT 46 (74) 1, 'Co-Ordinator's Working Party on World War II Intelligence Matters', 17 May 1974, CAB 190/74; 'Proposed New Guidelines on World War II Intelligence Matters', copy enclosed

in INT 46 (74) 5, 'Note by the Intelligence Coordinator', 24 June 1974, ibid.

214. Armstrong (PPS to PM) to Hunt, 'Marchetti and Marks and Winterbotham', 8 July 1974, PREM 16/670.

215. Goodall to Morrison, 6 June 1974, enclosed in INT 46 (74) 3, Note by Secretary, CAB 190/74.

216. 'Proposed New Guidelines on World War II Intelligence Matters', enclosed in INT 46 (74) 5, 'Note by the Intelligence Coordinator', 24 June 1974, CAB 190/74.

217. Hunt to Wilson, 5 July 1974, PREM 16/670.

218. This date is mentioned in Hunt to Wilson, 15 November 1974, PREM 16/670.

219. 'The Official History of Intelligence in World War II and Related Subjects', enclosed in Hooper to White, 7 November 1975, CAB 103/726.

220. Ibid.

221. One writer known to the PRO staff was Aileen Clayton, who lobbied her MP for continued access after the files were temporarily withdrawn, and later published a valuable book recounting her wartime experience in the 'Y' Service's intercept stations. See Wilson to Stainton, 25 November 1975, PREM 16/1290. Clayton's book was *The Enemy is Listening: The Story of the Y Service* (London: Hutchinson, 1980).

222. It also emerged that GCHQ had identified some references in PRO files in March 1974 'which a knowledgeable reader would know to be to their [GCHQ] work', but it had been decided at the time not to risk drawing attention by removing them. Upon its discovery, one official at the PRO minuted 'I must say that I would not have recognised the references'; see (unsigned) memo by PRO staff, 21 March 1974, PRO 69/219.

223. In his review of Winterbotham's book for *The Times*, Nicholas Bethell mistakenly reported that Ultra files were secretly transferred from the PRO in 1973. See Hunt to Wilson (PM), 15 November 1974, PREM 16/670.

224. JIC(74) 47th meeting, 18 October 1974, CAB 185/15; JIC(74) 48th meeting, 24 October 1974, ibid.

225. A brief summary of the deliberations can also be found in 'JIC Recommendations on Release of Intelligence Records and the Official History of Intelligence in World War II', n.d., CAB 103/726.

226. After Winterbotham's book appeared Peter Calvocoressi, Gordon Welchman, Ralph Bennett and Stuart Milner-Barry are recorded making requests for access; see Hunt to Stowe, 4 August 1976, PREM 16/1290.

227. GCHQ memorandum by Hooper, 'Unofficial Publications about Wartime Sigint', 9 August 1973, CAB 163/247; JIC(74) 47th meeting, 18 October 1974, CAB 185/15.

228. JIC(74) 45th meeting, 10 October 1974, CAB 185/15. On the presence of the Soviet official in the PRO see Romeril to Day, 30 July 1970, CAB 103/705.

229. Hooper to White, 18 July 1975, CAB 103/726.

230. 'JIC Recommendations on Release of Intelligence Records and the Official History of Intelligence in World War II', enclosed in Hooper to White, 18 July 1975, CAB 163/255.

231. Bridges to Hunt, 18 November 1974, PREM 16/670.

232. Hinsley, F. H. and A. Stripp, *Codebreakers: The Inside Story of Bletchley Park* (Oxford: Oxford University Press, 1993), p. 144.

233. JIC(74) 48th meeting, 24 October 1974, CAB 185/15. Bonsall's request was eventually met in a Parliamentary statement in January 1978; see enclosure in McIndoe to Morris, Annex, 28 April 1978, CAB 103/726.

234. See for example HW 25/4 and HW 25/5. These files – released in 2000 – comprise GCHQ's internal record of its campaign to break the Tunny machine.

235. Notably including Peter Calvocoressi, one of Bletchley's key Hut 3 assessors, in an informative review, 'The Ultra Secrets of Station X', *The Sunday Times,* 24 November 1974.

236. Beesly, P., *Very Special Intelligence: The Story of the Admiralty's Operational Intelligence Centre, 1939–1945* (London: Hamilton, 1977); Lewin, R., *Ultra Goes to War: The Secret Story* (London: Hutchinson, 1978); Bennett, R., *Ultra in the West: The Normandy Campaign of 1944–45* (London: Hutchinson, 1979); Calvocoressi, P., *Top Secret Ultra* (London: Cassel, 1980).

237. Jones, R. V., *Most Secret War: British Scientific Intelligence, 1939–1945* (London: Hamilton, 1978).

238. Hinsley et al., *British Intelligence in the Second World War: Vol. 1,* Appendix 1, 'The Polish, French and British Contributions to the Breaking of Enigma', pp. 487–95 (subsequently revised in *British Intelligence in the Second World War: Vol. 3, Part 2,* Appendix 30, published 1988).

239. GCHQ memorandum by Hooper, 'Unofficial Publications about Wartime Sigint', 9 August 1973, CAB 163/247.

240. Quoted in Erskine, R., 'Tunny Reveals B-Dienst Successes against the Convoy Code', *Intelligence and National Security,* 28, no. 6, 2013: 871, fn. 13.

241. 'Note for the Record: Colossus', 28 November 1974, CAB 163/230. For the balance between Colossus and hand attacks see Roberts, J., *Lorenz: Breaking into Hitler's Top Secret Codes at Bletchley Park* (Stroud: History Press, 2017).

242. Hinsley and Stripp, *Codebreakers*, p. 148.

243. Hinsley, F. H. et al., *British Intelligence in the Second World War: Its Influence on Strategy and Operations, Vol. 3, Part 1* (London: HMSO, 1984), pp. 477–83; Hinsley and Stripp, *Codebreakers*, chapter 14.

244. Nicoll (GCHQ) to Chamberlain (JIC), 17 May 1972, CAB 163/230.

245. This was acknowledged several months later by Hooper; see Hooper to Brearley, 14 May 1975, CAB 163/230.

246. Winterbotham, *The Ultra Secret*, p. 15, wrote of an 'oracle of Bletchley' which he saw in 1940. This almost certainly referred to the electro-mechanical bombe that was used to determine the Enigma's wiring and plugboard settings.

247. INT 37(75) 1, 'US Press Review of Winterbotham's Book', 8 January 1975, CAB 190/84.

248. Calvocoressi, *Top Secret Ultra*, p. 53.

249. Broadway (GCHQ) to Thorpe (FCO), 27 February 1975, CAB 163/230.

250. Randell, B., 'A Turing Enigma', in *23rd International Conference on Concurrency Theory* (Newcastle upon Tyne: Springer, 2012), p. 30.

251. Good's presentation was published as 'Some Future Social Repercussions of Computers', *International Journal of Environmental Studies*, 1, nos 1–4, 1970: 67–79. Michie's was 'The Bletchley Machines', in B. Randell (ed.), *Origins of Digital Computers* (Berlin: Springer-Verlag, 1973), pp. 327–8.

252. Hooper to Brearley, 14 May 1975, CAB 163/230.

253. Kirkland (JIC) to Bonsall (GCHQ), 17 December 1975, CAB 163/230; 'Opening of Science Museum Exhibition on Computing Then and Now', 17 December 1975, ibid.

254. Randell, 'A Turing Enigma', pp. 33–4.

255. Copeland, B. J., 'Colossus: Breaking the German "Tunny" Code at Bletchley Park. An Illustrated History', *The Rutherford Journal*, 2010, vol. 3, fn. 89. This open-journal article can be accessed at: http://www.rutherfordjournal.org/article030109.html

256. The withheld file is HW 76/7.

257. Nicoll on behalf of Tovey (GCHQ) to Richards (Cabinet Office), 13 October 1978, CAB 163/288.

258. Hinsley et al., *British Intelligence in the Second World War: Vol. 2*, pp. 28–31; Hinsley et al., *British Intelligence in the Second World War: Vol. 3, Part 1*, pp. 477–82.

259. Of the records released before 1996, HW 18/174-175 contain roughly 350 Tunny decrypts. There are at least 180 decrypts (headed ZTPG(T)) scattered among the naval Enigma decrypts in DEFE 3/100-112 and DEFE 3/180-206. I am indebted to Ralph Erskine for this information. See also Erskine, 'Tunny Reveals B-Dienst Successes Against the "Convoy Code"', p. 871.

260. 'Record of a Meeting held by the Intelligence Coordinator on 12th March 1969', DEFE 24/656.

261. Of the files released to the PRO, seventy were eventually determined as 'really sensitive' and most of those were said to be classed as such because they 'could reveal the identities of wartime agents working for the United Kingdom'. See Hunt to Wilson, 15 November 1974, PREM 16/670.

262. Hooper to White, 7 November 1975, CAB 103/706.

263. Enclosed in McIndoe to Morris, 28 April 1978, Annex, CAB 103/726.

264. Sir Maurice Oldfield, 1915–81. Head of SIS, 1973–8; Northern Ireland Office 1979–80; knighted in 1964.

265. Hooper to Hunt, 28 June 1977, CAB 163/256; Hooper's argument on this point was that '. . . [b]ecause World War II records of the service intelligence directorates are now being released into the public domain and failure to publish the Official History would probably mean that further inaccurate accounts based on incomplete material would be published by private writers'. See Hooper to Sykes (FCO), 23 February 1977, ibid.

266. Hooper spent some time in Oxford on postgraduate research on eighteenth-century English Catholics. From knowledge of him in later life it is difficult to imagine a more unlikely choice of subject. It was never completed. Oldfield may have been more serious and toyed with returning to medieval research when he first retired.

267. 'C' (SIS) to Palliser (FCO), 8 July 1977, CAB 103/726.

268. 'Official History of British Intelligence in World War II – Note of a meeting held in Sir John Hunt's Room', 21 July 1977, CAB 103/726; Hunt to Callaghan (PM), 26 July 1977, ibid. Sanitisation was to include removing details about intelligence operations against wartime allies and neutrals, methods and locations of intelligence activity which were still relevant to tradecraft, and details of liaison relationships. See JIC(A)(77) 42nd meeting, CAB

185/21. Historical references to early UKUSA intelligence collaboration before Pearl Harbor were also removed at the request of US authorities. See Theobald to Hooper, 20 April 1978, CAB 163/288.

269. Prendergast to Stowe, 3 October 1977, CAB 163/256.

270. 'Official History of Intelligence and Avowing the SIS', 16 June 1978, PREM 16/2081.

271. Stowe to Hunt, 10 October 1977, CAB 103/726.

272. Callaghan to Thatcher, 14 July 1978, PREM 16/2081.

273. For intelligence services' view of her 'robust and accurate' attitude, see Moore C., *Margaret Thatcher: Everything She Wants, Vol. 2* (London: Lane, 2015), p. 233.

274. Thatcher to Callaghan (PM), 17 July 1978, PREM 16/2081.

275. Theobald to McIndoe, 21 July 1978, CAB 163/288.

276. 'Official History of Intelligence: and Intelligence Related Records', 28 July 1978, PREM 16/2081.

277. The fourth volume (counterintelligence and security) was written by Antony Simkins, a former deputy director of MI5, with Hinsley brought in as editor and co-author after the review of the first draft. The fifth volume (strategic deception) was by the military historian Sir Michael Howard.

278. Butler (PPS to PM) to Armstrong, 8 May 1985, CAB 103/759.

279. Aldrich, 'Policing the Past', p. 950.

280. Howard, M. E., *Captain Professor: A Life in War and Peace* (London: Continuum, 2006), p. 191.

281. Welchman, G., *The Hut Six Story: Breaking the Enigma Codes* (New York: McGraw Hill, 1982).

282. Welchman, G., 'From Polish Bomba to British Bombe: the Birth of Ultra', *Intelligence and National Security*, 1, no. 1, 1986: 71–110. The correspondence was published in 'Gordon Welchman, Sir Peter Marychurch and "The Birth of Ultra"', *Intelligence and National Security*, 1, no. 2, 1986: 277–80. The defence of Welchman is by Sir P. Stuart Milner-Barry.

283. Mrs Thatcher's influence was also recorded late in the decade when a number of retired intelligence professionals, including the author, were requested not to attend an international conference on intelligence affairs at Ditchley Park in the UK, with varying results. For later problems when the Royal Institute of International Affairs sponsored the present author's book, see Chapter 1 in this collection, 'Profiles in Intelligence: An Interview with Michael Herman'.

284. Aldrich, 'Policing the Past', p. 953.

285. Hennessy, 'The Last Customer' (unpublished), p. 17.

286. Moran, *Classified*, p. 275; 'The Release of Sigint Records', JIC(58) 46, 13 November 1968, PREM 13/3252. Ironically Soviet knowledge of the Double Cross successes may have contributed to the regime's fear that the good secret intelligence it received was just Western deception.

287. Hooper acknowledged in 1973 that the focus in McLachlan's *Room 39* on the operations to seize codebreaking materials at sea was a useful distraction from the cryptanalytic exploitation at Bletchley; see Hooper, 'Unofficial Publications about Wartime Sigint', 9 August 1973, CAB 163/247.

288. On the position of the Cabinet Office Intelligence Coordinator in 1972–3, see Chapter 18 in this collection, 'The Joint Intelligence Committee 1972–5'.

289. Millward (GCHQ) to Richards (JIC Secretary), 25 July 1968, CAB 163/156. (Bill) Millward was Hooper's senior Assistant Director, in semi-retirement, and was a font of wisdom on Ultra matters. Uncatalogued papers at Bletchley some years ago included extensive exchanges between him and Hinsley on the Official History drafts.

290. Herman, M., *Intelligence Power in Peace and War* (Cambridge: Cambridge University Press/RIIA, 1996), p. vii.

291. Chapter 3 in this collection, 'GCHQ De-unionisation'.

292. Personal recollection.

293. Private letter Sir Michael Howard to author, 11 August 2003.

294. My predecessor as JIC Secretary, Brian Stewart, wrote in old age that White was valued in Whitehall as 'a widely experienced intelligence bureaucrat', and 'seen by the establishment as a safe pair of hands' (undated private letter).

295. Private conversation.

296. Aldrich, 'Policing the Past', p. 924; see also Chapter 17 in this collection, 'Up from the Country: Cabinet Office Impressions, 1972–5'.

3 GCHQ De-unionisation[1]

[1993]

No one needs to be reminded of the government decision of 25 January 1984 to ban national trade unions at GCHQ, the Sigint centre at Cheltenham. It has become an entrenched part of British political and trade union mythology; the sight of First Division civil servants marching in Cheltenham with the National Union of Mineworkers in the annual rally of protest sums up its lasting effects. Re-unionisation is well established as Labour's policy in opposition and will happen sometime; national unions were all set to offer attractive packages of cut-price membership after the expected Labour victory in 1992. The fact that Cheltenham is a marginal seat now gives the situation extra spin. Politics apart, the affair has a bearing on a raft of issues: trade union structures; patterns of public sector management; control of intelligence agencies; judicial review; the place of 'national security' in law and constitutional practice. In all these contexts a proper account of the affair is badly needed.

The short and readable book *A Conflict of Loyalties* by Lanning and Norton-Taylor – well produced as the first venture of a Cheltenham-based workers' cooperative – might seem to provide it, but the authors' backgrounds give fair warning that it is no dispassionate study. Lanning as a full-time trade union official was, and is, deeply involved in the action against the union ban; Norton-Taylor of *The Guardian* is a former Freedom of Information Journalist of the Year, and a long-term thorn in the side of the intelligence establishment. They have produced a campaigning account of a campaign. Indeed, with their penchant for military chapter titles like 'the battle' and 'the war', it reads rather like an old-style military history of one of the less successful episodes of Empire. Our soldiers die heroically for Queen and Country against overwhelming odds. But the cruel and treacherous fuzzy-wuzzies on the other side remain shadowy creatures. One hardly gets to understand why they attacked – and won.

One-sided campaign history of this sort is still useful, and the account here of union reactions and tactics has the virtues of first-hand recollection. The most informative chapter is on the negotiations of February and March 1984, particularly on the unions' 'no-strike' offer and its rejection by the government. Union politics and personalities are treated uncritically, as is the question whether a no-strike agreement would have survived criticism from the conference militants. Nevertheless the narrative has the whiff of the battlefield about it, and is valuable on that account.

The causes of war get less satisfactory treatment. The authors demonstrate that union problems at GCHQ went back to 1969 and pre-dated the service-wide pay disputes of 1979–81. They analyse the government's claim that GCHQ lost 10,000 days in strikes in that later period. But, though they have no compunction about publishing a wealth of information about GCHQ's classi-fied facilities and operations, they are surprisingly coy about the details of industrial action. The reader looks in vain for numbers, places and dates. The authors argue that the Civil Service unions were carried away by their own rhetoric in stating in 1981 that their actions were causing disruption and inconvenience; and they claim that the campaign was designed to cause embarrassment and not damage. This is a disingenuous *post facto* interpretation of history. Maybe no one on the union side now knows what really happened; all the more reason for trying to establish the facts. Freedom of information could start with the union records.

They are also determined not to give the other side an inch. GCHQ management is always shown as inefficient, authoritarian and paranoiac. The American relationship is caricatured as a 'master-servant arrangement of convenience . . . with GCHQ giving the Americans nearly everything of value, while NSA [its American opposite number] is highly selective in the intelligence it deigns to give to GCHQ'.[2] All the stale and unsourced canards about GCHQ are trotted out: illegal coverage of domestic targets; interception of the communications of Jane Fonda and Benjamin Spock; cooperation with South Africa; and so on. GCHQ is 'a uniquely privileged organ of the secret state. Its powerful position, its total lack of accountability, can only cause serious disquiet among those concerned with civil liberties.'[3] If only half this stuff were true, the mystery would not be why decent people got the sack from GCHQ, but why they ever worked there.

One example illustrates the rubbishing technique. The authors claim that Geoffrey Prime – sentenced in 1982 to thirty-eight years imprisonment as a Soviet agent – was not detected earlier because a woman who knew he was a spy was put off by a GCHQ investigating officer's manner, with the implication that this was an example of inefficiency. This is presumably the story of Miss Barsby, taken from the Security Commission's report on the case, but without the Commission's conclusion that her explanation was no more than 'an attempt at self-justification for a disgraceful action'.[4] Good campaign stuff, but is the liberal case best served by this selective use of evidence?

Thus, as a source the book should be treated with caution. How then can the historian, the politician or the man in the street reassess this important and continuing affair? It may be helpful to suggest some pointers.

Constitutional Settings

Two issues can be mentioned in passing that did not arise. First, the dispute was not about the need for secret intelligence; there was a surprising acceptance on all sides of Sigint's importance. Public opinion had probably been educated by the decisions taken in the 1970s – with much official hesitation at the time – to release details of Sigint successes in the Second World War. By 1984 the wartime contribution of Bletchley Park had become part of British political culture; without this background, the GCHQ debate could easily have taken a different turn. In this respect public opinion was genuinely and properly informed by official releases of information – a moral, perhaps, for the future.

Second, the affair did not raise questions of constitutional propriety or bureaucratic ineffectiveness. Intelligence agencies are usually portrayed as rogue elephants under inadequate Ministerial control. However, the deunionisation decision was taken by the Prime Minister and a small group of Ministers acting on official advice; it is difficult to fault this in purely constitutional terms. As for theories of bureaucracy, Lanning and Norton-Taylor rightly draw attention to the interview with Sir Brian Tovey, the former GCHQ Director, that made it clear that the initiative came originally from him.[5] Academic writers on British public administration have said for years that they wanted a more proactive higher Civil Service; here they got it in spades, thanks to the resonance between an official submission and a Prime Minister's instincts.

Secret Organisations and Public Bureaucracy

Most countries have Sigint organisations of some kind, often on a substantial scale. In some ways they are more like high-technology production lines than research centres. Secrecy tends to produce high morale and feelings of special value. But it also encourages the intensity of closed organisations, particularly since for most of those involved they are full-life careers without escape routes. Managing them is exhilarating but poses its distinctive challenges.

Secrecy also poses the question of unionisation. Some countries have it; others do not. GCHQ after the Second World War adopted the full-scale British Whitley system of national unions, and was rather proud of the marriage of secrecy and respectability. Nevertheless it sometimes seemed an odd arrangement. The author remembers sitting as a young man in a Departmental Staff Side meeting with a full-time union official from London said to be a Communist Party member – a curious situation in a secret establishment in the Cold War. Workable compromises evolved; thus, the book claims that one national union secretary was rather quaintly asked by GCHQ on his retirement if he would kindly return all the official material classified 'Confidential' from his files.[6] But it was all slightly anomalous. A few cases before industrial tribunals produced similar concerns about publicity and disclosures.

There were also questions about recruitment and staffing. The older intelligence organisations – the Secret Intelligence Service and Security Service – took their shape in the aftermath of the First World War and were not swept up into the standardisation of the Civil Service in the 1920s; in their degree of autonomy they were precursors in some ways of the 'Next Steps' agencies of today. GCHQ on the other hand, taking its modern identity in the late 1940s and 1950s, had aligned with service-wide Treasury-style gradings and conditions as the natural way to go. This had advantages for a new department, but there was some chafing at the constraints: were normal Civil Service structures and conditions the best basis for a secret intelligence organisation? The Security Commission's recommendation after the Prime case for introducing the polygraph illustrated the problem: could that transatlantic instrument of torture really be reconciled with a staid Civil Service regime? There is no evidence for Lanning's and Norton-Taylor's claim that the polygraph was a factor behind the de-unionisation decision; but it certainly encapsulated the underlying problems of GCHQ's status.

Industrial Action

Nevertheless, the central issue was industrial action and the role of national unions in it. Official secrecy still limits an account of the background, and only an outline can be given. GCHQ staff as a whole were singularly non-militant; GCHQ's reputation was of an efficient and well-managed department; a wide area of management/union relationships were relaxed and reasonably productive. But in one large group of staff (and one similar but smaller one) a set of long-standing problems had existed from the mid-1960s onwards: 'age bulges' through wartime recruitment, and their blight on promotion prospects; the impact of new technology on traditional skills; an 'us' and 'them' division between headquarters and 'outstations'; two unions competing for outstation membership – indeed all the elements of a standard business school exercise on 'managing change'. The two unions concerned discovered in a pay dispute of 1969, described by Lanning and Norton-Taylor, that 'working to rule' could produce more pay. The point was taken in the 1970s.[7]

By the chaotic standards of Britain at the time, the amount of serious militancy in GCHQ was minuscule. Even in the 'problem areas', staff support for strikes, working to rule and opposition to new technology was not solid, and there was usually some union effort to minimise damage. The managerial style was compromise, not confrontation, reflecting the Civil Service as a whole and the policy of the responsible Ministers. By the standards of the 1970s industrial action was reasonably well contained and the situation relatively civilised. The book goes out of its way to paint a black picture of management's staff relations, but the real atmosphere is conveyed in its cameo of the GCHQ trade union chairman setting out just before the surprise de-unionisation announcement for his regular lunchtime pint with the head of personnel. Nevertheless, management's relationships with these two unions and the staff they represented – substantial bodies, but not the majority – had an undercurrent of strain and a long-running threat of industrial action.

In 1979–81 this situation within GCHQ was overlaid by the wider Council of Civil Service Unions' campaign against the abolition of existing pay arrangements. The CCSUs' national calls for symbolic 'days of action' evoked mixed, fairly lukewarm responses in GCHQ as a whole. Even token actions went against the grain for most people; one of the senior officials in Lanning and Norton-Taylor's cast of subsequent baddies – a Labour supporter and a former local union chairman – resigned from the First Division Association in protest. But the two unions which had intermittently threatened action in the 1970s went further and targeted their own members with selective GCHQ action in 1981 as part of the national campaign; and some other groups of staff took some action. It would be interesting to know who decided on this, and why.

No one knows what intelligence was missed as a result. The show was more or less kept on the road. But Sir Brian Tovey's subsequent verdict that GCHQ was not at peak efficiency during the Afghanistan invasion in 1979 or the crises in Poland in 1980–1 is not unfair. It was a risk-ridden world, with heightened East–West tension, terrorism, the taking of Western hostages, etc. Intelligence as an insurance policy depends on regularity. No agency can operate properly under threat of lightning strikes. Nor can it command the confidence of allies with whom it cooperates. To Lanning and Norton-Taylor the American connection is of course anathema; but nations cannot cover international affairs without collaboration.

Reflections

Two questions therefore arise: why did the decision of January 1984 cause such a furore, and was it necessary? The book seeks to answer the first, but one point needs some extra emphasis. When it came to refusals to accept the new conditions, the union campaign got less support than it expected in the areas previously regarded as potentially militant. Where the campaign received unforeseen support was from the traditionally nonmilitant 'headquarters' areas. To a number of these people – some of them rather unwordly, boffin types without previous union connections – the ban and the way it was imposed touched nerves that the national campaign over pay had missed.

The result was quite impressive. In numerical terms the unions' campaign was a flop, and nothing in the book is more graphic than the description (presumably by Lanning) of the last-minute meetings at outstations, with support gradually melting away. Yet underneath some politicisation and martyrdom-seeking, what emerged was a movement of some integrity. The book paints a surprisingly cheerful picture of the campaigners; but there must have been a quota of unpublicised personal sacrifice. One must respect the stand.

Was de-unionisation necessary? The conventional wisdom at the time was that the trauma was worth it for a better organisation in the end. GCHQ acquired its management-approved Staff Federation, said to be effective. After de-unionisation there were substantial intelligence pay rises, in addition to the compensation paid at the time; in effect the taxpayer has picked up the bill. Presumably staff relationships have improved, despite the immediate effects of the 1984 affair. On the other side of the ledger there is all the management effort locked up for five years in sorting out de-unionisation and all its consequences, including the much-publicised dismissals that dragged on for some years; and the equivalent effort that will be needed for re-unionisation under a Labour government. Reinstating national unions and providing for the continued existence of the Federation will land some future Director with a dog's breakfast of union negotiations, and the Labour Party and TUC will have no incentive to make things easy for him.

Hindsight makes things clearer than they were, and adds some ironies. We can now see that union militancy was substantially defeated at the national Civil Service level in the strikes of 1981; de-unionisation in 1984 was tackling what had become a non-problem. The issue of GCHQ's place in the 'normal' Civil Service has been overtaken by Next Steps and devolved agencies; its links with national pay and conditions would have been loosened anyway. On the other hand those who criticised de-unionisation at the time because it would soon be reversed by a Labour government have been confounded by two Conservative victories. And the new Staff Federation can now be seen to fit a developing national pattern of single enterprise unions; what is good for Japanese factories on Tyneside may well be good for GCHQ.

In seeing 1984 without this hindsight, history may conclude that it was right to tackle the threat of GCHQ industrial action. Strikes elsewhere – in ambulance and fire services, for example – had been regularly threatening the manifold forms of 'public interest'. But 'national security' produced an additional dimension, and the Foreign Secretary's rationale that 'GCHQ is one of the security and intelligence agencies on which our national security, and to some degree the security of our allies, depends' was not unreasonable in the circumstances of the time.[8] And there is little doubt that national unions – or, to be precise, two of them – had actively and tacitly encouraged staff representatives within GCHQ to regard industrial action as a legitimate negotiating card.

Many people at GCHQ welcomed the fresh start but were unhappy about the authoritarian method. 'Couldn't it have been done by negotiation?' was a common reaction. A 'no-strike' agreement could indeed have been proposed to the unions, and what the Treasury subsequently paid out in pay rises could have been the carrot. But it is difficult to visualise a bargain: the Thatcher government was not normally in the business of making pay offers to civil servants, and the national unions had every reason for tough negotiation. Management was probably right to think that a complete exclusion of strikes could only be achieved by shock action. The practical alternative was to take on union militancy by appealing direct to the workforce on selected issues, as at British Leyland. This would probably have been wiser, but still bruising.

Once de-unionisation was announced, the unions' 'no-strike' offer provided a basis for a settlement. The book quotes a senior GCHQ officer who bore much of the burden in the 1970s as saying privately that 'When the unions put their teeth on the table in February 1984, I cannot understand why the Prime Minister didn't pick them up.'[9] Lord Howe (as he became) said in similar vein in a broadcast that (as the responsible Secretary of State) he personally favoured a 'card in the pocket' solution, presumably a no-strike agreement of some kind.[10] No doubt Ministerial memoirs will tell us more about the arguments. But the reality is that the affair generated too much political momentum to be stopped. In any case the memory of Mr Solomon Binding and other union declarations in the 1970s was too green. Most people quote the former Head of the Civil Service's judgement that 'What is beyond dispute is that the handling has been breathtakingly inept: a further exploration of the bloody fool branch of management science.'[11] But the affair was really Britain in microcosm. Union militancy of the 1970s was trumped by the 'can do', action-man style of government in the 1980s. Industry recognised the need to question assumptions and explore alternatives; of his time as Chairman of ICI, Sir John Harvey-Jones wrote that, 'I have said many times that I do not wish to hire yes-men . . . What we are looking for are what I call constructive no-men . . . It requires a lot of faith to believe that such questioning will actually be recognized, liked and rewarded.'[12] Of his time in the wartime Civil Service, Lord Franks spoke many years ago of the need for 'rational persuasion'; the difference between an ethos of 'what "They" have ordained rather than of what "We" are committed to carry through'.[13] But in 1984 the watchword in government and government service had become decisiveness above all.

The likely verdict on de-unionisation will be that the consequences were not sufficiently thought through, perhaps as was repeated with the poll tax. The two-party system, with conviction politics on both sides, did the rest. The most significant feature of the affair was that consultation with the Opposition seems to have been no part of the plan. It was not the Thatcher style; and there was no chance that the Opposition in 1983–4 would have played ball. But perhaps that was the most powerful reason against the proposal. Intelligence sits ill with political controversy.

The enduring result was a boost to intelligence's public profile and salience in political debate. The real casualty was the older and more subfusc view which saw it as a useful, inconspicuous supporting arm of government; at hand, on the fringes of power, but not using the main staircase or sitting in the Cabinet Room. Just after the announcement of the union ban, GCHQ's Director issued a circular in which he regretted the public debate and expressed the view that 'the important and unique character of our work [is] such that GCHQ needs to be insulated from external pressures'.[14] Just so. But 25 January 1984 made it a forlorn hope then, and not a much better one now.

Postscript

This is one of history's uncommon examples of things coming out right in the end. One of the first acts of the incoming Labour government in 1997 was to announce that the ban on national unions at GCHQ was to be rescinded, with a collective 'no disruption' agreement as part of the settlement. Possibly a Conservative government would also have sought a settlement of some kind had it been returned to office, but not so comprehensively and promptly. After the announcement, the management-approved GCHQ Staff Federation that had been established in 1985 moved smoothly towards affiliation as a branch of what eventually became the very large Public and Commercial Services Union, an amalgamation of most of the separate unions that formerly represented civil servants nationally. A 'no disruption' agreement was part of the settlement. The recalcitrants dismissed from GCHQ on disciplinary grounds had symbolic offers of reinstatement or retirement, and the thirteen-year campaign against deunionisation was formally closed. All concerned, including the Conservative Party, breathed sighs of relief. In the 1993 article published above I predicted that re-unionisation would produce a muddle, with national unions jostling for position with the GCHQ Federation. Happily this turned out to be wrong – as wrong as my expectation in 1984 that deunionisation would be overturned after a Labour victory in the next general election, or the following one.

This happy outcome springs partly from the national sea change in trade union militancy, but partly also from the restructuring of the national Civil Service unions that began in the 1980s and moved with increasing speed in the 1990s. In 1992, expecting a Labour victory, the national unions that still existed at that time were all set to compete with the GCHQ Staff Federation by offering cut-price membership. But by 1997 they had largely completed their merger into the new mega-union, and it had been established that existing staff associations could retain some separate identity within it. As the 1997 election grew closer the officials of the GCHQ Federation took a crucial and statesmanlike decision: to prepare for affiliation on these lines, rather than fighting to maintain their independence. Through this initiative they solved management's problem of reintroducing national unions without provoking a pitched battle between them and the Federation. It was lucky that the Labour victory was delayed until the Federation had developed quite deep roots in the department and the national trade union structure was able to absorb it.

Does de-unionisation now seem worth it? It can now be maintained that since 1984 the main objective – the continuity of operations at GCHQ – has been secured, and is now guaranteed. Though 'industrial action' in GCHQ in the 1970s and early 1980s was only of marginal significance in any direct ways, the action was real enough, and had wider indirect effects on efficiency, the transatlantic relationship and our own self-respect. I remember my own feelings of sadness and shame when present in the late 1970s when a Cold War 24-hour surveillance unit for which I was responsible closed down for a night watch as part of a departmental pay dispute. The closure was no more than a gesture, and our allies were able to take the strain; but it was humiliating nonetheless. The agreement to avoid industrial action of this kind is well worth having.

Yet there have been costs, as set out here. The 1984 decision and its prolonged repercussions produced major distractions for management for much of the period up to 1997. The widespread intelligence salary increases provided by the Thatcher government after de-unionisation meant that it was harder to fund the new technological investments needed in the 1990s. Media sensationalism and liberal distrust of the covert intelligence agencies were encouraged. Intelligence needed more openness, but could have done without the adversarial context in which it came about.

A general conclusion is that intelligence does not benefit from being too often handled as an exceptional, 'vital' activity, with special treatment and public excitement about it. It needs to steer clear of publicity and political controversy. A less dramatic appearance suits it better, and is probably a better reflection of its true place in national priorities. Fortunately the Parliamentary Intelligence and Security Committee established in 1994 has made this more practicable than previously; indeed this may be its greatest value. It is a pity that it was not available in the frenetic atmosphere of 1984.

As final afterthought: there were significant slices of luck in the final outcome. The Falklands War in 1982 secured Mrs Thatcher her subsequent electoral victory in 1983 and continued Conservative government up to 1997. And it was luck for GCHQ that its exemplary performance had been given in that war, before and not after the de-unionisation distraction.

Notes

1. Originally published as 'Review: GCHQ De-Unionisation 1984' in *Public Policy and Administration*, 8, no. 2, 1993: 74–80, which was revised with a postscript and reprinted as 'The Effects of Secrecy: GCHQ De-Unionization' in Herman, M., *Intelligence Services in the Information Age: Theory and Practice* (London: Frank Cass, 2001), pp. 180–90. Copyright © 1993 SAGE Publications, reprinted by permission of SAGE Publications and Taylor & Francis Group. It draws on Lanning, H. and R. Norton-Taylor, *A Conflict of Loyalties: GCHQ 1984–1991* (Cheltenham: New Clarion Press, 1991).

2. Lanning and Norton-Taylor, *A Conflict of Loyalties*, p. 33.
3. Ibid., p. 74.
4. Ibid., p. 49. See also *Security Commission Report*, Cmnd 8876 (London: HMSO, 1983), p. 22.
5. Lanning and Norton-Taylor, *A Conflict of Loyalties*, pp. 43–4; *The Sunday Times*, 5 and 12 February 1984. See also letter to *The Times*, 6 February 1984.
6. Lanning and Norton-Taylor, *A Conflict of Loyalties*, p. 86.
7. See Chapter 19 in this collection, 'GCHQ Directors'.
8. Sir Geoffrey Howe, Commons Debate, 27 February 1984.
9. Quoted by Lanning and Norton-Taylor, *A Conflict of Loyalties*, p. 103, from the Council of Civil Service Unions', *Warning Signal*, 22, 12 November 1984. The same CCSU piece referred, apparently with approval, to this officer's 'running a tight ship' in the 1970s. He was John Somerville, head of staff and financial matters; see Chapter 19 in this collection, 'GCHQ Directors'.
10. A. Howard's radio programme *The Brothers*, BBC4, 19 January 1993. Chapter 23 of Howe's autobiography *Conflict of Loyalty* (London: Macmillan, 1994) gives his views in more detail. 'Card in the pocket' would have meant retaining the right to belong to a national union but not to join in union action.
11. *The Times*, 4 February 1984.
12. Harvey-Jones, J., *Making It Happen* (London: Fontana/Collins, 1987), pp. 89–90.
13. Sir Oliver Franks, Sidney Ball Lecture 1947, quoted by Danchev, A., *Oliver Franks, Founding Father* (Oxford: Oxford University Press, 1993), p. 51.
14. Quoted by Lanning and Norton-Taylor, *A Conflict of Loyalties*, p. 137.

4   Intelligence and Ethical Foreign Policy[1]

[1999]

Intelligence services are integral parts of the modern state; as Sir Reginald Hibbert put it in the late 1980s, 'over the past half-century secret intelligence, from being a somewhat bohemian servant or associate of the great departments of state, gradually acquired a sort of parity with them'.[2] They have not withered away with the end of the Cold War. There has been some reduction in this decade, but not to the same extent as in the armed forces, and intelligence budgets have recently levelled off.[3] American expenditure has been declared as US$26 billion annually, around ten per cent of the cost of defence, perhaps with some recent increases in human source collection.[4] The equivalent British budget is probably more than £1 billion, rather more than the cost of diplomacy (contemporary figures).[5]

Does this investment pose questions of international morality? Most Western governments recognise issues of democratic accountability and restrictions on domestic targeting, but like the rest of the world accept the need for 'foreign intelligence'.[6] On coming to power in 1997 the Labour Foreign Secretary, Mr Cook, emphasised the ethical dimension of his foreign policy, but at the end of his first year spoke with unexpected warmth of the intelligence support he had received.[7] The Clinton Administration sponsored a study of the CIA's ethics, but what emerged focused on intellectual integrity, not morality.[8] The media make great play with intelligence leaks, whistleblowing and failures, but remain thrilled by secrecy. Its ethical concerns over intelligence tend to be inward-looking, concentrating on what it suspects to be part of the domestically repressive 'national security state', rather than on its foreign coverage. *The Times* pronounced in 1999 that 'Cold War or no Cold War, nations routinely spy on each other'.[9]

Nevertheless an underlying liberal distaste is evident for stealing others' secrets. Peter Wright's autobiographical account of his 'bugging and burglary' of foreign embassies in London is frequently quoted.[10] John le Carré's novels denigratingly portrayed Soviet and Western intelligence as two halves of the same apple.[11] CIA-bashing remains a world industry, an element in the *bien pensant* view that the US is 'becoming the rogue superpower'.[12] At a more thoughtful level, two British academics have dismissed all espionage as 'positively immoral' apart 'from certain extreme cases' (undefined).[13]

This points to a genuine if muted question about intelligence and ethical foreign policy. An Oxford student recently asked his college chaplain whether a Christian could apply in good conscience to work in intelligence; what was the right reply? Intelligence as an institution is an accepted part of the fabric of international society, but does it make for a better world or a worse one? Does it make any ethical difference at all? These are questions for intelligence practitioners as well as governments and publics. This chapter seeks to explore them.

Starting Points

Intelligence has to be judged in the first instance by its obviously observable consequences. One test is whether it increases or decreases international tension and the risks of inter-state war.[14] Another, more topical test is whether it promotes or retards international cooperation in a world that now has elements of 'a true world community, with global responsibility for the preservation of a just order'.[15]

Yet judging it solely in this pragmatic way seems incomplete. The code of conduct that deters individuals from reading each others' mail does not rest only on the risks and consequences of being found out, and states are arguably also bound by more than reciprocal self-interest. The American authority on the history of codebreaking concluded (even during the Cold War) that it was 'surreptitious, snooping, sneaking . . . the very opposite of all that is best in mankind'.[16] Kant condemned wartime espionage not only for its consequences (that it 'would be carried over into peace-time'), but also since it was 'intrinsically despicable' and 'exploits only the dishonesty of others'.[17] Ethics is right conduct. The moral absolutist or intelligence pacifist cannot be kept entirely out of the discussion.

The 'foreign intelligence' to be judged in these ways is basically the Western model: an institution with some commitment to telling truth to power, and some separation from the power itself. Contrary to Bacon's over-quoted dictum that knowledge is itself power, West-ern intelligence has on the whole not sought power or exercised it. Intelligence under communism and in other authoritarian states has a quite different tradition and would require a separate critique. But the Western ideal of objectivity is not a purely regional one, and has some wider currency. Military intelligence everywhere seeks to know its enemy, and Western intelligence applies the same aspira-tion more widely, as part of government by reason rather than ideol-ogy or caprice. It now has a place, albeit inconspicuously, in liberal democracy's worldwide baggage. However much it is criticised for its failures, democratic rulers are in trouble with their electorates if they are known to have disregarded it.

Intelligence on this Western model needs to be considered in its two different aspects: the knowledge it produces, and the activities through which it produces it. Their effects differ. Thus the knowl-edge gained from Western overflights of the Soviet Union in the 1950s benefited international security through scaling down some exaggerated Western estimates of the Soviet threat; yet the flights themselves were threatening and provocative, culminating in the Soviet shoot-down of the U-2 on 1 May 1960 which wrecked the East–West Paris Summit a few days later.[18] Knowledge and activi-ties can be examined separately but then have to be integrated into an ethical balance sheet.

Intelligence Knowledge: General Effects

Intelligence knowledge is itself of two overlapping kinds: first, the product of special, largely secret collection and, second, assessments on those foreign subjects – mainly bearing on national security – on which intelligence is the national expert.[19] The common factor to both is some separation between intelligence and policy-making.

Some of this knowledge has no obvious ethical connotations. Intelligence on the other side's negotiating positions may have figured in the 1999 US-European Union dispute over banana imports, but if so it is difficult to see a moral dimension for the intelligence or the diplomatic bargaining it served. Yet where intelligence knowledge bears on more obviously ethical issues of international security, justice and humanity it can have some moral influence on its own account. If truth-seeking by the intelligence producers is linked with governments disposed to listen, the result is an improvement in international perception which – arguably – reduces what have been termed national leaders' 'war-conducive' acts of insensitivity, thoughtlessness and recklessness.[20]

Of course these conditions do not necessarily apply. Evil regimes are served by self-seeking intelligence, and even in better states leaders use intelligence as selectively as domestic statistics. Intelligence cannot stop governments being wicked or misguided, and it provides no magic key to the future. But (like statistics) it can do something in favourable conditions about governmental ignorance and misperception. John Gaddis argues that the Soviet documents from the Cold War show 'the dangers of making emotionally based decisions in isolation' when authoritarians do not consult experts.[21] Recent writing about the Indo-Pakistan crisis in 1999 has brought out leaders' mutual sense of siege, and the importance of 'methods of deployment, intelligence capabilities and command-and-control systems' in reducing the risks of the antagonists' nuclear momentum. One hopes that intelligence in both countries is up to the job.[22]

Even if this has some credence as a general proposition, good intelligence can still be accused of applying its own institutional 'spin', a *déformation professionelle* towards hawkish, 'worst-case' assessments. Intelligence is partly a warning system; and as a former British Joint Intelligence Committee Chairman has put it, it specialises in 'the hard world of shocks and accidents, threats and crises . . . the dark side of the moon, history pre-eminently as the record of the crimes and follies of mankind'.[23] So it is not surprising if intelligence exaggerates threats and demonises enemies. It is bound to be sometimes misleading (again like statistics),[2] but the charge is that it tends to be misleading always in the same direction, giving policy and decisions a systemic bias.

Yet historically this is a caricature, not a measured judgement. There is indeed a danger of military intelligence reflecting the interests of the military-industrial lobby in increased defence expenditure, as was an element in the Cold War. Soldiers in any circumstances have to dwell on 'worst cases' since they pay the price of complacency. Intelligence's secrecy – 'if you knew what we know' – does not make criticism of hawkish assessments easy. But the overall intelligence record is far more varied than this image suggests. There are more instances of failing to detect surprise attacks than of ringing alarm bells for imaginary ones, and as many examples of underestimating opponents as exaggerating them. Moreover institutional checks and balances can be devised to provide some safeguards against bias, as in the way the British JIC system allegedly produces an interdepartmental synthesis of military pessimism with diplomatic optimism – itself another caricature, but with a grain of truth in it. International discussion of intelligence estimates is even more effective in improving standards. Intelligence can err by striving too hard to be 'useful' to its customers, but this is balanced by the ethic of professional objectivity, the practitioner's self-image of exposing 'all those who won't listen to all the things they don't want to know'[25] and the importance of international reputation. The effect over time is that governments that take note of Western-style intelligence behave as better international citizens than those that operate without it.[2]

Intelligence Knowledge: Specific Applications

This conclusion is supported by more specific connections with international morality, many of them springing from America's world role and its unmatched superpower intelligence. Intelligence is part of the American security umbrella over China's and North Korea's intentions towards their Pacific neighbours. It figures in America's role as international mediator, providing stabilisation and reassurance. As part of the settlement after the 1973 Yom Kippur War Henry Kissinger undertook to provide Egypt and Israel with intelligence from regular airborne sorties.[27] The power of satellite surveillance has subsequently given a new dimension to this part of the American security toolkit. The effect of intelligence briefings given to India and Pakistan in 1990 to prevent their drifting towards war illustrates intelligence satellites' place in the *mana* of American power.[28] Similar intelligence support will presumably be offered to Israel in compensation for eventual withdrawal from the Golan Heights.

Nevertheless intelligence contributions of this kind to international security are by no means limited to the American ones, and they extend beyond specific situations to a group of worldwide and long-term security issues. Terrorism is one such; the limitation of weapons of mass destruction and other arms proliferation is another, through the Missile Technology Control Regime, the Nuclear Suppliers Group and others of this kind; and international sanctions are a third category of wide-ranging, intelligence-driven cooperation. International arrangements between intelligence professionals underpin these political agreements. National intelligence tips off collaborating nations, or is used to keep them from backsliding.

It also supports the many agreements that now exist for arms control and other confidence-building measures. Historically it bore the main weight of arms control verification in the Cold War; the US–Soviet strategic arms control agreements of the 1970s depended entirely on intelligence for verification, since on-site inspection was still unacceptable to the Soviet Union. These agreements even had provisions for cooperative displays to each party's imagery satellites, and limitations on the encipherment of radiotelemetry from missiles. Astonishingly, the superpower antagonists undertook in this way to facilitate each other's secret intelligence collection.[29]

Arms control and confidence-building agreements now have large symbolic elements, but where there are real tensions, as between India and Pakistan, intelligence still operates in synergy with any agreements reached for transparency. Intelligence triggers treaty-based inspections; inspections plus declared confidence-building data provide leads for intelligence; each checks and steers the other. National Technical Means of collection (the Cold War euphemism for intelligence) were recognised in 1996 in the Comprehensive Test Ban Treaty as legitimate triggers for international on-site inspection.[30] The power of modern intelligence is a prop, perhaps not sufficiently recognised, for the advocates of nuclear reduction or elimination.

Intelligence's most dramatic impact in recent years has however been in support for international intervention. Iraq since the Gulf War has been a classic intelligence target of almost Cold War difficulty, and UNSCOM-IAEA inspections of Iraqi compliance with the Gulf War peace terms leaned heavily on national intelligence inputs, with as many as twenty nations contributing data.[31] Action over the no-fly zones and the Kurdish sanctuary has been similarly intelligence-steered.

Iraq may be *sui generis*, but Bosnia and Kosovo have represented what seems the new pattern of intelligence support for international intervention of all kinds. All those responsible for such operations, from the UN Secretary-General downwards, have emphasised the need for good intelligence.[32] A deluge of information is available from the many non-intelligence sources – the media, diplomatic reporting, deployed military units, NGOs, international officials – but all concerned echo T. S. Eliot's cry in *The Rock:*

> Where is the wisdom we have lost in knowledge?
> Where is the knowledge we have lost in information?

National intelligence is relied upon to fill gaps, validate other sources, and above all assess. The concept of graduated force, surgical strikes, low casualties and minimum collateral damage is intelligence-dependent. Military forces deployed in peace enforcement and peace building need virtually the full range of wartime intelligence support, and providing evidence on crimes against humanity now adds a whole new set of intelligence requirements.[33] International intervention is snowballing and – as put in one of the British agencies' recruitment literature – 'government cannot make the right decisions unless it has the full picture'.[34] The West's operations over Kosovo have dramatically demonstrated the paradox of highly public international operations depending crucially on secret intelligence.

Meeting the need poses many problems. America's leading role cannot be guaranteed,[35] and in any case other participating nations have to be accommodated in the intelligence structure. Its intelligence dependence on America is a current issue for the European Union; coalitions of the willing need shared information, with some confidence that it is not being rigged by the US with British connivance. Small powers have the dilemmas posed by supporting international action while taking others' intelligence assessments on trust.

Yet the problems should not obscure modern intelligence's ability to deliver the goods. Satellites' scope is ever-increasing, as is the capability of high-flying aircraft and drones. So too are the opportunities provided by the electronic world in which every detachment commander, insurgent leader, terrorist director, hostage-taker or international drug dealer has his mobile phone or communicates via internet. The cases of collateral damage in the bombing of Serbia should not divert attention from what the campaign showed of the power of sophisticated technical collection combined with precise weaponry. 'There are now no places on Earth that cannot be subjected to the same relentless harrowing . . . The World Order looks better protected than it did the day before the bombing began.'[36]

This support for international order may at last be making intelligence respectable; or at least some intelligence. In her aid programme for developing countries Ms Clare Short as Britain's left-wing Secretary of State for International Development has endorsed strengthening 'the capacity of [local] intelligence services to assess genuine outside threats'.[37] Considering her radical background, this could be taken as game, set and match for intelligence's ethical justification.

Intelligence Activities: The Ethical Spectrum

But if this applies to intelligence's knowledge, there is still the problem of its activities. About 90 per cent of intelligence expenditure is on secret collection; is this a form of anti-social international behaviour? Absolutists hanker after a Woodrow Wilson-like world of open information openly acquired. Pragmatists may have no objection to covert methods *per se* but may worry about the effects. International law suggests some constraints; though actually not many. From any of these viewpoints it might be held that intelligence's activities undo the good done by the knowledge they produce.

Here, a first approach is to consider the collection methods intelligence uses, to recognise their variety and broad ethical spectrum. At one extreme no questions of propriety are posed by intelligence's use of public information and the results of military and diplomatic observations and contacts. Something of the same applies to some of its own peacetime collection, despite the secret intelligence label. Ships and aircraft collect intelligence in international waters and airspace without accusations of illegality, as do armies when deployed overseas (though the media always tag similar civilian observations as 'spying').[38] Satellite photography violates no international law and is now more or less accepted as a commercial as well as an intelligence activity.[39] *Pace* Kant, wartime intelligence-gathering is free from any legal or moral restraint, except on the torture of prisoners under interrogation. (There is also a legal concept of 'treachery',[40] but it has not yet been applied to intelligence.) Yet a wartime effort has to be operational in peacetime and cannot sit twiddling its thumbs.

Other types of intelligence collection and exploitation have less legitimacy but are tolerated provided that they remain undeclared. Most electronic interception is at relatively long ranges and provides no indication of its precise targets; despite national privacy legislation, transmission via the ether is intrinsically a public means of communication. Routine anti-Americanism does not usually extend to condemning US technical collection.[41] Russia now has a separate and probably effective codebreaking organisation but no one loses much sleep over it. Armed forces assume intelligence coverage of them, and diplomats are not fussed by having their telegrams intercepted. Intelligence collection in these categories does not seem particularly intrusive. Governments' attitudes to it have echoes of current American policy over homosexuality in the armed forces: 'don't ask, don't tell'.

Some other collection has bigger ethical question-marks against it. The Western overflights of the USSR in the 1940s and 1950s, by balloons as well as aircraft, were clear breaches of territorial integrity, as was the West's intelligence collection in Soviet territorial waters, incompatible with maritime law on innocent passage.[42] There is also the doubtful status of embassies, as both intelligence targets and intelligence bases. Suborning foreign embassy staff to provide documents or ciphers has a long history, but the Cold War added the new dimension of bugging and electronic attacks against their premises. The new US Embassy in Moscow has had to be abandoned, unused, hopelessly penetrated with microphones and bugs.[43] Gordievsky's autobiography recounts the claustrophobic precautions taken in the Soviet Embassy in London.[44] An American diplomat has written with honesty of the effects on his diplomatic judgement of being under intelligence siege in Moscow: 'it was hard not to let that situation impact on your own view of the former USSR'.[45]

The converse of this targeting of embassies has been the development in this century of 'diplomatic cover' for agent-runners and recruiters, after diplomats became too respectable to do this work themselves. Some embassies subsequently became bases for electronic interception; Soviet listening posts of this kind were reported to be in action late in the Cold War.[46] On most counts these various features of twentieth-century diplomatic life sit awkwardly with the 1961 Vienna Convention which governs it. On the one hand this provides for the inviolability of diplomatic missions and their premises. On the other it describes diplomacy's function as ascertaining conditions in the host country *by all lawful means*, with the stipulation that diplomatic premises are not to be used 'in any manner incompatible with the function of the mission as laid down in the present Convention or by other rules of general international law or by any special agreements in force between the receiving and sending state'.[47]

Most questioned of all is peacetime espionage, irrespective of any diplomatic involvement. In reality some human agents are just extensions of diplomatic sources; governments need some inconspicuous and unavowed contacts, as with the IRA before the 'peace process'. Others are like confidential press sources. But the dominant image is of the spy engaged in deeply concealed espionage. Even some of this deep espionage is defensive, part of the conflict between intelligence attack and defence; despite the American shock-horror over Ames as a Moscow agent in CIA, his effect was to reveal US espionage in Russia.[48] Some spies have patriotic or ideological motives, though avarice and other human weaknesses loom equally large; in 1995 the CIA was restricted over recruiting 'unsavoury' agents.[49] Whatever the motives, espionage is feared for the damage it can do, and evokes the reaction associated with the betrayer, the Judas, the traitor, akin perhaps to the 'moral panic' over some domestic crime.[50] In England the betrayal of secrets to the Crown's enemies was identified with treason even before the 1351 Treason Act. The same feeling attaches itself to foreign covert action, for which intelligence is usually the executive agent. The intensity of Soviet espionage and covert action left a deep imprint on Western attitudes, reinforcing atavistic fears of the enemy within, and ambivalence about using such methods oneself.[51] Authoritarian regimes share the fears, though not the scruples.[52]

This survey suggests some inverse correlation between ethical acceptability and the degree of intrusion in intelligence's methods, but the picture is not clear, and international law does little to clarify it. The laws of war permit the execution of spies, but wartime espionage is not itself illegal; 'the spy remains in his curious legal limbo; whether his work is honourable or dishonourable, none can tell'.[53] No one knows what the Vienna Convention's 'lawful means' and 'rules of general international law' actually signify for diplomatic collection methods. Violations of national territory are illegal, but there is no code of conduct for information-gathering *per se*. The liberal repugnance for covert means cannot be discounted, but there is no international law of states' privacy. Moreover the state cannot defend its own secrets properly without being up to date on offensive techniques; the effective gamekeeper has to be a competent poacher.

Thus considering methods *in vacuo* does not get us very far. In reality the scale of intelligence operations may be as important as the precise methods used, particularly since all intelligence tends to be tarred with the brush of espionage (as in the way the media always refer to the British Sigint agency, quite inaccurately, as 'the Cheltenham spy centre'). Most Western airborne and shipborne collection around the Soviet periphery did not infringe national airspace; yet the sheer weight of it probably reinforced Cold War tensions and threat perceptions. Some forty American aircraft were shot down in the first decade and a half of the Cold War, as well as the two innocent South Korean passenger aircraft much later, with grievous losses.[54] The political circumstances are equally impor- tant; the Indian shoot-down of a Pakistani electronic aircraft in August 1999 reflected the state of tension as well as exacerbating it. Ethical judgements probably need to link methods with scale and cumulative effects, but the nature of the targets and reasons for targeting are also a factor.

Targeting of Non-States and International 'Baddies'

Here a shift over the last decade is important. Foreign intelligence is now directed more than previously towards two relatively new targets. One is the 'non-state' category, ranging from frag- mented and dissolving states, through independence movements, terrorists, international criminals and illegal dealers in nuclear material, to others at the security-threatening end of the trad- ing spectrum. The other, linked with the first group, is the small group of rogue states, exemplified by the Milosevic regime or states supporting terrorism. Many of these new targets, whether state or non-state, are either international 'baddies', or actors in scenes of actual or incipient mayhem. In targeting them most governments have altruistic motives overlaying narrow national interests, with intelligence's tasking manifesting ethical foreign policy in a direct way.

Arguably this combination of targets and policy objectives moves intelligence's ethical goalposts virtually to a wartime position; in a sufficiently good cause, against such targets, almost anything goes. Intelligence may be needed on potential victims of violence to effect their protection. Foreign non-state entities and failed states have no international rights of privacy, and rogue states have for- feited them by bad conduct, especially if they are gross violators of human rights. The baddies are at war with international society, deliberately or implicitly by rejecting civilised standards. Unlike armed force, intelligence does not kill or cause suffering. Though he was speaking of military intelligence rather than covert collection, a thoughtful Victorian officer pointed out that 'the pursuit of intelligence has not, like swollen armaments, any tendency to bring about war'.[55]

Yet it can still be argued that some intelligence methods are ethically unacceptable in any circumstances. Using robust methods in special cases may be seductive; 'the exception would become part of the norm'.[56] Intelligence may be harmless in itself, but there is a danger of slipping into the defence that 'guns do not kill people; people kill people'. Whatever the morality of the West's bombardment of Serbia, intelligence power was a prime element, not just an incidental supporter.

Ideally such problems of conscience might be solved by UN mandates. Thus at the end of the Gulf War the Security Council's request to all states to give UNSCOM 'maximum assistance, in cash and in kind' was interpreted to include intelligence.[57] Yet it is difficult to see the UN leading with ethical criteria over intelligence methods. Its image is one of rectitude and transparency, and indeed has suffered from the allegations that UNSCOM cover was used for covert CIA operations.[58] It can be expected to favour the 'don't ask, don't tell' approach to the sources of the national intelligence it receives. In the long run the UN will need to sponsor some intelligence collection and assessment on its own account, in the way UNSCOM had its own analysis unit plus American U-2 collection at its disposal; but that is a separate issue. For the time being the absolutist has to deal with intelligence's ethical problems without much UN guidance.

For the pragmatist, of course, reflecting on these targets – the limitation must be repeated – these absolutist concerns do not carry great weight. The greater the ethical emphasis in foreign policy, the less concern is needed over intelligence's methods and scale, always assuming that this collection is necessary. The scale of international suffering and crimes against humanity is a powerful warrant for intrusive collection, as is rogue states' sponsorship of terrorism and assassination of their political opponents overseas.

Targeting of Legitimate States

But most intelligence is still directed against normal states whose behaviour does not put them beyond the pale, and here other considerations apply. International society is a society of states bound by cooperation, or at least toleration; they do not behave as if in a complete state of nature. The avoidance of inter-state aggression and war remains one of the world's highest priorities. Governments' reticence about intelligence collection is not related only to source protection, and implies a conflict with a tacit code of international behaviour over information-gathering, albeit a shadowy one. Some states with particularly close relationships refrain from regular covert collection against each other; much as they would like it, the US and Canada probably do not tap each other's telephones to get access to the other's bottom line in their many economic and other negotiations. Even where special relationships do not exist, responsible states think twice about using the more intrusive and risky intelligence methods against others; not all states are fair game for anything. Even against antagonists, issues of prudence arise over covert operations which (if discovered) will be taken as insults or confirmations of hostility. Cold War documents show British Ministers balancing the intelligence benefits from airborne collection, including U-2 flights based on Britain, against the effects on Anglo-Soviet relations.[59]

Of course states' behaviour depends on the facts of particular cases: the targets, the methods and the risks of being found out. But generally speaking it has not been assumed in the West that peacetime intelligence had complete *carte blanche*, whether the targets were friendly states or unfriendly ones. Vestiges persist of British Victorian rectitude over covert methods and the pre-Second World War American maxim that 'gentlemen don't read each others' mail', even though neither has been observed with any consistency (and the American quotation was a post-1945 rationalisation).[60]

These inhibitions exist; yet over the last decade they do not seem to have significantly limited intelligence's scale and methods. Press reports suggest the opposite; more espionage cases hit the media now than in the Cold War. Most of the permanent members of the Security Council have been accused of spying on each other, and membership of the European Union does not seem to convey immunity from being targeted by fellow members. Russia seems to have sought an intelligence *détente* in the early 1990s – the last head of the KGB handed over the bugging plans for the new US Moscow Embassy; there was some release of Soviet intelligence records; public statements claimed that its successor Foreign Intelligence Service was contracting its overseas collection and sought international cooperation[61] – but this period has now passed. The KGB's foreign intelligence successors are now flourishing, active and influential, and China's coup in acquiring American nuclear secrets is said to rival the Soviet successes of the late 1940s. The Russian Federal Security Service claimed to have caught eleven foreign agents and thwarted thirty-nine attempts to send secret information abroad in the first half of 1997.[62] Other countries are following these leads. Early in the 1990s a respected historian foresaw that claimants to regional dominance would seek superiority in intelligence collection, producing 'upward spirals and a new intelligence war'.[63] Reports that intelligence expenditure in the Far East had doubled from the end of the Cold War to 1997 may support his prognosis, as has the Chinese and North Korean concern reported over Japanese proposals to launch intelligence satellites within four or five years.[64] The media may exaggerate, but it seems that the global Information Age has in no way reduced states' interest in acquiring others' secrets.

Does it Matter?

Does this affect inter-state relationships? Much of it is accepted as part of the international system. Except in special relationships, intelligence collaboration between states has never been seen to rule out some discreet targeting of each other. It cannot be demonstrated that collection on either friends or enemies has affected the climate of the 1990s. Its economic espionage has not caused France to be blackballed in the European Union. Intelligence threats have not consistently increased military confrontation in Korea, South Asia or South Lebanon, and did not provoke the war between Eritrea and Ethiopia. Conventional wisdom tolerates espionage on *The Times*'s grounds that everybody does it.

Yet it seems unrealistic to exclude intelligence from the unquantifiable grit of international friction. Collection is necessarily against someone; attack necessitates defence. Even if collection has been somewhat reduced from the Cold War scale, it is difficult to believe that its more intrusive aspects do not have cumulative effects in reinforcing conflicts and impairing international cooperation. The targeting of diplomacy, and the facilities which diplomacy itself provides for intelligence, hardly promote the diplomatic function described by Alan James as 'the communications system of the international society'.[65] Ernest Bevin as Foreign Secretary said that a better world would involve being able to cross the Channel without a passport; his modern successors might say that it would involve discussing secrets abroad without worrying about foreign bugging. Being able to operate without reckoning with covert intelligence attacks may be a factor – if only a minor one – in the special quality of the English-speaking transatlantic and Old Commonwealth relationships, and perhaps of those of the Scandinavian countries. Intelligence-gathering within the EU hardly makes it easier for it to stagger towards its Common Foreign and Security Policy. Espionage is said to be a factor in the low state of US–Chinese relations.[66] Most important of all, the continuation of the Cold War pattern of intelligence attack and defence surely has some influence on relationships between Russia on the one hand and the US plus NATO on the other.[67]

Perhaps the more open modern world helps to make covert intelligence more disturbing. In the age of worldwide investigative journalism intelligence is now far more exposed than formerly; few secrets remain secrets. Foreign policies are now more influenced by domestic politics, and it is difficult for politicians and opinion-formers to accept foreign intelligence attacks as natural parts of the international game. The modern humanitarian morality that 'something must be done' takes effective intelligence for granted, yet at the same time prizes international legality and clean hands. Even before the present British government's ethical foreign policy, its predecessor endorsed a 'moral base' for its defence doctrine; the 'concept of propriety, which seeks to ensure that the activities of the armed forces are viewed universally as being justifiable, fair, and apolitical'.[68] It can be argued that intelligence everywhere – an aspect of national power, like armed forces – needs a similar ethical foundation.

Balance Sheet and Desiderata

Despite intelligence's modern status, what states do is worth more ethical scrutiny than the intelligence they use and the activities that produce it. Some intelligence knowledge does not affect the ethical standards of the foreign policies it influences, and many intelligence activities have no ethical significance in themselves. Nevertheless part of intelligence's knowledge and a smaller proportion of its activities probably have some general (and contradictory) effects on the morality of international society.

The ethical case for its knowledge is fairly clear. Despite intelligence's failures and distortions, its rationales of information-seeking and objectivity tend to make those leaders who draw on it behave 'better' internationally than those less concerned with an intelligence view of reality, or less exposed to it. (Governments that encourage objective intelligence may well be inclined anyway to 'better' international behaviour than those that do not, but intelligence probably has some institutional influence on its own account.) The international community working *qua* community depends upon national intelligence inputs, particularly from American technical collection. It needs intelligence as much as the population, health and environmental data that are other foundations for international action.

Yet a minority of intelligence collection poses ethical problems. On some targets the ends justify the intelligence means, though perhaps not completely. (Should one torture terrorists to forestall imminent operations?[69] Perhaps one should.) On the other hand, the more intrusive methods of peacetime collection – espionage, some bugging, and perhaps diplomatic targeting and the exploitation of diplomatic immunities – probably are disturbing factors when used against legitimate states. The situation is not static. 'Since the end of the Cold War a universal international system has come into existence marked by the unprecedented situation in which almost all states are in diplomatic relations with other states.'[70] This aspect of globalisation sits uncomfortably with the prospect that 185 states and statelets may all invest in covert intelligence collection to keep up with the international Joneses. If international arms limitation is a desirable objective, why not limit intrusive intelligence?

This balance sheet suggests three desiderata for strengthening the international attitudes and norms that already exist. The first is to recognise that the Western idea of objective, all-source intelligence assessment on foreign affairs, with some separation from policy-making, is a necessary part of the modern, global standard of government. All states should be encouraged to develop this machinery, in the spirit of Ms Short's commendation of intelligence to the developing world.[71] The CIA's Directorate of Intelligence with its remit for analysis and assessment should be an international role model, and it is tragic that historical accident has caused it to be identified with the covert collection and covert action of the Agency's Directorate of Operations.

Second is to emphasise the place of international exchanges between states at this 'finished intelligence' level. International action is no more cohesive than the intelligence exchanges that underlay it. The UN, EU, NATO and other regional institutions will eventually develop machinery for supranational intelligence assessment, but it will be a long haul, and will have to build on inter-state exchanges. Two former American DCIs argued some years ago that American intelligence should become an international good,[72] and the US subsequently committed itself to intelligence support for international organisations.[73] To some extent this is already a de facto underpinning of international society, yet for its credibility the American input needs to be complemented by national intelligence institutions capable of critically assessing it for their own governments. States cooperating internationally need some kind of peer review of their own intelligence estimates. One wonders how far the impasses between NATO and Russia over Kosovo reflected different national intelligence inputs.

The third is to borrow the criteria of restraint, necessity and proportionality from Just War doctrine to discourage gung-ho approaches to intrusive covert collection. Morality reinforces the considerations of cost-effectiveness that covert methods should only be used where overt material is inadequate. The more intrusive the methods the greater the justification needed; recruiting additional human sources to fill the gaps in technical collection runs its own ethical risks. Ethics should be recognised as a factor in intelligence decisions, just as in anything else, and the Western notion of elected leaders' accountability for sensitive intelligence operations provides one way of reinforcing the ethical dimension. Similar considerations should be applied to covert action, though the essential difference should be recognised between the morality of information-gathering and action. Perhaps more should be done to separate the two.

This restraint implies some reordering of collection priorities. National security matters should remain central and legitimate requirements. But to these can now be added those bearing on international security, justice and humanitarian concerns. John Keegan has argued that democracy's professional soldiers are now international society's check upon violence; 'those honourable warriors who administer force in the cause of peace'.[74] *Mutatis mutandis*, national intelligence should now be seen in this light.

The counterpoint to this approach is some limitation over collection for purely national purposes, especially those unrelated to security. Throughout the 1990s it may have been fashionable outside the English-speaking countries to target covert collection on other countries' non-military secrets of economic, financial and technological kinds. Russia has seen this as a means of solving its economic problems vis-à-vis the West. French publicists have been rather proud of collection of this kind, though it is by no means a purely Gallic activity.[75] The issues over government activity of this kind are complex, but as a generalisation it is both provocative and overblown. The Soviet aircraft industry is said to have copied stolen plans of Concorde; much good it did them. Immediately after the Cold War some argued that US intelligence should be redeployed to the 'trade war' with Japan and Western Europe, and Washington deserves credit for substantially rejecting the case.[76]

Even for governments that want to get into this field, using open and 'grey' sources and commercial information brokers is a better bet than tasking their intelligence agencies.

This restraint also implies extending the existing limitations on targeting other states for 'bargaining intelligence' on matters of purely national interest. Covert intelligence increases diplomatic effectiveness, but sometimes with the long-term costs already suggested. Firms in the private sector depend on reading their competitors' hands, but those that care about their reputations are careful about how they do so. Perhaps governments should exercise similar care over the intelligence methods used against friendly powers, and rely instead on journalists as the experts on intrusion.

These are desiderata for multilateral action, not for unilateral intelligence disarmament. They reflect Western views and Western cultural power – though a doctrinal restraint on intrusive methods would not come easily to the major Cold War powers, East or West. The US, Russia and Britain all have strong (and differing) reasons for keeping intelligence power unfettered. Yet the case remains for developing the present loose code of conduct through reciprocal or multinational understandings, probably inconspicuously. The problem is to demystify intelligence's role and make it a fit subject for international discourse.

Two features of international norms may be helpful. First, some evolve gradually through informal international contacts and the influence of 'world opinion'. The international patchwork of multilateral and bilateral intelligence relationships already provides scope for confidential discussion of intelligence purposes and priorities. In particular, Western intelligence already has well-publicised links with Russia on international terrorism, drugs and other criminality, and evidence of war crimes, plus the military opportunities presented by the Partnership for Peace programme and other contacts. The publicity now given to intelligence objectives by Britain and America provides a basis for further discussion, with Russia and more widely.[77]

International understandings of any kind may seem an unlikely outcome but are not impossible. Before the SALT I and II and ABM agreements of the 1970s it would have seemed quite inconceivable that the superpowers would in effect legitimise aspects of each other's secret collection, yet they did.[78] Recently the OECD nations plus some others signed a 'bribery convention' in which 'the United States has got all the rich countries to play by roughly the same rules'.[79] This is still far removed from intelligence; but it is a reminder that unexpected things can happen when states are persuaded of common interests. Russia is reported to have pressed the UN Secretary-General in 1998 for an international treaty banning information warfare.[80] The possibility of mutual US and Russian reductions in espionage was raised, apparently from the American side, in July 1999 in Washington discussions between the US Vice-President and Russian Prime Minister, and was remitted for further examination. The Prime Minister was removed from office shortly afterwards, but the idea has at least got to the conference table.[81]

Second, international law has a momentum of its own. An American naval officer writing on intelligence argued that there are limits of behaviour which 'create definable customary international norms . . . To those who must work with these subjects, the norms are real, the boundaries tangible, and the consequences of exceeding them unacceptable – personally and professionally, nationally and internationally.'[82] Geoffrey Best takes us further by reminding us that 'much international law of the contemporary age . . . is "normative". Normative means standard-setting; adding to established State practice, the aspirational concept of State practice as it is expected, intended, or hoped to become at some future date.'[83] International law need not remain as silent on intelligence as it is now.

To sum up; intelligence is now a permanent part of the nation state. Even lesser states need it and will soon have it. There is plenty for it to do. But the new millennium should seek to emphasise internationally:

1. The value of accurate knowledge and policy-free intelligence assessment of foreign affairs, based on all sources of information and not necessarily the product of covert collection. This should be recognised as a condition of good government in the globalised world.
2. The increased relevance of national intelligence, both covert collection and all-source analysis, to the working of international institutions, and to other international action in

the interests of security, justice and humanitarianism. International exchanges are a necessity for international society. International action is no more cohesive than the intelligence assessments that underlie it.

3. Restraint in the use of the more intrusive methods of collection for purposes not geared to national security or support for the international community. Ethics should be a factor in intelligence decisions, as in all others.

In short, *The Times*'s dictum that 'Cold War or no Cold War, nations routinely spy on each other' provides a realistic starting point for considering intelligence ethics, but is not the last word.

Notes

1. Originally published as 'Intelligence Services and Ethics in the New Millennium', *Irish Studies in International Affairs*, 10, 1999: 249–65. Subsequently revised and reprinted as 'Modern Intelligence Services: Have they a Place in Ethical Foreign Policies?', in H. Shukman (ed.), *Agents for Change: Intelligence Services in the 21st Century* (London: St Ermin's Press, 2000), pp. 287–328, and 'Intelligence and International Ethics', in M. Herman, Intelligence Services in the Information Age: Theory and Practice (London: Frank Cass, 2001), pp. 201–27. Reproduced by permission of the Royal Irish Academy and Taylor & Francis Group.
2. Hibbert, R., 'Intelligence and Policy', *Intelligence and National Security*, 5, no. 1, 1990: 115.
3. Contrary to the 'peace dividend' elsewhere, France planned a considerable expansion after the humiliation of depending on American intelligence in the Gulf War. See Kemp, P., 'The Rise and Fall of France's Spymasters', *Intelligence and National Security*, 9, no. 1, 1994: 12–21.
4. 'Reborn CIA dusts off Cloak and Dagger', *The Observer*, 14 March 1999. Expenditure for FY97 was US$26.6 billion, and for FY98 US$26.7 billion. (Press references summarised in Canadian Association for Security and Intelligence Studies, *Newsletter 34*, 1999: 20.)
5. The three intelligence agencies had a published budget of about three-quarters of a million pounds, but the cost of MoD and other strategic intelligence needs to be added. For costs of 'the national

intelligence capability' see Chapter 12 in this collection, 'Post-Cold War Issues and Opportunities'.

6. Within the European Union the Republic of Ireland may be an exception.

7. Speech, 23 March 1998.

8. Pekel, K., 'Integrity, Ethics and the CIA', *Studies in Intelligence,* spring 1998: 85–94.

9. Leader, 26 May 1999.

10. Wright, P., *Spycatcher: The Candid Autobiography of a Senior Intelligence Officer* (New York: Viking, 1987), p. 54.

11. For a criticism of le Carré's moral stance see Burridge, J., 'Sigint in the Novels of John le Carré', *Studies in Intelligence,* 37, no. 5, 1994: 125–32.

12. Attributed to Professor Huntington (as a comment on international opinion) by Chomsky, N., 'Now it's a Free For All', *The Guardian,* 17 May 1999.

13. Lustgarten, L. and I. Leigh, *In from the Cold: National Security and Parliamentary Democracy* (Oxford: Clarendon Press, 1994), p. 225. This work concentrates on intelligence's domestic aspects, but incidentally provides some ethical criticism of foreign intelligence.

14. Discussed in chapter 20 of Herman, M., *Intelligence Power in Peace and War* (Cambridge: Cambridge University Press, 1996), written from the perspective of the early 1990s.

15. Howard, M., 'Introduction', in R. Williamson (ed.), *Some Corner in a Foreign Field: Intervention and World Order* (London: Macmillan, 1998), p. 9.

16. Kahn, D., *The Codebreakers* (London: Sphere, 1973), p. 456.

17. Reiss, H., *Kant: Political Writings* (translated by H. B. Nisbet) , (Cambridge: Cambridge University Press, 1991), pp. 96–7.

18. A US policy-maker of the time had claimed that the timing of the flight, on May Day before the conference, was taken by Khrushchev as a deliberately offensive US signal. See Robert Bowie, *Baiting the Bear,* BBC2, 8 October 1996.

19. In Russian usage the first is 'Razvyedka' or 'Shpionazh', the second 'Svedyeniye'.

20. See Suganami, H., 'Stories of War Origins: A Narrativist Theory of the Causes of War', *Review of International Studies,* 1, no. 4, 1997: 401–18, for a typology of 'war-conducive' acts comprising contributory negligence and insensitive, thoughtless and reckless acts.

21. Gaddis, J. L., 'History, Grand Strategy and NATO Enlargement', *Survival,* 40, no. 1, 1998: 145–51.

22. *The Economist*, 22 May 1999, p. 5.

23. Cradock, P., *In Pursuit of British Interests: Reflections on Foreign Policy under Margaret Thatcher and John Major* (London: Murray, 1997), p. 37.

24. Compare intelligence with the many statistical failures such as over British earnings in 1997–8, set out for example in *The Economist*, 5 March 1999, p. 38.

25. Le Bailly, Vice-Admiral Sir Louis, letter to *The Times*, 3 August 1984.

26. For a discussion of American intelligence and policy in the Cold War see Andrew, C., *For the President's Eyes Only* (London: Harper-Collins, 1995). For the CIA's record in estimating the Soviet Union see MacEachin, D. J., 'CIA Assessments of the Soviet Union', *Studies in Intelligence*, 1, 1997; and Lundberg, K., *CIA and the Fall of the Soviet Empire: The Politics of 'Getting It Right'* (Harvard Intelligence and Policy Project, 1994).

27. Kissinger, H., *Years of Upheaval* (London: Weidenfeld and Nicolson, 1982), p. 828. Similar proposals were also made as part of the Israeli–Syrian settlement, p. 1254.

28. Statement by Robert Gates in *Open Secrets*, BBC Radio, 21 March 1995.

29. See chapter 9 in Herman, *Intelligence Power in Peace and War*.

30. Article 23 (Verification) permitted NTMs to be used to back up a call for on-site inspection if the data has been collected 'in a manner consistent with generally recognized principles of international law'.

31. An early team leader from the UN Special Commission in Iraq wrote that 'In the face of the highly efficient Iraqi deception, the inspection could not have gone forward without accurate intelligence.' See Kay, D., 'Arms Inspections in Iraq: Lessons for Arms Control', *Bulletin of Arms Control*, 7, 1992: 6–7. For a more complete account see Trevan, T., *Saddam's Secrets: The Hunt for Iraq's Hidden Weapons* (London: HarperCollins, 1999).

32. As early as 1971 the UN Secretary-General complained of the 'lack of authoritative information, without which the Secretary-General cannot speak'. See U Thant letter of 30 March 1971, quoted by Dorn, A. W., 'Keeping Tabs on a Troubled World: UN Information-Gathering to Preserve Peace', *Security Dialogue*, 27, no. 3, 1996: 263. This theme was taken up again in the early days of intervention in the former Yugoslavia in statements by military officials. For example, 'intelligence is a vital element of any operation and the UN needs to develop a system for obtaining information without compromising its neutrality', in Tod, J. R. R., 'UK Perspectives of

Current Security Arrangements', *RUSI Journal*, 139, no. 1, 1994: 35; and 'I have asked for numerous reforms in the structure of the UN in Yugoslavia, especially in the use of information, the capacity to analyse and reflect' – a French general quoted by *The Independent*, 31 January 1994.

33. Lloyd, A., 'Aerial Photographs and Phone Intercepts are Giving Instant Evidence of Atrocities', *The Times*, 14 May 1999.
34. GCHQ graduate careers brochure 1996.
35. As in its (reported) refusal to provide satellite results during the period of disunity before mounting the NATO-led Implementation Force in Bosnia and Herzegovina.
36. Keegan, J., 'So the Bomber Got Through After All', *The Daily Telegraph*, 4 June 1999.
37. DFID Policy Statement, *Poverty and the Security Sector*, p. 6. This formed the basis of an address by Short at the Centre for Defence Studies, 9 March 1999.
38. As in the TV programmes at various time about British Cold War observations from trawlers in northern waters.
39. For this legal position see Jasani, B., 'Civil Radar Observation Satellites for IAEA Safeguards', *Journal of the Institute of Nuclear Weapons Management*, 27, no. 2, 1999. UN resolutions such as A/RES53/76 have however stressed the need for transparency on the use of outer space and the avoidance of a space arms race.
40. For a brief description see British Defence Doctrine JWP 0-01 1996, Annex B.6.
41. Though for many years a British protest group had alleged that the American Sigint station at Menwith Hill in Northern England was intercepting British communications.
42. The well-attested American U-2 observations of Anglo-French preparations in Cyprus for the Suez operation perhaps entailed overflights of what was then a British island but might have been possible by oblique photography from outside territorial limits. On maritime collection, the relevant law is United Nations Convention on the Law of the Sea 1982, articles 19 and 29. 'Innocent passage' excludes 'collecting information to the prejudice of the defence or security of the coastal state' (19.2.(c)).
43. For a summary see Nelson, D. and J. Koenen-Grant, 'A Case of Bureaucracy "In Action": The US Embassy in Moscow', *International Journal of Intelligence and CounterIntelligence*, 6, no. 3, 1993: 303–17.
44. Gordievsky, O., *Next Stop Execution* (London: Macmillan, 1995), pp. 257–8.

45. Herspring, D. R., 'The Cold War: Perceptions from the American Embassy, Moscow', *Diplomacy and Statecraft*, 9, no. 2, 1998: 200.
46. For Soviet activities see Ball, D., *Soviet Signals Intelligence (Sigint)*, Australian National University Papers on Strategy and Defence No. 47, 1989, pp. 38–70.
47. Vienna Convention 1961, Articles 3.1 and 41.3.
48. A Soviet defector, himself betrayed by Ames, claimed that up to forty-five CIA agents had been identified. See *The Times*, 18 February 1997. Other press reports quoted lower figures.
49. Gerber, B. L., 'A Discussion of Intelligence Ethics', paper delivered to the International Studies Association Convention, Toronto, March 1997, p. 6.
50. Compare with Cohen, S., *Folk Devils and Moral Panics: The Creation of the Mods and Rockers* (Oxford: Blackwell, 1987).
51. The liberal view also includes the belief that the agent can be induced to 'betray obligations of loyalty which may be legitimately demanded of him'. See Lustgarten and Leigh, *In from the Cold*, p. 225. (This assumes, of course, that the regime spied upon deserves loyalty.) Other elements are the risks to the agents, and the corrupting effects on the officers running them; according to a former CIA General Counsel, 'the constant pressure of the clandestine life can try the moral ballast of the most honest man or woman', quoted by Gerber, 'A Discussion of Intelligence Ethics', p. 30.
52. Thus China and Iran, in signing the Comprehensive Test Ban Treaty, made separate declarations that verification should not be interpreted as including the results of 'espionage or human intelligence'; see Declarations and Reservations in 'Comprehensive Nuclear-Test Ban Treaty', *United Nations Treaty Collection*, Chapter XXVI, section 4, accessed on 18 January 2021 at: https://treaties.un.org/doc/Publication/MTDSG/Volume%20II/Chapter%20XXVI/XXVI-4.en.pdf
53. Best, G., *War and Law Since 1945* (Oxford: Oxford University Press, 1994).
54. The second of these incidents, of KAL-007 in September 1983, also exacerbated a period of high East–West tension.
55. Brackenbury, Major C. B., 'The Intelligence Duties of the Staff Abroad and at Home', *RUSI Journal*, 19, no. 80, 1875: 265.
56. Lustgarten and Leigh, *In from the Cold*, p. 496.
57. UN Security Council resolution 699 (1991).
58. Accusations by Scott Ritter, reported for example in *The Guardian*, 30 March 1999.
59. See Aldrich, R. J., *Espionage, Security and Intelligence in Britain 1945–70* (Manchester: Manchester University Press, 1998), pp. 33–4,

100–1, 103–4. For intelligence cases and diplomatic expulsions as an irritant in Anglo-Soviet relations see Deighton, A., 'Ostpolitik or Westpolitik? British Foreign Policy, 1968–75', *International Affairs*, 74, no. 4, 1998: 896.

60. The official history of the Crimean War is said to have concluded that 'the gathering of knowledge by clandestine means were [sic] repulsive to the feelings of an English Gentleman', quoted by Parritt, B., *The Intelligencers* (Intelligence Corps Association, Ashford Kent, 1983), p. 80. On the other hand Lord Salisbury wrote in 1875 that 'we receive pretty constantly copies of the most important reports and references that reach the Foreign Office and War Office at St. Petersburg' (from John Ferris, quoted by Herman, *Intelligence Power in Peace and War*, p. 22). For 'reading each other's mail' see the correspondence in *Intelligence and National Security*, 2, no. 4, 1987: 192.

61. For Vadim Bakatin's handover of bugging details see Waller, J. M., 'Russia's Security Services: A Checklist for Reform', *Perspective*, 8, no. 1, 1997. Earlier reports of the handover were confirmed, with disapproval, by the Director of the Russian codebreaking organisation in a Russian television interview of 25 October 1997. For statements by V. A. Kirpichenko, the SVR Director, see *Krasnaya Zvezda*, 30 October 1993, p. 6.

62. Reuters, quoted by *Jane's Intelligence Watch Report*, 1 July 1997.

63. Ferris, J., 'Intelligence After the Cold War: A Global Perspective', in A. Bergin and R. Hall (eds), *Intelligence and Australian National Security* (Canberra: Australian Defence Studies Centre, 1994), p. 8.

64. Quoted from Desmond Ball in *Far East Economic Review*, 9 June 1997. Chinese and North Korean reactions are referred to in VERTIC, *Trust and Verify*, 83, 1993: 6.

65. James, A., 'Diplomacy', *Review of International Studies*, 19, no. 1, 1993: 95.

66. Not limited to the alleged Chinese nuclear espionage. A Chinese academic had previously been arrested on his return from Stanford University and accused of betraying Chinese secrets. See Liu, M. and B. John, 'Spy-for-Spy Justice', *Newsweek*, 29 March 1999.

67. 'The Russian National Security Blueprint', published 26 December 1997 (*Rossiyskaya Gazeta*, Moscow) laid surprising emphasis on defence against 'leaks of important political, economic, scientific-technical and military information', 'the threat of foreign intelligence services' agent and operational-technical penetration of Russia', and the need for 'information security' far more than in any comparable Western statement of national security policy.

68. *British Defence Doctrine (JWP 0-01)* (London: HMSO, 1997), p. 3.10.
69. For some time Israeli courts approved the use of 'moderate physical pressure' in such circumstances. See Gerber, 'Discussion of Intelligence Ethics', p. 7. This was overtaken by a Supreme Court decision in 1999 (*The Guardian*, 7 September 1999).
70. Cohen, R., 'Diplomacy 2000 B.C.–2000 A.D.', paper delivered to the British International Studies Association annual conference, 1995, p. 1.
71. The Russian national blueprint cited in note 67 also highlights 'the objective and comprehensive analysis and forecasting of threats to national security'.
72. Turner, S., *Secrecy and Democracy* (New York: Harper and Row, 1986), pp. 280–5; Colby, W. E., 'Reorganizing Western Intelligence', in C. P. Runde and G. Voss (eds), *Intelligence and the New World Order* (Bustehude: International Freedom Foundation, 1992), pp. 126–7.
73. 'To the extent prudent, US intelligence today is . . . being used in dramatically new ways, such as assisting the international organizations like the United Nations . . . We will share information and assets that strengthen peaceful relationships and aid in building confidence'. See *National Security Strategy of the United States* (Washington DC: White House, 1993), p. 18.
74. Concluding words in Keegan, J., *War and Our World* (London: Hutchinson, 1998) (Reith Lectures 1998), p. 74.
75. For accusations and counteraccusations see Farrell, N., 'Hark Who's Talking (and Listening)', *The Spectator*, 21 November 1998.
76. For a survey of the issues and of US thinking see Johnson, L., *Secret Agencies: US Intelligence in a Hostile World* (New Haven, CT: Yale University Press, 1996), chapter 6; also Clarke, D. and R. Johnston, 'Economic Espionage and Interallied Strategic Cooperation', *Thunderbird International Business Review*, 40, no. 4, July/August 1998.
77. US objectives were regularly aired by holders of the DCI office and through Congressional reports and special investigations. The annual reports of the Parliamentary Intelligence and Security Committee provided a British viewpoint.
78. The US–USSR Incidents at Sea agreement of 1972 also had some implications for intelligence collection at close quarters.
79. *The Economist*, 16 January 1999, p. 28.
80. *The Sunday Times*, 25 July 1999, p. 21.
81. Russian accounts of the press conference refer to 'total mutual understanding' having been reached on 'one sensitive topic', and

existing agreements 'to work in a fairly correct sort of way'. See FBIS and BBC translations of 28 and 29 July 1999 items.

82. Bowman, M. E., 'Intelligence and International Law', *International Journal of Intelligence and Counterintelligence*, 8, no. 3, 1995: 330.

83. Best, *War and Law Since 1945*, p. 7.

PART 2

The Cold War

5 Intelligence as Threats and Reassurance[1]

[2011]

Intelligence mattered in the Cold War mainly through governments' use of the knowledge it produced. But it was at the same time an activity, principally in its covert means of information collection, and also a capability: a power that governments felt able to count on in planning for the present and future. Both these had effects on the psychology of the two sides. The collection activities (or some of them) were seen as intrusive threats by the opponent against whom they were targeted. By contrast the intelligence capabilities that depended on this collection gave their own governments in the West – perhaps also in the East – some assurance in facing the Cold War's future. They were some restraint on the fears and distortions of uncertainty.

The two effects interacted in ways that posed an intelligence version of the 'security dilemma' of military power, in which seeking more security nationally through developing more forces increases perceptions of insecurity internationally and leads to a ratcheting of military procurement.[2] This did not apply to intelligence's verification of the US–Soviet strategic arms agreements in which, remarkably and exceptionally, the intelligence coverage of the two sides was legitimised so that it provided mutual reassurance without additional threats. But everywhere else intelligence increased the confidence of its own side by drawing on the product of collection activities that alarmed the other. This chapter discusses this combination of its threats and reassurance and the place of the two in Cold War psychology, though it is written mainly from an Anglo-American perspective and adds only limited aspects of the Soviet Union's perspective.

Threats

Human and Technical Collection

Most intelligence activity was in collection and the first-stage exploitation that went with it. The image of this collection everywhere was of espionage, the covert use of human agents, and this can be discussed first. The agents were of all kinds: those seeking to talent-spot, recruit and run them and the recruited agents in place, but also the defectors who changed sides with information to offer, the emigres, travellers and other occasional sources of all kinds, the whole gamut of human contacts with the other side. The image of 'spying' was popularly extended to all other intelligence collection, even merging into legitimate information-seeking. Both sides also used diplomatic cover for their intelligence officers overseas, and they sometimes extended intelligence functions as a result to providing covert government contacts and unattributable diplomacy. Covert technical collection was also mounted from diplomatic premises, as well as being a means of host countries' and others' external attacks on them. Embassies were both intelligence bases and intelligence targets.

Espionage was of course nothing new. On the Soviet side the large-scale effort of the Cold War had been foreshadowed in the pre-revolutionary Tsarist Okhrana, the inter-war pursuit of émigré and other perceived threats abroad, and the effort against both enemy and allies in the Second War; but the worldwide scale and professionalism the system developed after 1945 were unprecedented in peacetime. This was even more the case with its much smaller British and American counterparts. Covert US collection in peacetime was starting virtually from scratch, and the small pre-war British effort against Soviet targets had been discontinued after 1941.

Counterespionage developed in parallel, and the spy cases and spy trials it produced became regular reminders of espionage's Cold War significance to governments and publics on both sides. In the West the defection of the code clerk Igor Gouzenko from the Soviet embassy in Ottawa in 1945 led to public revelations of the scale of wartime Soviet espionage on its allies, and the effects were reinforced by the trials of the Soviet 'atomic spies' in the United Kingdom and United States in the following years. Other spy cases followed regularly on both sides, and the diplomatic cover these involved led to the recurrent tit-for-tat expulsions of diplomats and pseudo-diplomats. Both sides chose to publicise these trials and expulsions, along with some (not all) of the valuable human defections from the other side, and these glimpses of the secret war came to be regularly quoted in the East–West war of words. The intelligence war was held to be deeply secret, but some aspects of it were surprisingly public.

This was the public face of espionage, but it was closely linked on both sides with the less publicised activity of covert action, in its wide range from unattributable information services and confidential contacts at one extreme to support for paramilitary operations at the other. In the Soviet view these 'active measures' were complementary to espionage and doctrinally inseparable from it in the communist struggle.[3] The West distinguished more sharply between the two, and unlike the Soviet Union tended to see covert action as the subsidiary and more controversial of the two activities. Yet over the Cold War as a whole it was a significant American activity, although the effort in it waxed and waned;[4] and though Britain was more cautious it made its contributions. Covert action on both sides – and reactions to it – may indeed have been a major strand in Cold War history, particularly of the East–West conflict in the Third World. It may indeed have been an important element in the loss of both Western and Soviet empires. But we lack a synoptic view of it, and one is not attempted here. The chapter limits itself to the psychological effects of these human activities– both espionage and covert action – and does not distinguish between the two.

Despite the importance of this human component, most intelligence activity was in fact technical and not human in character. This was overwhelmingly the case in the West, and was probably also true of the Soviet Bloc where the technical effort is now known to have been larger than once thought. Part of technical collection on both sides was photo-reconnaissance, initially by aircraft and later with the addition of the extensive programmes of imagery satellites. But most of it was signals intelligence (Sigint), overwhelmingly so in the West, and probably also so in the East.[5] Despite the development of space satellites, most of Sigint's interception effort was at sizeable, fixed, terrestrial sites. These were not publicly declared, but could not be completely concealed. Each side was aware of the other's efforts, though sketchy on the details. Each side also gave them the popular but misleading label of 'spying', which has stuck. For the British media, for example, the national Sigint headquarters has for many years been, erroneously but irretrievably, the 'Cheltenham Spy Centre'.

The location of the interception stations was determined on both sides by the physics of radio propagation. The principal classes of Soviet military transmissions could be intercepted reasonably well by the West at ranges of hundreds of miles, but not when these got far into the thousands. They could not be adequately heard from the American homeland. Hence the United States needed Sigint bases nearer the Soviet Bloc, or arrangements with friendly services in suitable places, or both. Most of America's NATO allies, including the United Kingdom, could meet this geographic requirement: even from North America Canada was able to provide coverage of the Barents Sea and the Soviet Far North from its Arctic sites. The same considerations dictated the location of sites outside NATO around the southern Soviet periphery and Soviet Far East. Geography was also a factor in other kinds of technical collection, as in the use of British and Norwegian locations to provide some of the shore ends for the American acoustic devices that detected submerged Soviet submarines en route between northern waters and the Atlantic. But Sigint was the main technical activity dictating the search for sites.

As the Cold War developed, this geographical dimension was sharpened by the growing volume of Soviet transmissions and radar-like emissions that operated in higher frequency bands that necessitated interception at much closer ranges, comparable with those of the domestic FM radio receivers we all use today: rather further than line-of-sight distances across the earth's curvature, but not by much. Those Western states with Soviet forces across their borders or just over their horizons therefore offered particularly valuable locations, and the ring of longer-range Western sites was complemented by an inner ring of close-access ones in locations that included northern Norway, Baltic islands, the Federal

Republic of Germany's East–West border, northern Turkey, Iran and northern Japan. For the same reason West Berlin was a prime location behind enemy lines.

This collection was all from fixed sites, but the need to get close to the targets also led the West to mount mobile collection from ships and aircraft where land-based collection was impossible or incomplete. For the same reason there was even a brief attempt to operate from an Arctic ice-floe. Aircraft flying high had a special ability to provide an especially deep Sigint 'look' into Soviet Bloc territory, as well as oblique photography. Thus there were constant aircraft flights along Warsaw Pact borders, over international waters off the Soviet coastline, and in the sea areas used by the Soviet fleets. Naval surface vessels and submarines collected intelligence in the course of suitable deployments, and there was some Western use of specialised intelligence vessels that could spend lengthy periods on station. A result on the Western side was an intensive, multinational Great Game with the opponent, played not only along the German border but also over and in the Baltic, the Barents Sea, the North Pacific and elsewhere. Aircraft of almost all Western countries packed with technical equipment flew every day, and tough men rolled for weeks in small ships. Though the United States led, most of its allies took some part.

The Soviet Union had the same collection needs but the combination of geography and radio propagation worked against meeting them. It had large-scale efforts within the Soviet Bloc's borders, but lacked any sites close enough to the American enemy's home base, except for its station in Cuba which remained an irritant to the United States long after the USSR had ceased to exist. It mounted extensive flights along the East–West German border and over the Baltic and the Norwegian Sea, but it was difficult for its aircraft to fly close to Britain or the United States for any length of time. There was covert interception from Soviet diplomatic premises, and there were persistent reports of other clandestine operations, for example in civilian lorries transiting through divided Germany. The main Soviet investment in mobile operations was however in shipborne interception, in which there was a much greater effort than in the West, with regular patrols by the specialised collection vessels, the so-called 'intelligence trawlers'. Even here geography meant that these were widely dispersed by comparison with the West's concentrated efforts around the Soviet periphery.

The operations of both sides were undeclared, but many of them were virtually overt, and some produced contacts between attackers and defenders. There was no deep mystery about the regular aircraft flights of both sides, or the East's intelligence trawlers. Each side tracked the surface warships of the other and assumed them to be collecting whatever intelligence they could. Submarine operations were more covert, but the Russians had no illusions about the operation of Western boats in their fleet areas, and the same applied to the comparable Soviet operations around Western deployments and exercises. There were deeply secret American submarine missions in the 1970s and 1980s to tap cables off Soviet coasts, and also to retrieve fragments of Soviet missiles from the seabed, but they were eventually detected.[6] Close contact of a quite different, non-technical kind between the opponents was also provided by the 'licensed espionage' – actually observation and photography – by both sides' military missions in East and West Germany, and by the activities of their military attachés everywhere.

Technical Collection and Incidents

Most of these technical operations were conducted by both sides without intentionally infringing international law, and some became Cold War routines, but they were fragile ones, liable to produce East–West incidents, particularly through the airborne Sigint operations and the urge for them to get close to their targets. There were accidental Western incursions into Soviet airspace through navigational limitations and human errors, particularly in the Cold War's early years. Soviet Bloc fighters would normally be sent to intercept any flights not recognised as scheduled civil ones, and there were shoot-downs of Western aircraft when positional errors of one side or the other produced unwonted Soviet reactions, especially in times of political tension. The Western flights' objectives also regularly included provoking and testing the Soviet defences to study their responses. An aircraft would approach low under Soviet radar cover and suddenly go high to test the speed and accuracy of the defender's tracking and reporting system; or as in one American account, '[S]ometimes we would fly missions over the Black Sea . . . To tickle the Soviets a little and create more activity we would do a straight approach towards Sevastopol, turn and run out. Then we would listen to the racket [on the air defence radio communications].'[7]

In these circumstances it is not surprising that as many as thirteen intelligence-gathering American aircraft were shot down around and over the Soviet periphery between 1947 and 1960.[8] In 1952 a Swedish intelligence aircraft was also a victim over the Baltic, and the same happened to a flying boat sent to rescue the crew.[9] No British intelligence aircraft was ever shot down. There were no further shoot-downs of these kinds after the summer of 1960, perhaps through more sophisticated navigation systems or more caution on both sides. Minor incursions still continued (by both sides) around the East–West border in Germany, and in and around the Western air corridors to Berlin, but none of them led to significant incidents. But accidental overflights of Soviet territory by others could still take place, and Soviet fears of intelligence incursions could give them tragic consequences. In April 1978 a South Korean airliner was shot down over the north-west USSR, though without heavy casualties,[10] and on 1 September 1983 there was a more publicised repetition in the Far East, when an aircraft of the same airline was shot down after accidentally overflying Kamchatka and Sakhalin, with the loss of all 269 people aboard.[11]

Even more significant than this activity around the Soviet periphery in forming Soviet attitudes was the succession of deliberate Western penetrations of Soviet airspace in the years through the 1950s. These were to various depths, and for the varying purposes of photography, radar mapping, technical interception, testing defence reactions and (some writers have argued) demonstrating American military machismo. Many were detected though none was lost. They began in 1950, and for the first half of the decade including 1956 were by US Air Force (USAF) (mainly Strategic Air Command (SAC)) and US Navy aircraft in separate operations that in total ran well into the teens, some by multiple aircraft in different areas.[12] The penetrations were mainly of the USSR's remote Far East and Far North, but some were of Eastern Europe into Byelorussia, Ukraine and Metropolitan Russia. Two (multiple) operations, in 1952 and 1954, were by Royal Air Force crew in American military aircraft painted with British insignia.[13] There were also concentrated operations in spring 1956 that according to unofficial American accounts consisted of 156 flights in seven weeks into Soviet airspace, ending with a squadron flying in formation in daylight several hundred miles over (remote) Soviet territory.[14] There were also programmes of unmanned American balloons from Western sites to drift across the USSR to record imagery and radar emissions. Nearly 500 were released in the mid-1950s, and another smaller balloon project was mounted two years later.[15]

The overflights by military aircraft were all superseded after the end of 1956 by the CIA-led programme of operations by the specially constructed, high-altitude U-2 aircraft, principally for photo-reconnaissance though they also had a subsidiary Sigint capability. There were twenty-four U-2 overflights of varying depths, including two by Royal Air Force pilots in 1959–60 (not to be confused with the earlier British-manned operations just mentioned). The overflights ended with the well-known shoot-down of one of these aircraft on 1 May 1960 deep in Soviet territory, near Sverdlovsk, and the subsequent trial of the pilot.[16] No more U-2 operations took place over the Soviet Union, though there may have been incursions by military aircraft in the Far East much later, in the early 1980s, as part of the Reagan Administration's demonstrations of power.[17]

Other kinds of close-range collection also produced their own incidents. At sea, the underwater trailing of opposing submarines produced East-West collisions, though none became public knowledge. An unofficial account shows thirteen involving American boats and two involving the British.[18] An officer of the American military mission in East Germany was shot and killed in 1985, after a member of the French mission had been road-rammed and killed the previous year.[19]

Apart from the maritime collisions, the incidents were all Soviet reactions to Western collection of an intrusive or potentially intrusive kind. There were no comparable examples of intrusive Soviet operations and violent Western reaction. Soviet aircraft flying off the US homeland seem to have stayed outside a fifty-mile limit.[20]

Intelligence trawlers were stationed off Western naval bases but their presence became accepted as a routine. The only authenticated case of a substantial Soviet maritime incursion was of the Whisky-class submarine that ran aground off the Swedish coast in October 1981, much publicised by the Western press as the 'Whisky on the Rocks'.[21] Compared with its adversary the West suffered fewer close approaches and was much more restrained in its responses.

These, then, were the sensitive activities – human and technical – in which each side was engaged and the incidents that followed, but what effects did they have on the Cold War? Did they make it hotter, or did leaders accept them as no more than part of the background noise?

Effects on Allies

The effects were mainly on opponents; but there were some between allies and not enemies. The United States was sometimes an intelligence paymaster, and would provide the smaller countries with equipment or funding in return for operating in their territories or receiving their intelligence product; but despite this material quid pro quo the allied agencies would also insist on some Sigint assistance and collaboration. Their attitude was rarely that of mercenaries, or real estate agents only concerned with maximising rent for their sites. The need for suitable intelligence sites reinforced not only America's need for a large overseas presence but also the cooperative character of the relationships it developed.

Proximity to the USSR was also a factor in the tenor of these individual relationships. The UK–US Sigint partnership was *sui generis* within the transatlantic alliance, but one element in it – though by no means the most important – was the UK mainland's position as an unsinkable aircraft carrier within intelligence range of the adversary. The same applied even more to the UK's 'useful geography' elsewhere, as in its presence in Cyprus and its retention after Cypriot independence as a striking case of an influence of intelligence requirements on the retention of sovereignty. Countries such as Norway and Turkey offered unique access to important areas and received particularly generous American treatment. With the presence of UK and US forces on its territory,

West Germany could not provide special access of its own, but its combination of sizeable Sigint resources and well-placed locations was nevertheless felt to make it particularly useful in 'taking the strain' (the idiom of the time) in helping the UK–US effort on the European mainland. By contrast, France's lack of well-placed sites held it back as an influence in the Western intelligence club, and perhaps contributed a little to its semi-disengaged political stance.

Such geographical effects also applied outside the NATO area. The value of its site in Iran for monitoring Soviet missile tests was a considerable factor in the US's uncritical support for the Shah before his fall. Japan's value for coverage of the Soviet Far East figured similarly as a factor in its American relationship. Australia's geographical suitability for a ground control site for American intelligence satellites became a factor in its emergence as a US ally in its own right, no longer so tied to the British connection. Similar factors applied to the alliance's relations with friendly neutrals: a history of Swedish Cold War policy would be incomplete without considering the value to the West of its window on to Soviet forces and activities in the Baltic area. Geographic access was even the basis of the secret Sino-American agreement for Sigint operations in China targeted against Soviet missile tests.[22]

We know less about any comparable effects within the very different Soviet Bloc. The East European countries offered little access not open to the USSR, but Moscow nevertheless depended heavily upon East German intelligence for its high-quality coverage of the many Western targets in West Germany: we do not know if this gave East German leaders any leverage with Moscow. We do not know if Polish intelligence influenced its governments in pro-Soviet or nationalist directions. An account of Romanian intelligence's place in the extraordinary history of Soviet–Romanian relations is now available,[23] but otherwise the English literature on Warsaw Pact intelligence arrangements is limited.

What is clearer, however, is that this Soviet-controlled effort as a whole had its political effects at one remove on the politics of the Western alliance. The politics of NATO was influenced throughout by the accurate UK–US assessment about the Soviet penetration of the alliance's continental members: the assumption was that anything passed to them would reach Moscow. This was a factor in the emergence of the half-acknowledged English-speaking, 'CANUKUS Eyes Only' community within NATO, and the ramifications this had in the strain between the alliance's continental and transatlantic strands.

Covert Agents: Enemies Within

The main interest here is however in activities' effects on adversaries. Of these, some individual episodes are established parts of Cold War history. The scale of Soviet espionage against its wartime allies had its part in fixing the Western view of post-war Soviet intentions in 1945–6, and was confirmed by the spy cases that followed later. Those of Hiss and Fuchs may have contributed a little by their timing in early 1950 to the hard line of the American National Security Council's policy report NSC-68 issued that summer. The shooting down of the American U-2 on 1 May 1960 led to Nikita Khrushchev's break-up of the East–West Paris Conference that began shortly afterwards. The same fate of a U-2 over Cuba during the 1962 crisis increased the tense situation. The expulsion in 1971 of 105 Soviet intelligence officers from their diplomatic cover in London, and the Soviet response, froze UK–Soviet relations for some time, and set a pattern for the next twenty years of substantial expulsions by Western governments and counter-expulsions from Moscow, though none was on the London scale. The fate of the South Korean airliner in September 1983 exacerbated a situation of already high US–Soviet tension.

But these were major episodes, and the question remains whether the many unpublicised activities of these kinds had a comparable psychological influence through the nature of the activities and the scale of their repetition. Part of the answer is in Raymond Garthoff's comment on the shoot-down of the South Korean airliner in 1983, that

Each side thus converted its ready suspicions and worst assumptions about the other into accusations that could not be proved or disproved, but that tended to be believed by its own side and bitterly resented by the other. The upshot was to set American–Soviet and Soviet–American relations considerably further back and undercut tentative steps towards an improvement in relations.[24]

What was known about the other side's secret activities was no doubt magnified by what was suspected about them and became the unseen parts of the adversary's intelligence iceberg. But it must be asked whether experienced leaders and officials regarded this iceberg in reality as a nuisance rather than a threat, and something best insulated from Cold War policies as far as possible. How seriously was it really taken as evidence of a threat?

It may be sensible here to separate reactions to human and technical 'spying'. On the first, the expert view in the West seems to be that Western espionage and covert action were genuinely seen by the Soviet regime as evidence of a serious Western intent to overthrow the system. The demonology of the West's 'special services' in Soviet thinking went back to the West's intervention in the regime's early days, and the solid evidence of the Western spy cases and support for anti-Soviet partisan movements after 1945 bore out its Cold War relevance.[25] Inside government's top echelons the KGB's exaggerated accounts of Western machinations in Eastern Europe were accepted before the invasion of Czechoslovakia in 1968 and the other actions considered to preserve the Bloc's integrity. The West's covert activities were routinely blamed for most of the regime's domestic and international failures: the shakier its empire became, the more was attributed to the CIA's subversion. Julie Fedor describes the grand scale of the KGB's myths about the West's intent and action that were developed in the Cold War and are devoutly put around now.[26] We have no reason to disagree with Vojtech Mastny's conclusion that in the Soviet Union the 'reports showing vast penetration by Western spies were not merely invented for public consumption to justify the repression of imaginary enemies, but were taken seriously by the security services as working assumptions'.[27] The preservation of secrecy had acquired an absolute value in the Soviet system, almost beyond analysis.

Western reactions to these human activities by the Soviet side were more diverse. Hawkish opinion-formers made the same exaggerations in the West as their Soviet opposite numbers, but the succession of spy cases and the large scale of covert Soviet operations also nourished rather wider, visceral, less ideological Western fears of treachery, the betrayal of the open society's trust, the enemy within. Typical was the long-running speculation in the British media about the penetration of the Establishment by the KGB's 'Cambridge Five' agents. Fears of Soviet subversion and support for communist parties in Western Europe loomed large in the Cold War's early years and were never completely stilled. They reappeared at a top official level in the British Joint Intelligence Committee's 1972 assessment of 'The Soviet Threat' which gave prominence to the presence in continental Europe of 'more than 800 identified or suspected Soviet intelligence officers with official cover'. It forecast that 'the Soviet Union will increase the number of agents of influence and sympathisers . . . in order to influence Western policies and undermine Western resistance to Soviet aims'.[28] This was a bleaker assessment of Soviet motives than that Committee usually produced. Nevertheless the writer recalls genuine official concern in subsequent years that Spain and Portugal might 'go communist' when the two dictators Francisco Franco and Antonio Salazar died.

On the other hand, some more relaxed attitudes could be found among Western politicians and officials. The published volume of internal Foreign and Commonwealth Office documents leading up to the British expulsions of the Soviet intelligence officers from London conveys an impression of measured professionalism: documents with that provenance would be unlikely to convey anything else. They suggest that the decisive factor was the foreign secretary's robust anger at the scale and shamelessness of this Soviet effort. It was no way for a state to behave that aspired to be treated as a respectable great power, and an impediment to developing any normal relationship, but not necessarily a threat to national security.[29]

Yet even under this professional carapace the diplomats' experiences within the Soviet Bloc may still have had their effects. An American diplomat has written with honesty about life under constant hostile intelligence targeting in the Moscow Embassy, and concluded that 'it was hard not to let that situation impact on your own view of [what is now] the former USSR'.[30] (Possibly the same applied in reverse: the autobiography of Oleg Gordievsky records the claustrophobic precautions taken in the heavily curtained Soviet Embassy in London to counter the UK's technical eavesdropping against it.[31]) Even if diplomats managed to remain impassive in their attitudes, it is difficult to believe that governments as a whole did not share the public view of the opponent's espionage and subversion as threats to national ways of life, the more corrosive for being for the most part invisible.

Effects of 'Technical Spying'

Here the bulk of intrusion was by the West. There were indeed numerous Soviet Bloc operations, and Western publics were regularly reminded of the threats posed by the Soviet long-distance flights over the Atlantic, the patrols by the intelligence trawlers, and the suspicions of covert activity by Soviet merchant ships and other Soviet 'technical spying'. There was enough evidence to provide ammunition for the hawkish Western commentators whose influence on Western policies is a fact of Cold War history. Nevertheless the proportion of activity that could reasonably be deemed threatening was small, and it is difficult to believe that Western opinion was ever as influenced by the USSR's technical operations as by the scale of its agent-running.

The threat of the opponent's technical operations must have seemed much more substantial to the Soviet side. The worldwide location of the West's Sigint facilities around the Soviet periphery was part of the Cold War's political geography: the West looking in and the USSR looking out. The sites were much less conspicuous than the main military deployments, but their link with 'spying' probably gave them some place in the worldview of Soviet strategists, though by no means a dominating one. There must have been more definite effects from the scale and intrusiveness of the West's mobile collection operations, particularly the airborne ones. After the American creation of SAC in 1946 an airborne nuclear attack on the Soviet Union was part of Western military planning, and was quickly reflected in the Soviet creation of the air defence force in 1948 as a separate service to counter it. Evaluating this air defence and ways of defeating it was always the principal target of the Western intelligence flights, though not the only one. Treating the flights as potential threats must have seemed especially important on the Soviet side in the periods when SAC had its 24-hour nuclear-armed patrols airborne.

With this sensitivity it is not surprising that the Russians presented their shoot-downs of American aircraft as national defence, and reported in the official primer on Soviet armed forces' organisation issued in Moscow in 1978, that '[A]t the beginning of the fifties, when violations of USSR air borders became more frequent, the National Air Defence Forces successfully intercepted all attempts to penetrate Soviet airspace'.[32] The high-level command's involvement in the Soviet shooting-down of the South Korean civilian aircraft in September 1983 illustrated the importance that the defence of the airspace was still given.[33] For the Americans these incidents were all evidence of Soviet ruthlessness and warlike attitude. In all they lost some 170 USAF and Navy aircrew around the total Soviet Bloc periphery between 1946 and 1991, most though not all on intelligence missions.[34]

There were also regular Soviet protests over the deliberate overflights of the 1950s. When these began there were American hopes that they would not be detected and tracked, but the Soviet radar coverage improved throughout the 1950s, though the defending fighters were still unable to reach the intruders. There were also American press leaks about them. At one point the Russians displayed one of the American intelligence-gathering balloons in Moscow. So for Khrushchev the flight and shoot-down of the U-2 deep over Soviet territory on May Day 1961 may have been a last straw, and his wrecking of the subsequent Paris conference was not the only result. High feelings were raised again on both sides when a SAC reconnaissance aircraft was shot down in international airspace off the Kola Peninsula shortly afterwards, on 1 July,[35] and it seems that Khrushchev decided at that stage to abandon further cooperation with the Eisenhower lame-duck Administration and wait until the following year for his successor.[36]

Yet it is still not clear that the Soviet reactions to these overflights and other Western close-range technical collection were quite as visceral as to the covert activities attributed to the Western 'special services'. The protests over overflights before the U-2 shoot-down were relatively muted, though there may have been practical explanations: the radar contacts may have been uncertain, and in any case the regime may not have wanted to draw its citizens' attentions to the limitations of its air defences.

Khrushchev did not raise the subject of overflights with Dwight Eisenhower in his visit to the United States in September 1959.[37] It also seems that after the U-2 shoot-down Khrushchev was initially prepared to accept the expected American excuses and apologies, and it was only Eisenhower's soldier-like acceptance of responsibility and refusal to apologise that moved him to take a much harder line in Paris than he had intended.[38] Khrushchev may indeed have seen the U-2 operations as an insult to Soviet pride rather than more evidence of a basically aggressive American intent.

We also do not know what the Soviet leadership really thought of all the Western peripheral flights that passed without incident, and indeed of the maritime deployments in Soviet sea areas. Some of the naval operations were intended as assertions of American power and no doubt the political message was taken, but their intelligence collection was subsidiary.[39] Close encounters between the two sides' surface warships were frequent, but the American writers on the covert submarine operations concluded that 'even the most violent submarine encounters never sparked real crisis'.[40] Limitations were agreed in the signature of the US–Soviet Incidents at Sea agreement in 1972 to avoid accidents, and for the navies of both sides much of the regular intelligence-gathering probably became accepted as part of the Cold War choreography of demonstrating power, 'tailing' the other side and observing. The Soviet authorities became aware of the West's much more intrusive submarine operations, but there is no indication of any top-level reaction to them. A Soviet general dealing with the British Military Mission in East Germany drew a distinction between acceptable 'reconnaissance' and unacceptable 'espionage',[41] and comparable tacit understandings about what was acceptable may have developed among the air and maritime authorities most often involved. Despite the intrusions and shoot-downs, the West's airborne and maritime technical operations probably did not arouse quite the same feelings in Moscow as the image of the West's covert agents and 'special services' and their undermining of communism from within. Yet at the very least the scale of the West's technical operations and their intrusion or near-intrusion must have been a constant reminder, to attackers and defenders alike, of the Cold War's nature as a very unusual period of peace.

Playing Hardball with the Adversary

The big question for each side was to assess the balance of offence and defence in the other's worldviews, and their scope for change. To apply to the Cold War a term coined earlier to discuss the post-1918 peace, was the other side a 'satisfied' power, or an 'unsatisfied' one, seeking to change the situation in its favour? Each side took the other's activities as evidence of hostility, but there is no evidence that either side went further and scrutinised them for clues to whether the other's politico-strategic aims were offensive or defensive.

Neither did either consider the effects of its own side's total covert activity – human as well as technical, those of its allies or subordinates as well as its own – on the opponent's assumptions on what the Cold War was about. To think of such terms was hardly Moscow's style: even Mikhail Gorbachev, who sought to improve the KGB's objectivity, did not as far is known curtail its collection. In the West those drafting the assessments on the USSR were never aware of the full scope of Western activities against it and the effects they might have. Even if they had tried they had no means of getting complete information.

On the other hand, the West was not completely insensitive about intelligence's effects. There was an official study for President Eisenhower of the limits to be set on American intelligence activities, and there is published information on some presidential and prime ministerial decisions on particular operations in the Eisenhower period. They provide little indication of any guiding view about intelligence's effects on the adversary, but they merit examination.

The report was by a commission under General Doolittle convened by President Eisenhower in 1954 to consider policy on covert activities, including intelligence-gathering. The conclusions were hardline:

> We are facing an implacable enemy whose avowed objective is world domination by whatever means and at whatever cost. There are no rules in such a game ... We must develop effective espionage and counterespionage services and must learn to subvert, sabotage and destroy our enemies.[42]

Eisenhower wrote in reply that 'I have come to the conclusion that some of our traditional ideas of international sportsmanship are scarcely applicable in the morass in which the world now flounders.'[43]

Yet the actual decisions over the airborne operations of that period were more nuanced. The American flights around the Soviet periphery had initially been given stand-off distances of 40 miles from Soviet borders,[44] but after the outbreak of the Korean War this was usually reduced to 12 miles, though the United States still claimed a (contested) right to approach to a three-mile limit.[45] The military overflights of Soviet territory in the first half of the 1950s had approvals from Presidents Harry Truman and Eisenhower.[46] By the mid-1950s Eisenhower was making his remarkable proposal to the Soviet side for an Open Skies inspection agreement[47] and had become more hesitant about the overflights. He was assured at one stage that the specially designed U-2s would be undetectable, and authorised some flights by them. The assurance was found to be optimistic and he became more parsimonious with his authorisations. By the end of the decade he was insisting that the U-2 missions should all take off from Pakistan to exploit the remaining gaps in the Soviet radar coverage. After further detections he was even more torn between the risks and the pressing need for intelligence on the size of the Soviet missile threat.[48] Even had it succeeded, the overflight of 1 May 1960 which he authorised may well have been the last, as usable satellite photography was about to become regularly available.

The British decisions over participation in these series were also taken at top level. The two RAF operations in the first half of the 1950s had Churchill's approval as Prime Minister. In 1956, after the much-publicised failure of a quite different British covert operation,[49] his successor Anthony Eden withdrew the British cooperation with the U-2 programme. After Eden's resignation in early 1957 Harold Macmillan renewed the British stake in it, including the two RAF-piloted U-2 overflights already mentioned.[50]

This is no more than a snapshot of Western decisions over these overflights, but it is clear that they all had proper political authority, even though the military commanders may have exceeded the discretion they were initially given. (Though few details are available, there also seems to have been presidential awareness of the intrusive American submarine operations then and later.[51]) The need for intelligence was undeniable: it was intolerable and dangerous that the American intercontinental ballistic missile (ICBM) programmes were being driven by guesswork about the Soviet competition. The underlying American mood was as set out by Doolittle, of playing hardball and signalling toughness, but there seems in practice to have been ample presidential weighing of pros and cons of the operations.

Eisenhower's judgements seem to have been careful, but there is little indication of his rationales. It must be remembered that at the time of the early overflights American aircraft (and British) had just been engaged in the undeclared air battles with the Soviet air force in the Korean War. The survival of the U-2 pilot to be put on trial in Moscow had also been judged to be an unlikely outcome. Nevertheless, with hindsight, given the place of nuclear air attack in American strategy and Soviet fears of it, the succession of overflights in the 1950s now seems among the most provocative of the West's intelligence-related activities, next only to the support of the armed resistance movements in the Soviet Bloc in the early years. Neither side's intelligence was good at seeing things accurately through the opponent's eyes, least of all in assessing the conclusions he would draw from one's own intrusive collection against him. Eisenhower in his decisions on the U-2 operations was caught here between intelligence's two psychological effects, of promoting reassurance in its own side and perceptions of threat in the other, before the development of American intelligence satellites removed the need for any further aircraft overflights.

These were the threat perceptions. The international and national dimensions of reassurance can now be examined.

Reassurance

Arms Control[52]

Intelligence's capabilities – what it could be relied on to provide – served national ends. Yet they also played an important part in the American government's initiative in launching East–West strategic arms control in the late 1960s, and in reaching the agreements with the Soviet Union in the 1970s and later. Negotiations would never have got underway without the factual baseline about the Soviet strategic forces that American intelligence was by then able to provide: 'it was in large but unrecognised measure US confidence in the quality of the intelligence on Soviet forces during the late 1960s and early 1970s that allowed strategic arms limitation negotiations to begin at all'.[53] It continued to be available throughout the negotiations.

But counting on this intelligence for the future was even more important. The concept of arms control turned on the ability to verify, and on-site inspection for this purpose was at that stage unacceptable to the Soviet side. Confidence about long-distance verification by intelligence was therefore a foundation of the American proposals and the eventual agreements. Domestically it was essential for the American Congressional approvals on which so much depended. More than that, intelligence determined not only the mechanism for verification but the subjects of the agreements. The Strategic Arms Limitation Talks Agreement (SALT I) was cast in terms of launchers (at missile sites and as missile tubes in submarines), not missile production, because launchers were what imagery satellites could see. The limitations on throw-weights and multiple independently targetable warheads in SALT II were possible because US interception and analysis of radio-telemetry from Soviet missiles could yield the necessary data on them.

All this received treaty recognition. The USSR had accepted the existence of intelligence satellites from 1963 onwards, but only tacitly; and there were American fears that they might be disarmed in some way, as through the operational deployment of anti-satellite programmes for knocking them out in space, or by extensive camouflage to conceal launchers from satellite imagery. The result was the provision incorporated as Article XII of the 1972 Anti-Ballistic Missile (ABM) Treaty and Article V of the SALT I Agreement, repeated as Article XV of SALT II, that:

> For the purpose of providing assurance of compliance with the provisos of this Interim Agreement [Treaty], each Party shall use national technical means of verification at its disposal in a manner consistent with generally recognised principles of international law.

Each Party undertakes not to interfere with the national technical means of verification of the other Party operating in accordance with paragraph one of this article.

Each Party undertakes not to use deliberate concealment measures which impede verification by national technical means of compliance with the provisions of this Interim Agreement [Treaty]. This obligation shall not require changes in current construction, assembly, conversion, or overhaul practices.

The US–Soviet Standing Consultative Committee was created as a mechanism for handling complaints about treaty breaches, with the 'national technical means' (NTMs) accepted as legitimate inputs. In commentaries these NTMs have often been identified exclusively with satellite collection, but the wording did not limit them in this way. Soviet missile-telemetry was collected by US aircraft and by ground-based sites in Iran as well as by satellites; and Soviet intelligence vessels in the Atlantic probably did the same against the American test firings from Florida.[54] Nevertheless, it was the development of satellite collection by both sides that made this intelligence verification possible.

This special importance of NTMs declined when on-site inspection became acceptable to the USSR and assumed the major verification role in the arms control measures of the 1980s. Nevertheless, inspection still benefited from synergy with NTMs, as for example in the signatories' ability to trigger the limited numbers of on-site 'challenge inspections' permitted by treaty.[55] The NTM provisions were repeated in the later Intermediate-Range Nuclear Forces (INF) Treaty and Strategic Arms Reduction Treaty (START), along with mutual agreements for some specific displays of equipment to imagery satellites.[56]

For intelligence this was all breaking new ground. The agreement not to camouflage missile silos from satellites was new enough, but more surprising still was the explicit agreement in conjunction with SALT II that the NTM provisions covered not only the interception and analysis of radio-telemetry but also a limitation in the encipherment of its channels. Both parties' imagery satellites were by then an open secret, and in any case the practical scope for hiding ICBM silo construction from them was limited.[57] By contrast, telemetry interception and analysis had previously been part of the closely guarded intelligence world. After SALT I the SALT II negotiations in the 1970s turned increasingly on parameters verifiable from this material, and there were US fears that its access to them would be cut off by increases in the Soviet encipherment of it that had begun some years earlier.[58] From 1977 onwards the United States demanded assurances that further telemetry encipherment was covered by the ban on 'concealment measures which impede verification by national technical means', and after two years the Soviet Union accepted as part of the SALT II settlement that neither party would 'engage in the deliberate denial of telemetric information, such as through the use of telemetry encryption, whenever such denial impedes verification of compliance with the provisions of the Treaty'.[59] The spread of encipherment was halted, and the later START I agreement of 1991 banned it completely and took other measures to ensure that recorded telemetry data was available to the other party.[60]

This recognition of intelligence collection, and the agreement not to interfere with it, became what John Gaddis has described as the 'reconnaissance satellite regime' between the superpowers.[61] It was still quite a strange one. It had no definition of NTMs, nor of the 'recognized principles of international law' to be applied in using them.[62] Their legitimisation applied only to verifying the arms control treaties, and not to technical collection for any other purposes.

It is also not at all clear whether it was even-handed between the two sides. The United States may well have been the main gainer, perhaps the only one, since the evidence about American programmes from published and leaked information available – to say nothing of the product of Soviet espionage – may have meant that its NTMs could not add a great deal to what Moscow knew already. Checking Soviet encipherment was a major US interest, but we do not know whether the equivalent American telemetry transmissions were encrypted at all, and whether the Soviet side exploited them. But the Soviet fear of American deception was so deep that the regime may well have felt it needed all it could get from the NTMs. In any case no agreement would have been acceptable to Moscow without the appearance of complete reciprocity.

Whatever the oddities, the agreements were of lasting significance. The enemies were prepared to discuss what hitherto had been their secret means of collection and the fruits from them. The American side's revelation of its exploitation of the intercepted telemetry, and the store it set by preventing its encryption, was an unprecedented revelation of intelligence's capabilities; and there were also no precedents for the undertakings to send radio transmissions *en clair*. Agreements with the other side on what had previously been among the most sensitive parts of the intelligence war were possible in a good cause. Intelligence in the form of USAF's late 1950s estimates of the 'missile gap' had had some responsibility for the Cold War's inflated strategic nuclear arms race that followed. In its contribution to arms control intelligence subsequently did something to check this arms race and bring it under control. The significance for Cold War history is not for discussion here, but there is probably not much modern dissent from the conclusion of Michael (later Sir Michael) Howard at the time that '[F]ew would deny that the development of reconnaissance satellites has been highly stabilising'.[63]

Reducing National Uncertainty: Taking the Opponent's Pulse

This creation of mutual East–West reassurance was exceptional, and intelligence's other reassurance to its leaders was national. In trying to assess what this contributed to Cold War psychology it is not easy to reconstruct the changing and sometimes fickle moods of the period. Nevertheless, it can be recalled that as the Cold War continued the British national mood moved from the widespread fear of nuclear war in the years after the Cuban crisis to a degree of confidence that the Cold War could be managed. In the United States the interest in civil defence and fallout shelters was at its height in the early 1960s and then declined.[64] One can guess that in both countries intelligence's improving performance was a factor in a greater government confidence which rubbed off on popular opinion.

The accompanying chapter 'What Difference Did it Make?' (Chapter 6) in this collection outlines Western intelligence's improvement. It was never able to provide compelling insights into long-term Soviet intentions, and we still do not know if the views that it endorsed struck the right balances between expansion and defence in Soviet motives, and allowed enough for changes over time. But its main contributions were on Soviet military power. On this its record in the early part of the Cold War was a mixture of realistic judgements, exaggerations and uncertainties, but from the 1960s onwards the American imagery collection by satellite helped to improve it greatly. 'Worst-case' exaggerations were reduced, though by no means eliminated. The intelligence estimates became more precise and less fuzzy, and governments had less scope for choosing what suited their political stances. There was less fear of destabilising surprises. An improved warning role was joined with a better understanding of Soviet military capabilities, and the two rubbed off on each other. The imponderable of reassurance was one result.

The fear of Soviet surprise attack was bound to be part of the Western stance: Pearl Harbor had seared itself into the American consciousness. Britain had not had quite the same experience of surprise, but the Joint Intelligence Committee (JIC) had developed from the experience of the German attacks in spring 1940 and the threat of German invasion that followed, and the influence of Churchill's instruction for it to produce urgent appreciations as needed 'at any hour of the day or night'.[65] Warning arrangements got some limited attention in Washington after 1945, but were given their impetus by the surprises of the invasion of South Korea and the subsequent Chinese intervention, and warning machinery was set up.[66] Britain responded to an invitation to join, and it became a tripartite system with Canadian participation.

The assumption behind the warning system was that there would never be direct evidence of a Soviet intent to attack, or a decision to do so. These would have to be inferred from departures from normality over wide ranges of government activity, mainly by Soviet and satellite armed forces, and the 'warning indicators' that these would present. This warning role was implicit in the coverage of these forces for other purposes, including the analysis of Soviet Bloc capabilities and order of battle needed for many other reasons. But the speed and comprehensiveness of surveillance for effective warning greatly influenced the effort towards the development of information technology (IT) and the speed and comprehensiveness it could provide. IT devices and early computers had been developed in the Second World War for cipher-breaking, but from the early 1950s onwards there was a parallel development of them, along with communications, for large-scale data-handling and exploitation. It became a prime characteristic of the US effort and of the British and other allies who cooperated with it.

What was presented as a result was never complete. It was in a sense a two-dimensional picture of military activities, without explicit insights into purposes and intentions, and it needed interpretation. But when it was set against the static and initially delayed pictures available from satellite imagery, it provided the West with a dynamic and timely picture of changes, movements and preparations. In the jargon of the day it indicated the Soviet 'military posture'. It was likened at the time to 'taking the pulse' of the target. Perhaps the modern medical analogy would be with using MRI scans of human brain activity to give clues of the subject's preoccupations and intentions. Scanning activity in this way for 'warning indicators' became a specialist activity by military intelligence staffs. If the exciting part of the West's Great Game was close-range collection around the Soviet periphery, its substantive complement was the 24-hour operation of the warning and reporting offices that sought to monitor what the other side was doing.

This effort was never solely for strategic warning. The West's own naval and air operations around the Soviet periphery needed the supporting surveillance that could alert them to reactions that might threaten their safety. The development of this kind of mission warning may indeed have been a reason for the absence of Soviet shoot-downs of American aircraft after 1960. It was inconceivable in any case that Western authorities should not have some current awareness of what Soviet forces were doing. But timely reporting and evaluation became a top priority, and the provision for surveillance at a near-wartime tempo became one of Western intelligence's distinctive features. Of all the megatons of paper that Cold War intelligence consumed, a considerable proportion must have been for the ephemeral product of this system, of little practical use except as a precaution. Never before had intelligence sought to provide warning of attack on such a scale in peacetime, and for so long.

No one will ever know how effective the system would have been against a real Soviet attack. It had to be geared to the imaginable scenarios that were unlikely to happen, and not the unpredictable circumstances of war by accident, error or leaders' impetuosity. Its record on Soviet moves against targets outside the Western alliance was actually unimpressive. It failed to provide clear warnings of the moves to crush Hungarian and Czechoslovakian independence in 1956 and 1968. It provided indications of Moscow's preparation to take action against Romania in 1968 and China in 1969, but its warning of the Soviet invasion of Afghanistan in 1979 was muted. On the other hand it did better in following the aborted Warsaw Pact preparations for military moves into Poland in 1980 and 1981, and the American use of this intelligence to drive the diplomatic signalling of the time may have helped to deter Moscow from the military solution it was contemplating. Yet the Soviet alert of some kind in November 1983 was not discerned until some time after the event.

But these events were all different from a prepared Soviet attack on the West, and the record on them is hardly relevant. There were endless NATO debates about the warning times that could be expected in varied scenarios, but the bottom line was that warning was central to the West's formal stance. Nuclear deterrence needed some warning of a Soviet bolt from the blue, and NATO's plans for conventional resistance depended on warning time for its large-scale mobilisation and redeployment. The West needed warning and had no alternative. The real value was that it reduced the risk of war by misperception, or by accidents in the automated detection of missile launches on radar screens. Confidence in the system may have encouraged the Americans not to invest for longer in SAC's continuous airborne deterrent, and not develop other hair-trigger arrangements for a strike. As the sophistication of the warning system developed, statesmen felt more protected against surprise and the fog of crises. Even at the worst times of East–West tension, American presidents never believed that they were about to be attacked. For the top political level this was the real, peacetime pay-back for the large-scale coverage and analysis of Soviet Bloc forces – the often-despised 'bean-counting' – that was criticised by the civilians in Whitehall as serving no purpose except meeting military needs for the war that would never happen.

Understanding Soviet Power

This confidence over Soviet attack was part of a wider intelligence effort. The warning system depended not only on harnessing IT and communications for the speed and scope they could provide, but also on the understanding of the Soviet military machine that improved as the Cold War continued. For those running the Western effort there were difficult decisions on the balance of effort between 'current intelligence' and 'research': producing a better and quicker picture of today's activities and the indications they provided of tomorrow's, or promoting more understanding in depth? Yet the two were at opposite ends of a common intelligence spectrum: each infused and strengthened the other.

The same applied to the effect of reassurance. As the Cold War went on, Western confidence grew not only in the ability to detect a Soviet attack but also to understand the extent of the military threat. Even in the early years this had never been a complete mystery; and at no time afterwards was this understanding complete. Nevertheless, as intelligence improved, the military balance of men, *matériel* and deployments between the two sides could be used as policy rationales by Western governments with more confidence than before. Fears of new Soviet wonder-weapons and widespread Soviet deception still had their effects in the 1970s and 1980s, but were kept in check better than the earlier 'missile gap' had been. There was no policy panic in the later period on the scale of the reaction to the Soviet Sputnik in 1957. No American government could have embarked on arms control without confidence in its intelligence on Soviet missile deployments and characteristics. Mrs Thatcher was probably strengthened in her belief that she could do business with Mr Gorbachev by the confidence that the JIC was capable of checking on his veracity, and in the event was only too anxious to find evidence of concealment or deception.

Hence intelligence helped all those, hawks and doves alike, who saw the West's objective as 'managing' the Cold War. The confidence it provided in the military balance did not necessarily encourage any particular style of Cold War politics. It may indeed have supported the confident and aggressive style of the first Reagan Administration just as much as the milder approach of President Jimmy Carter's before it. But it may nevertheless have encouraged considered approaches, and reduced the risks of panics and hasty decisions by leaders. In the reflection of a thoughtful British diplomat much involved in dealing with the Soviet Union, 'those responsible for day-to-day affairs proceeded on the assumption that there would be no doomsday'.[67] The fact that Soviet power was no longer quite as secret as it had seemed immediately after 1945 may have been a factor in what the same diplomat described as 'a consensus on both sides – conscious in some cases, unconscious in many – to allow the confrontation to play itself out rather than to bring it to a head'.[68] Western intelligence's improved quality as the Cold War progressed had been a factor in this confidence, and it was fortunate that the improvement had come about in large measure through the American intelligence satellites that operated at safe distances in the sky, and had not needed the continued violations of Soviet sovereignty of the overflights up to May 1960.

Soviet Reassurance?

We know little about the Soviet regime's view of intelligence as an insurance against surprise. It adopted its new national warning system (RYaN) in the early 1980s when fears of Western attack increased, and this was raised to alert status in late 1983, and then retained for some time though with declining priority. There is earlier evidence of special daily reporting during the Berlin crisis of the late 1950s and early 1960s,[69] but not of any other comprehensive warning arrangements before RYaN. Perhaps the need for warning in the 1980s was felt to justify copying the West's system, which the USSR must have known about by then.

On the wider issue of managing the East–West conflict, we do not know whether Soviet leaders drew confidence from the information they had on the Western diplomatic hand, or always feared Western surprises and deception. Perhaps there was a mixture of both. Intelligence's role in the verification of the strategic arms control agreements certainly seems to have been taken seriously. Presumably the Soviet satellite imagery programmes used for this verification gave its operators some new dimensions of Western visibility, though we have no idea how effectively the satellite source (run by Soviet military intelligence) was integrated into other top-level reporting in Moscow. The Soviet fears of a Western strike in the first half of the 1980s, and the related crisis alert in November 1983, demonstrated the Soviet leaders' continued capacity for misinterpreting American intentions, but presumably by then Soviet intelligence as a whole (including the absence of alert messages from the warning system) had some balancing effect.

A Balance Sheet

Intelligence's main importance in both East and West was in its reports and assessments and governments' use of them; but its activities and its capabilities also had these other effects on the psychology on both sides. The West always felt threatened by the large scale of Soviet espionage and the subversion associated with it. The corresponding activities by the West were less extensive, but the Soviet regime felt even more deeply menaced by them. Next only to the threat of war, the Cold War was felt everywhere to be about these covert, internal attacks on the two regimes and societies. The publicity given to spy cases and tit-for-tat diplomatic expulsions kept the threats in the minds of governments and publics.

Both sides' collection by technical means had comparable effects, but they were less visceral and also less symmetrical, with the Soviet side more obviously threatened than the West. Geography and the requirements of radio interception produced concentrated Western efforts around the Soviet Bloc's periphery. American aircraft involved in them were shot down through the 1950s up to the summer of 1960, and the same period saw the deliberate American and British overflights of Soviet territory. Up to the end of the Cold War the West's close-range airborne collection must have had particular links in Soviet eyes with the threat of US–UK nuclear attack.

On the other side of the coin, the two sides' technical collectors were mutual confidence-builders in their legitimised verification of the US–Soviet strategic arms control agreements. On other things the West's improving intelligence on Soviet military targets increased its governments' confidence that it would get warning of an impending

Soviet attack, and similarly would not be surprised by the appearance of new Soviet weaponry that would overturn the military balance. It increased leaders' confidence that the Cold War could be managed. In the early part of the Cold War this service of intelligence had needed the intrusive collection operations that frightened Moscow, but from the 1960s onwards its improvement came substantially from the American satellites, and the overflights of the USSR ceased: better intelligence had ceased to require more intrusion. The inherent dilemma – that Western reassurance came through activities that nourished Soviet fears – did not disappear but became rather less acute.

Soviet intelligence may have provided some similar reassurance. Its intelligence satellites may also have provided valuable coverage of a non-threatening kind, though we are guessing about its contribution. The total effect on the Soviet side may have added a little (though not much) there to Western intelligence's contribution to all those running the Cold War who, in the words of the diplomat quoted earlier, 'had a vested interest in keeping the show on the road' so that in the end 'Armageddon came to be side-stepped, at least this time round'.[70]

Despite this, threats were intelligence's bigger psychological contribution. I argue in 'What Difference Did It Make?', Chapter 6 in this collection, that, at the level of formal inputs to policy, intelligence's knowledge was important to both sides on matters of military power, but much less so on the adversary's long-term intentions. These judgements by each side about the other – as put by the British JIC in 1948, 'What is Russia trying to do?'[71] – were based more on what each saw of the other's behaviour than on intelligence assessments. Yet for each side the intrusive intelligence activities of the other were an important and continuing element of this behaviour. The knowledge they produced may eventually have given Western governments – and possibly the Soviet regime – the confidence that the Cold War could be managed without disaster, yet for both sides the adversary's intrusive collection demonstrated the hostility that made the conflict continue. All in all, this psychological effect probably did more to keep the Cold War going than intelligence's reassurance could do to wind it down.

Notes

1. Originally published in *Intelligence and National Security*, 26, no. 6, 2011: 791–817, and reproduced in Herman, M. and G. Hughes (eds), *Intelligence in the Cold War: What Difference did it Make?* (Abingdon and New York: Routledge: 2013), pp. 37–63. Reprinted by permission of Taylor & Francis Ltd, http://www.tandfonline.com

2. For a fuller discussion of this dilemma over intelligence effects see Herman, M., *Intelligence Power in Peace and War* (Cambridge: Cambridge University Press/RIIA, 1996) pp. 368–75.

3. The KGB's official definition of intelligence-gathering was as 'a specific form of political struggle used by the intelligence agencies of a state to help it to fulfill its internal and external functions', not far different from the role of active measures in 'exerting useful influence' on the target country and misleading and disrupting its activities generally. See Mitrokhin, V., *KGB Lexicon: The Soviet Intelligence Officer's Handbook* (London: Frank Cass, 2002) pp. 13, 200.

4. Well-known examples of American covert action are the funding of the Italian anti-communist parties after 1945, the backing for the Mujahidin in Afghanistan, and the provision of printing presses and other covert support for Solidarity in Poland.

5. One description is in Andrew, C. and O. Gordievsky, *KGB: The Inside Story of its Foreign Operations from Lenin to Gorbachev* (London: Hodder and Stoughton, 1990) pp. 510–12. Andrew has also quoted the combined strength of KGB and GRU Sigint as 350,000 people. See 'The Nature of Military Intelligence', in K. Neilson and B. C. J. McKercher (eds), *Go Spy the Land: Military Intelligence in History* (Westport, CT: Praeger, 1992), p. 5. This seems a high figure, but probably included military tactical Sigint and electronic warfare. For the particularly important East German effort see Fisher, B., '"One of the Biggest Ears in the World": East German Sigint', *International Journal of Intelligence and CounterIntelligence*, 11, no. 2, 1998: 142–53.

6. For details see Sontag, S. and C. Drew, *Blind Man's Bluff: The Untold Story of American Submarine Espionage* (New York: Perennial, 2000) pp. 171–98.

7. Price, A., *The History of U.S. Electronic Warfare* (Alexandra, VA: The Association of Old Crows, 1989), p. 87. Other examples of the means used to stimulate Soviet defences, with and without official sanction, are given in Lashmar, P., *Spy Flights of the Cold War* (Stroud: Sutton, 1996), pp. 117–19.

8. I am indebted to Chris Pocock for this figure in March 2010. Lashmar's *Spy Flights of the Cold War* Appendix 2 gives a total of twenty Western aircraft shot down in this period, including some he lists as on transport and training flights.

9. Lashmar, *Spy Flights of the Cold War*, p. 169.

10. Flying from Paris to Alaska to refuel and fly on to Seoul on 20 April 1978, it managed with astonishing navigational ineptitude to change course by almost 180 degrees and overfly the Murmansk area. After being fired on by a Soviet fighter it landed on a frozen lake. Two passengers were killed (Wikipedia, accessed 23 January 2010).

11. For a full account see Wikipedia.

12. Details here are summarised from Cargill Hall, R., 'The Truth about Overflights', in R. Cowley (ed.), *The Cold War: A Military History* (New York: Random House, 2006), pp. 161–88. Cargill Hall was Chief Historian at the National Reconnaissance Office.

13. There have also been claims that an RAF flight in a British aircraft was mounted in this period. For a discussion of the evidence and doubts about the conclusion see Pocock, C., 'Operation "Robin" and the British overflight of Kapustin Yar', *Intelligence and National Security*, 17, no. 4, 2002: 185–93.

14. Barrass, G., *The Great Cold War: A Journey through the Hall of Mirrors* (Stanford, CA: Stanford University Press, 2009), p. 90. A rather more restrained account is given by Cargill Hall in 'The Truth about Overflights', pp. 182–5. The flights were indeed concentrated, though the incursions were all over the Soviet Far North.

15. Unsinger, P. C., 'Whales in the Air', *International Journal of Intelligence and CounterIntelligence*, 6, no. 3, 1993: 406; Pocock, C., *The U-2 Spyplane: Toward the Unknown* (London: Schiffer, 2000), pp. 42, 131.

16. Pocock, *The U-2 Spyplane*, pp. 158, 161–2. I am indebted to him for confirmation of this total of twenty-four U-2 overflights (correspondence March 2010).

17. MccGwire, M., *Perestroika and Soviet National Security* (Washington, DC: Brookings Institution, 1991), p. 389.

18. Figures compiled from Sontag and Drew, *Blind Man's Bluff*, Appendix A.

19. Geraghty, T., *Beyond the Front Line* (London: HarperCollins, 1996), pp. 247–8.

20. Cargill Hall, 'The Truth about Overflights', p. 163.

21. Details can be found in Wikipedia (accessed 23 January 2010).

22. Garthoff, R., *Detente and Confrontation: US–Soviet Relations from Nixon to Reagan* (Washington: Brookings Institution, 1985), p. 719, fn. 726.
23. Watts, L., *With Friends Like These: The Soviet Bloc's Clandestine War Against Romania* (Bucharest: Military Publishing House, 2010).
24. Garthoff, *Detente and Confrontation*, p. 1016.
25. For brief references to the scale of Western support for these movements after 1945 see Garthoff, R., *Assessing the Adversary: Estimates by the Eisenhower Administration of Soviet Intentions and Capabilities* (Washington, DC: Brookings Institution, 1991), pp. 16–19.
26. Fedor, J., 'Chekists Look Back on the Cold War: The Polemical Literature', in M. Herman and G. Hughes (eds), *Intelligence in the Cold War: What Difference Did it Make?* (Abingdon and New York: Routledge, 2013), pp. 88–109.
27. Mastny, V., 'On the Soviet Side', in M. Herman, J. K. McDonald and V. Mastny, *Did Intelligence Matter in the Cold War* (Oslo: Norwegian Institute for Defence Studies, 2006), p. 60.
28. Bennett, G. and K. A. Hamilton (eds), *Documents on British Foreign Policy Overseas series III, Vol. I: Britain and the Soviet Union 1968–72* (London: HMSO, 1997), p. 528. The paper was the work of the JIC's then Chief of the Assessments Staff (Sir) Percy Cradock, later its chairman 1985–92.
29. Official papers published at note 28 above.
30. Herspring, D. R., 'The Cold War: Perceptions from the America Embassy, Moscow', *Diplomacy and Statecraft*, 9, no. 2, 1998: 200.
31. Gordievsky, O., *Next Stop Execution* (London: Macmillan, 1995), pp. 257–8.
32. US Air Force translation, *The Soviet Armed Forces: A History of Their Organizational Development* (Washington, DC: US Government Printing Office, no date; original in Russian by S. A. Tyushkevich, 1978), p.3 91.
33. See Wikipedia account at note 10.
34. Cargill Hall, 'The Truth about Overflights', p. 188. Barrass suggests after correspondence with Hall that this figure includes losses around Eastern Europe, China and North Korea. See Barrass, *The Great Cold War*, p. 90. Some others were also lost on non-intelligence flights.
35. Pocock, *The U-2 Spyplane*, p. 234.
36. Gaddis, J. L., *The Cold War* (London: Allen Lane, 2005), p. 74.
37. Pocock, *The U-2 Spyplane*, p. 157.
38. Gaddis, J. L., *We Now Know: Rethinking Cold War History* (Oxford: Clarendon Press, 1997), p. 247.

39. Those close to the Soviet Far East in 1983 were a particularly large demonstration of power. See MccGwire, *Perestroika and Soviet National Security*, p. 389. American and British surface deployments in the Barents Sea also had political objectives mixed with collection.
40. Sontag and Drew, *Blind Man's Bluff*, p. 301.
41. I am grateful to Col. Roy Giles for this observation.
42. Quoted by Greenberg, H. M., 'The Doolittle Commission of 1954', *Intelligence and National Security*, 20, no. 4, 2005: 687–94.
43. Quoted by Gaddis, *The Cold War*, p. 165.
44. Cargill Hall, 'The Truth about Overflights', p. 166.
45. Ibid., p. 166. Also Pocock, *The U-2 Spyplane*, p. 142.
46. Cargill Hall, 'The Truth about Overflights', pp. 167–8, 174, 176.
47. For Eisenhower's 'Open Skies' proposal see Gaddis, J. L., *The Long Peace: Inquiries into the History of the Cold War* (Oxford: Oxford University Press, 1987), pp. 195–202.
48. Pocock, *The U-2 Spyplane*, chapters 7–9.
49. An MI6 operation using an ex-naval diver to investigate underwater features of the Soviet cruiser, which had brought the Soviet leadership to Portsmouth in April 1956 in a visit to the UK. The diver, Commander Crabb, was drowned and the operation became known to the press. A permanent result was a tightening of the British procedures for the authorisation of intrusive operations, and this remained a feature of the British system for the rest of the Cold War.
50. Lashmar, *Spy Flights of the Cold War*, chapters 5–7, 14; Pocock, *The U-2 Spyplane*, pp. 157–61.
51. For indications of presidential (and Congressional) briefings see Sontag and Drew, *Blind Man's Bluff*, pp. 179–80, 227–31, 242–4. See, however, p. 222 for the fudging of reports to disguise the risks submarine captains had taken.
52. These paragraphs are adapted from Herman, *Intelligence Power in Peace and War*, pp. 158–63.
53. Kincade, W. H., 'Challenges to Verification: Old and New', in I. Bellany and C. D. Blackmore (eds), *The Verification of Arms Control Agreements* (London: Frank Cass, 1983), p. 26.
54. An official American description of NTMs was as 'assets which are under national control for monitoring compliance with the provisions of an agreement. NTMs include photographic reconnaissance satellites, aircraft-based systems (such as radar and optical systems), as well as sea- and ground-based systems (such as radar and antennas for collecting telemetry).' See *Verifying Arms Control Agreements: The Soviet View* (Washington DC: US Government Printing Office, 1987),

p. 84, quoted by Kunzendorf, V., *Verification of Conventional Arms Control* (Adelphi Paper 245) (London: IISS/Brassey's, 1989), p. 74.

55. For this synergy see Herman, M., 'Intelligence and Arms Control Verification', in J. B. Poole (ed.), *Verification Report 1991* (London: VERTIC, 1991), pp. 187–96; and Kunzendorf, *Verification of Conventional Arms Control*, pp. 52–9.

56. Thus Article XII of the INF Treaty provided for each side to be able to request six open displays per year of road-mobile ground-launched missiles at operating bases; not later than six hours after receiving a request, roofs of all launcher structures were to be slid open, and missiles and launchers moved into the open for a period of twelve hours; see Leggett, J. K. and P. M. Lewis, 'Verifying a START Agreement: Impact of INF Precedents', *Survival*, 30, no. 5, 1988: 413. The START I Agreement included similar provisions for monitoring mobile ICBMs; see Krass, A. S., 'Update: Verification and START: A Progress Report', in J. B. Poole and R. Guthrie (eds), *Verification Report 1992* (London: VERTIC, 1992) p. 57.

57. Though it was thought necessary to agree as a 'Third Common Understanding' attached to Article XV of the SALT II Treaty that 'no shelters which impede verification by national technical means . . . shall be used over ICBM silo launchers'.

58. For an account of the US attitude and subsequent negotiations see Talbot, S., *Endgame: The Inside Story of SALT II* (London: Harper Row, 1979) pp. 194–202, 221, 237–60.

59. 'Second Common Understanding' attached to Article XV. For an account of these negotiations see Labrie, R. P., *SALT Handbook* (Washington, DC: US Enterprise Institute for Public Policy Research, 1979), pp. 410–12.

60. The treaty required the broadcasting of all telemetric information and banned any practice – including encryption, encapsulation and jamming – that denied access to it by NTMs. It also required the provision of full telemetry tapes and certain information that helped in their interpretation. This was 'a new and highly significant commitment to transparency in military affairs' (details and quotation from Krass, 'Update: Verification and START', p. 59).

61. Gaddis, *The Long Peace*, pp. 195–214.

62. Though there is an echo of them in a UN resolution on the principles of arms control verification that 'any verification system should correspond to the generally recognized principles and norms of the UN Charter and other fundamental sources of international law' (Final Document UN 1st Special Session 1978 on Disarmament

(UN Document A/S – 10/2), quoted by Tuzmukhamedov, B. R., 'Verification of Disarmament', in A. Carty and G. Danilenko (eds), *Perestroika and International Law* (Edinburgh: Edinburgh University Press, 1990) p. 49.

63. Howard, M., 'Is Arms Control Really Necessary?', 8 October 1985 Address (London: The Council for Arms Control 1985), p. 12.

64. See Wikipedia entries for 'Fallout Shelters' and 'Civil Defense' including the initiation of the Community Fallout Shelters Program in September 1961 (accessed 11 August 2010).

65. Hinsley, F. H. and E. E. Thomas, C. F. G. Ransom and R. C. Knight, *British Intelligence in the Second World War: Vol. I* (London: HMSO, 1979), appendix 6.

66. Grabo, C. M., 'The Watch Committee and the National Indications Center: The Evolution of U.S. Strategic Warning 1950–75', *International Journal of Intelligence and CounterIntelligence*, 3, no. 3, 1989: 363–86.

67. Alexander, M., *Managing the Cold War: A View from the Front Line* (London: RUSI, 2005), p. 238.

68. Ibid.

69. Uhl, M., 'The Professionalization of Soviet Military Intelligence and its Influence on the Berlin Crisis under Khrushchev', in T. Wegener Friis, K. Macrakis and H. Muller-Enbergs (eds), *East German Foreign Intelligence: Myth, Reality and Controversy* (London: Routledge, 2009), p. 209.

70. Alexander, *Managing the Cold War*, p. 2.

71. *Russian Interests, Intentions and Capabilities*, JIC(48)9(O)Final, 23 July 1948 (London: India Office Library and Records, now administered at the British Library, L/WS/1/1173), first paragraph of Annex I, the summary.

6   What Difference Did It Make?[1]

[2011]

Intelligence was a major strand in the Cold War for East and West alike. The two sides started from different positions, with very different standards of openness and secrecy. Soviet intelligence could exploit the West's relatively open society and draw on the wide swathes of information available from it, while the West was confronted throughout by the Soviet regime's ferocious level of secrecy. Yet both gave high priority to their intelligence effort. Soviet secrecy made the West depend extensively on it, while despite Western openness the Soviet regime could not believe anything it had not learned by covert means.

Intelligence's institutional positions also differed greatly in the two systems. In the Soviet Union it was part of the ruling elite, while in the West it had some bureaucratic independence from policy and (in the United States) could speak with varied voices. The Soviet system was ruthless and professional in collecting Western secrets and protecting its own but was weak in assessing what they meant. The United Kingdom and United States for their part went some way to redress the information imbalance by drawing on their Second World War intelligence standards and applying them to the post-war Soviet target. But for both sides the struggle to acquire knowledge of the adversary remained a mixture of success and failure up to the end. It was a continuous struggle on a quasi-wartime scale between the two intelligence systems that were in some ways replicas of each other, and in others as different as the regimes they represented. This was the intelligence war, in some ways a model of the Cold War as a whole.

But what difference did it make? This chapter focuses on intelligence's product and its effects on its governments' politico-strategic policies. This was not intelligence's only influence on them: it had other applications with less direct top-level effects, and these are summarised here. But the effects of its information and assessments are the main subject. The examination of the subject is limited. The chapter refers to the 'East' and 'West' but restricts itself mainly to the United States and United Kingdom plus some comparisons with the Soviet Union, omitting allies and satellites. China is also ignored. I hope it will encourage more extensive commentary elsewhere.

The Cold War was substantially about military threats and military competition, and most Cold War intelligence in the West – perhaps also in the East – was military intelligence about military power. In the West – though not to the same extent in the East – intelligence was not only the collector of evidence about the adversary but also the expert on him, providing the interpretations and assessments that became the estimates of the military capabilities and political intentions. Capabilities and intentions combined as judgements of 'the threat'. I begin with the Western view of the Soviet capabilities within it.

This was where intelligence most counted. Governments' defence decisions were taken and justified largely on a basis of numbers: of men, machines, destructive power and everything else in the military lexicon. Leaders could not dream up the Soviet numbers themselves, and intelligence had to supply them. The United Kingdom and United States started from considerable ignorance but made progress quite quickly. This was the case even on the highly secret Soviet nuclear programme. Historians now take their detection and evaluation of these first tests for granted, but these were considerable collection and analytic successes at the time, and on this most important question the West was no longer in the dark.

Yet up to the 1960s there were still big gaps and uncertainties, and substantial errors. Despite intelligence's progress the Soviet Union remained the deeply secret colossus, virtually closed except to technical collection from outside. The West did well in the 1950s in following Soviet missile tests and development, but as late as 1960–1 the UK and US intelligence communities were still uncertain whether the Soviet Rocket Forces had hundreds of operational inter-continental ballistic missiles (ICBMs) or none at all.

This situation changed radically with the advent of American satellite imagery in the early 1960s and the synergy it developed with other sources. This satellite effort had its limitations, including a lack of timeliness which was not remedied until much later, but as it developed it came to mean in principle that any Soviet military *matériel* that could be seen could eventually be measured and counted, and its significance estimated. Soviet defensive countermeasures had their successes, but Western intelligence as a whole came on to a rising curve in its scope, accuracy and confidence, with fewer black holes in its knowledge. When data was exchanged and verified in the East–West arms control agreements of the 1970s and 1980s, the Western estimates were found to be substantially accurate. It was a triumph of collection and analysis: mainly an American one, but with significant British assistance.

This did not mean that intelligence was always complete or reliable. It got better at producing hard and semi-hard facts, but many important 'soft' ones were still derived from analysis and were open to question. In the first half of the 1980s the CIA doubted whether the use of chemical weapons was still part of Soviet planning for conventional war, while other American agencies (and the British) argued that it was.

It also remained difficult to estimate military effectiveness. Despite all the knowledge of methods and equipment, it was never clear whether the Soviet adversary was a paper tiger or ten feet tall. Intelligence had no particular skill in comparing 'them' with 'us'; its expertise was on the adversary, not its own side. American attempts to develop a new discipline of objective 'net assessment' of the two sides did not get very far. The Russians' own assessments of the military balance would have been instructive but remained (and remain) elusive.

Moreover, the big Western decisions turned on future Soviet capabilities rather than current ones and, despite the insights into Soviet weapons' testing, the forecasts of what would come into service, with timescales and numbers, still had large elements of guesswork. Intelligence still tended to emphasise 'worst-case' possibilities that could be taken up as gospel by policy advocates.

The forecasts of Soviet capabilities came to draw on assumptions about Soviet intentions which were influenced by the capabilities that had been created in the past. Intelligence could never free itself completely from this circularity and from the assumptions of the leaders it served, and its threat assessments had their own effects in ratcheting the arms race.

Apart from these inherent difficulties there were the effects of intelligence structure and defence politics, particularly in Washington. The American estimates' system did not demand consensus. It sought to tell truth to power, but even after its improvements its truth was often fuzzy, and power could pick what suited it. Not all this applied in other capitals, but Washington was where intelligence most mattered. The record on Soviet capabilities was a mixture of success and error, certainty and uncertainty, all in a setting of considerable improvement as the Cold War continued. But to apply Robin Winks's much-quoted question 'so what?' about intelligence history,[2] what difference did it make?

The record shows two major errors in the period up to the early 1960s. In the first of these, in the late 1940s, the current (not future) Soviet strength of the post-war Soviet army was judged to be around 170 divisions. The analysis involved was of high quality, but it made the assumption that the divisions were all fully manned and active. It was not until the late 1950s and early 1960s that it was properly appreciated that their actual status was of the order of one-third full strength, one-third partial strength, and one-third cadre,[3] and by then the Western image of overwhelming conventional Soviet superiority had taken firm hold. A related assumption was that the armed forces of the European satellites could be counted as Soviet assets, and early reservations about their reliability diminished after the Warsaw Pact's creation.

Hence the message taken by policy-makers was that, despite the USSR's exhaustion, a sizeable part of the massive force that had defeated Germany had been retained and deployed outside the USSR opposite the West. With the satellite forces added, there was a military mass that the West could not rival and could march to the Rhine or the Atlantic at will. The conviction of gross numerical inferiority set the form of the West's defence policy and remained part of its worldview until the end.

The other early error, rather later, was the exaggerated US Air Force estimate in the second half of the 1950s of the so-called 'missile gap', following its earlier alleged 'bomber gap'. The US Air Force (USAF) figures were not generally accepted throughout the US and UK intelligence communities, but they had the effect of pulling the others' estimates some way towards them. Joined with the Soviet launch of the Sputnik satellite in 1957 and Nikita Khrushchev's boasting about his missiles, they raised the fear that the United States was losing the nuclear arms race almost before it had begun, and the result was the skewing of American nuclear policy from the late 1950s onwards, with important and long-lasting results. These included the crash deployments of US missiles in the United Kingdom and Turkey, the missile gap's prominence in the Democratic campaign for the presidency in 1960, and the enhanced American ICBM programmes after John F. Kennedy's election. Subsequently there was the Soviet response of the larger-than-forecast ICBM programmes of the 1960s and 1970s, the claims that an American 'window of vulnerability' was emerging in consequence, and the results in the increased programmes under Ronald Reagan. This long-standing nuclear instability was a major Cold War feature and went back to these early USAF exaggerations.

On the other side of the balance sheet for the early period, it can be argued that although intelligence was still struggling it produced quite realistic forecasts in the late 1940s of how Soviet military power could develop over the next ten years. The conclusion was that the USSR could not be in a condition for war until after the mid-1950s, but by then it could have operational nuclear weapons as well as forces re-equipped with modern conventional weaponry in what was dubbed the West's 'period of danger' in the second half of the 1950s.

This forecast was important in the early decisions about Western defence policies, for example the size and timing of the British V-Force programme, and was not far from what actually happened on the Soviet side. It now seems obvious; and it had its self-fulfilling quality. Nevertheless, nothing in the Soviet Union was obvious at the time, and we were reminded in 2003 over Iraqi weaponry just how wide of the truth expert intelligence analysis can be. A less competent effort after 1945 could have produced something quite different.

Things changed after the American satellite imagery became available. Uncertainty and error were reduced, and there was less scope for false alarms and special pleading. There was less doubt about operational Soviet weaponry, and the photography gave the intelligence about it a particular credibility. Policy-makers became convinced that analysts could measure and count. Despite continued Soviet secrecy, the arms race became a matter of relatively open debate in the West, and surprisingly like its predecessors in the less secretive worlds before 1914 and 1939.

There were still errors: the American forecasts between 1974 and 1986 of Soviet nuclear force modernisation were consistently on the high side,[4] and outside government there were exaggerated claims in the second half of the 1970s that the United States was falling behind and becoming liable to decapitation by a Soviet first strike. The CIA's former chief historian referred to the [US] Air Force's 'stubborn dissent' from February 1960 for the next thirty years in its belief that the Soviet Union was working to attain a decisive military superiority over the United States.[5] These exaggerations had some effects, but fewer than earlier. Intelligence had developed some authority in its estimates of the USSR's current strength and what it *could* produce in the future, even if there was guesswork about what it *would*.

This seemed of particular relevance in the world of strategic nuclear forces. It had its new theology of mutually assured destruction and deterrence but applying it to policy always depended on having comparative figures on the two sides' numbers, payloads and accuracy. For the Americans the Soviet data was available from their satellite imagery and the interception and exploitation of radio-telemetry from Soviet test firings, and it was used to construct the specifications of Soviet missiles that the West has never seen except sometimes on Moscow parades, and to model them into a kind of virtual reality. The same could apply on the Soviet side. Intelligence for this application became part of the mutually agreed verification procedures agreed by the United States and the USSR in the 1970s, perhaps its first international legitimation.

Much of this top-level value must also have been true in the planning and procurement of non-nuclear forces. In Britain it was said in the second half of the Cold War that a battle tank programme had been cancelled after intelligence appeared to show weaknesses against its likely Soviet opponent; that the security of the nuclear V-Force bomber bases was being strengthened in the light of intelligence of a threat from Soviet Spetsnaz forces; that the air defences of the United Kingdom were receiving greater attention after intelligence on new Soviet bombers stiffened earlier threat assessments. There must be many more numerous recollections of this kind in American experience.

Yet these are recollections of corridor gossip, and research would be needed to establish how much intelligence really counted in governments' decisions of those kinds. Industrial policy, jobs and domestic politics could have major influences on procurement policies. The armed services drew on their own experience and doctrine, and used intelligence for their own interests, as in the way the US Navy's doctrine of 'forward deployment' and its development into the 600-ship navy of the 1980s drew on the intelligence about the Soviet deployment of submarine-launched ballistic missiles (SLBMs) in the Soviet 'bastion' in Arctic waters. With so many varied factors in play in national defence policies it is difficult to judge where intelligence stopped and others took over. It counted somewhere, but who can now judge the relationship between the original threat assessments and what emerged so many years later as NATO's Eurofighter?

Despite the uncertainties, Soviet capabilities were where Western intelligence was most useful; yet Soviet intentions were always more important. The Cold War turned on intentions and how they were perceived: no hostile intentions would have meant no threat, except war by misunderstanding. Soviet intentions were the central puzzle. As put by the British Joint Intelligence Committee (JIC) at the beginning of one of its reports in 1948: '[W]hat is Russia trying to do?'[6] This was an answerable question, not futurology. The Soviet regime had its objectives and intentions, even though they had to be elucidated, and could change; and the secrecy surrounding them gave intelligence a special responsibility for eliciting them if it could. Western intelligence certainly tried to elucidate them, but I suggest that it was with only modest effect. Intelligence was important as the watchdog for the 'worst-case' eventuality of a Soviet attack, but on actual Soviet policies its judgements seem to have been mainly confirmatory, corroborating the general Western view that had been formulated mainly by others in the Cold War's formative years from 1945. The knowledge by then of the Soviet Union's wartime espionage against its allies contributed something to the views formed about the threat, but much more was based on overt Soviet behaviour and statements. Intelligence was the professional authority on Soviet espionage and military power, but it never had the same weight on Soviet intentions.

This was partly for organisational reasons. Post-war American intelligence was based for some time on the separate armed services, and there was no effective structure for inter-agency coordination and civilian inputs. A military Joint Intelligence Committee had been formed in 1941 (at British insistence) and continued well into the 1950s but had only limited influence. The idea of community-wide assessment of the USSR has a basis in the creation of the Central Intelligence Group in 1946 and its successor the CIA the following year.[7] But the CIA's talented team for the drafting of the National Intelligence Estimates was not gathered together until the early 1950s. For the Truman Administration the important official inputs on Soviet motives in 1945 and afterwards were those of State Department and its Moscow embassy, notably George Kennan's 'Long Telegram' of February 1946 which in John Gaddis's view was to 'shape American policy over the next half century'.[8]

This was not quite the same in London, where the JIC from the end of the war produced assessments that covered Soviet intentions as well as capabilities. They now read well, especially in emphasising the caution in Soviet short-term intentions. But it is arguable that they represented the Foreign Office view and not a distinctly 'intelligence' one. The JIC had lost the talented wartime 'civilians in uniform' in its drafting staff; the new Joint Intelligence Bureau was restricted to defence subjects; no intelligence body was then (or ever) tasked with studying Soviet policy at the top.[9] The political passages in JIC reports were then drafted in the Foreign Office, whose views were developed in its own 'Russia Committee'.[10] The assessment in Frank Roberts's telegram from its Moscow embassy, written in conjunction with Kennan's, was probably as influential in London as its American counterpart in Washington.[11]

In some ways this situation changed subsequently in both countries. After the shock of the Korean War, Washington developed the style of intelligence assessment that, despite all the changes in organisation and nomenclature, now remains more or less the same. The Board of National Estimates and the Office of the same name that prepared them came into action in late 1950 and had circulated 150 reports by the end of 1953.[12] The CIA's Directorate of Intelligence developed as a high-quality Soviet centre. The same applied to the State Department's intelligence and research centre, and military intelligence became more professional. Diplomatic and State Department influence declined as intelligence's rose.

Yet this professionalism was accompanied by the characteristic American tolerance of dissenting intelligence views amid Washington's highly politicised debates on national security. Intelligence was much prized in them, but often as handy ammunition rather than a search for truth. It had no single, authoritative view of Soviet intentions, and political leaders tended to encourage assessments best in tune with their own. CIA analysts had a high reputation, but even they had to bend to be useful. They have been criticised by their former official historian for their caution, a result in his view of the CIA's continuing need to defend anything it said against 'the Pentagon's belief in a Soviet Union hell-bent on world domination'.[13]

This was not the situation in London, where Cold War policy was less controversial. The JIC acquired a powerful Assessments Staff in 1968 with members no longer bound to represent their parent departments. Yet the Foreign Office's influence remained strong, and it is difficult to see that the JIC's contribution was more than a fine-tuning of existing Whitehall thinking, or that it had distinctive effects. When Gorbachev's rise to power made Soviet intentions a major issue, the Committee is said to have been over-cautious about him, but this did not dictate Mrs Thatcher's reactions.[14]

Far more important than these matters of organisation and procedure was, however, the simple fact that neither UK nor US intelligence was ever able to develop covert sources as its own transparent window on to Soviet policies and policy-making. Agents and defectors produced useful knowledge of the regime they hated, but they were never close or sympathetic enough to its top leadership to have a deep understanding of its inner workings and aims. Those who were so close did not become spies or defectors. The reading of the Soviet Venona traffic cast light on the regime's espionage but not its policy. An American human source provided extensive copies of Soviet diplomatic traffic in the mid-1970s, but these were probably more valuable on Soviet negotiating positions than on basic attitudes and intentions.[15] These had to be judged from the indirect evidence available, and in this intelligence was in the same boat as everyone else and had no special authority.

There was a partial exception in the British discovery of the fears in Moscow in the early 1980s of a pre-emptive American strike, culminating in Soviet alert measures of November 1983.[16] But the evidence was fragmentary and the effects may have been marginal. Robert Jervis has commented pessimistically that in understanding the other party there is no reason to expect analysts to do better than policy-makers,[17] and Soviet secrecy certainly made this true of the Cold War. Intelligence's special contribution to governments was on Soviet capabilities and not mindset.

On the Soviet side we are still guessing about its intelligence on the West and its effect on the regime. Ideology ruled out the Western concept of 'objective', policy-free assessment. For KGB chairmen and their predecessors, intelligence was a basis of their power, not a service to the rest of government. Reports were expected to consist of evidence rather than assessment and judging what they meant was a matter for the readership. Official KGB doctrine has scant reference to analysis on the Western model,[18] and a snapshot of the analysis staff in the KGB's huge machine in the 1970s showed that it comprised only 250 people, whose concern was editing field reports from stations overseas. It produced little analysis in the Western style, and indeed some station reports are said to have gone direct to the party's Central Committee.[19] As late as 1985, of 8,000 KGB reports sent to high authorities only 186 were analytical estimates.[20]

The machine for covert collection was extensive and professional at its best, and mendacious and corrupt at its worst. It seems that, whatever the quality and subject, the evidence reaching Moscow was selected and presented there in the light of the regime's bleakest assumptions about Western attitudes, intentions and deception. There is an account for example of the British and American military planning papers of 'worst-case' kinds early in the Cold War that were sent to the top leadership, and which out of context must have been taken as hard evidence of the West's aggressive intentions.[21] There is the direct evidence of the KGB's institutional slanting in Gorbachev's strong criticism in December 1985 of the distortions in its reports, and his demand for more objectivity in them.[22] Gordon Barrass in his study of the Cold War quotes the verdict of an insider that its reporting reinforced the image of the West by blaming the Americans for everything: 'People were not praised for their objectivity, but for providing information that was in line with policy.'[23]

But this was on the West's motives, and it is unclear how the system handled Western military capabilities. There was ample evidence: 'it is clear that practically every military secret of any significance was betrayed'.[24] One might presume that, like its opposite numbers, Soviet military intelligence tended towards exaggerated, 'worst-case' estimates of the opponent. It seems clear, for example, that the Soviet military fears in the early 1980s were heightened by inaccurate assumptions that Reagan's Strategic Defense Initiative (SDI) could be available quite soon, and that the American deep and precise battlefield strike was a current capability and not still a concept.[25] On the other hand, it has been powerfully argued that Soviet military intelligence assessed the evidence objectively and developed strategic policies that were realistic in the context of the assumed Western threat and risk of conflict.[26]

An informed view is that our source base of top-level Soviet archives is still so sparse that it is risky to reach any general conclusions about intelligence's effects.[27] One exception however is the significance of the scientific and technical Western data collected by the KGB and GRU and passed to the Soviet designers who could use it. The KGB's annual report for 1985 claimed that in that year it had provided the Soviet scientific establishment with

40,000 pieces of information and 12,000 'model types', presumably specimens of hardware. The figures should be taken with the same scepticism as those in annual intelligence self-audits anywhere,[28] but there seems to be agreement that this intelligence was extensive and useful in the struggle to keep Soviet military development up with the West. In Christopher Andrew's view its volume 'helps to explain one of the central paradoxes of a Soviet state which was famously described as "Upper Volta with missiles"'.[29] The wartime penetration of the UK–US atomic bomb project and the kick-start it gave to the Soviet response made up what was probably the intelligence's biggest Cold War success on either side.[30]

These were the direct effects of evidence and estimates, but intelligence affected governments in the other ways touched on in the introduction. This chapter can end with a brief discussion of these influences in the West, and even briefer comments on the East.

One effect of intelligence was, of course, when it became a cause of major Cold War episodes or an identified participant in them. Particularly important were the shooting-down of the American U-2 over the Soviet Union on 1 May 1960 that provoked the breakdown of the Paris conference that followed it, and the U-2's discovery of the Soviet missiles in Cuba in October 1962 and all that followed. In a different way there was its publicly avowed place in the strategic arms control agreements of the 1970s. In these cases, intelligence was itself the substance of East–West conflict or negotiation.

At this level of high diplomacy between leaders there were also the tactical side effects of intelligence's politico-strategic assessments. The CIA's demonstration to President Kennedy in summer 1961 that, contrary to what was previously thought, the ICBM inferiority was all on the Soviet side, is said to have changed the chemistry of his subsequent contacts with Khrushchev, particularly after the American reassessment was made known to the Russians.[31] Confidence in their intelligence no doubt had some bearing on leaders' psychology.

What is less clear is the extent of intelligence's behind-the-scene effects on the other East–West diplomacy that was so much of the Cold War's action. Possibly the most useful intelligence provided for the West was on Soviet activities in Third World countries, particularly the Middle East. Sources there provided good insights into Soviet policies before the Arab–Israeli War in 1967, and covered the later deployment of Soviet Bloc air defence forces to Egypt. Later there was all its monitoring of the vicissitudes of the Soviet presence in Afghanistan. Yet British diplomats have been rather dismissive about this support. One concluded that 'the intelligence agencies and their product . . . do not have a central impact of government decision-making in peacetime – even when the peace is a Cold War'.[32] Perhaps intelligence supplied useful bits and pieces but not the main parts of the pictures.

Diplomatic support probably counted for more to the East. There is good evidence, for example, of the way the Soviet diplomatic hand was strengthened over action on Berlin from the late 1950s onwards by excellent covert reports on the Western planning for military responses.[33] The West may indeed have been generally intimidated by the success of Soviet covert collection: the British diplomat just quoted also recorded that 'a misplaced belief during much of the Cold War that the Russians would always triumph in negotiation helped to undermine Western self-confidence on a number of occasions'.[34] But we do not know how much the covert Soviet intelligence really counted. In 1989 John Gaddis discussed the high-quality Western information that was available to Stalin before and during the Korean War but concluded that: '[W]hat we do not know is what role, if any, the reports of his spies played in shaping this [his] behavior'.[35] Our picture of the Soviet side has not changed much since.

In terms of resources involved and volume of output, however, diplomatic support was a minority intelligence activity in the West, and perhaps also in the East. By far the biggest activity was military intelligence, the monitoring, analysis and reporting of the other side's armed forces. Barrass remarks of the detente area that 'the best intelligence available to both sides was about military matters'.[36] It was what was most extensively used in the West, and those using it were the military authorities responsible for planning, preparing and training their own forces. Despite Soviet secrecy they were probably at least as well informed about the potential enemy as their predecessors had been in 1914 and 1939.

Much the same may well have been true on the Soviet side. It is unlikely that any campaign has ever been war-gamed for so long and so intensively by both sides as the Soviet blitzkrieg on the North German Plain that never took place.

This military intelligence of course had its top-level applications. The use of the formal estimates of military capabilities has already been discussed, and the military evidence that underlay them was also the basis of the Western surveillance of Soviet activities for warning of hostile moves, as described in my 'Intelligence as Threats and Reassurance', Chapter 5 in this collection. Here and elsewhere the extent of the military information provided important reassurances to Western governments. Washington was not going to be Pearl Harbor-ed overnight; NATO could have some confidence in implementing its alerting and reinforcement plans; the Cold War balance would not suddenly be upset by unforeseen Soviet weaponry. As its quality improved it helped governments towards their belief that the Soviet threat was knowable and the risk of war manageable.

Nevertheless, its bread-and-butter use was the military one, preparing armed forces for the war that never came and providing for the support they would need if it ever did. All possible detail was needed, and the large-scale effort involved was sometimes denigrated by British civilian officials as military intelligence's 'bean-counting'. Despite the top-level relevance just described, a substantial part of its peacetime justification was helping the armed forces to prepare for war when the West's object was to avoid it. Intelligence managers faced the conundrum: what level of this (invisible) intelligence support was needed in peacetime to maintain these forces' (visible) effectiveness in the eyes of publics, allies and opponents?

Other effects of intelligence were not in the knowledge it provided but as one of the Cold War's actors. 'Intelligence as Threats and Reassurance' discusses the extent to which intrusive intelligence collection on both sides encouraged fears and resentments about the other's human and technical 'spying' and made these fears permanent parts of Cold War psychology. The same was true of intelligence's covert action. 'Intelligence as Threats and Reassurance' also suggests that, psychological effects apart, covert action was an important weapon for both sides, and a study of its effects will be a necessary part of a complete Cold War history. But that would take us beyond the present study.

Lastly there were also effects of the defensive side of the intelligence war: advising on or controlling the defensive measures needed to nullify the opponent's intelligence attacks. Intelligence in both East and West was the defensive gamekeeper as well as offensive poacher. Inside this wide-ranging secret war was the narrower mini-war of intelligence versus intelligence, or counterintelligence: the detection and neutralisation of the adversary's attacks, and perhaps 'turning' them for one's own deception purposes: the 'wilderness of mirrors'[37] of the Le Carré novels.

These were important activities to which both sides rightly devoted significant effort, probably much more in the East than the West. Raymond Garthoff concluded in 2004 that 'the most notable achievements of espionage on both sides were for counterintelligence purposes'.[38] By the end of the Cold War the two sides' counterintelligence successes and failures more or less balanced each other out: a significant achievement of the West considering how it had started in 1945.

There were some top-level effects. Individual spy cases on both sides reinforced Cold War hostility, and the espionage threat had a specific impact on East–West relationships in the British government's expulsion of the 105 Soviet intelligence officers from London in 1971. Professionally this was a major counterintelligence success and put the Soviet effort there on the defensive for the rest of the Cold War, but it also had its diplomatic reverberations. It gave a political message to Moscow, froze Anglo-Soviet relations for a while and probably enhanced the UK's Western standing.

There was also the remarkable effect of the ingrained myth on the Soviet side of great British and American effectiveness at deception within this counterintelligence contest. The value of the excellent Soviet sources in the West was constantly negated in Moscow by this fear of deception in what they produced. The balance of advantage in the overall intelligence war may indeed have been determined as much by this Soviet fear of deception as by the West's improving security procedures.

Yet with such exceptions the work of defensive security was technical and specialised. Where there were political effects outside the intra-intelligence war of offence and defence they were mainly of a very general kind. Effectiveness against Soviet Bloc penetration was one index of national standing in the Western alliance: the UK benefited from its reputation of having 'good security'. 'Making NATO secure' against the Soviet attack was a recurrent political issue for the United Kingdom and United States. The success of the Soviet penetration of NATO's continental powers was a particular reason for the UK–US–Canadian exclusivity within the alliance, and the resentment it caused to the others. But these effects were general and long term. Governments sought information security for its own sake, and the political effects were relatively rare.

Did it all matter? Did it make governments act more wisely? Did it make the Cold War hotter or colder? Intelligence was a major activity for both sides and permeated much Cold War thinking. Its scale, the importance attached to it, and some of its activities (allied with its covert action) all helped to fix the idea of the Cold War everywhere as a relationship of hostility and threat, a most unusual kind of peace. It supported and hardened the adversary images of both sides, and what has been described as the Cold War's 'sheer intensity'.[39]

But how far were governments driven by the intelligence they received? In the West (and probably also the East) they drew particularly on its estimates of the adversary's military capabilities, and they used them in fashioning their own military power. Soviet secrecy made the Western estimates imprecise and sometimes exaggerated, especially in the early years, and there were long-lasting effects on governments' decisions. But they always provided government with some tether with reality, and their quality improved as time went on. They did something to keep Western policies on the level. This may also have been true on the other side, in its much easier task of estimating Western strength.

Intelligence did not have the same effect at the Cold War's centrepoint: the other side's intentions. On these the Western view was set early in the Cold War without much intelligence input. Intelligence's status then increased, but it never had the luck to find covert sources close enough to Moscow's centre to provide a direct window on to it. The assessments it produced were prestigious, but the main effect was to confirm existing government views. On the Soviet side the evidence is that intelligence's reports were presented and selected in ways that emphasised Western hostility and threats. Presumably there were cumulative effects there on leaders' judgements, but Soviet intelligence was such an integral part of the regime that it is hard to disentangle cause and effect.

So there may have been some symmetry in intelligence's influence. For the West it was important in the Cold War's arms race. It kept governments in some touch with reality, and more sensible than they might have been. Something of the same may have been true in Moscow. But this applied to military strength, not more widely. Neither intelligence system contributed much on what (in the West) we see as its prime task: to see the world, including oneself, realistically through the target's eyes, and convince its masters of the results. The most important Cold War judgements for each side were of the balance of offence and defence in the opponent's politico-strategic aims, and how this might be changing; and both sides may have got this balance wrong. The Soviet leaders' view that there was a consistent US aim of undermining their system was exaggerated, though not without foundation. The same may be true of the West's view of the comparable Soviet threat, and its modifications as the Cold War progressed. But so little is known even now of the inner levels of Soviet policy-making that this is still speculation.

Notes

1. Originally published in *Intelligence and National Security*, 26, no. 6, 2011: 886–901, and reproduced in Herman, M. and G. Hughes (eds), *Intelligence in the Cold War: What Difference Did it Make?* (Abingdon and New York: Routledge, 2013), pp. 132–47. Reprinted by permission of Taylor & Francis Ltd: http://www.tandfonline.com
2. Winks, R., *Cloak and Gown: Scholars in America's Secret War* (London: Collins Harvill, 1987), p. 63.

3. Evangelista, M., 'Stalin's Postwar Army Reappraised', *International Security*, 7, no. 3, 1982–3: 112, quoting an opinion of Paul Nitze. The distinction between cadre strength, low strength and combat-ready divisions was not incorporated into US intelligence estimates until the early 1960s. See Garthoff, R., 'Estimating Soviet Military Force Levels', *International Security*, 14, no. 4, 1990: 93–116.

4. Kerr, R. J., 'The Track Record: CIA Analysis from 1950 to 2000', in R. George and J. B. Bruce (eds), *Analyzing Intelligence: Origins, Obstacles and Innovations* (Washington, DC: Georgetown University Press, 2008), p. 38. The statement draws on Haines, G. and R. E. Leggett, *CIA's Analysis of the Soviet Union, 1947–1991* (Washington, DC: Center for the Study of Intelligence, 2001).

5. McDonald, J. K., 'How Much Did Intelligence Matter in the Cold War?', in M. Herman, J. K. McDonald, and V. Mastny, *Did Intelligence Matter in the Cold War?* (Oslo: Norwegian Institute for Defence Studies, 2006), p. 3.

6. *Russian Interests, Intentions and Capabilities*, JIC(48)9(O)Final, 23 July 1948 (London: India Office Library and Records, now administered at the British Library, L/WS/1/1173), first paragraph of Annex I, the summary.

7. The CIA actually made its first report on the Soviet Union in September 1947. See Aronsen, L., 'Seeing Red: US Air Force Assessments of the Soviet Union, 1945–1949', *Intelligence and National Security*, 16, no. 2, 2001: 122.

8. Gaddis, J. L., *We Now Know: Rethinking Cold War History* (Oxford: Oxford University Press, 1997), p. 20.

9. Though one senior officer, Malcolm Mackintosh, had the remit to do this single-handed in the Cabinet Office Assessments Staff for many years after its creation in 1968.

10. The 1948 JIC report quoted at note 6 strikes the modern reader as a rather crude 'cut and paste' compilation from separate departmental contributions, in the style of 'joint service writing' that was then the military fashion. It is made up of a (brilliant) two-and-a-half-page summary, and main sections with A4 page lengths as follows: Fundamental Principles in the Outlook of Soviet Leaders (1½), Capabilities (Economic and Military) (15), General Soviet Policy (9), Soviet Interests and Intentions by Area (36). By comparison, the JIC's 1972 equivalent entitled *The Soviet Threat* (concentrating on intentions rather than capabilities) had a single author and as now published is on seventen (smaller) book pages in Bennett, G. and K. A. Hamilton (eds), *Documents on British Policy Overseas Series III*,

Volume I: Britain and the Soviet Union, 1968–72 (London: HMSO, 1997). One JIC member who dissented from the Whitehall consensus of this period was Rear-Admiral Buzzard, Director of Naval Intelligence 1951–4. Some details are given in Clark, I. and N. J. Wheeler, *The British Origins of Nuclear Strategy 1945–55* (Oxford: Clarendon Press, 1989) pp. 181–200.

11. See Cradock, P., *Know Your Enemy: How the Joint Intelligence Committee Saw the World* (London: John Murray, 2002), pp. 41–6.
12. McDonald, 'How Much Did Intelligence Matter in the Cold War?', p. 50.
13. Ibid., p. 55.
14. Urban, M., *UK Eyes Alpha: The Inside Story of British Intelligence* (London: Faber and Faber, 1996), pp. 70–83.
15. Barrass, G., *The Great Cold War: A Journey through the Hall of Mirrors* (Stanford, CA: Stanford University Press, 2009), p. 392.
16. Discussed in Scott, L., 'Intelligence and the Risk of Nuclear War: Able Archer-83 Revisited', in Herman, M. and G. Hughes (eds), *Intelligence in the Cold War: What Difference Did It Make?* (Abingdon: Routledge, 2013); and Chapter 20 in this collection, 'Harry Burke and Able Archer'.
17. Jervis, R., 'A Look Back on the Soviet Menace', *International Journal of Intelligence and CounterIntelligence*, 18, no. 1, 2005: 171.
18. In the 419 pages of Mitrokhin, V., *KGB Lexicon: The Soviet Intelligence Officer's Handbook* (London: Frank Cass, 2002) the references to analysis are limited to pp. 13, 46, 297.
19. Pringle, R. W., 'The Heritage and Future of Russian Intelligence', *International Journal of Intelligence and CounterIntelligence*, 11, no. 2, 1998: 178.
20. Ibid.: 179.
21. Tsarev, O., 'Intelligence in the Cold War', in H. Shukman (ed.), *Agents for Change: Intelligence Services in the 21st Century* (London: St Ermin's Press, 2000), pp. 22–40.
22. Andrew, C. and V. Mitrokhin, *The Mitrokhin Archive: The KGB in Europe and the West* (London: Allen Lane, 1999), p. 280.
23. Barrass, *The Great Cold War*, p. 385.
24. Ibid., p. 393.
25. Ibid., pp. 275, 319.
26. This view was set out impressively in MccGwire, M., *Military Objectives in Soviet Foreign Policy* (Washington, DC: Brookings Institution, 1987). See also Barrass, *The Great Cold War*, p. 385 for the role of the 'military intellectuals' in the General Staff and Soviet Military Intelligence.

27. I am indebted to Mark Kramer for this comment on an earlier draft. He has pointed out that neither the Soviet Politburo (now Presidential) Archive nor the SVR archive has ever been accessible, but that the available material confirms that Soviet foreign intelligence officials shared the outlook of Soviet Politburo members.
28. Pringle, 'The Heritage and Future of Russian Intelligence', p. 179.
29. Andrew and Mitrokhin, *The Mitrokhin Archive*, p. 723. For a short account of the value to Soviet projects see pp. 280–7.
30. Ibid., pp. 173–5.
31. Gaddis, *We Now Know*, pp. 256–7.
32. Alexander, M., *Managing the Cold War: A View from the Front Line* (London: RUSI, 2005), p. 193.
33. It was described in Uhl, M., 'Soviet Espionage and Policy: Decision-Making under Khrushchev', paper presented at the conference Intelligence in Waging the Cold War: NATO, The Warsaw Pact and the Neutrals, 1949–1990, at the Norwegian Institute for Defence Studies in Oslo, 28 April–1 May 2005.
34. Alexander, *Managing the Cold War*, p. xi.
35. Gaddis, J. L., 'Intelligence, Espionage, and Cold War Origins', *Diplomatic History*, 13, no. 2, 1989: 191–212.
36. Barrass, The *Great Cold War*, p. 393.
37. Title of Martin, D. C., *Wilderness of Mirrors* (New York: Harper and Row, 1980). Taken from T. S. Eliot's poem 'Gerontion'.
38. Garthoff, R., 'Foreign Intelligence and the Historiography of the Cold War', *Journal of Cold War Studies*, 6, no. 2, 2004: 34.
39. Kramer, M., 'Ideology and Cold War', *Review of International Studies*, 25, no. 4, 1990: 573. He argues there that '[i]deology goes a long way towards explaining the sheer intensity of the Cold War'. Intelligence probably added to it.

7   The Intelligence War: Reflections on Sigint[1]

[2013]

I was an intelligence official from 1952 to 1987, almost the whole duration of the Cold War. On reflection I would now describe that historical period in two ways. The first is a particular succession of international events, in which intelligence knowledge usually played a significant part, or when intelligence collection provoked events.[2] The second is a mental state of permanent rivalry between East and West, with its set of attitudes, fears, ambitions, adversary images, precautions and preparations on both sides. The West was heavily dependent on intelligence because of the Soviet regime's ferocious secrecy, while the Soviets refused to believe anything they had not learned by secret means. The result was an intelligence war of great intensity, which incidentally established intelligence organisations as a substantial element of the peacetime Western state.

How did Sigint fit into this general picture? We now have the authorised history of GCHQ;[3] in conjunction with earlier accounts of the US National Security Agency (NSA), including the redacted version of Thomas Johnson's internal history,[4] it can be said that Western Sigint has finally been given a place in the post-1945 historical record. Partly because the Soviet intelligence archives remain inaccessible, the evidence is still incomplete at what we might call the technical-cum-strategic level of the intelligence war: the constant game of snakes and ladders between intelligence and secrecy in East and West, the mixture of advances and defeats for each side, and the cumulative effects they had on policy-making. There is also always something of a tension between the historian's judgement and one's own memories of events – fallible, distorted, yet with the conviction that 'I was there'. I therefore confine myself to some generalisations of Cold War Sigint which may help historians to draw conclusions from the evidence they get as more materials become available. I rely on official revelations about Sigint, particularly those of the US, and cite relevant observations from Professor Ferris's history without seeking to elaborate on them.

First, the size of the post-war effort: GCHQ was easily the biggest UK agency. Why so big compared with the others? Resources were not planned in 1945 on a community basis, and there was never a proper intelligence community budget until the Cold War was over. The size of post-war GCHQ was first settled after a review in 1946, and the impetus for its subsequent growth was in keeping up with the transatlantic partnership and preserving the world-class service of Sigint which Her Majesty's Government received through it. In this GCHQ's consistent strategy was to avoid being a second- or third-class American subsidiary, relegated to the minor role of picking up uninteresting but necessary bread-and-butter coverage. We managed this by seeking to play some part in sophisticated and important operations, including investing in the hi-tech, expensive facilities they needed.[5] One of the key episodes in this strategy was the Treasury's critical testing of GCHQ's expanded financial bids in the first half of the 1960s and the general endorsement it gave them.[6] We used to say that Soviet targets absorbed at least 60 per cent of our Sigint effort, though all such figures were to be taken with caution. On this task we had rather below 1,000 staff directly involved at the headquarters, a large share of the military and civilian collectors in the field, and a share of all the computer and other supporting facilities.

Next there is the question often put, about the degree of UK–US success against Russian ciphers. Writers have tended to describe us through the prism of Bletchley's wartime cryptanalytic success, disparaging our Cold War efforts as 'mere traffic analysis'. On this I would point to a distinction I have previously made between textual and non-textual sources: access to the target's own messages, information systems and meanings on the one hand, and observation of the target's appearance and behaviour on the other.[7] Using this distinction I would accept that if Sigint in the Second World War was predominantly textual, then over the fifty years of the Cold War its product was predominantly, though not exclusively, non-textual.[8]

I would qualify this in various ways, however. There is a tendency to lump under the heading of 'traffic analysis' the low-grade code messages and plain language which can be exploited and analysed in depth. The identification of secret callsigns, and target location from direction finding, have also been underestimated along with other non-textual sources. Historians perhaps have not reflected on what could be achieved by fusing these techniques to produce order of battle, accounts of military activities and forecasts of moves.[9] This applied particularly when American satellites extended the scope for collection. As a pointer from the Second World War record, I commend the account in the Hinsley history of establishing the size of the German bomber force through callsign analysis.[10] Nevertheless, the absence of consistent and rich textual material made Cold War Sigint in a sense two-dimensional, compared with Bletchley's more three-dimensional quality. We were usually guessing about the Soviet mind, not reading it. There is a parallel with the way archaeologists' hypotheses from the objects they find are enriched if they also have some inscriptions to work on.[11]

Next, I would highlight the influence of the transatlantic relationship, far more intimate in Sigint than elsewhere.[12] I would emphasise the importance of the formal post-war agreement for complete exchanges: I was consistently surprised at the trouble our American colleagues took to observe the letter of the agreement somehow, even in tricky political circumstances.[13] For us, thinking in transatlantic terms became almost a professional reflex. My first job in 1953 was working in a combined section with members of the US Navy, and most of my subsequent jobs had an American dimension of some kind.

The British motives for the relationship were clear enough: access to a first-class power's intelligence product. On the American side it was driven by personal friendships as well as powerful professional convictions, but I always wondered how the relationship seemed to the top political levels in Washington. It is now known that Henry Kissinger briefly cut off part of the intelligence exchange to bring pressure on the Heath government, but he was exceptional.[14] I suspect that the intelligence alliance was usually accepted by American administrations as part of the politico-military furniture they inherited and had no particular reason to shift, but we await a full study of the transatlantic relationship as seen through American eyes.

How did the alliance affect the way we worked? One was the emphasis it gave to speed and current surveillance. Bletchley had seen the introduction of mechanised processing to the needs of war, but the Cold War then saw the progressive development of IT to provide something like wartime surveillance in peacetime.[15] Most of this activity was military intelligence, a natural adjunct to military power: preparing for war or providing warning of an attack that never came. Any picture of Cold War intelligence as a scholarly accumulation on Soviet capabilities is misleading without depicting the timely monitoring of Soviet forces on a near-wartime scale, by worldwide civilian and military resources. Pearl Harbor drove the tempo of what we did and how we did it. What has the target been doing recently? What is he doing now? Most important, what is he intending to do? NATO's military posture came to depend on warning of Soviet attack, and American influence in the alliance made warning a major intelligence objective. It should be remembered that the Sigint organisations of both the UK and US were federations of central institutions and the separate armed forces, all participating in twenty-four-hour coverage and electronic reporting from around the Soviet periphery.[16] Tests for this warning were provided before the Soviet military moves into Czechoslovakia in 1968 and Afghanistan in 1979, and the preparations for similar moves into Poland in 1980 and 1981.[17]

In this there was always some tension in GCHQ between speed and depth. There were the occasional grumblers who complained that our effort was 'just keeping up with the Americans' rather than doing a more thoughtful job. One aspect of Bletchley's wartime success had been the speed of some of its Enigma exploitation: a speed which, when the intelligence product was passed quickly to responsible commanders, could drive immediate tactical decisions as well as contribute to long-term operational and strategic ones.[18] Much of Bletchley's intelligence – though not all of it – had a perishable quality. There was a wartime requirement to know what the enemy was doing today, and if possible what he was preparing to do tomorrow. When I was in charge of our contribution in the late 1970s and early 1980s, I opted for putting more effort into speedy exploitation, for both national and transatlantic reasons. I later diverted some talent into deeper research, to try for example to study our detailed military evidence for answers about Soviet objectives: what war were the Soviet forces designed to fight, and what did this indicate about Soviet aims? Perhaps I should have moved earlier, but I doubt whether we would have ever had success without more interest from London.

This leads me to discuss our working relationships with the Americans on the one hand and with London Ministries on the other. With our American opposite numbers we had liaison officers, exchanges of analysts, and easy communications, all added to the complete exchanges of material.[19] Collaboration also extended to agreements for divisions of effort to reduce duplication. For two independent nations the relationship was remarkably close.[20] By contrast, our interchanges with the DIS and its predecessor departments in London were cordial, but circumscribed. Relations had a background in the wartime history of Bletchley's struggle to establish its independence in assessing all relevant Sigint evidence, and not just reporting so-called 'raw facts', and this battle was re-fought in the 1950s over the emerging evidence of Soviet missiles. Such battles over institutional boundaries were far more intense in the US, and since they raged over British as well as American reports they led to agreed UK–US rules for limiting the inclusion of technical Sigint detail in published reports. Other factors in our relations with the DIS were the physical distance between Cheltenham and London, the inexperience of some of the uniformed officers there, and security restrictions on our reports that constantly got stricter through American attempts to stop their persistent Washington press leaks.

A result was that on the whole we kept our independence in Sigint research and reporting, with more coordination with the Americans than with London, where our customers welcomed what they received and usually did not try to influence what we did and the conclusions we offered. With the institutions and people involved it worked reasonably well, but it was not an optimum meeting of minds. Drawing on someone else's bright idea, I eventually sought to move our analysts towards negotiating their research programmes with customers to take account of their Whitehall priorities. It was interesting that, apart from analysts' caution over changing well-established practices, it was sometimes surprisingly difficult to get customers keen on the innovation.

My general picture is of a large-scale knowledge factory, partly dispersed to the military stations. The factory produced reports for British departments and commands worldwide, plus the Americans and other allies including NATO. Equally important, it acted as the conduit to customers for the much greater flow of American reports, and some from other collaborators. It was all a massive international service, increasingly electronic, much of it comprising ephemeral military intelligence in ever-increasing volume.

Running it all was partly like optimising the factory, but it was also like directing a large-scale research organisation that sought new knowledge. Its reports certainly influenced military procurement programmes, though no one has analysed precisely how, and it would be difficult to do so. Along with American satellite imagery the Sigint effort also reassured British governments against surprise. It was most tested in forecasting the Soviet regime's military moves against its East European satellites, and did quite well,[21] but was less successful in convincing the JIC system of its findings. In Whitehall some of the reports they received seemed rather non-British in tone (as indeed many of them were), and were sometimes not well understood.

To sum up, our Cold War Sigint was up against a target that was big and difficult but fairly static. We collaborated with an ally that operated in great power style. Above all, we were working in peace, but joined in monitoring our target with a near-wartime intensity. This was a characteristic of our operations, and of the Cold War itself.

Notes

1. Adapted from a presentation to the sixth biennial Centre for Intelligence & International Security Studies (CIISS) Aberystwyth conference at Gregynog Hall, Wales, UK, 23–25 May 2013.

2. Chapter 5 in this collection, 'Intelligence as Threats and Reassurance'.

3. Ferris, J., *Behind the Enigma: The Authorised History of GCHQ, Britain's Secret Cyber-Intelligence Agency* (London: Bloomsbury, 2020).

4. Johnson, T. R., *American Cryptology during the Cold War, 1945–1989*, 4 vols (Washington, DC: Centre for Cryptologic History, 1995).

5. Ferris, *Behind the Enigma*, pp. 361–6. See also Aldrich, R. J., *GCHQ: The Uncensored Story of Britain's Most Secret Intelligence Agency* (London: Harper Press, 2010), chapter 14; Easter, D., 'GCHQ and British External Policy in the 1960s', *Intelligence and National Security*, 23, no. 5, 2008: 685–9; and Mainwaring, S. and R. J. Aldrich, 'The Secret Empire of Signals Intelligence: GCHQ and the Persistence of the Colonial Presence', *The International History Review*, 43, no. 1, 2021: 54–71.

6. Aldrich, R. J., 'Counting the Cost of Intelligence: The Treasury, National Service and GCHQ', *The English Historical Review*, 128, no. 532, 2013: 613–21; Ferris, *Behind the Enigma*, pp. 297–303.

7. Herman, M., *Intelligence Power in Peace and War* (Cambridge: Cambridge University Press/RIIA, 1996), pp. 69–72.

8. Johnson, T. R., *American Cryptology during the Cold War: Book I: The Struggle for Centralization, 1945–1960*, pp. 184–6.

9. American Sigint historians have explored the NSA's use of these techniques in Cold War analyses. See Aid, M., 'NSA and the Cold War', *Intelligence and National Security*, 16, no. 1, 2001: 37–9; Bamford, J., *Body of Secrets: Anatomy of the Ultra-Secret National Security Agency* (New York: First Anchor Books, 2002), pp. 254, 566; Budiansky, S., *Code Warriors: NSA's Codebreakers and the Secret Intelligence War Against the Soviet Union* (Vintage Books: New York, 2016), pp. 232–5, 266–8.

10. Hinsley, F. H. and E. E. Thomas, C. Ransom and R. C. Knight, *British Intelligence in the Second World War: Vol. 1* (London: HMSO, 1979), pp. 299–302.

11. Herman, *Intelligence Power in Peace and War*, p. 82.

12. Johnson, *American Cryptology during the Cold War: Book III: Retrenchment and Reform, 1972–1980*, p. 157; Ferris, *Behind the Enigma*, pp. 324–6.

13. The Johnson history observes that, even amid the UK–US political fallout over the Suez crisis, 'COMINT between the two centres continued to flow, people continued to work together, information continued to be exchanged. Such a strong alliance could not be torn asunder by Suez.' See Johnson, *American Cryptology during the Cold War: Book I*, p. 235.

14. Aldrich, *GCHQ*, pp. 289–90; Ferris, *Behind the Enigma*, p. 381.

15. Johnson, *American Cryptology during the Cold War: Book II: Centralization Wins, 1960–1972*, pp. 361–72.

16. The GCHQ history describes the post-war UK–US Sigint agreement as 'a memorandum of understanding between two national interde-partmental intelligence coordinating groups'; see Ferris, *Behind the Enigma*, p. 344.

17. On the Soviet intervention in Afghanistan, the Johnson history notes that '. . . December of 1979 marked a high-water mark of sorts . . . After years of struggle, it was now possible to predict with some clarity and speed the intentions of the major antagonist. It had been a long walk from Pearl Harbor'; see Johnson, *American Cryptology during the Cold War: Book III*, p. 254.

18. Kahn, D., 'Intelligence in World War II: A Survey', *Journal of Intelligence History*, 1, no. 1, 2001: 10–13.

19. Aldrich, *GCHQ*, pp. 96–7; Ferris, *Behind the Enigma*, pp. 347–9, 353–5, 358–9.

20. For instance, on the NSA–GCHQ relationship, the Johnson history observes that 'the two SIGINT operations had become virtually inseparable by 1970'; see Johnson, *American Cryptology during the Cold War: Book II*, p. 415.

21. The 1982 Nicoll Report commended the performance of intelligence warning before the Soviet–Polish crisis, finding that 'the provision of intelligence very rapidly in the building up late-November 1980 and in late-March 1981, enabled sustained and high-level diplomatic action to be taken', with the JIC 'ready to accept immediately the evidence of an "intervention contingency force"'. See the expurgated copy of this report reprinted in Goodman, M., 'The Dog That Didn't Bark: The Joint Intelligence Committee and Warning of Aggression', *Cold War History*, 7, no. 4, 2007: 542.

8   National Requirements[1]

[2019]

I mentioned in an earlier chapter that my approach to intelligence at GCHQ was that of a factory manager interested in volume, accuracy and value, as well as customer satisfaction. On the one hand we strove to deliver a slicker and cheaper product, on the other to make progress in the permanent battle against Soviet security measures. There was a constant striving for quality, with the memories of what Bletchley achieved in the war as an ideal objective. It is from this standpoint that I offer reflections on the system for intelligence requirements and priorities which notionally drove our Cold War activity. Philip Davies has described this formal machinery more extensively in his comparative study of UK and US intelligence,[2] but I add some personal thoughts on it here.

I start with the minutes of a JIC review of Defence Intelligence Targets on 28 April 1955.[3] This meeting was held in the light of a recent JIC assessment that any war with the Soviet Union was likely to be nuclear rather than conventional. It was one of the Committee's more thought-provoking discussions of its intelligence objectives, after a striking and controversial opening statement by Eric Jones, later Sir Eric, who had been GCHQ's Director since 1952. Jones was an unusual leader who had left school at fifteen to join the family textile business before establishing his own firm. He had joined the Royal Air Force in 1940 and then distinguished himself at Bletchley, staying with GCHQ after 1945.[4]

At the JIC, of which GCHQ had just become a full member by 1955, Jones argued that the new assessment of nuclear war meant that Cold War intelligence was now more important than preparations for 'hot' war. He therefore questioned the importance of the JIC's requirements for collecting intelligence on the Soviet order of battle, arguing against detailed specifications of what was sought from GCHQ. Instead he advocated for broad collection objectives with bilateral consultation over implementation. This was in some ways a replay of the wartime debates about Bletchley's role, forcefully brought out in Sir Arthur Bonsall's presentation some years ago at our Oxford Intelligence Group about Bletchley's air section and its struggle to become a Sigint centre.[5] His section had sought to report its exploitation of German communications to whoever needed the results, and not remain a codebreaking agency whose output was only for Air Ministry intelligence to assess and handle. Jones was in a sense putting the same argument for a degree of GCHQ independence in 1955.

Others at the JIC supported the case for flexibility and opportunism, but there was also a sensible military view that commanders in war would use the results of their staffs' studies in peacetime based on what GCHQ could then provide. For forces to have credibility they needed intelligence, including detailed order of battle information, much as they needed effective weapons and training. There was also the need for warning. Armed forces were devised to fight, but their Cold War objective was to deter enemies and encourage allies, particularly through the ability to provide warning of surprise attack. With all these considerations, what priority should be attached to Soviet order of battle – the task that civilians in Whitehall disparaged as 'bean counting' – at a time when analytical thinking was moving towards missiles and nuclear weapons and away from conventional warfare?[6] I recall a later decision that all aspects of the Soviet threat were important, but strategic nuclear capabilities and warning of attack had priority. But the requirements problem raised by Jones was never settled, and many years later Sir Leonard Hooper as GCHQ Director reprised the same argument for more selective Sigint reporting.[7] The question Jones had posed for his Whitehall customers was whether they really needed extensive daily accounts of all Soviet military activities, or just the significant and unusual ones? But how 'unusual' and 'significant' would be defined raised difficult questions that were the nub of the problem.

Against this background, studying Soviet order of battle became the symbol of a running MoD–FCO disagreement in the Cold War over the necessary tasks of intelligence. The British intelligence community was then said to deploy at least sixty per cent of its resources on Soviet and Warsaw Pact collection, mainly against military targets. At GCHQ we tended to say that the Soviet Union absorbed most of our effort, but when we received thanks for useful intelligence they were usually from the Foreign Office and other departments for material on other, smaller targets. It was the difference between helping diplomacy (including economic diplomacy) to achieve tactical successes and monitoring the Soviet military target on which intelligence had fewer immediate demonstrable applications.

In reality I now judge that the intelligence community really exercised five capabilities against the Soviet target. These were peacetime coverage for warning of attack; peacetime coverage of other significant present and future activities, capabilities and intentions inside the Soviet Bloc; the same of Soviet activities in the rest of the world; similar coverage to provide the military data useful in war, including details of Soviet military power; and provision for a continued service if war happened. The last capability was the most problematical of the five, with the heavy costs of providing for any kind of wartime survivability. There had been early post-war plans for Cheltenham to be a combined UK–US wartime Sigint centre,[8] but these were abandoned after the Sandys White Paper of 1957 ruled that major war would be all-out and nuclear if it occurred. The armed services were particularly worried about providing intelligence during war, but no one did much – or could do much – about survivable facilities. The history of Teufelsberg in Chapter 10 of this volume illustrates different ways of meeting the problem. The Royal Air Force opted for Berlin for maximum peacetime effectiveness (including warning) from the location amid its Soviet and East German targets, while the army kept most of its Sigint resources near the Dutch border with vague hopes of wartime survivability.[9] For one of the occasional studies of GCHQ's wartime role it was officially assessed in the 1980s that we would be a target for Soviet air attack in conventional war, and I remember making the unpopular suggestion that, if war seemed imminent, the sensible thing was for most of us to be told to go home and survive for later operation.

This was the background to the JIC's requirements and priorities which developed after 1945. Concerns over wartime intelligence were magnified by warning failures in the Korean War, with the surprise North Korean attack in 1950 and Chinese intervention later that autumn all adding to the American determination not to have a repetition of Pearl Harbor.[10] An American alert system accordingly developed into a Tripartite System with British and Canadian collaboration. There is a received view that Cold War Sigint was all centred on a 'Five-Eyes' US, UK and Old Commonwealth club, with others excluded, but this is a distortion. Soviet success in penetrating other Western allies was such that the product of some UK–US Sigint was indeed not generally shared; but most allied countries were hooked to a significant extent into a near real-time surveillance system for monitoring Soviet military activity. Apart from security questions, speed and technical compatibility of Sigint data were essentials for participation. Hence from GCHQ our priorities were not a purely national matter, and they should be understood in the context of this alliance network.

When I became JIC Secretary I was therefore puzzled by the fact that SIS valued national intelligence requirements so highly. From GCHQ I had seen requirements differently, as useful lists of customers and interests that helped in distributing our reports and those received from allies, but not in driving what we ourselves produced. Our predecessors at Bletchley operated under some formal oversight of their wartime priorities but it did not amount to much; Bletchley's success in breaking and exploiting cipher traffic took place without any formal decisions by its customers over day-to-day priorities in the use of its machines.[11] This independence largely continued in the post-war years, and in my time I probably thought along the lines set out by Jones in 1955. For Humint, however, the status of intelligence requirements was different, and its origins can be found in Philip Davies's account of MI6's creation in 1909, when they were designed so that the military services and Foreign Office could formally task the new Secret Service Bureau's espionage to meet their precise needs, and supply the results for them to handle.[12] Sigint developed differently after 1914 because, though it was a natural adjunct to military and naval intelligence, it developed with more independence through the technicalities of interception and the sensitivities of codebreaking. The two approaches to customer requirements merge but there was a difference of balance between them.

Statements of requirements and priorities appeared periodically on the JIC's agenda after 1945. The post-war continuation of the Committee made it possible for the first time to think of British intelligence as a community, and what was needed from it, although these statements were designed as guidance and did not have the prescriptive authority of the earlier Humint requirements.[13] The requirements system then attracted more attention with Britain's imperial retreat in the 1960s, when the Cold War had settled into a mood of détente after the Cuban crisis, and it was also a period of economic decline and withdrawal from imperial positions in Africa and 'east of Suez'. This produced a conviction in Whitehall that money could be saved by cutting intelligence requirements appropriately, often with the Soviet order of battle quoted as a target for reduction. An ambitious JIC study was undertaken to establish Whitehall's total information needs, intelligence and non-intelligence, but it ran into the sand by the late 1960s. As with an attempted inventory of economic requirements, connected with the economic JIC created in 1968, this project was sunk by the sheer scale of all the relevant information and the undefined boundaries of intelligence assessment.[14] It was just too difficult, and eventually a clever diplomat instead produced a moderate report on the changed requirements in the Far East that satisfied everybody.

In the late 1960s the guidance role was shuffled to the newly established Coordinator and his annual review. In 1972 as JIC Secretary I brashly persuaded his successor (Wilkinson) to abandon the lists of requirements. Aside from SIS, the GCHQ attitude was passive, and it was never clear whether the Security Service was bound by the JIC's requirements and priorities, while the DIS needed to have its formulations rubber-stamped by the Chiefs of Staff. No one objected to the changes, but in the second half of the 1970s the lists gradually crept in again. I had suggested that a machinery be established to consider specific conflicting customer demands, but within a short time this reverted to producing annual documents. These were limited to the collection agencies and became

progressively more elaborate. Sir Antony Duff as Coordinator subsequently tried to give the system some teeth in the use of resources,
and I recall an argument with him when warning of Soviet preparations for war had formal priority over insight into Soviet objectives,
which was lower down the list.

I have no recollection that requirements and priorities documents ever changed anything we did. On balance they did no harm
but produced little good. They were blamed in the official inquiry
into the Argentine invasion of the Falklands since they gave a low
priority to intelligence coverage of the threat: not a good advertise-
ment for the system, though this may have been a convenient excuse
after the event.[15] I now think my own attitude was too dismissive,
overlooking the extent to which formal requirements and priorities may have at least offered a back-up to the individual relationships between collection agencies and Whitehall customers. Annual
meetings with customers to prepare the lists were useful, but I still
see them mainly as an exercise in legitimisation.[16]

Jones was probably right in 1955 to resist tight control of what
GCHQ did and how it reported the output, but the corollary was
that GCHQ should work closely with the military staffs and programme its effort to meet their needs. This sounds easy, but with
the peacetime structure it was not as easy as it sounds, not least
because there are varying priorities with multiple customers at different levels of command. I think it a pity that the requirements
and priorities developed quite as they did, in mainly geographical
terms. I would have preferred more consideration of priorities in
terms of the varied kinds of government activity that intelligence
supported. An example might be weighing its tactical assistance
for Britain punching above its diplomatic weight against the value
of its contribution to military planning. I have an impression that
the intelligence priorities we heard tended to be those of Whitehall
rather than those operating abroad. But changing this would have
required a new approach to intelligence strategy, and – even if it
had succeeded – it would never have produced a perfect solution.

This is not pessimism. I was impressed some time ago by the academic literature on the complexity of human affairs, and the role of
imperfect and partial understanding in dealing with them: in effect
the value of so-called 'satisficing', taking short cuts in economic and

administrative decisions.[17] Intelligence as we know it is an entrepreneurial activity with its own dynamics, but it needs some democratic accountability. If we believe that the British intelligence community is more than a collection of independent agencies working across departments, then government must have a means of directing it as a whole. But effectiveness in this task needs a light touch. Satisficing to provide adequate direction of intelligence may depend less on formal requirements and priorities than on the character of its leaders, and their reliability in following general guidance from government – in the ethics as well as the priorities of intelligence collection.

This brings me back to my opening picture of Sir Eric Jones and his leadership. I do suggest that the character and impact of intelligence leaders – though difficult to assess – is something that those studying Cold War history should consider in their future research.

Notes

1. Adapted from a presentation to the Study Group on Intelligence at the Royal United Services Institute, London, 17 May 2019.
2. Davies, P. H. J., *Intelligence and Government in Britain and the United States: A Comparative Perspective, Volume 2: Evolution of the UK Intelligence Community* (Santa Barbara, CA: Praeger, 2012).
3. Confidential Annex to JIC (55) 34th meeting, 28 April 1955, CAB 159/19, The National Archives (UK); Ferris, J., *Behind the Enigma: The Authorised History of GCHQ, Britain's Secret Cyber-Intelligence Agency* (London: Bloomsbury, 2020), p. 508.
4. Nicoll, D. R., 'Sir Eric Malcolm Jones, 1907–1986', in *Oxford Dictionary of National Biography*. Jones's post-war contribution to GCHQ is discussed in Chapter 19 of this collection, 'GCHQ Directors'.
5. This was first delivered to the Oxford Intelligence Group at Nuffield College in 2007, and later published as 'Bletchley Park and the RAF Y Service: Some Recollections', *Intelligence and National Security*, 23, no. 6, 2008: 827–41.
6. Dylan, H., *Defence Intelligence and the Cold War: Britain's Joint Intelligence Bureau, 1954–1964* (Oxford: Oxford University Press, 2014), pp. 126–36.
7. I recall Hooper's advocacy on this point in the early 1970s, and recently seeing material to this effect, but cannot recall the reference.

8. Ferris, *Behind the Enigma*, p. 270.
9. Chapter 10 in this collection, 'Teufelsberg'.
10. Johnston, T. R., 'American Cryptology During the Korean War: Opening the Door a Crack', *Studies in Intelligence*, 45, no. 3, 2001: 33; Grabo, C. M., 'The Watch Committee and the National Indications Center: The Evolution of U.S. Strategic Warning 1950–75', *International Journal of Intelligence and Counterintelligence*, 3, no. 3, 1989: 363–86.
11. Ferris, *Behind the Enigma*, pp. 178–89, 213–20.
12. Davies, P. H. J., *MI6 and the Machinery of Spying* (London: Frank Cass, 2004), p. 50.
13. A copy of one such statement is reprinted in Aldrich, R. J. and M. Coleman, 'The Cold War, the JIC and British Signals Intelligence, 1948', *Intelligence and National Security*, 4, no. 3, 1989: 546–9.
14. Davies, *Intelligence and Government in Britain and the United States*, pp. 206–10, 221–2.
15. Intelligence requirements are mentioned in paras 304, 311 and 318 of the report; see *Falkland Islands Review: Report of a Committee of Privy Counsellors* (London: HMSO, 1983), pp. 82–6.
16. Herman, M., *Intelligence Power in Peace and War* (Cambridge: Cambridge University Press/RIIA, 1996), pp. 288–92.
17. This concept was developed by the American economist and psychologist, Herbert Simon. See for example Simon, H., *Administrative Behaviour: A Study of Decision-Making Processes in Administrative Organisations*, 4th edition (New York: The Free Press, 1997).

9 Manual Morse and the Intelligence Gold Standard[1]

[2009]

Wartime Bletchley was the centre for Britain's development of a 'gold standard' of intelligence professionalism, which the UK and US then applied to the challenges of the Cold War.[2] I have argued elsewhere that, despite the limitations in its understanding of the Soviet Union, intelligence became a steadying influence on Western governments. On balance it was an antidote to fears that we might be hit by a Soviet bolt from the blue, or that new Soviet weaponry would suddenly outclass Western military forces.[3] The legacy of Bletchley's professionalism was a force for sanity on these and other questions, and part of this intelligence gold standard was the basic skill of interception – plucking radio signals out of the sky – on which most of the Sigint process depended. This is a note on the introduction to this skill which I was given when I first joined GCHQ.

After its move from Bletchley at the end of the war GCHQ had retained part of the site as a training school for the civilian radio operators still employed by the three service ministries as well as GCHQ. As a newly joined trainee I was sent to Bletchley in the winter of 1952–3 to learn something about interception. I have mixed memories of the time: no Milton Keynes existed, and old Bletchley town was not exactly a centre for swinging youth. But I was introduced there to the craft of signals interception, at a time when the basic technology and skills were still essentially unchanged from wartime.

To understand interception as it was then, I was taught to think of two distinctive features of communications in the immediate post-war period: high frequency (HF) radio, and the morse code used on HF transmissions. Radio in the First World War had used the low frequencies now found on the long and medium wave-bands of domestic receivers, but by the Second World War military communications had largely moved to HF, or what was then labelled 'short-wave'. This technique used radio transmissions at frequencies that bounced off layers of the ionosphere and facili-tated long-distance contacts, sometimes through multiple bounces. The heights of these ionospheric layers at any time determined what signals could be picked up, and where and when, but they were constantly changing, particularly between night and day and by the different seasons of the year. Predictions about the iono-sphere were said to be about as reliable as weather forecasts, then well below modern standards, and these communications were also beset by fading, background noise, and interference from other signals. As for the 'manual morse' used on these frequen-cies (morse code spelt out by hand), this had been the staple of radio communications since their first invention, and experienced communicators sent and received it at what seemed like impos-sibly high speeds. Some languages had special morse characters for certain letters, and there were also distinctive regional styles of sending.

All this meant that communicating and receiving radio signals was itself a skilled business, and the eavesdropper had to cope with the additional difficulties of his task. He would only rarely be in an optimum location for hearing his target signals, and he could not communicate with the senders to ask them to stop and repeat things he had missed, as an intended receiver normally could. The targets probably used encrypted and frequently changing secret callsigns to identify themselves, and would transmit on undeclared frequencies that changed from day to night, by season, and often more regularly for security reasons. The two ends of a radio link might also communicate on different frequencies. In difficult cases the intercept operator might have to search a crowded frequency band for his target with no guidance except his knowledge of the sort of traffic it passed, or a memory for particular transmitter notes or the morse styles of individual operators.[4] This was all made more difficult by the fact that, in the post-war years as in wartime, the radios used by targets and interceptors still relied on thermionic valves that could be unstable in the frequencies of the signals they produced, and that needed constant tuning to receive them properly. A bottom line of our training was that all target signals were liable to be 'difficult' signals, and the trained interceptor could be satisfied by nothing less than one hundred per cent accuracy in the traffic he copied, or success in getting the direction finding of a brief signal.[5]

This was the craft explained by my admirable instructors at Bletchley. They were fatherly men, with long radio experience in the Post Office or Merchant Navy, sometimes going back to before the First World War. I learned to copy morse, though not to a useful operational speed, and they taught me how to operate my receivers – two, to cope with the two ends of a target link if on different frequencies – and select the best aerial for each. One's left hand had to be free for constant retuning to cope with frequencies 'wandering' in one's receiver or in the target transmitters. The intercepted traffic was written down in pencil with one's right hand, with multiple carbons and as near an approach to copperplate as one could manage. The Americans were then starting to use typewriters, but this was frowned on by the Bletchley perfectionists: one hand always had to be free for wandering signals, while copying with the other. At that time there was still a wartime assumption that we were the teachers, and the Americans the pupils, although this prejudice soon disappeared.[6]

These HF morse transmissions had not been the only wartime targets. Still higher frequencies – including those now labelled FM on our personal radios – were already being used for radio telephony, especially by aircraft, and automated transmissions were also expanding.[7] After the war there were moves towards higher frequencies for all applications but HF morse tasks still predominated, particularly in the coverage of the conscript Soviet/Warsaw Pact and Chinese armies, and they lasted into the final decade of the Cold War. I understand that much of this technology – certainly the reliance on the morse code – is now part of vanished history. Yet the lessons I learned in 1952–3 about the skill of finding and copying 'difficult' HF morse signals was a reminder that the gold standard of intelligence was a matter of collecting evidence as well as exploiting its content. Bletchley's wartime successes drew on the operator's ability to pluck transmissions out of the air as much as the task of steering interception and extracting value from it.[8] This apparently unexciting twenty-four-hour work at the intercept sites was a principal investment of manpower, and the large civilian effort to recruit and train radio HF morse operators gave the GCHQ workforce some of its characteristics for as long as the Cold War lasted.[9] It was at the centre of the staff problems that led to de-unionisation in 1984, and all that followed. My comments written shortly after this incident are reproduced in Chapter 3, though I add a further speculation in the conclusion below.

These were not the only effects of the HF morse targets, however. The business of interception also influenced the organisational structure of Cold War Sigint. The challenge of reliably intercepting HF signals had produced stations with suitable aerial fields on flat areas without obstruction, and at some distance from towns to avoid electrical interference. Having multiple interception sites of this kind provided some diversity against the vagaries of the ionosphere, and direction finding produced its own need for multiple, dispersed sites coordinated to produce location fixes. The value of this diversity combined with the mixed management of armed forces' and civilian resources produced a pattern of small-to-medium size interception stations dotted around the British Isles by the time of the Second World War, not close to towns and not co-located with Bletchley. Throughout the Cold War there was a gradual rationalisation of these stations, but the basic separation and difference between them and Sigint headquarters remained.[10] This became an imprint on our occupational psychology: everyone thought of himself or herself as either a 'station' or 'headquarters' person, with quite different roles, careers, rewards and positions in the hierarchy, and with different reactions to trade union pressures and inducements. All this was the pattern of twentieth-century Sigint organisation that can be traced back to the properties of the ionosphere.

The technical requirements for intercepting Soviet transmissions were also part of the dynamic of the intelligence war itself.

As pointed out in another chapter,[11] HF radio transmissions could be intercepted at considerable distances, but not everywhere; the historian should generally think in terms of hundreds of miles rather than thousands. Some wartime Japanese transmissions were regularly intercepted in the UK at certain times and seasons, but that was exceptional. Most HF interception had to be in the same theatre of war as its targets. In the Cold War, Soviet Bloc and Chinese transmissions could not be heard properly on American home territory, and without such a home base American Sigint needed to have intercept stations on allies' territories, or arrangements to receive allies' own 'take', or combinations of both. One effect of this was to underline the cooperative nature of the Western alliance: Washington could not fight the intelligence war without partners, or at least the cooperation of allies in the use of their territory.[12] Another was to reinforce the geopolitical landscape of the East–West divide, with Western Sigint stations deployed around the Soviet periphery looking in, and the adversary inside it looking out. What seems like mundane radio technicalities thus had their influence on the form of the Cold War itself and the organisations that fought it.

This brings me back to a detail in the history of GCHQ's relationship with its operators' unions. After the two unions' 'work to rule' in 1969 I was shown a copy of the official brief to the first, rejected arbitration of that year, and was struck at the time that the official side claimed less than usual for operators' skills in finding and following their targets. It drew instead a mechanistic analogy with the brain and the hand: GCHQ told the hand where to look for the target, and the hand looked and found it.[13] I speculate that this may have reflected an unobtrusive change over the previous twenty years as radio transistors systematically replaced valves, and operators no longer had to cope to the same extent with wandering signals. How far this was a significant factor in changing the interception business needs a more informed discussion than I can offer, although I note that Professor Ferris's history also lays emphasis on automation as a cause for discontent among some veterans by the late 1960s.[14] I include it here as an addendum to the professionalism of these operators and their craft.

Notes

1. Adapted from a presentation at the Buckingham University conference 'Bletchley Park and British Intelligence: Confronting Security Challenges, Past and Present' at Bletchley Park, 20 May 2009.
2. The literature on wartime Bletchley is now quite large. On the characteristics of Bletchley's performance compared with its German counterparts, see Ratcliff, R. A., *Delusions of Intelligence: Enigma, Ultra, and the End of Secure Ciphers* (New York: Cambridge University Press, 2006).
3. Chapter 6 in this collection, 'What Difference Did it Make?'.
4. One account of allied codebreaking suggests that 'the style, habits and eccentricities of virtually every enemy wireless operator were recorded somewhere on a card index' by the end of the Second World War. See West, N., *GCHQ: The Secret Wireless War, 1900–86* (London: Weidenfeld and Nicolson, 1986), p. 214.
5. Ralph Erskine quotes an internal history of the wartime Y service observing that 'a good operator was nine-tenths of the battle' for the HF Direction Finding intercept stations. See Erskine, R., 'Shore High-Frequency Direction-Finding in the Battle of the Atlantic: An Undervalued Intelligence Asset', *Journal of Intelligence History*, 4, no. 2, 2004: 13.
6. A historian of the US Army Security Agency notes that '. . . having relied mostly on the British for wartime cryptanalysis in Europe, the Americans in late 1945 lacked the technical equipment and adequately trained personnel to intercept communications from deep within Soviet-controlled areas of Europe'. See Boghardt, T., 'Semper Vigilis: The US Army Security Agency in Early Cold War Germany', *Army History*, 106, winter 2018: 16.
7. Very high frequency (VHF) for aircraft communications was already developed for use in the Korean War. See Johnson, T. R., 'American Cryptology During the Korean War: Opening the Door a Crack', *Studies in Intelligence*, 45, no. 3, 2001: 35–6.
8. This contribution was emphasised by Alan Stripp, a wartime codebreaker posted to Delhi, who recalled the 'hundreds of Indian wireless operators whose patriotism at such a time, coinciding with the "Quit India" campaign, could easily have pulled them in another direction. When signals were appallingly faint, the temptation to write down gibberish must, one would think, have been strong.' See Stripp, A., 'Breaking Japanese Codes', *Intelligence and National Security*, 2, no. 4, 1987: 147–8.

9. The ability to copy morse was also the main skill of the uniformed operators in the three services, though there was also a significant proportion of voice operators. Some of the entrants as GCHQ operators were former uniformed operators who had been accepted at the completion of their service engagements.

10. Ferris, J., *Behind the Enigma: The Authorised History of GCHQ, Britain's Secret Cyber-Intelligence Agency* (London: Bloomsbury, 2020), pp. 460–6.

11. Chapter 10 in this collection, 'Teufelsberg'.

12. Budiansky, S., *Code Warriors: NSA's Codebreakers and the Secret Intelligence War Against the Soviet Union* (Vintage Books: New York, 2016), pp. 172–3.

13. Ferris, *Behind the Enigma*, p. 469.

14. Ibid., pp. 466–7.

10 Teufelsberg[1]

[2016]

In 1950 the West Berlin authorities began dumping debris from wartime bombing in the Grunewald, in the British sector. The rubble pile was known as the Teufelsberg and it soon became the highest point in the city with a summit about 400 feet above sea level. From the early 1960s this man-made hill hosted a joint British and American Sigint site which operated until the end of the Cold War. I was involved at one stage in planning this site, and offer here some recollections of the experience.

Why were important Sigint resources located in West Berlin, in the middle of the deployed Soviet and East German armies and air forces, and why in particular were they placed on a rubble pile? The answer lay in the physics of radio transmissions. Radio waves travel in straight lines and do not bend around the earth's circumference, or not much. At some frequencies they bounce off layers of the ionosphere between 75 and 250 miles above the earth, and thus are suitable for long-distance communication. Many of our Soviet targets in the Cold War were of this kind: high frequency (HF) transmissions which could be effectively intercepted at ranges of some hundreds of miles. Other targets operated differently, using higher frequencies which did not have this ionospheric effect; instead they transmitted over a limited range, akin to those of personal VHF radios. This second category included Soviet radio-relay systems, radars and other Elint emissions, battlefield radio and air-ground plain language. For all of these targets the interceptor had to get close, ideally within line of sight of the transmitters, with audibility increased by the height of the target, the intercept site, or both. Our Sigint targets in Germany were a mixture of those which needed this type of close access (particularly air-ground voice) and those in the HF range, which were interceptable over longer distances. Many other factors influenced the location and tasking of the British Sigint stations, but all depended on the audibility of their targets.

Radio interception of both kinds had provided Allied commanders with tactical intelligence in the wartime re-conquest of Europe, and after 1945 the British Sigint units in occupied Germany were deployed to provide similar coverage of the Soviet and Warsaw Pact forces confronting them across the East–West border. They continued to be service-manned, not civilian, and to provide tactical intelligence direct to the headquarters of the British Northern Army Group and 2nd Tactical Air Force, as well as GCHQ and a wide range of other British, American and Canadian recipients.[2] By the end of the 1950s the British Army and Air Force had established their principal stations deep inside the territory of West Germany; the army near the Dutch border in Birgelin, and the RAF near Cologne. These stations conducted long-distance interception of army and air targets in the Soviet Forward Area, but it was soon recognised that they also needed forward detachments to intercept short-range transmissions, particularly the plain language air-ground messages to and from Soviet Bloc aircraft. Detachments were deployed on the East–West border but the richest interception site turned out to be West Berlin, in the midst of the Soviet army deployments and Soviet and East German airfields.[3] An RAF detachment for this purpose was established in 1951 at Gatow, the pre-war German Air Force station, and an army detachment soon followed it there.[4]

By the 1960s this was still not an optimum arrangement. Communications trends were making Berlin an increasingly advantageous site, but its intercepted material was signalled to the main stations in West Germany to be exploited for tactical intelligence. It made professional sense to concentrate more resources in Berlin, including reporting, but there were practical reasons against a major relocation there, including the risk of exposing more young servicemen to the approaches of the KGB and GRU.[5] Underlying all this planning in Germany was the open question about intelligence support in wartime. Armed forces needed Sigint in a military conflict, but what survivable arrangements should be provided for nuclear or conventional war, and at what cost? Moreover, how important was this wartime requirement set against the peacetime task of monitoring Soviet intentions and building up knowledge of Soviet forces, for which Berlin was so obviously suitable?

These questions about Western Sigint rumbled on as a whole without clear resolution.[6] There were worries about intelligence survivability, but while NATO planned for war, intelligence collection itself was not a NATO subject. The British answers were pragmatic, perhaps reflecting the instincts of an island power. Soviet forces were the prime intelligence target, but with priority given to peacetime coverage rather than the more difficult, expensive and competing goal of wartime survivability. It was judged better to have successful collection in peace than catering for the war everyone sought to avoid, although this could never persuade the military commanders whose professional role had to involve preparations for a battle in Germany.[7]

In the event, a striking clarification came unexpectedly from the RAF in the mid-1960s through one of the Labour government's financial crises. Perhaps because it was having problems with recruitment – service conscription had ended some years previously – the RAF offered up widespread Sigint economies, including closing its Cologne station and moving everything to Berlin. GCHQ embraced this idea for its combination of economy and operational efficiency, and intelligence in the RAF's wartime role was largely set aside. The army worried more about war and kept the division between the main unit in West Germany and its forward detachments including Berlin.[8] Eventually it found the money for a sizeable Electronic Warfare unit expressly for a tactical wartime role, with no formal part of peacetime operations; I understand that it was subsequently important in post-Cold War operations overseas. The end of the 1960s therefore saw the whole RAF effort and the small army detachment well established in the facilities at Gatow. This was assumed to be as permanent as anything in the Cold War could be, but it did not last: the new arrangements were soon jettisoned for the appeal of Teufelsberg five miles away.

This change arose from a combination of front-line enthusiasm, a senior GCHQ analyst's pursuit of excellence, a couple of personal relationships, and – above all – unexpected financial backing. I became responsible at GCHQ for interception planning at the beginning of 1964, and the American army had been experimenting with Sigint on the summit of Teufelsberg from 1961. The attraction of this unconventional site lay simply in its height advantage for intercepting the short-range Soviet Bloc communications we otherwise covered at Gatow. It was also in what was still technically the British occupation sector of Berlin, and the RAF had taken advantage of this fact to establish a hut there alongside the Americans, as part of its effort against the distant Polish and Czech air forces. The position in 1964 was that the American army had ambitious ideas for the site, while the US Air Force's Sigint unit was well established elsewhere in Berlin and had no wish to move. The UK had its small Teufelsberg operation, but had declared at a high level that it had no other claims on the site.

Local initiative then took a hand. The RAF officer who commanded the Gatow detachment took a couple of voice operators to Teufelsberg and assessed the audibility there of the RAF's main targets at Gatow. This trial bore out the theoretical figures he hoped for: Teufelsberg's height advantage provided a modest increase over Gatow's interception range, and a significant one in the actual ground area covered. Particular advantages were found in the coverage of important Soviet airfields at the limits of Gatow's normal range, and of the low-altitude operations that were increasingly practised by Soviet tactical units. The officer's report recommended a substantial redeployment to Teufelsberg.

At first no one took the report seriously, but then personal networks came into play. The RAF officer was friendly with the deputy head of the GCHQ production branch that controlled the unit's operations, and he passed her a copy of his report in the hope she could do something about it. It happened that this GCHQ official was – and still is – a lady of energy, talent and wartime experience, who could be impatient with peacetime procedures. It also happened that she and I were on good terms from working together in our previous jobs, in which I had developed great respect – sometimes fear – for the ability and passion she brought to our profession. The upshot was that I was bombarded with the case for Teufelsberg and persuaded to act on it. Looking back it was perhaps more akin to a surrender. Whatever the motives, the planning machinery swung into action to transfer virtually all of the RAF's Comint effort from Gatow to Teufelsberg, where it and the British army detachment would operate alongside the US Army station. The Elint effort would remain at Gatow. This concept was accepted by the British and American authorities, and successive RAF unit commanders threw themselves into solving the many problems arising from the relocation and operation on this site shared with the Americans, five miles away from their base.

There were many delays, but by the second half of the 1970s the unit was working effectively in impressive new facilities. It happened with remarkably little friction. Striving for the improved interception promised had a professional attraction for the RAF unit, especially if it would give them a technical edge over their American Air Force colleagues elsewhere in the city. The American army already stationed on Teufelsberg could have treated the British as unwelcome latecomers, but they showed a high degree of cooperation in the planning and sharing that was needed. At the planning stage there were technical concerns about mutual interference between the proposed British and American aerials, but these eventually ended when the Americans agreed to the British bid for an unusually high aerial mast, thereby accepting a degree of interference with their own direction finding operations. It was a striking example of effective joint planning, and I flatter myself that it may have owed a little to the early meeting of all concerned, in the American Embassy in London, for which with the rashness of youth I booked a good lunch for everyone in an impressive club, ignoring all the rules for obtaining prior financial approval.

This may have helped, but any goodwill it produced was icing on the cake. What made the Teufelsberg project possible was that it was substantially funded by what was in effect free money, through the anomaly of what was known as the Berlin Budget. Until the end of the Cold War the city remained frozen in its nominal 1945 state of occupation by the four military powers. West Berlin was not included in the creation of the Federal Republic in 1949, and was not part of NATO. The Western Powers were still reimbursed for the so-called supporting costs of their Berlin garrison, in annual agreements reached discreetly with the West Berlin authority; though no doubt the Federal government blessed this financial assistance for the Western Allies' protection of Berlin as its Cold War outpost. As far as I know, the other British projects for the Budget had been of a military welfare character, such as family accommodation and sports clubs, not overt military support, and from my experience there were no precedents for using it to support intelligence.[9] Nevertheless, the RAF suggested that a case should be made for funding Teufelsberg, and in the event it was an important part of the whole scheme. Perhaps it helped that the technical equipment would be purchased locally as a boost to the booming West German electronics industry. However it happened, the money was a slice of good fortune. The RAF was able to specify and obtain state-of-the-art technical equipment. For once, a British military station was well equipped on equal terms with its American ally, and did not have to operate in the top league with cut price equipment.

Are there lessons for the historian in this episode of Cold War intelligence? One is its reminder that an important part of the combined British and American Sigint effort was made up of the uniformed, armed services elements, and that these bore the main load of forward interception and tactical reporting in Germany and elsewhere. GCHQ was the British Sigint authority, but its relationships with its national armed services were those of a federation rather than a commanding hierarchy. Bletchley had emerged from wartime as the coordinating centre for Sigint,[10] at the heart of shared military and civilian resources, and this was the basis for GCHQ's post-war role. The same was basically true on the American side, though their national inter-agency tensions tended to be more acute. The close UK–US cooperation that developed under the UKUSA Sigint agreement embraced the relationships between the UK and US military elements as well as those between the civilian GCHQ and NSA. It is not always recognised now that cooperation was as real in the field as it was between the headquarters.

Was Teufelsberg worth it? I doubt whether it ever had a proper cost-effectiveness study. Governments do not look backwards in this way, except in the search for scapegoats. I now think that our

Teufelsberg project owed something to the impetuosity of youth: our modern successors may be far more rigorous in their decision-taking. But I have no reason to regret it. NATO's air forces needed to know how the potential enemy would fight and how effective he would be. It was no secret on either side of the Cold War divide that Berlin was the West's prime listening post for seeking answers out of stereotyped, security-conscious Soviet conversations studied in depth. The urge to get the best quality for this material through the collection on the rubble pile was surely a professionally healthy one. It is also a reminder how much Cold War intelligence production was a matter of squeezing valuable insights from unpromising material, as on the Teufelsberg.

Notes

1. Adapted from a presentation at the 22nd annual conference of the International Intelligence History Association (IIHA) in Dresden, Germany, 15–17 April 2016.
2. Aldrich, R. J., 'Intelligence within BAOR and NATO's Northern Army Group', *Journal of Strategic Studies*, 31, no. 1, 2008: 102–3, 112–14.
3. In the words of an internal NSA history, 'Berlin became a SIGINT gold mine, a window into the heart of the Communist Bloc military system'. See Johnson T. R., *American Cryptology during the Cold War, 1945–1989: Book I: The Struggle for Centralization, 1945–1960* (Washington, DC: Centre for Cryptologic History, 1995), p. 118.
4. Kevin Paul Wright has also written about the separate intelligence-gathering flights to and from Gatow airfield. See Wright, K. P., 'Cold War Reconnaissance Flights along the Berlin Corridors and in the Berlin Control Zone 1960–90: Risk, Coordination and Sharing', *Intelligence and National Security*, 30, no. 5, 2015: 621.
5. Geoffrey Prime and Brian Patchett were two such examples in the 1960s. Prime, the Soviet agent at GCHQ, first offered his services to the Soviet Union during his RAF deployment to Gatow; see Aldrich R. J., *GCHQ: The Uncensored Story of Britain's Most Secret Intelligence Agency* (London: Harper Press, 2010), pp. 370–6. Patchett defected to the East from Gatow in 1963 after making several requests for a transfer; see Croxson, P., 'Sergeant Brian Patchett and Other Wall-Crossers', The Military Intelligence Museum, accessed

on 6 October 2020 at: http://www.intelligencemuseum.org/assets/pdf/articles/news12_patchett.pdf

6. Aldrich, *GCHQ*, pp. 448–9, 451–2.

7. The history of GCHQ notes Sigint efforts to enhance tactical support for operations during the 1980s, but argues that 'the NATO Sigint system would have collapsed in a hot war'. See Ferris, J., *Behind the Enigma: The Authorised History of GCHQ, Britain's Secret Cyber-Intelligence Agency* (London: Bloomsbury, 2020), pp. 513–14 (quote on p. 551).

8. Ibid., p. 526.

9. Although Richard Aldrich cites a presentation by Col. Roy Giles describing the BRIXMIS missions as being paid for by the West Berlin Senate. See Aldrich, 'Intelligence within BAOR and NATO's Northern Army Group', p. 105.

10. Grey, C., 'The Making of Bletchley Park and Signals Intelligence 1939–42', *Intelligence and National Security*, 28, no. 6, 2013: 785–807. See also Sir Arthur Bonsall's account, 'Bletchley Park and the RAF Y Service: Some Recollections', *Intelligence and National Security*, 23, no. 6, 2008: 827–41.

PART 3

Organisation and Reform

11 1945 Organisation[1]

[2011]

A report on post-war organisation of intelligence was presented to the Joint Intelligence Subcommittee of the Chiefs of Staff (the JIC, hereafter 'the Committee') on 10 January 1945 and was given the striking subtitle of 'The Intelligence Machine', in itself a sign of the new way of thinking about intelligence that had developed during the war. The idea of intelligence as a single entity had some ancestry. Shakespeare wrote of it in the singular, as in 'Where hath our Intelligence been drunk, where hath it slept?' in his *King John*, and the 1945 report followed this antique usage in referring to 'our Intelligence Service' and 'our Secret Service'.[2] But this idea of 'the intelligence' as a collective had always been a shadowy one. This report was the first serious British attempt – possibly the first attempt anywhere – to set out a plan for it as a complete, interlocking, peacetime system, perhaps the first recognition of intelligence power as part of the modern state.

The individual intelligence institutions in it were of course older. The British Navy and Army had acquired their intelligence directors and staffs in the last quarter of the nineteenth century, but there was no particular thought then about a collective identity or cooperation between them. A wide-ranging investigation of intelligence led to the creation of the Secret Service Bureau in 1909, but the result was to separate covert collection from the naval and army directorates, not bring all the elements together. Though the First World War produced intelligence activity on a quite unprecedented scale, it remained organised mainly in single-service bodies, not joint-service ones. Even before 1914 the offices just established for espionage and counterespionage were developing separately, and from the post-war reviews of 1919 and 1921 they emerged as the separate civilian Security Service (MI5) and Secret Intelligence Service (SIS or MI6), divided roughly between home and foreign targets. (This chapter uses these two organisational titles but otherwise uses 'service' and 'services' to denote armed forces.) The post-war reviews also established codebreaking in the civilian Government Code and Cypher School (GC&CS) under C, the head of SIS (the abbreviation 'C' for 'Chief' dates back to the first occupant of the post and is still used). The inter-war period saw varied relationships between these new bodies and the older service directorates, and there was a hint of the future in the creation of the small, non-departmental, civilian Industrial Intelligence Centre (IIC) to study the economies of potential enemies. Nevertheless, the post-1918 system was mainly one of separate institutions without formal coordinating machinery. There was still a particular gulf between the civilian collectors of secret intelligence and the military intelligence authorities who used the results. Treating it all as a whole was some way ahead.

This began in a small way with the creation of the JIC in 1936 for the coordination of Service Intelligence by the three armed forces' directors, reporting to the Chiefs of Staff. It acquired its Foreign Office membership and chairmanship in 1939, and the SIS, Security Service, and Ministry of Economic Warfare (MEW) became members in the following year. It received directions in the summer of 1939 for coordinating, reporting and assessing intelligence for top government (its expert assessment role), and for managing intelligence to include consideration of 'any further measures which might be necessary in order to improve the efficient working of the intelligence organisation of the country as a whole'.[3] Much was subsequently made in the official intelligence history of this reference to 'intelligence as a whole' as a landmark, an idea that 'had been evolving for twenty years, but evolving slowly, haphazardly and only in response to events in the absence of a single coordinating authority'.[4]

Ideas were certainly changing, but there is a danger of reading too much into the wording produced in that 1939 summer of preparation for war. The civilian agencies were by then well aware of the JIC: the IIC director, Desmond Morton (with an SIS affiliation) had attended some of its meetings, and Security Service and SIS representatives had been present occasionally.[5] But the civilian-military gap remained: in 1945 Morton, who had been the director of intelligence at the MEW in 1939–40, wrote later that even in that first year of war 'the military men . . . could not bring themselves to admit that war was really the concern of men in plain clothes'.[6] The JIC's purpose was still to get the military services to talk to each other, and the civilians were incidental. There is no evidence that they had been consulted about the 1939 wording which on the face of it brought them within the military's purview.

What is more important is that wartime intelligence was subsequently not quite as close-knit as has sometimes been presented. The JIC's assessments were important at the top politico-strategic level, but below it the war was run mainly through single-service command structures with single-service intelligence staffs. In its managerial role, the JIC and its subcommittees were a success in the establishment and control of new joint-service organisations, but in this the civilian agencies were less involved. Signals Intelligence (Sigint), the most important wartime intelligence source, had its own nominal supervisory machinery, and remained outside the JIC's control. So did the disputes between SIS and the Security Service, though those between SIS and the Special Operations Executive (SOE) did come to the Committee. The war certainly closed the military-civilian gaps, but by no means completely.

Nevertheless, by 1944–5 the idea of 'the intelligence organisation as a whole' was catching on. The January 1945 report put it that the JIC 'has developed into a forum for discussion of all matters of common "intelligence" interest to its members, and thus into a kind of Board of Directors laying down interservice intelligence and security policy at home and abroad'.[7] This was still gilding the lily, but was nevertheless not far from what was happening and what people thought was happening. Intelligence had developed greatly since 1939, and the 1945 report's title of the 'machine' captured the wartime shift from cottage industry towards mass production, speed and interconnection, though we now prefer to call it the less mechanistic 'community'.[8] It needed a peacetime structure, and it got it from the 1945 report and how it was implemented. These are subjects of this chapter.

Background

The government's planning of post-war Britain began in early 1943, and in intelligence the post-war future of its effort on economic targets was raised by the MEW in the summer of that year. The JIC's chairman proposed in a minute dated 13 October that post-war planning should have some consideration, and at a committee discussion on 26 October there was agreement that 'it was most desirable that the present machinery for collecting and collating intelligence' should continue after the war, and that 'if possible, there should continue to be a central coordinating body'.[9] In the first half of 1944 the three service directors were asked to produce papers on the future of the wartime interservice bodies for which they had taken responsibility, but these do not seem to have appeared.[10] In September the Director of Naval Intelligence raised the future of the interservice topographical studies that he ran, but this study seems to have been held up until the JIC's report appeared in January 1945.[11]

Post-war planning was by then a growth area everywhere, and this report was by no means the only intelligence study under way. It mentioned the separate study of topographic intelligence.[12] It also referred to the 'enquiries being made under other auspices' into the future of SIS and the Security Service.[13] The fate of SOE was being canvassed. A further study was also in progress that led to the creation of Government Communications Headquarters (GCHQ) as the national Sigint centre, replacing GC&CS. Bletchley had begun its own work on this in September 1944, and in the process developed its own ideas about intelligence as a whole.[14] On scientific and technical intelligence (hereafter S and T) we have the similar recollections of R. V. Jones, the Air Ministry's wartime Assistant Director (Science), who recorded Whitehall's interest in this work's post-war future from summer 1944 onwards, and his own strong belief in combining the separate single-service efforts into one organisation.[15] From naval intelligence there is a similar memory of papers in 1944 that 'advocated a postwar organization which would concentrate economic, scientific, and much non-secret intelligence in a department that would be, so to speak, supra-service'.[16] There was a movement for change.

226

This was the background when work on the JIC report started. It was in progress by 24 October 1944, though its genesis is not clear.[17] The authors refer in the report's first line to the JIC's 'invitation' to them to prepare it, but the JIC minutes of the period do not record any commission of this kind. It is also not clear whether the work was approved by ministers, and how the various intelligence studies were to be coordinated. The JIC was still supposed to be a military subcommittee. The civilian agencies had been nominally overseen since the First World War by the high-level Secret Service Committee, but it had rarely met. Churchill enquired in 1940 who was in charge of intelligence, but the answer was no clearer in 1944. He could have ordered a comprehensive post-war study, but there is no evidence that he did so.

Hence the paper for the JIC was only part of the post-war planning, but it was the nearest thing to a complete survey. The authors took their remit for post-war organisation to allow them to discuss the whole machine, but they were careful to limit their formal recommendations to the JIC itself and the temporary wartime organisations that no one else was looking into, while also offering observations and suggestions (but not formal recommendations) about almost everything else. They presumably sought to make the report as influential as possible without being told by those looking at the civilian agencies to mind their own business.

This seems an untidy way of planning, though it was made less so by the wartime JIC's collegiality and personalities. The wartime Committee had been a constant meeting point – several times a week – for the top intelligence people, military and civilian. C, as head of both SIS and GC&CS, had been a regular attendee, as was MEW's intelligence head; the Security Service less so. There was also the personal standing of those who produced the report and put their names to it: the Committee's Chairman and Secretary. JIC reports were normally prepared by the drafting staff and departments, and this report by the Chairman and Secretary over their joint names was unprecedented and must have carried unusual weight. They referred archly in it to the 'enquiries under other auspices' that were taking place about the civilian agencies, but this was formulaic. The Chairman was one of the group looking into the post-war SIS, with the JIC secretary as its group secretary, and it is a reasonable guess that the two had comparable fingers in the other post-war pies.[18] They were probably what kept the post-war planning together.

Their influence needs explanation. Both had been with the JIC throughout the war and were among wartime Whitehall's quintessential insiders. The Chairman was Victor (Bill) Cavendish-Bentinck of an aristocratic family, career diplomat, in the chair since 1939, and longer in place than any of his colleagues.[19] At the beginning of the war he was still quite junior, and, even after promotion to counsellor in 1942, was still a nominal grade down from the service directors. But he had handled them with skill and aplomb and had a reputation for independence and impartiality. One who saw him in action recorded that he was 'both astute and prescient' yet 'had the gift of producing harmony among the service chiefs'.[20] He had a high standing with everyone, and historians credit him with much of the JIC's wartime success.

The Secretary, Colonel Denis Capel-Dunn, was a more mysterious character. A pre-war civilian of obscure background, he had risen to become JIC Secretary and subsequently combined this with heading the Cabinet Office's Joint Staff Secretariat. As such, he was Secretary for some of Churchill's top meetings, attended the allied conferences in Moscow and Yalta, helped to plan the United Nations at Dumbarton Oaks in the autumn of 1944, and is among the six people listed as the top British delegation to the UN's inauguration in San Francisco the following year. He was killed while flying back from it in early July 1945, and Cavendish-Bentinck was then joint author of an unusually warm tribute to him in *The Times*.[21] By contrast, the few post-war recollections of him give an unattractive picture of a careerist, a schemer, trying so hard that he was almost a figure of fun; though they endorse his ability and wartime influence, and suggest that he would have had a successful post-war future. He and Cavendish-Bentinck must have been a powerful combination. One can guess that he was the 'ideas man' behind the report as well as drafting it, with Cavendish-Bentinck adding authority and common sense.[22]

Concepts and Doctrine

The report's principal question was the future of the JIC itself, but its continuation was virtually taken for granted. The other pressing question was the future of the temporary wartime bodies, and on these it made detailed proposals. The rest of the machine – the pre-war service intelligence directorates, Security Service, SIS and Sigint – was accepted more or less as it stood, but this did not stop the authors in their observations from conveying their lack of empathy for the military, and from offering to the civilian organisations 'certain general points which have come to our notice and which we feel it useful to record'.[23] It is a sign of their standing that they could toss these *obiter dicta* into the other post-war studies.

The declared aim of their report was not just to adapt the wartime arrangements to peacetime, but to produce something better. Hence it was a mixture of a reform agenda, post-war doctrine and practical recommendations. For reform the immediate rationale was the need for post-war economy and the elimination of duplication: 'we should strive not merely to ensure that our Intelligence Service after the war is the most efficient possible, but to ensure that it is as economical as can be without sacrifice of efficiency'. The wartime arrangements had been marked by 'some overlapping of responsibilities and duplication of work which should not be acceptable or permissible in peace-time, and should, if possible, be avoided in war'. In their view 'a more symmetrical organization could have done at least as well at less cost'. Wartime intelligence had had too many masters. 'There were no doubt excellent reasons for the decisions that led to this state of affairs. It may have been right under the pressure of war to avoid the dislocation that any attempt at rationalization would have caused.' Nevertheless the country 'cannot afford in peace (or even perhaps in war) the kind of intelligence organization we have today'. Economy was worthy in itself, but for Cavendish-Bentinck and Capel-Dunn it was linked with the greater aim of reducing the dominance of the three single-service directorates by making organisation more interdepartmental and 'national', less single-service. This had happened in the war but needed consolidation and extension.[24]

The report therefore opened with a short argument that modern war needed more varied intelligence than the traditional single-service studies of enemy forces. It went on to lambaste the service directorates for their pre-war state. Intelligence was as important to the military as ammunition, fuel and food, yet 'no one would be so bold as to contend that our Service Intelligence Staffs entered this war adequately equipped for the task confronting them'. They had been allowed to 'wither'. The Admiralty had been 'rather better' than the others, but the Air Ministry had been 'less impressive' and in the pre-war army 'intelligence was a dangerous branch of the Staff for an ambitious officer to join'. There had been first-class Sigint in the war but 'full value could not be got unless the machine at the centre was properly equipped to collate and assess it against cognate intelligence from other sources'. Yet there was no guarantee that the post-war military would do anything about it. Those in control, like their predecessors, could not be blamed if they give preference to 'ships, aircraft, guns, and warlike stores'. Despite intelligence's wartime importance, 'it would be rash to assume . . . that the lesson will be remembered'.[25]

In a report for the military JIC this was strong stuff, but it now seems consistent with the wartime record. The three big intelligence successes were Sigint, deception and the work of the Joint Intelligence Staff (the JIS) serving the JIC, none of them under the military directorates' immediate control. Collectively, the military in Whitehall were not the heroes of Sir Harry Hinsley's official intelligence history. Noel Annan (later Lord Annan) recalled from his time in the JIS that 'our masters in the JIC were not an impressive team', and his reminiscences are of producing agreed JIS assessments and having to water them down through single-service opposition at the JIC level.[26] On the services' management of intelligence, we have recently had Sir Arthur Bonsall's judgement on the Air Ministry's attitude to Bletchley's so-called low grade Sigint sources, that 'it will probably never be known how much the allied cause could have gained, or not suffered, if there had been no delay [by the Air Ministry] in recognizing that useful intelligence could be produced from very unpromising material'.[27] With some naval exceptions, intelligence's wartime stars were not the military regulars who got drawn into it.

The report's criticism of the single-service directorates also fitted the mood of the day. There was anger about pre-war inadequacies everywhere and little sympathy for military hierarchy. There were already intimations that intelligence might be a key to post-war survival, and there was a mood for radical thinking about it. There was also a generational factor: the intelligence war had been a young man's war, and the young men now had influence. Neither Cavendish-Bentinck nor Capel-Dunn was a young radical – their ages were at the two ends of the forties – but they would be receptive to the radical view.[28] Neither had any stake in the pre-war military or intelligence establishments.

So single-departmentalism was the problem, and the solution was in the JIC's joint-service organisations, or 'jointery' as this became known in military jargon.[29] Reducing single-service duplication to economise was bound to get Whitehall's support, but the report also set it out as intelligence doctrine. Single-service approaches were not only wasteful but also liable to be incomplete, blinkered by service self-interest, and wrong. Handling intelligence should not depend on the colour of uniforms: the organisation best fitted for a particular kind of intelligence should do it. Material should be collated and evaluated so that all relevant information was brought together, including all non-intelligence data. Analysis should include some 'quite objective check' that stopped policy-makers from interpreting reports in the light of their preconceptions. 'One who is concerned in devising and recommending policy and assisting in its execution is likely, however objective he may try to be, to interpret the intelligence he receives in the light of the policy he is pursuing.' Hence 'no Department has anything to lose by bringing the intelligence directly available to it to the anvil of discussion and appreciation among other workers in the same field'. The results should be made available to all needing them. To these ends the system 'should be controlled at the top by a strong interservice and interdepartmental body representing the needs of producers and consumers'. It was an impressive articulation of what had emerged in war, as good a summary of the JIC philosophy for assessment as has ever been produced, and still just as relevant.[30]

But this was only half the philosophy. The wartime system had also depended on the temporary joint service, non-departmental organisations that had been created for the tasks that would otherwise have been left in separate single-service packets. Single-departmentalism had been countered not only by the JIC, but equally by creating the single, integrated organisations for topographical intelligence, photographic interpretation, strategic interrogation and intelligence support for political warfare. The intelligence department of the wartime MEW was in the same category, though with different origins; so too was the emergence of Bletchley as the controlling and coordinating centre for all the service and civilian Sigint effort. Britain had been successful as an intelligence builder as well as an intelligence assessor. The wartime success was in the combination of committees and centralisation, with the second as important as the first.

Not everyone had seen the force of the combination. The young men did not like committees. R. V. Jones was explicit in his criticism of the JIC – which had been particularly weak in handling the German V-1 and V-2 threat in the later years of the war[31] – and wanted a single S and T organisation. (He did not get it and went back to academe.)[32] Cavendish-Bentinck and Capel-Dunn were wedded to the JIC but sought equally to build on the wartime joint-service organisations. What shines through their report is a surprising enthusiasm for what they had seen in them of the squeezing of valuable intelligence from apparently unrewarding evidence, including publicly available material. Someone – presumably Capel-Dunn or one of his minions – had been bitten by the excitement of applying large-scale scanning, indexing and collation to produce gold dust from low-grade ore, a striking prevision of intelligence as it evolved in the computer age.

Thus, the report's philosophy was two-pronged: coordination by committees combined with moving towards centralised institutions. The conclusions and recommendations in which it can be traced can now be discussed.

Recommendations: The JIC Itself

The Committee was to have 'as far as possible all intelligence producing and using agencies' represented on it.[33] It was to be the 'principal interservice and inter-departmental body', to make sure the civilians' organisations were included.[34] The official membership would follow the wartime one (except for the wartime MEW): the Foreign Office, the three service directors, and C. The position of the Security Service was left open. The Board of Trade might be represented, though surprisingly the wartime MEW intelligence effort, by then being administered by the Foreign Office in its Economic Intelligence Organisation, was said not to be needed.

The chairmanship was not mentioned, but when the report was considered by JIC members the Foreign Office occupancy of it was 'generally agreed' to be 'preferable in principle'. Cavendish-Bentinck's biographer reports that only his success in the job made the appointment of another civilian acceptable to the military.[35] Capel-Dunn privately argued at the time that the Foreign Office should keep the post, as otherwise it would lose interest altogether.[36]

Despite civilian involvement, the Committee was to remain responsible to the Chiefs of Staff, as it did until its transfer to the Cabinet Office in 1957. As a Chiefs of Staff body, it remained a committee of equals, proceeding by consensus, and this was reinforced at first by continuing to have a civilian chairman junior to his uniformed colleagues. When Air Chief Marshal Sir Douglas Evill reviewed it two years later, he got its chairmanship upgraded, but that did not affect its consensus character.[37]

So what was this high-powered body to do? The report said very little about its assessment role. There was a marker that it should not be limited to military needs: 'the practice that has grown up, of the committee giving advice on request to other Departments and authorities, should be preserved'.[38] The JIS would continue to prepare the Committee's reports. Otherwise, the service to top government was taken for granted.

There was more attention to the management role, which may have been seen as the Committee's main post-war function. The report's language about it was robust: 'We think it essential that all the intelligence authorities should be brought under the J.I.C. umbrella.' The post-war machine was described as an organisation with the JIC as its head, 'directing its general policy'.[39]

The Committee would have its standing subcommittees 'dealing with the various aspects of intelligence', including a general requirements subcommittee 'to lay down the priorities to be accorded to the nation's "intelligence effort" [original quotation marks], to coordinate the work of the different collection agencies, and to allocate responsibilities between them'. It would also 'exercise general supervision over the Central Intelligence Bureau [a new body, see below]'.[40] It reads as if the JIC and its subcommittees would be involved in everything, with 'policy' and 'direction' as the themes, but what these meant was not expanded.

The report also dealt with S and T matters but did not move much beyond the wartime single-service situation that R. V. Jones coordinated where he could. We have seen that Jones wanted a single post-war organisation: 'a single Head of Intelligence is far better than a Committee'.[41] Critics thought he wanted the job, and there was strong service opposition.[42] The report pointed out that 'while the Joint Intelligence Staff is well equipped to prepare for the J.I.C. papers on enemy intentions generally, there exists no similar interservice body to draft papers for the J.I.C. on enemy technical developments'. It wanted technical intelligence to be 'integrated', and recommended a committee from the three services' technical sections, but stopped there. Despite further investigation the situation was not properly sorted out for another decade. It was a political hot potato, subsequently made hotter by the complex sensitivities of atomic intelligence, and Cavendish-Bentinck and Capel-Dunn presumably judged that they could not shift the single services over it. But it was a weak part of their report.[43]

Imagery and the Central Intelligence Bureau

Some of the wartime organisations would not be needed in peacetime, and the report conscientiously made recommendations for the disposal of their records or the maintenance of their expertise.[44] Of those that were to continue there were important but straightforward recommendations for the Central Interpretation Unit, the interservice photo-interpretation establishment that had operated under a JIC subcommittee's direction and RAF administration. The report discussed the potential of imagery and speculated on its worldwide civilian applications, and argued that 'the interest of the consumers is so considerable that we do not believe that any one Ministry should be burdened with the exclusive responsibility for the general control and direction of this branch of intelligence'.[45] It suggested that a variety of RAF and army photo-interpreter training and equipment provision might be taken over centrally, implying that imagery was too important to be left entirely to the RAF.[46]

Nevertheless, the recommendations essentially continued the wartime arrangements, with the joint-service unit under RAF command, and a Photographic Reconnaissance Committee reporting to the JIC for policy direction and 'the production, interpretation and distribution of aerial photographs'.[47] The Air Force subordination of what became the Joint Air Reconnaissance Intelligence Centre made good sense, since the RAF was the main collector and interpreter of photography as well as a principal customer. The JIC's post-war oversight eventually withered in favour of exclusive Ministry of Defence control, in contrast to what later evolved in the United States for the development of imagery, including satellite imagery, as a major national source with agency status.

Much more innovative was the report's proposal for the new Central Intelligence Bureau. It was to be formed around the wartime Interservice Topographical Department (ISTD), which had been established in 1940 under JIC direction and Admiralty administration, and had made topographical intelligence an important wartime subject, for example on European transport facilities and the targeting of them in the assault on Western Europe. It was also to take over the records and expertise of the Political Warfare Executive (PWE), whose intelligence effort had supported its black propaganda and had become a leading authority on the non-military aspects of the enemy, *inter alia* through the exploitation of foreign press and broadcasting sources.[48] The same would apply to a nucleus of the wartime Postal and Telegraphic Censorship Department.

The Bureau was evidently created to be the centre for handling the low-grade evidence *en masse*, about which the report was so enthusiastic. ISTD's publications, files and registries 'seem to provide the best possible basis for the Central Bureau we have in mind'.[49] The report rejoices over the 'some 7,000 files and records of some 190,000 personalities'[50] that could also accrue from the

PWE. It also had two long appendices on the organisation and methods of the Censorship Department, which were said to reflect the 'efficiency of its administration and the wisdom with which it has been directed', and were recommended for the Bureau's information-handling methods.[51]

So the Bureau was to be an analysis centre, but on what, apart from the ISTD's topographic remit? Here the report was expansive but unclear. It spotted the significance of publicly available ('open') sources such as newspapers, fifty years before they became a fashionable intelligence topic. Apart from government's needs, the Bureau might meet those of private interests in trade and industry for this material and some official sources such as overseas trade reports, and hence might be divided into classified and unclassified sections.[52] Both sections would serve government. 'We have in mind that information required as a basis of high policy should be collected and collated in the first instance in the non-secret branch of the bureau. It should then be tested in the light of any secret information that is available,'[53] and then, if necessary, put to the JIS and the JIC itself. For 1944–5 this was indeed visionary, and it anticipated the concern in the 1960s and 1970s for economic intelligence, as well as our current enthusiasm for the information society.

This was a response to the young men's urge for a central body of some kind. Yet it needed more teeth to be convincing. Cavendish-Bentinck and Capel-Dunn must have had economic intelligence in mind; and their warm words about the wartime ISTD, PWE and censorship could have been applied even more to MEW Enemy Branch, for example, for the value of its work on the German economy as the basis for the allied strategic bombing campaign. Its representative was a powerful member of the wartime JIC.[54] Yet economic intelligence is barely mentioned in the report. One can only guess that its post-war future was another political hot potato, connected with its transfer to Foreign Office control in April 1944 as part of its Economic Intelligence Organisation.[55] In the event, the omission was rectified when the report was first discussed by JIC members.

Central analysis was not all. The Bureau was also to have a role derived from another wartime creation, Intelligence Section (Operations), or IS(O), which had been created in early 1942 to cope with the increased demand for the detailed intelligence needed to plan the invasions of North Africa, Italy and France. Multiple and often duplicative requests were being addressed to different producers, creating overload and confusion. IS(O) was established under JIC control and War Office administration, and it became what the official historians later described as 'more of a clearing house than an agency to collate intelligence', in order to 'regulate and rationalise' the many demands for this kind of information.[56]

This body was to be in the Bureau, but much expanded. It was to receive information from all intelligence sources, and 'within the Bureau, this information should be brought together and reproduced in the form required by the different customers of the intelligence machine'.[57] Each intelligence-producing organisation would collect intelligence from its own sources, but 'should not normally receive intelligence from other Departments and organisations save through the medium of the Central Bureau'.[58] It reads like a mixture of collation, clearing house, intelligence warehouse, a summarising centre, and the provision of what the Americans now call 'tailored intelligence' to meet individual customers' requirements.

It would go even further, and would have liaison sections from departments that needed intelligence to state their requirements, and decide what agency was best fitted to meet them. It would support the JIS by providing 'in the shape of memoranda or reference books such factual information as was required', and the report also suggests that the information required 'as a basis for high policy' could be collected and collated in it. The intention was clear: 'we believe that if our recommendation is accepted, the central machinery will sufficiently justify itself to encourage Departments to refrain from duplicating its work'. Hence the Central Bureau in its varied ways would be the heart of what Cavendish-Bentinck and Capel-Dunn summarised as 'an uncertain amalgamation' of existing interservice and interdepartmental bodies, so as to provide a central intelligence agency and to leave it to departments to work out the alterations in their own organisation that would be possible and desirable were that proposal accepted.[59]

It would have suitably heavyweight management. It was asserted that ideally C would direct it, but he could not be the public figure. A deputy would be needed for 'the public side of his activities'. He would be the Bureau's director general, an ex officio member of the JIC and all its subcommittees, and would run a common secretariat for the JIC and the Bureau.[60] These would be responsible, under him, for 'ensuring the coordination of the different branches of the national intelligence machine'.[61] The vision of the strong centre was therefore of a powerful JIC and its subcommittees, plus the Bureau and its director general, all at the expense of single-service approaches.

The Pre-war Institutions

The observations – not recommendations – about the rest of the intelligence effort can be summarised briefly. On the civilian agencies, the report criticised the division of counterespionage between the Security Service and SIS, and opined that 'we doubt whether any case can be made for the retention of the present system, under which the responsibility for counterespionage is divided between two authorities with no better basis for division than that of geography'.[62] This was a sore spot then, and perhaps still is. Otherwise the authors steered clear of the Security Service.[63] On SIS, the report argued that it should incorporate the post-war rump of the wartime SOE and keep it; it was on the winning side in that Whitehall battle.[64] Nothing was said about the military directorates explicitly, but there was a passing kick at them over the quality of their attachments to SIS and Security Service, since 'in the early days of the war there existed an impression that . . . certain of . . . [them] were officers for whom it was not easy to find employment elsewhere'.[65]

For Sigint, despite the wartime successes, 'some pulling together of the strings appears to us to be desirable'. GC&CS should remain under C's direction. (It did not, and became GCHQ, and nothing happened to this and the other proposals about C's responsibilities.[66]) The Sigint board should no longer be independent of the JIC (this never happened). Sigint funding should no longer be shown on the Foreign Office budget (this remained a complicated issue for many years). The three services' intercept organisations should continue, but the idea of a central intercept organisation should be studied. (A consolidated civilian one was created over the next two decades.) The Radio Security Service should be brought under the Sigint board, and its independence reviewed. (Its integration into the main interception force followed soon afterwards.) Sigint reporters should not be banned from including 'appreciations' in their reports. (A sensible point, but Bletchley had already won most of this wartime battle, even though some of it had to be fought again later.[67]) It is not clear what effect these observations had on the other post-war studies, but the remarks about Sigint give an impression of rather gratuitous observations from the side-line. It was as well that the advice was not all followed.

The Outcome

The report's issue on 10 January 1945 was followed by a delay, perhaps as a result of JIC members' absences at the Yalta conference. They then had a 'preliminary discussion' of it (not recorded as a formal meeting) on Sunday, 11 March. As noted above, they agreed that 'an outline of the history and achievement of the economic intelligence organization' should be included, and they favoured the continued Foreign Office chairmanship. The Central Bureau was welcomed in principle, and a subcommittee was to go into the details. Another subcommittee would be established for the S and T issues. There were conflicting views about the JIC's proposed oversight of Sigint, but otherwise the report had a smooth passage.[68]

The report was then rewritten as a normal, much shorter one, minus most of the discussion, approved by the Committee on 29 May, and submitted to the Chiefs of Staff as 'the broad lines on which we are thinking' plus specific proposals for the new Bureau as an appendix. The main paper repeated the criticism of the pre-war single-service arrangements and the ad hoc expansion of wartime, and also promoted the use of open sources as a major objective. The rest of the first version was omitted and with slight changes the kernel of the report became the January recommendations.[69]

The appendix about the new Central Bureau was more detailed, and very different from the original scheme. It was now to be the

Joint Intelligence Bureau, with analysis restricted to defence subjects, and without the managerial functions envisaged for it. It would take over the ISTD's topographic work. It would also have the economic intelligence that originally had been omitted, but all this was to be only in respect of military needs, so that it became 'collating and appraising' the 'economic intelligence required by the Service Departments'.[70]

This still produced quite a wide remit. 'In the field of defence' it was to 'collect, assess and, where appropriate, appreciate, intelligence material of interdepartmental significance', including overt material.[71] It was to 'cover subjects concerning more than one Service, which in the interests of efficiency and economy can best be studied on an inter-Service basis'.[72] The specified subjects were quite broad and ranged from obviously military ones such as static defences and armaments production to the study of more diffuse economic, industrial and other targets. But these were all 'in relation to any probable war condition', and on anti-aircraft defences and shipbuilding there were caveats about further demarcation discussions with the RAF and Navy; some S and T subjects were included with similar provisos.[73]

We do not know how this trimming happened between the discussion of the original report on 11 March and the JIC meeting on 29 May. Individual absences may have played a part, notably Capel-Dunn's, which may well have prevented him from explaining and defending the original proposals.[74] Departments may have weighed in with their own interests: the Foreign Office will have wanted to keep its non-defence economic portfolio, and the service directors will have wanted something to meet their needs and not those of the Board of Trade. Whatever the motives, the revision to the defence-oriented JIB had the merit of coherence. It was not the central organisation the young men wanted, but they were still busy with the war and perhaps were persuaded (though R. V. Jones never was) that the JIB was a big step towards it. It has to be added that the job description for the proposed director general of the Central Bureau and JIC Secretariat now seems so close to Capel-Dunn's wartime position of power that it may have been thought he was thinking of a job for himself.

A further report on the JIB was sent to the chiefs in late July.[75] The organisation would be mainly civilian, but with a strong service and ex-service flavour. Some demarcation lines with the single services still had to be established. The separate S and T studies had recommended that the single-service staffs should have common accommodation with the JIB, but without integration. The plan for the JIB was approved and it came into existence the following year.

As for the rest of the post-war proposals, a final version of the JIC report was considered by the chiefs on 11 September for submission to the Prime Minister as a defence requirement.[76] There were some shifts in emphasis. There was an explicit statement of the need for 'a first-class system in peacetime'. As before, intelligence should be centrally directed, but the emphasis was now on interdepartmental assessment: thus 'the *collating* staffs should work as far as possible on an interservice basis [my emphasis]'. The JIS teams were reduced from two to one, and the members were now permanent members of departments, more clearly limiting their non-departmental independence. On S and T arrangements there were now to be separate scientific and technical subcommittees, but still without any joint-service element. In addition to other tasks, the JIB would collect and collate open source material to avoid duplication elsewhere, but this never came to much. For the first time, a worldview was set out of the London JIC's position at the hub of a post-war system of JICs overseas and complementary committees in the Dominions.[77]

The post-war arrangements were completed the following year. They were reviewed by Evill in 1947 but no major changes ensued. There have been some since,[78] but the main feature of the system – a community operating by consensus in and through the JIC – has been unchanged. A JIC member transposed from 1945 would not be much surprised by what he would now find. The Cavendish-Bentinck and Capel-Dunn report and the 1945 decisions that followed it settled the form of the British system. How well was it all done?

Lessons Learned

The post-war organisation was not preceded by any comprehensive study of intelligence requirements or institutions. The civilian agencies had separate investigations of them, and we have seen how Cavendish-Bentinck's and Capel-Dunn's report established the post-war JIC's role and the community structure under it, but made only detached comments on some of the components. It was produced at some speed, amid wartime pressure, and we have seen that it was not fully implemented. Some of its exposition was brilliant and of lasting importance. It was a vision of a post-war system written from the centre of wartime action, but it was stronger on vision than on reflection, or indeed some of the detail. It might have considered the nature of its post-war machine rather more deeply.

This includes what the JIC was actually to do. The authors assumed that the Committee's dual role of intelligence management and assessment would continue, and did not discuss whether it was sensible for it to combine the two. The joining of the two functions had happened almost by accident in 1939 and was never questioned until 2009 when some separation of them took place.[79] In a similar way the Committee's chairmanship was not covered, and in the event it was accepted as a Foreign Office commitment without apparent examination of alternatives. Two years later Evill posed the option of filling the post from the (new) Ministry of Defence,[80] but without result.

Indeed, a weakness of the report was that it did not consider the Foreign Office's special position as the non-intelligence body among intelligence specialists, *inter alia* for the effect this had on the nature of the JIC's peacetime product for government: did its assessments present an intelligence view, or a consensus of intelligence and policy-makers' judgements? The report sought to reduce the single-departmental influences of the three military directorates, but apparently regarded the Foreign Office's departmental position as off limits. There was also the report's omission of the Foreign Office's economic intelligence effort (the omission was rectified later on others' insistence), and of its wartime research and political intelligence departments. The omissions presumably reflected the Foreign Office view that it did not 'do' intelligence – one that still applies to the present (non-intelligence) Research and Analysis Department that succeeded these wartime bodies.[81]

Yet it is understandable that Cavendish-Bentinck and Capel-Dunn did not delve so deeply. Their aim in 1945 was not to produce a new system from scratch, but to build quickly on the wartime successes that commanded widespread support. Making the JIC the peacetime centre, and sorting out the wartime organisations, was pushing at an open door, but they did it in style, with their positive message of developing the committee approach while moving from single-service institutions towards national or joint-service ones. But what effect did their message have? It was intended to influence intelligence's management as well as its production, and the effects on the two can best be discussed separately.

For post-war management, their enthusiasm for the JIC's central role was clear from their tone. The Sigint board was to come under it; had it happened, it would have been a considerable increase in the JIC's responsibilities. The JIC would have been strengthened by the management role proposed for the Central Intelligence Bureau and its director general, but this never happened, and other specifics were lacking. No draft terms of reference were produced at the time. So we do not really know how far what became the JIC's style of peacetime management reflected the hopes of Cavendish-Bentinck and Capel-Dunn and those who supported their ideas in 1945. But the indications are that they 'intended that coming under the JIC's umbrella' would signify a higher management profile for the Committee than it actually developed.

This may have been because JIC did not have the best of peacetime starts in the high summer and autumn of 1945. By then Capel-Dunn was dead. Cavendish-Bentinck had been away in the United States in April and was again absent, presumably on leave, for some weeks before a valedictory JIC appearance in mid-August. His Foreign Office successor then took a long time to appear, and longer to take the chair, so the Committee was leaderless for much of the transition to peace. Two years later Evill was still critical that the Committee was not providing the post-war leadership that intelligence needed.[82] The Foreign Office subsequently filled the chairman's post at a more senior level, but by then the post-war mould would have been established and difficult to change.

It is equally possible that Cavendish-Bentinck and Capel-Dunn had expected too much of management by consensus in peacetime. They may have allowed too little for the special circumstances of war that had made it effective (and indeed underestimated their own personal contributions), and for the renewed importance in peacetime of proper lines of command and budgets. It has been suggested that Britain as a nation was at that time too enthusiastic about committees, and did not consider how authority and responsibility fitted into them as carefully as we would now.[83] The report used the analogy of the JIC with a board of directors and did not consider the place of a chief executive. Attlee's submission to Churchill in the autumn of 1940 that 'there should be one directing mind at the head of the Intelligence Service' remained in limbo.[84] The report writes of the JIC's 'policy' and 'direction' but does not explore the responsibilities for finding resources and ensuring effectiveness.

Whatever the causes, the reality has been that the post-war community has always needed some central authority that the JIC could not provide, and has met the need by a gradual growth of Cabinet Office power and influence. The JIC's position as a forum for managerial issues has remained a key part of the system, and its collegial style has promoted more inter-agency cooperation than can be found in other countries. The result has been a system that has combined authority and collegiality within a relatively loose federation. In some respects this has been a national asset, and in others it has been a feature once characterised by the Committee of Parliamentarians as its 'weakness in the centre'.[85] It has had a high reputation and has served the United Kingdom reasonably well, but it is difficult not to feel that in following the wartime committee model it has failed to incorporate something of the authority, and leadership, which Churchill had radiated from the centre.

On the community's assessment role the effects of the report's message have also been mixed. The JIC's system of assessment by committee under Foreign Office chairmanship has been highly regarded. It has done well in producing relevant and useful product for top government: the close linkage of intelligence and policy has been a world success. There has always been some inherent tension between the merits of assessment by consensus compared with the advantages of having a single chief intelligence officer figure, not tied to being a committee spokesman; and the balances between the two have varied considerably. Yet the needs of the day have been met reasonably well, and recent years have seen a more consistent recognition of the chairman's personal standing within what is still much prized as a consensus system.[86]

Yet it has had its assessment failures. A disinterested observer might conclude that in getting things right it has done no worse than the comparable American and Commonwealth systems, but not much better. The main lesson drawn from its performance on Iraqi weapons of mass destruction before the war of 2003 has been to improve the quality of the professional analysis that underlies the Committee's judgements.[87] Cultivating this quality was implicit in Cavendish-Bentinck's and Capel-Dunn's vision of better analysis through the Central Intelligence Bureau and the reduction of single-service approaches, but it was not recognised. In 1945 the wartime successes in single-source collection and exploitation (especially Sigint) and in JIC assessment had obscured for most people the importance of the unglamorous analytic work that linked the two.

That said, we should still recognise that despite the rejection of Cavendish-Bentinck's and Capel-Dunn's Central Bureau the decision to go as far as the JIB was a brave move in the right direction. As approved by the Chiefs of Staff it was to have an establishment of 212 people plus clerks, as well as outposts overseas.[88] The peacetime total for the three service directorates in Whitehall was then being planned as 249 officers and civilians, so the Bureau would be almost the same size as those it was created to support.[89]

It was also a success as far as it went. It became a strong player in the West's work on Soviet defence production, and despite the early problems over S and T organisation it became particularly valuable in assessing the rate of Soviet missile production in the late 1950s and early 1960s when the missile threat was the hottest Western topic. It recruited the young civilians who later became the backbone of the Defence Intelligence Staff (the DIS). It was a genuine move away from single-department analysis towards a new model. But the glass was half empty as well as half full. Major-General Sir Kenneth Strong, the JIB's first and only director, wrote later that 'the Bureau had a considerable battle for existence. The armed forces never really liked it and many of their senior men regarded it as a threat to the traditional forms of service intelligence'.[90] In his old age Cavendish-Bentinck said the same.[91] Though some of its Cold War analysis was important, a substantial part of its work served military contingency planning and war planning, for example through its inventory of world air-fields and their characteristics. It periodically broke out from the yoke of military requirements, notably stepping into the breach in the 1960s on the effect of sanctions on Rhodesia's economy after its government had declared its independence of United Kingdom authority. But it was always restricted by its defence remit and was never able to become a proper national centre. Most important, it was too small to offer analysis as a career to compete with intelligence's other specialties. Its image came to be of retired officers studying obscure subjects that might be useful sometime – in fact just what the military directorates had wanted in 1945. It was never staffed to be intelligence's research centre on Soviet policies and intentions, and no other intelligence body ever was.

Those opting for it in 1945 can hardly be criticised. The case put for the Central Bureau was too vague, and where it was more precise it was a mixture of good ideas and bad. It did not have enough critical scrutiny. Yet inside it was something that deserved a better fate. The January 1945 report was full of foresight – on the place of economic, scientific and technical intelligence, the need to exploit open sources as well as low-grade intelligence ones, the potential of imagery, the future of non-military subjects as well as defence ones – and the same was true of its enthusiasm for central analysis. But the case for it was not well made, and it was left to the United States to lead it in the decade that followed.

In Britain the idea was not completely forgotten. The JIB managed *de facto* to meet Whitehall needs on some non-defence subjects, mainly on matters of foreign economics and technology. Field Marshal Sir Gerald Templar in his report on service intelligence in 1960 proposed that the Bureau should become part of the Cabinet Office. The JIC chairman proposed separately in 1963 that the integrated tri-service and JIB organisation that was to become the DIS should be a 'Combined Intelligence Bureau' in the Cabinet Office, perhaps harking back to the proposal of twenty years earlier. The idea of a central economic intelligence body still rumbled around Whitehall until the end of the 1960s, but died.[92]

There must be some regret that the United Kingdom did not go further towards the Central Bureau in 1945. Yet the British situation was always stacked against it. Like Cavendish-Bentinck's and Capel-Dunn's hopes for powerful JIC management, their idea of central analysis was ahead of its time. Intelligence's value was still thought in 1945 to be rooted in war and military power, and British military power was still single service, with the Chiefs of Staffs' committee of equals at the top. The post-war machine was bound to stick with the system. It was another twenty years before the JIB could be amalgamated with the military intelligence directorates, and by then Britain had become comfortable with its own mixture of departmental organisation and intelligence by committee. The new, amalgamated organisation became the DIS, part of the Ministry of Defence, and still a departmental body. Probably it would now need a national disaster for the idea of central analysis to be revived.

Notes

1. Originally published as 'The Postwar Organization of Intelligence', in Dover, R. and M. Goodman (eds), *Learning from the Secret Past: Cases in British Intelligence History* (Washington, DC: Georgetown University Press, 2011), pp. 11–77. Copyright by Georgetown University Press, and reprinted with permission (www.press.georgetown.edu). All archival references are from the UK National Archive (TNA). Unless otherwise indicated, the paragraph numbers are from a report – 'The Intelligence Machine' – found in CAB 163/6; numbers at the end of a paragraph refer to all the quotations in it from that report, and references at the end of a paragraph in the text apply to all quotations in it.
2. *The Intelligence Machine. Report to the Joint Intelligence Committee*, 10 January 1945, paras 11 and 49, CAB 163/6. Emphasis added.
3. Hinsley, F. H. with E. E. Thomas, C. F. G. Ransom and R. C. Knight, *British Intelligence in the Second World War: Vol. I* (London: HMSO, 1979), p. 43.
4. Ibid.
5. I am indebted to Gill Bennett for this information.
6. Bennett, G., *Churchill's Man of Mystery: Desmond Morton and the World of Intelligence* (Abingdon: Routledge, 2009), p. 207.

7. Para. 16. Quotation marks of 'intelligence' in original.
8. First used in the United States in 1952, according to Andrew, C., *For the President's Eyes Only* (London: HarperCollins, 1995), p. 197. The source is not quoted.
9. JIC(43) 53rd meeting (O), item 1, CAB 81/91. Earlier correspondence is also in this file.
10. JIC(44) 4th and 18th meetings, items 6 and 3, CAB 81/91.
11. JIC(44) 50th meeting (O), item 1, CAB 81/92.
12. Para. 24.
13. Para. 11.
14. GCHQ's own post-war planning committee of Welchman, Hinsley and Crankshaw is said to have called for 'a more centralised Foreign Intelligence Office'. See Aldrich, R. J., 'GCHQ and Sigint in the Early Cold War', in M. Aid and C. Wiebes (eds), *Secrets of Signals Intelligence during the Cold War and Beyond* (London: Frank Cass, 2001), p. 69. Exactly how comprehensive this organisation would be is not clear, but I remember being told around 1959–60 by William Millward at GCHQ that Hinsley had wanted a unified all-source intelligence organisation of some kind, something that did not happen.
15. Jones, R. V., 'Scientific Intelligence', *RUSI Journal*, 92, no. 567, 1947: 364. His criticisms of single-service organisation are set out at more length in his *Reflections on Intelligence* (London: Heinemann, 1989), pp. 7–34.
16. McLachlan, D., *Room 39: Naval Intelligence in Action 1939–45* (London: Weidenfeld and Nicolson, 1968), p. 369.
17. On that date Capel-Dunn visited the Security Service to discuss its future as part of his JIC investigation and was sent packing. Cavendish-Bentinck then had to smooth feathers by confirming to the Security Service's Director General that the study was in progress at the JIC's invitation, but would not significantly involve his Service (JIC/1494/44, Cavendish-Bentinck to Petrie, 27 October 1944, CAB 163/6). The note of the contretemps that occasioned this letter is West, N. (ed.), *The Guy Liddell Diaries: Vol. II* (Abingdon: Routledge, 2005), p. 237. If the report had been commissioned in the normal JIC way Petrie would surely have been well aware of it.
18. Howarth, P., *Intelligence Chief Extraordinary: The Life of the Ninth Duke of Portland* (London: Bodley Head, 1986), p. 199.
19. Victor Frederick William Cavendish-Bentinck, 1897–1990. JIC Chairman, 1939–45; Ambassador to Poland, 1945–7; became 9th Duke of Portland in 1979. See Howarth, *Intelligence Chief Extraordinary*.

20. Annan, N., *Changing Enemies: The Defeat and Regeneration of Germany* (London: HarperCollins, 1996), pp. 61–2.

21. Letter signed VFWC-B and EICJ ([Sir] Ian Jacob), *The Times*, 25 July 1945, p. 7. I am grateful to Michael Goodman for the reference.

22. Denis Capel-Dunn, 1903–45. Said to have been the son of a Leipzig consular clerk; undergraduate at Trinity College, Cambridge, 1922–4 and 1930. Described by a member of the JIS as an 'elusive, secretive barrister'; see Annan, *Changing Enemies*, p. 17. A man of mystery, drawn on for an unsympathetic character in Anthony Powell's post-war novel *A Dance to the Music of Time* (confirmed in Powell's *Journals 1990–2* [London: Heinemann, c. 1998], pp. 151, 161–2). The few other personal recollections of him are equally uncomplimentary, completely at variance with the tribute in the Cavendish-Bentinck/Jacob letter. Biographical details obtained from Trinity College, Cambridge.

23. Para. 49.

24. Quotations in this paragraph are from para. 8, except the final one from para. 9.

25. Quotations from para. 2, except the final two from para. 4.

26. Annan, *Changing Enemies*, p. 63, also pp. 59–68. He had previously served in the Military Intelligence Directorate and was subsequently a distinguished academic. For Cavendish-Bentinck's own criticisms of his service colleagues see Howarth, *Intelligence Chief Extraordinary*, pp. 165–6.

27. Bonsall, A., 'Bletchley Park and the RAF Y Service: Some Recollections', *Intelligence and National Security*, 23, no. 6, 2008: 827–41. See also the criticisms of the estimates of German aircraft production in mid-1943 to mid-1944: 'These miscalculations arose generally from lapses in organization within the Air Intelligence Branch' (Hinsley, *British Intelligence: Vol. 3, Part 1*, pp. 62–3).

28. Cavendish-Bentinck was born in 1897; Capel-Dunn was born in 1903. Capel-Dunn was already arguing for a central post-war organisation in the spring of 1943. I am grateful to Huw Dylan for this reference, 'Defence Organisation after the War', 29 April 1943, CAB 163/6.

29. The noun 'jointery' did not itself appear until after the Joint Services Staff College's opening in 1947, described in Thornton, M. D., *Latimer Remembered* (Latimer, UK: National Defence College, 1983), pp. 43–53.

30. Paras 12 and 13. See also the description of the JIS's methods in McLachlan, *Room 39*, particularly pp. 251–2.

31. Described in Jones, R. V., *Most Secret War: British Scientific Intelligence 1939–1945* (London: Hamish Hamilton, 1978), chapters 44–6. For confirmation see Hinsley, *British Intelligence: Vol. 3, Part 1*, section V, particularly pp. 411, 444, 455.
32. Jones, *Most Secret War*, chapters 50–2.
33. Para. 17.
34. Para. 17. Emphasis added. Compare the inclusion of 'interdepartmental' for the post-war role with the narrower 'interservice' (armed service), used to describe the wartime role in para. 16.
35. His successor was the future Lord Caccia; see Howarth, *Intelligence Chief Extraordinary*, p. 203.
36. J.S./72/45, Capel-Dunn to Cavendish-Bentinck, 20 February 1945, CAB 163/6.
37. *Review of Intelligence Organisation*, by Air Chief Marshal Sir Douglas Evill, 6 November 1947, CAB 163/7.
38. Para. 59.
39. Quotations up to this point in the paragraph are from para. 59.
40. Para. 70.
41. Jones, *Most Secret War*, p. 517. The same view is set out in his 1947 lecture 'Scientific Intelligence', p. 364.
42. A recollection of a contemporary view that Jones 'felt he had won the war single-handedly' is recorded in Goodman, M., *Spying on the Nuclear Bear: Anglo-American Intelligence and the Soviet Bomb* (Stanford, CA: Stanford University Press, 2007), p. 135.
43. Para. 19.
44. These were the wartime Combined Service Detailed Interrogation Centre, the Secret Communications Organisation, and the Inter-Service Security Board. On this last subject, the JIC had established important wartime subcommittees for radio and cipher security. The 1945 report and the decisions of that year gave the JIC a post-war security role, which was significant but subsidiary to the Committee's intelligence activities, and it is not discussed here.
45. Para. 37.
46. Para. 39.
47. Para. 68.
48. Note, however, the rather different explanation of the official history, that PWE was a user rather a supplier of intelligence, except for its valuable studies of enemy propaganda that had a bearing on studies of enemy morale; see Hinsley, *British Intelligence: Vol. 2*, note 7. The Foreign Office's Political Intelligence Department (see note 81) was located with PWE at Woburn Park. It is not clear whether it was part of it or used as a cover term for it all.

49. Para. 25.
50. Para. 44.
51. Para. 46.
52. Para. 60.
53. Para. 71.
54. Charles Geoffrey Vickers VC, 1894–1982. Lawyer, administrator, writer and pioneering systems scientist; recommissioned in the Second World War as colonel; knighted 1946; junior in wartime rank to the military JIC members, but his ability (and the Victoria Cross) must have made him an influential member.
55. Hinsley, *British Intelligence: Vol. 3, Part 1*, p. 54 fn.
56. Hinsley, *British Intelligence*, Vol. 2, pp. 11, 15.
57. Para. 59.
58. Ibid.
59. All quotations from para. 71 except the last, which is from para. 10.
60. Para. 63.
61. Para. 62.
62. Para. 49.
63. The scanty treatment of the Security Service may have stemmed from Capel-Dunn's unhappy visit to it. See fn. 17.
64. Para. 56.
65. Para. 51.
66. If all the suggestions in the report had been followed, C would have remained responsible for GC&CS and become chairman of the Sigint board, and would have become responsible via a deputy for the new Central Bureau. His job as head of SIS would have expanded to take on a large proportion of Security Service's effort if the suggested rationalisation of counterespionage had ended in SIS's favour. At the JIC's meeting to discuss the report, it was suggested that he should also be responsible for exploiting open sources. Had this all happened he would have become the most important intelligence person, the absolute éminence grise. But the recommendations for his responsibilities outside SIS all fell by the wayside.
67. Sigint discussion in paras 52–5, 58, 64.
68. J.S./108/45, The Intelligence Machine, 21 March 1945, CAB 163/6.
69. JIC(45)181(0)(Final), 1 June 1945, CAB 81/129.
70. Ibid., outline in para. 5(c) of report and expansion in Annex. Quotations are from para. 4(j) of report and para. 8 of Annex.
71. Ibid., para. 5(c)(i) and Annex para. 19.
72. Ibid., para. 5(c).
73. Ibid., details in Appendix to the Annex, quotation in its first item.

74. The working party to consider the original proposal for the Central Bureau was due to meet on April 18 under Cavendish-Bentinck's chairmanship (JIC(45) 27th meeting, item 13, 17 April 1945, CAB 81/93). The record did not survive. Cavendish-Bentinck then went to Washington for the rest of the month; see Howarth, *Intelligence Chief Extraordinary*, p. 197. The 18 April meeting may well have been a decisive one, with staff left to work out the details of what had been agreed and to prepare the report that was eventually considered by the JIC in late May. JIC minutes show that, after JIC directors had considered the original report proposing the Central Intelligence Bureau on 11 March, Capel-Dunn was absent from all the Committee's meetings from 13 March onwards, except for one attendance on 27 April, not on this subject. The San Francisco conference that he attended began on 25 April, but it went on until early July and presumably he travelled out by air and skipped the beginning.

75. JIC(45)226(Final), 24 July 1945, CAB 81/130.

76. COS(45) 220th meeting, item 2, 11 September 1945, taking the paper at note 76, CAB 79/39.

77. JIC(45)265(O)(FINAL) Post-War Organisation of Intelligence, 7 September 1945, CAB 81/130. Quotations are from paras 1 and 3, and Annex, part I, para. 6.

78. The peacetime machine was the JIC itself, its JIS support, and its members the Foreign Office, the three single-service directorates, and the Security Service, SIS and JIB. GCHQ became a member some years later. Subsequently the Committee became part of the Cabinet Office; the service directorates and JIB were rolled into the Defence Intelligence Staff; the JIS became the Assessments Staff. Another change has been for more civilians from policy departments to become committee members since 1983.

79. Cabinet Office paper of July 2009 (released 8 October that year) *Improving the Central Intelligence Machinery* (www.cabinetoffice. gov.uk/sites/default/files/nim-november2010.pdf). This emphasised the JIC's responsibilities for assessment, with the transfer of managerial functions to the Cabinet Office. For revised terms of reference and explanation see: www.cabinetoffice.gov.uk/security_and_ intelligence/community/central_intelligence_machine (accessed October–November 2009).

80. *Review of Intelligence Organisation 1947*, by Air Chief Marshal Sir Douglas Evill, 6 November 1947, CAB 163/7.

81. Brief references to wartime arrangements are in Foreign Policy Document (Special Issue) No. 263, Longmore, R. A. and K. C. Walker,

Herald of a Noisy World – Interpreting the News of All Nations: The Research and Analysis Department of the Foreign and Commonwealth Office (London: Foreign and Commonwealth Office, 1995). I am indebted to Patrick Salmon for drawing this history to my attention.

82. *Review of Intelligence Organisation 1947*, by Air Chief Marshal Sir Douglas Evill, 6 November 1947, CAB 163/7.
83. I am indebted to Pete Davies for this suggestion.
84. Bennett, *Churchill's Man of Mystery*, p. 267.
85. Intelligence and Security Committee, *Annual Report 1999–2000* (London: HMSO, 2000), para. 23. The same section also has 'the Agencies need stronger coordination'. The weakness appears as a 'void' at para. 41 of that report.
86. The most important recent influence has been the conclusion of the Butler Committee that 'We see a strong case for the post of Chairman of the JIC being held by someone with experience of dealing with Ministers in a very senior role, and who is demonstrably beyond influence, and thus probably in his last post'. See *Review of Intelligence on Weapons of Mass Destruction: Report of a Committee of Privy Counsellors* (London: HMSO, 2004), para. 63.
87. Ibid., chapters-5–8.
88. JIC(45)293(Final), 13 October 1945, CAB 81/131.
89. Ibid.
90. Strong, K., *Intelligence at the Top: The Recollections of an Intelligence Officer* (London: Cassell, 1968), p. 224.
91. Howarth, *Intelligence Chief Extraordinary*, p. 199.
92. I am indebted for the contents of this paragraph to Pete Davies and his then-draft of British defence intelligence, subsequently published as 'Estimating Soviet Power: The Creation of Britain's Defence Intelligence Staff 1960–65', *Intelligence and National Security*, 26, no. 6, 2011: 818–41.

12 Post-Cold War Issues and Opportunities[1]

[1997]

The British government's 'intelligence' is based on specialised intelligence organisations and their activities. Their main output is 'foreign intelligence' – on a range of foreign affairs, including military and other external threats – plus 'security intelligence' on terrorism, espionage and other threats with covert and domestic components. Intelligence also contributes to the protection of government's information ('information security'), typically through personnel security and the protection of communications and information technology ('ITSEC'). The offensive role of penetrating foreign security defences is combined with acting defensively to protect national secrets; intelligence acts as gamekeeper as well as poacher.

In 1940 Winston Churchill provocatively asked how 'the Intelligence Service' was organised.[2] This 'Service' – or for the last half-century the 'intelligence community' – is based on four organisations.[3] Three of them are officially the 'intelligence and security services', or 'the Agencies', and are:[4]

- Government Communications Headquarters (GCHQ), the national agency for the production of signals intelligence (Sigint), from the monitoring of communications and other electronic emissions.
- The Secret Intelligence Service (SIS), producing foreign intelligence from human and technical sources.
- The Security Service which gathers, analyses and assesses security intelligence, as well as advising and acting upon it.

254

The fourth member is the Defence Intelligence Staff (DIS), which analyses defence-related intelligence for 'the Ministry of Defence (MoD) and the Armed Forces and other Government Departments'.[5] (Strictly speaking its Whitehall element is now the Defence Intelligence Assessment Staff – DIAS – but DIS remains the common usage and is retained here.) To weld the community together there is the interdepartmental machinery of the Joint Intelligence Committee (JIC), with the twin roles of coordinating intelligence assessment and community management. It is served by the Cabinet Office Assessments Staff and a Secretariat.

Four features are important for understanding this community. The first is the continuum between security intelligence and foreign intelligence. Terrorism is international, and even when home-based it almost always has international connections; like espionage and the other targets of security intelligence, it manifests itself overseas as well as at home, as threats to British forces, ships, aircraft, embassies and citizens abroad. It can be supported by rogue states or directly practised by them. Security intelligence is increasingly globalised. Nevertheless, its responsibilities retain a domestic element of detecting covert 'enemies within' which distinguishes the Security Service's orientation from that of the other agencies.

Second, there is the basic difference between the 'single-source' collectors/exploiters (GCHQ and SIS) who are experts on their own techniques for producing covert intelligence, and the 'all-source' elements (the DIS and the JIC) who are government's experts on the particular subjects on which they produce finished intelligence.[6] GCHQ intercepts and exploits foreign communications, and SIS recruits and runs human sources. By contrast, the *raison d'être* of the DIS is the analysis and understanding of foreign military power using all available information. The JIC machinery operates on the same all-source basis, producing interdepartmental assessments and forecasts for the top level of government on 'events and situations relating to external affairs, defence, terrorism, major international criminal activity, scientific, technical and international economic matters'.[7] All-source work of this kind draws not only on covert sources but also on public material and official information such as diplomatic telegrams and military reconnaissance and observation.

The distinction between single- and all-source intelligence is by no means complete; thus, the single-source agencies use other material as background in exploiting their own, and the DIS controls some of its own single-source collection and exploitation. Nevertheless, there is a key difference between single-source and all-source responsibilities, between collecting/exploiting single-sources and producing finished, authoritative, all-source output. The Security Service in its own specialised area is also an all-source producer in this sense, as well as a collector.

The third feature is the institutional variation in status. The three agencies are self-standing, with Heads personally responsible to Ministers – SIS and GCHQ to the Foreign Secretary, the Security Service to the Home Secretary. Policy on them is kept under collective review by the Ministerial Committee on Intelligence Services (IS) and the Permanent Secretaries' Committee on the Intelligence Services (PSIS), chaired by the Cabinet Secretary, and their combined budgets form the Single Intelligence Vote (SIV). The Parliamentary Intelligence and Security Committee established by the 1994 Intelligence Services Act is also charged with reviewing their 'expenditure, administration and policy'.[8] The DIS on the other hand is one of MoD Central Staffs, managed as part of defence.

The fourth is the inadequacy of describing national intelligence solely in terms of this central community. Within the MoD, the military Chief of Defence Intelligence (CDI) is responsible not only for the DIS but also for 'the overall direction of intelligence within the *defence community*'[9] (emphasis added), including the 'strategic-level' resources of the armed forces. Chief among these is the Joint Air Reconnaissance Intelligence Centre (JARIC), the national centre for producing photographic intelligence (imagery). This had some post-war status under JIC supervision, but evolved as an MoD resource, controlled and tasked mainly by the DIS.[10] CDI also oversees the Military Survey Agency, with important intelligence components, and the Defence Intelligence and Security Centre, for training.

Also under armed forces' control are some expensive airborne assets which are nominally 'tactical' electronic collectors but are really of national significance, and at one time were budgeted as strategic intelligence.[11] There is also the military intelligence staff in Northern Ireland, and the staff at the Permanent Joint Forces Headquarters at Northwood, of growing importance in current arrangements for operations overseas; thus the effective use of intelligence in the Falklands War depended on an improvised Northwood staff of that kind, and not on Whitehall.

Additionally, there are the military and civilian elements that have significant part-time or fringe intelligence roles yet are not categorised as national intelligence resources. Armed forces' ships and aircraft may be engaged on temporary intelligence operations, or regular ones supplementary to their operational roles. The Security Service has close links with police forces' Special Branches, and the Special Branch of the Royal Ulster Constabulary retains special responsibilities for Irish terrorism in its area, even though like other Special Branches it is also linked with police responsibilities for public order and other law enforcement. The JIC itself still has some subordinate coordinating machinery in British territories overseas. Most important of all, within the central community the Foreign and Commonwealth Office (FCO) plays a major part in the JIC assessment process, and the same applies, though less significantly, to other non-intelligence departments in Whitehall. In short, the central intelligence community is linked with an outer ring of other bodies, of varied degrees of size and central relevance.

There is nothing odd about the imprecision. All organisation involves anomalies and imperfect boundaries, and these do not prevent intelligence from being a distinctive activity based on identifiable institutions. But it comprises rather more than just the central community. Hence this chapter is concerned with the total *national intelligence capability*: the central community, plus the outer ring of those associated and subordinate activities that have more than merely local or tactical significance.

Resources

This capability suffered considerable reductions at the end of the Cold War, and further contraction continued through the last decade, though more in people than in total costs. The 1996

Estimate for the three civilian agencies showed planned financial reduction by 3.25 per cent over the following four years, with manpower cuts over the same period of 13 per cent, from 9,642 to 8,366.[12] The 1999 Estimate and its forecasts for the next two years suggested that manpower was on a plateau at around 8,350 people. There appeared to be an upward trend in overall spending; £774 million for 1999/2000 was preceded by £730 million and £724 million in 1997/98 and 1998/99.[13] The figure available for 1996/97 for the DIS and other defence intelligence, shown as the CDI slice of the Defence Budget, was £152.6 million. The picture of present strengths used as a basis here is derived from a mixture of public data and working assumptions, and is as follows:

- A Sigint effort of about 4,500 civilians plus a considerable military effort, perhaps now of 2,000, all controlled from GCHQ.
- SIS and Security Service strengths in the region of 1,750 civilians in each.
- MoD (CDI) resources (1996/97) of 4,700 (3,100 uniformed and 1,600 civilian), of which the most important components are probably:
  o the military Sigint manpower controlled by GCHQ;
  o the DIS (or DIAS) with a military and civilian strength now of perhaps 500, mainly for all-source analysis but with some effort devoted to the control and support of the other defence intelligence;
  o JARIC about 500 strong, divided on a 70:30 basis between military and civilians;[14]
  o Military Survey, about 1,150 strong and roughly one-third military;[15]
  o the Defence Intelligence and Security Centre.
- The current Cabinet Office effort (the Joint Intelligence Organisation) of 50 in all, divided between the Assessments Staff and JIC Secretariat.

To these figures must be added the other armed forces' resources already referred to, plus the Special Branch officers linked with the Security Service.[16] In all, the cost of the national intelligence capability to be discussed here can be assumed to be at least £1 billion annually. By comparison with the total intelligence budget, Britain spends significantly less on diplomacy, not quite twice as much on overseas aid, and over twenty times as much on defence.[17]

Status

In purely financial terms this effort is commensurate in some respects with intelligence in France and Germany, but there are significantly greater British efforts on Sigint and also, albeit on a much smaller scale, on imagery interpretation. British intelligence as a whole probably has a higher public standing than its opposite numbers in continental Europe. In its combination of size and quality Britain is, uniquely, an 'upper second class' intelligence power in international terms, still with an unusual degree of world reach.

This work provides HMG with intelligence not only from its own efforts but also foreign liaison sources, and its value is the sum of the two; national investments in intelligence are in some respects subscriptions to a set of international clubs. Britain's high reputation for quality, reliability and source protection underlies its extensive foreign liaisons, but among these the relationship with the United States is paramount and unusually close. Hence the academic 'upper second class' analogy does not quite convey the effect of the UK's large-scale access to the output of the American intelligence superpower. To pursue the academic analogy: Britain enjoys postgraduate status without having paid all the fees. As recipients of national plus American intelligence, as well as the product of other foreign liaisons, British governments receive a quasi-superpower level of intelligence support: perhaps a last vestige of the *Pax Britannica*.

Value

Intelligence in an Unstable World

Intelligence as a substantial, permanent feature of Western states was a product of the Cold War, and throughout the 1990s there was substantial discussion of its future. Initially there was a tendency to dwell on requirements outside the traditional security field: not only economic intelligence but also environmental and other new international issues. Terrorism then appeared at centre stage. For the first half of the decade the British community was also preoccupied with the scope for intelligence assistance to law enforcement, particularly on drugs and other organised international crime. Over the last few years 'information warfare', including threats to the 'national information infrastructure', has been topical as 'a new form of combat',[18] relevant to terrorism and subversion as well as war between states.[19]

The thread through the 1990s has however been the intelligence challenges placed upon the turbulent post-Cold War world, including a nuclear-tipped, unstable and discontented Russia; all posing 'concerns' rather than threats as previously conceived. American writers have recently distinguished between new policy priorities: List A, threats to national survival (the Soviet Union in the Cold War); List B, threats to national interests but not survival; List C, 'contingencies' indirectly affecting national security without directly threatening national interests.[20] A senior British official some years ago put forward a comparable diagnosis that

> although the big threat has gone, the second order threats are proliferating. The chances of a second order threat turning nasty will be greater . . . Usually there will be no direct threat to Britain or the West, but not always . . . Technology, communications, the media have transformed the world over the last 50 years.[21]

For purposes of an intelligence strategy these features of the modern world can be taken as read, without translation into precise intelligence requirements and priorities. Some general points will suffice:

- There is a continuing need for covert intelligence on a wide range of issues. The modern world is indeed increasingly open, and covert sources less unique than during the Cold War; but the open sources are often incomplete and misleading. Deeply secretive regimes still exist, along with the wide and increasing range of opaque, often clandestine non-state targets like terrorist groups and illegal arms traffickers.

- Intelligence's ability to provide useful information continues to increase. Despite the international spread of encryption, the explosion in electronic communications provides ever-increasing intelligence access, and the technology of imagery and other means of surveillance continues to lead the counter-measures of 'stealth' and 'signature reduction'. On technical methods as a whole there is some hyperbole in the American claim of a move to 'a world in which the many kinds of sensors, from satellites to shipborne radar, from unmanned aerial vehicles to remotely planted acoustic devices, will provide information to any user who needs it';[22] but it does reflect something of modern technical intelligence's power. At the same time the world of increasing travel and migration – travel and tourism is said to have become the world's largest single industry[23] – provides increasing scope for developing and exploiting human sources.
- In quantitative terms the biggest intelligence requirement remains military intelligence in support of armed forces. Military forces in the variety of peace support and peace enforcement operations in Bosnia and elsewhere have needed virtually the full range of wartime intelligence support. Targeting intelligence is vital to exploit the power of precision weaponry. Whatever the limitations of the NATO air campaign, Kosovo reinforced the general lesson of the Gulf War that 'what can be seen on the modern battlefield can be hit, and what can be hit will be destroyed'.[24]
- Nevertheless, the immediately valuable day-to-day application of good (mainly covert) intelligence is often geared not to military contexts but to 'diplomatic support' to national governments in their international interactions, irrespective of subject. A generalisation of some years ago probably still applies, that intelligence sources add perhaps 10 per cent on the subject-matter of diplomatic reporting.[25]
- Despite this direct value of covert single-source reports, the basis of any sound application of intelligence to major decisions remains intelligence's all-source assessment. The relatively small resources engaged in this part of the process remain the main determinant of intelligence's overall cost-effectiveness.

On these foundations it is easy to make the general case for modern intelligence. For military commanders it is an integral part of the so-called Revolution in Military Affairs, but the revolution runs wider. International affairs as a whole are increasingly dominated by information and its speedy use, and intelligence has a firmly established place in this scene. But how much of it is needed by Britain? How important is the remarkable level of intelligence support that HMG receives, and the national effort that sustains it?

Intelligence and the UK's Role

Intelligence's value can sometimes be illustrated quantitatively, in terms such as saving and losing lives, avoiding and incurring physical damage, and financial and economic gains and losses. It was officially claimed before the 'peace process' that security intelligence has prevented four out of five operations planned by Irish terrorists,[26] and annual Defence White Papers gave tallies of terrorist explosives, weapons and ammunition seized. Effects on international negotiations can sometimes (though not often) be expressed quantitatively as the benefits of getting a good deal. Intelligence failures can sometimes be measured similarly. Intelligence warning of Argentine plans to invade the Falklands might have spared HMG the costs of the war and the subsequent capital and running costs of the permanent military garrison and airport; intelligence helped to win the war but failed to prevent it.

Yet the great mass of intelligence does not lend itself to cost-benefit calculation of this kind. Some of it can certainly be related to specific national commitments, threats and interests, as when intelligence requirements are based on British responsibilities for the security of its overseas territories and other specific overseas commitments. The requirements on Irish and international terrorism are clear enough, and these threats largely set the scope of the Security Service and its supporting resources from the other agencies. Something of the same applies to counterespionage and intelligence assistance to law enforcement.

But these are still relatively small demands on the total intelligence capability, and likely to remain so. The main expectations of intelligence are related to much broader aspects of policy. In the late 1980s it was asserted that 'British foreign policy since the war

has seen successive governments attempting to maintain international responsibilities without the [material] resources necessary to
meet them'.[27] Intelligence had been a constant if unpublicised support. Since the end of the Cold War Britain's improved economic
position and heightened military reputation have reinforced the
nation's view of itself as an influential world power, an international leader in the Security Council, one of the natural managers
in world society.[28] Despite Parliamentary criticism there is effective
bi-partisan agreement on the ethical dimension of foreign policy;
as put by one of Mr Cook's predecessors, 'it is now, and perhaps
has always been, part of the interests of Britain to do what we can
with others to achieve a more decent world'.[29] The same consensus
underlay the findings of the Strategic Defence Review (SDR) and
its concept of expeditionary forces and support for international
intervention.

This largely elective, wide-ranging foreign and military policy
needs comparable intelligence support – sometimes for specific
decisions, but also for more general educational, cumulative and
generalised effects. Intelligence reduces the quota of government's
mistakes and misperceptions in its chosen world role, and enables
it to do better than if it had had to manage without it. Current
British defence planning – for intervening for international causes,
with surgical precision and mobility and low casualties – requires
the 'information superiority' set out in NATO's 1999 Strategic
Concept.[30] Having superpower-standard intelligence is an unstated
assumption in the British worldview and expectations. 'Britain
plays with the hand it has been dealt; intelligence is one of the
strong cards'.[31] Codebreaking's part in fighting Hitler is part of
British folk memory. Britain sees itself as an intelligence winner,
not a loser, and in the last resort cares more about intelligence than
trade promotion. In Germany and Japan, by contrast, intelligence
successes have no particular place in national history, and intelligence receives lower national expectations. Arguably since 1945
they have needed it less.

Of course it can still be argued that since the early 1980s, perhaps since the Falklands War, successive British governments have
had love affairs with intelligence; that it gets too well treated compared with the FCO, BBC external broadcasting and monitoring,

the British Council, overseas aid, and the Defence Budget;[32] that, even with their present foreign policy objectives, Ministers could rely more on reading diplomatic dispatches and *The Economist*, and less on the JIC's weekly intelligence survey. There may be something in this. The highly classified intelligence in Ministerial boxes may sometimes get more attention than it deserves. Yet in general terms the connection between high-profile foreign policy and intelligence support cannot be gainsaid. Proactive British governments without good intelligence would be international loose cannons.

There are also the indirect effects. Britain's international reputation for sound judgement is significantly intelligence-driven, and is a factor in the national influence, inside and outside the transatlantic alliance, the EU and the Commonwealth. Britain's leading part vis-à-vis other European countries in the current NATO command structure rests partly on its intelligence superiority. Intelligence is an aspect of British power, both 'soft' and 'hard'. Additionally, the defensive security of the 'national information infrastructure' also turns on the quality of the offensive intelligence advice available.

Value – The Transatlantic Factor

Even if the intelligence requirements of Britain's international position are accepted, it can still be argued that the US will meet them anyway. But this is not the normal British view, and for the last half-century Whitehall has assumed that the transatlantic relationship has to be worked at. Intelligence liaisons are ultimately subject to international politics, even though they also shape them. The US was known during the Cold War to withdraw services of intelligence material as a signal or punishment, and not merely to New Zealand. A future Suez Crisis would not leave UK–US intelligence relations as unaffected as they were in 1956.

UK policy has therefore been to shore up the relationship by creating as many areas as possible in which Americans can point to substantial British burden-sharing, or at least a British quid pro quo. A grumpy but knowledgeable American has described the British as 'superb intelligence diplomats' in 'making an extraordinarily astute investment buying into the US system, particularly in Sigint'.[33] Britain has sought to make the British connection indispensable to the US, and this has had a bearing on the size of the present effort. Its quality and modernity have also been influenced by the need to remain America's intelligence ally and keep a foot in the door in expensive, sophisticated, US-led fields. Britain has sought to remain a partner, even if a junior one, rather than be a dependant.

On the whole, the resulting quasi-superpower service to HMG has come cheaply. The American intelligence budget is nominally about sixteen times the British total suggested here, though different budgetary conventions for 'tactical' military systems make it difficult to compare like with like; the figure includes American 'tactical' military resources, and the comparison overstates the American predominance. But for Britain the transatlantic alliance has been by no means costless. There is no way of computing a precise cost for the future; the many and varied UK–US intelligence relationships are not simple 'on-off' devices. Yet there is no reason to question the conviction that they depend on visible British contributions. Their nature would change drastically if they became seen as an American provision of free goods.

Intelligence and National Stance

These twin features – Britain's chosen role as an active world power, and the importance for it of the American intelligence connection – underlie the broad endorsement of previous intelligence investments by the present government. Intelligence's share of the foreign policy and national security cake can be a matter of detailed argument, but the bottom line is that no British government with its present high-profile foreign and defence policies can afford to run unnecessary risks of intelligence failure, especially if resulting in military casualties. It is illustrative that a complete and updated stock of intelligence on fifty foreign countries is now said to be required to cover the list of contingencies in which new-style British military power may be deployed; and no doubt events will show that even this long list is incomplete.

British intelligence therefore needs to be evaluated in this context, and not in the more traditional terms of threats, interests and commitments. In current military jargon the British army is now capabilities based and not threat based, and intelligence has to be seen in the same light.

Quality and Central Management

Budgets are only one element of Britain's intelligence status; quality is equally important. It is the intelligence multiplier and needs to be sought for purely national reasons irrespective of its transatlantic and international effects. It costs money but is also a matter of using resources well. It is determined mainly at the single-agency level, but central management also comes into the picture. The remainder of this chapter deals with some issues of this kind.

The British community is managed on a basis of agency autonomy, collegial discussion and limited central intervention. There is a surprising degree of inter-agency cooperation. The results command international respect, indeed envy, and compare well with the much more elaborate American arrangements. The Whitehall instinct is therefore not to tamper with what seems to work. In his provocative 1940 question about a single Intelligence Service Churchill was probably renewing his attempt twenty years earlier to be an organisational mover and shaker,[34] but by 1943 he had come to a different view: 'I have a feeling that it would be a mistake at the present time to stir up all these pools.'[35] In not going back to the drawing board the present government has taken the same view, and rightly so.

Yet British pragmatism carries with it the risk of complacency, of not pursuing improvements from the centre with the energy shown within the individual agencies, of changing things only after post-mortems such as those following the Falklands invasion, the Gulf War and the Scott 'arms to Iraq' Report. Of those three sets of changes, the post-Falklands decision to make the JIC Chairman a non-departmental, Prime Ministerial appointment had been advocated in print by a former Director General of Intelligence thirteen years earlier;[36] the need demonstrated in the Gulf War for CDI's direction of the overall defence intelligence community had been recognised within the DIS some five years earlier;[37] and Whitehall's shortcomings of intelligence-handling seized upon by Scott had been common knowledge for many years. The British are inclined to view American intelligence as the product of an engineering culture, always trying new solutions for insoluble problems, and ignore what this US restlessness achieves. Hence the three central issues to be considered here. All these are relevant to Britain's international intelligence standing, but merit – and need – consideration in their own right.

Balance between Analysis and Collection

Detailed Analysis and Institutional Memory

Britain's reputation rests on its covert single-source collection and exploitation on the one hand and on its JIC output on the other. Collection and related exploitation absorb at least 90 per cent of the total budget, and the resources for JIC assessment seem trivial by comparison. Since 1968 the Cabinet Office Assessments Staff, as the kernel of the JIC process, has been staffed by perhaps twenty-five or thirty secondees, including a strong element from the FCO. Talent is what counts there, with a positive advantage in keeping the numbers low.

But between single-source collection and the JIC is the separate stage of detailed all-source analysis, integrating and evaluating all available evidence, monitoring current developments in detail, and acting as the national expert. This analysis provides the community's archive and institutional memory. It serves intelligence customers directly on subjects that do not need the top-level JIC imprimatur. Its output ranges from ephemeral situation reports to the results of research and assessment of varying depth, plus the updating of basic information on foreign countries.

Throughout the Cold War Britain under-invested in work of this kind and the 'subject' expertise that goes with it. Folk-memories of the Second World War emphasise Bletchley Park and occasionally the JIC; analysis by the wartime army, navy and air force intelligence staffs are less well remembered.[38] All-source desks have a peacetime image of rather mundane military 'collation' and have not had first claim on the community's numbers and quality. Observers have assumed that the Assessments Staff and JIC do everything needed after the single-source agencies have done their own analysis and selection and distributed the results.

Yet the Assessments Staff was never set up for detailed analysis. It was introduced in 1968 when 'think tanks' were in vogue. The Central Policy Review Staff, created two years later and located just above it in the Cabinet Office building, typified the faith of the time (in the words of a Cabinet Secretary many years later) in assembling 'a team of outstandingly talented people who have the capability of coming up with original perspectives and original questions which departments, with all their back-up and resources, haven't found'.[39] The Assessments Staff was conceived in the same spirit, to draw on others for detailed analysis and research, but to bring clear and uncommitted minds to the difficult assessment task, described by a former head of its Australian equivalent as being 'to illuminate what is otherwise unknown, pull together the overall picture, examine choices and possibilities, put this all on one page and get it to policy principals at the opening of business'.[40] The Assessments Staff has remained in this mould. It has occasionally recruited or developed its own gurus, but in most cases its members' knowledge of their subjects has been gained *in situ* during their two-year secondments.

Part of its strength is indeed that it is not self-contained. It draws upon the whole JIC community and provides 'guided collectivism' for the assessment process. Some argue that assessment as an activity needs detachment rather than subject expertise, but sometimes it can be no better than the detailed analysis and institutional memory on which it leans. Hence all-source analysis is needed to support it, as well as to meet the daily and weekly needs of Whitehall's lower- and medium-level policy desk officers on subjects that do not cross the JIC's thresholds of top-level relevance. There are also the threat assessments which contribute to expensive decisions on defence procurement that do not normally go through the JIC route. In short, the success of the Rolls-Royce JIC assessment system can obscure the need for all-source analysis of kinds not possible within the Cabinet Office.

The account given in Sir Richard Scott's report illustrated this need for analysis to pull things together. A succession of different desk officers in policy departments failed to recognise the accumulated significance of a succession of individual, single-source reports which arrived at their desks where they had no machinery for recall and collation. The problems of intelligence's security regulations were compounded by backwardness in information technology; an FCO official had written in 1991 on his department's management that 'the main blot is IT. Our approach appears antediluvian. We are being left behind.'[41] But the situation described by Scott also reflected the underlying shortage of all-source resources for the integration of all available evidence on the Iraqi arms industry. As Scott put it:

> individual items of intelligence taken in isolation might have been passed off as inconclusive . . . The cumulative volume of intelligence could not be so passed off [without an equivalent to] the Nelsonian use of the blind eye. But this, of course, assumes that the user of the telescope had been made aware of all the relevant intelligence. It is probably true that no one person was familiar with all the accumulated intelligence until, in June 1990, the JIC made the assessment required for the Iraq Note [on the Iraqi arms industry].[42]

There was a dearth of the consolidated reports from multiple sources that would have rung alarm bells earlier.

Government reactions to the Scott Report list some shutting of stable doors, mainly in policy departments and over their relationships with single-source collectors.[43] But they did not identify the key difference between single-source production and all-source analysis, nor consider the balance between the two. A former Chief of the Assessments Staff is reported to have described the British emphasis on single-source reports as delivering 'farm gate intelligence – you picked it up from the end of the drive at Cheltenham in a completely raw form . . . there wasn't a proper mechanism for digesting it'.[44] Scott's account illustrates the need for better all-source digestion. The best test of an intelligence system is the all-source memory it builds up, whether in old-fashioned index cards or through modern information technology.

What has been termed the 'Open Source Revolution' has made it all the more important to get a better balance between collection and analysis. It is now said that there are a hundred million internet sites worldwide, and a million new internet users each month. The ability to search what the American Presidential Commission on

US Intelligence (the Brown Commission) described in 1996 as 'the vast universe of information now available from open sources'[45] is now a necessity. DIS experts were said to have calculated some years ago that there were 8,000 relevant databases then available worldwide.[46] There is also the volume of 'grey' intelligence, defined as 'information which is not published or widely diffused but to which access can be gained, provided that one knows it exists and has adequate channels of communication'. It was argued in the 1980s in connection with US–Japanese economic competition that 90 per cent of the relevant information was openly accessible, 9 per cent from grey sources such as conference reports, trade association reports and unpublished doctoral theses, and less than 1 per cent from secret sources.[47]

This does not mean that intelligence analysis should become government's universal expert. There are many other specialists and forecasters, particularly on economic, commercial and financial matters. Intelligence cannot be the expert on all the factors which shape international relations. But analysis needs to be able to draw on other specialisms and integrate their material with political, defence and other elements in the matters it is required to understand. Even where this work can be let out to the private sector, intelligence will still need to control it and integrate it with covert material. Its all-source analysis should be led by high-quality staff, with good information technology and funds for subscription to international databases.

Compared with covert collection this is cheap. The modern world needs marginally less emphasis on covert collection and rather more on analysing its results, often in conjunction with non-intelligence sources. Measures for implementation can now be considered.

Contribution of the Defence Intelligence Staff

Excluding the special contribution of the Security Service, the DIS is the only intelligence agency charged with the detailed all-source analysis just discussed. Defence intelligence organisations have problems in all countries: the difficulty of developing intelligence as a specialist career for uniformed officers; problems of civilian careers; constant turnover of senior uniformed officers; vulnerability to the pressures of military interests. The DIS has compared well with its foreign counterparts, including those of the United States. In the Cold War its main preoccupation was with the USSR, but then and subsequently it has also provided London with detailed analysis and community memory on all overseas targets and situations in which foreign military and paramilitary forces have been involved. It has been Whitehall's main intelligence centre in British military operations. Subjects like the proliferation of weapons of mass destruction have helped to keep its work at the top of post-Cold War priorities. Additionally, it has habitually taken on wider, non-defence tasks such as the monitoring of economic sanctions which no one else could do. It has upheld in intelligence the military tradition of pulling governments' chestnuts out of the fire.

Despite all this, it has never been the jewel in intelligence's crown. Its performance in the Cold War has been criticised by the present author for accepting and reinforcing an uncritical and convenient view of the Soviet threat.[48] Successive generations of intelligence professionals combined respect for the DIS's individuals with criticism of it as an institution. It has not normally had potential three- and four-star service officers posted to it as part of their career development, and it was not noted for recruiting and keeping high-class civilians. For many years it deployed its graduate intake in one specialist area, with few wider opportunities. The main analyst areas were staffed by retired officers, reporting to serving officers on short intelligence tours. Some distinguished intelligence practitioners emerged, but in spite of the system rather than because of it. Its military component lacked stability, and criticism of it had some resonance with the future Bomber Harris's protest (in 1938) – about the lack of continuity in the Bomber Group he then commanded – in which he stated that 'we cannot run a highly technical and complicated business on the floating population of a casual ward'.[49]

Some welcome changes have been made in recent years, but the DIS is still not seen as a centre of excellence. It still needs to develop a handful of first-class people (military as well as civilian); more continuity in its uniformed and civilian scientific elements; and the institutional *esprit de corps* and independence that develop more easily in the intelligence agencies than in the DIS's position as part of the central MoD staff. People should be keen to join it. It should be more formally recognised and tasked as an intelligence producer serving a variety of Whitehall recipients as well as its primary MoD and military customers and the JIC. Materially and psychologically, it needs parity of esteem within the intelligence community.

The DIS and National All-Source Analysis

This would not resolve the question whether its analytic remit should be widened. For some decades after 1945 there was a British vision of a 'total' all-source intelligence institution, studying and understanding foreign countries and overseas situations as a whole. In America the CIA Directorate of Intelligence – quite distinct from the Agency's covert collection activities – emerged with this role, with a remit for detailed study of foreign countries and situations in a holistic way, free of any departmental tie. Australia has developed its Office of National Assessment along something of the same lines. Canada some years ago re-subordinated its small External Affairs research group to the Privy Council Office, to work for its equivalent to the JIC in a non-departmental way.

Britain has never created an analogue with this part of the CIA, and has emphasised departmental analysis, with political and defence analysis separated between the FCO and DIS, and foreign economic research shuffling uneasily between various parts of Whitehall. The Joint Intelligence Bureau (JIB) formed after the Second World War had only limited responsibilities, but the 1945 vision did not die completely. When the DIS was formed in 1964 through the amalgamation of the JIB with the three services' intelligence departments, some visualised it as the basis of a central, national institution. Thus, its successive heads were civilians, just retired from the services, Deputy Chairmen of the JIC, and held the title 'Director General of Intelligence' (DGI) – not 'Chief of Defence Intelligence', as the post became when converted to three-star serving level in the early 1980s.

The Cold War's emphasis on the Soviet target indeed made the DIS the nearest thing to a British analysis centre on the USSR. It studied the Soviet economy, its science and technology and its Third World aid, trade and penetration, besides Soviet military power and the many things connected with it (though not its internal and external politics and policies). It produced first drafts of JIC papers on these subjects, and on the Soviet target it had a major input at the JIC's Current Intelligence Groups and the JIC itself.

Some of this analysis continues, accompanied by a continued service on the rest of the word. Defence intelligence is a broad subject. Most of the assessments of the unstable world draw on it in some way, and studying foreign military power is itself incomplete without regard to the non-military factors that bear on it. DIS analysts are touchy if accused of knowing about the Ruritanian army but not about its politics and economics, and are usually familiar with this background.

Yet the fact remains that the DIS's job is defence intelligence, and it is not a multi-subject agency like the CIA's Intelligence Directorate. By contrast the responsibilities for economic intelligence outside the old USSR have always been uncertain, and there have been successive attempts to establish it elsewhere. An inquiry in 1969 found against the establishment of a separate Central Overseas Research Department with an economic slant, but recommended that the DIS effort on the Soviet economy should be incorporated in a new Sino-Soviet research unit in the FCO. An economic assessment effort was established in the Cabinet Office in 1968 as part of the new Assessments Staff, but subsequently was run down before being partly re-established. Since the end of the Cold War successive MoD economies have forced the DIS to cut back on what appear to be the non-military frills. There has been a recurrent pattern of the DIS accepting cuts in this way, then having to take on urgent new topics which no one else was equipped to study. There is ambiguity about where the limits of the DIS's responsibility for defence intelligence actually lie.

Hence it is tempting to reorient it towards the pattern of the CIA or the Central Overseas Research Department discussed in 1969. It is a seductive idea, but one to be resisted. Military forces need something like the DIS committed to meeting their military needs and supporting command intelligence staffs. A central agency without military affiliations would never be satisfactory; an American lesson of the Gulf War was the inadequacy of the CIA's direct support of deployed forces.[50] Incorporating the Research and Analysis Department (RAD) of the FCO into a central agency would meet the same objection, that the FCO as an operational department needs its intelligence analysis in-house. Central analysis of terrorism would similarly cut across the Security Service's close relationship with the Special Branches and with the operational arms of police forces and other counterterrorist actors.

Thus, the advantages of central analysis are offset by the loss of close relationships between intelligence customers and 'their' intelligence staffs. The corollary in the US of the CIA's Intelligence Directorate is its widespread duplication by departmental analysis units: the Defense Intelligence Agency and the many other armed forces' organisations; the Intelligence and Research Bureau in the State Department; and so on. The American system thrives on duplication and rivalry, and can afford them. They would not suit the British scale of resources, and the dislike of interdepartmental competition.

In practice the present situation works tolerably well in a pragmatic British way. The DIS works closely with the rest of the intelligence community and provides a service to London departments outside the MoD when it can. Whitehall is not given to black-and-white terms of reference. Yet in times of stringency the DIS's fortunes are determined by the MoD's view of it as a departmental defence asset, and not by wider needs. This suggests that others in addition to the MoD and the armed forces should have a say in determining what the DIS does, and what it needs. Its study of foreign subjects on the periphery of defence intelligence should be formally recognised, as should its services of intelligence to non-MoD departments. As a key part of the national capability, it should be subject to (and involved in) nationally supported priorities, resource allocation and community planning. In the military term, it should become formally 'double-hatted' in its analytical role, with responsibilities to the MoD and armed forces on the one hand, and national intelligence management on the other. Its role in the control of national imagery and other sources points in the same direction, and is discussed later in this chapter, along with the budgetary and other implications of double-hatted status.

Complementary Approaches

Nevertheless, the DIS must remain largely defence oriented, and formalising its wider role would not completely meet the challenge of understanding foreign countries holistically. The Western inability to forecast the collapse of the Soviet Union reflected a preoccupation

274

with studying it as a rival and threat, rather than as a society; and the lesson must have some relevance for the post-Cold War world. Understanding Islamic fundamentalism might be a parallel. Understanding 'difficult' foreign areas/countries needs some insight into national character, the Gestalt, 'the functional whole whose properties are not derivable from the sum of its parts'. Hence there is the question whether Britain's posture of 'world reach' is supported by enough provision for area experts, with relevant language and other competence.

The question goes beyond intelligence boundaries. On one view there is no problem. The FCO has an amassed and living knowledge of foreign countries. To quote a working diplomat: 'the Foreign Office is the custodian of information about countries throughout the world . . . [It] must be prepared when the next crisis in the world arises'.[51] Diplomats are in touch with journalists, bankers and businessmen, and with non-governmental studies of international affairs; Chatham House was established precisely for this purpose. Defence attachés link the diplomats with military developments abroad. Backing up all the working contacts is the overseas expertise of the FCO's eighty-strong RAD and its dozen Economic Advisers; the Bank of England on financial matters; and experts in the other Whitehall Departments dealing with overseas matters. Policy officials everywhere digest the open literature. The accumulated knowledge of the DIS and the civilian agencies is on tap to the JIC. What with the high calibre of the Assessments Staff, the non-stop circulation of drafts around Whitehall, the wide range of CIGs, extensive departmental pre-JIC briefings and discussion at the JIC itself, is anything lacking?

Yet manifestly things go wrong, and reality can be different. Many senior diplomats have become area experts, but the mid-career pattern is of expertise in dealing with successions of foreign countries rather than understanding particular ones deeply. An FCO team itself recognised the difference between its diplomatic 'generalists' and its more knowledgeable Research Officers:

> Policy towards a country should not be formulated solely by a political department only one of whose members has ever served in the region, and none of whose members is capable of uttering more than courtesies in the vernacular of the country concerned.[52]

At one period covered in the Scott Report, FCO's Middle East Department had three heads in a year; out of twenty desk officers only three had had experience of the countries they were dealing with, and their average time in post was six months.[53] In Whitehall as a whole everyone is always taking over or moving on, and even when policy-makers are genuine experts they lack what the FCO team cited as the 'intellectual and operational independence that comes from freedom from policy commitment'.

Hence the need for area specialists. But the staff of RAD have borne their share of FCO cuts, beginning with a 17 per cent reduction conceded in 1978 in response to the CPRS survey. There has been repeated heart-searching about their position, and the in-house scrutiny in 1993 sought to make better use of their expertise through a controversial reorganisation.[54] The DIS has never systematically encouraged the learning of foreign languages, though it has benefited from the presence within it of former defence attachés. The FCO's and DIS's research classes are separate from each other, small, and with career prospects that do not rival those of the policy-makers, nor those offered by the intelligence agencies. In the post-imperial era Britain cultivates specialist overseas expertise in a rather casual way.

There is no clear correlation between area expertise and intelligence performance. The CIA is full of experts with academic backgrounds, but this does not guarantee success. It failed to forecast the Shah's fall, despite having an Iranian expert of great experience on its staff.

Yet in reviewing the record of intelligence failure it is difficult not to conclude that area knowledge has a place in reading foreign leaders' minds. The misinterpretation of the evidence on preparations for the Yom Kippur attack on Israel turned on a failure to believe that Sadat could choose to attack for reasons other than clear-cut military victory. It is still not clear to what extent NATO's expectation of a speedy Serbian collapse over Kosovo drew on incomplete understanding of Serbian politics or of Yugoslav military doctrine of camouflage and concealment. The same applies to the need to understand foreign terrorists' mindsets, and those of the IRA.

The DIS has already been discussed. Other inexpensive ways of developing and using a bigger pool of area expertise can be suggested as follows. First, as the author has advocated elsewhere, there should be some tinkering with the composition of the Assessments Staff to build up a rather greater proportion of intelligence professionals within it, complementing but not replacing the diplomatic secondees from the FCO.[55] Second, continued efforts should be made to tap expertise outside government, not just by cultivating contacts but also by developing consultancies with Chatham House, Oxford Analytica and similar institutions, perhaps with some central, JIC funding of 'Team B' assessments to complement official ones. The present 'Foreign Office Fellowships' scheme of temporary expert appointments in RAD might also be extended to the Assessments Staff and DIS. The practical problems over securing senior, well-qualified academics should not be underrated. But 'area studies' developed as a recognised academic discipline through American academics' experience of intelligence in the Second World War, and academia might be able to do something to return the compliment.[56]

Third, there should be some interdepartmental planning of overseas analysis. The JIC has its programme for finished reports and papers, and RAD and the DIS have their equivalent lists of work-in-progress to meet department requirements. There is ample contact and discussion of drafts, but no national system for coordinating research and study. The JIC could usefully develop a strategic, annual, interdepartmental analytic programme. The fact that Whitehall departments are increasingly driven by immediate, short-term needs makes it all the more important to have a strategy of some kind for research, whether in-house or by contract. It is odd that the JIC produces priorities for single-source collection, but not for the all-source work that exploits it.

Alongside these practical suggestions, there is also the more tantalising vision of a Central Overseas Research Department, on the lines of the Government Statistical Service and Office of National Statistics. British government statistics grew up on a departmental basis in almost exactly the same period as organised intelligence developed in the second half of the nineteenth century in the Admiralty and War Office Intelligence Departments. A. J. P. Taylor's description of government statistics in the 1930s – 'four separate departments collected industrial statistics; five classified employers of labour; two produced rival and conflicting figures concerning overseas investment'[57] – could have been applied to intelligence of that period. The JIC subsequently evolved to produce coordinated assessments on the enemy, and the Central Economic Intelligence Service (renamed the Central Statistical Office (CSO) in 1941) to do the same on Britain's war effort. The CSO cooperated with Washington to produce joint wartime statistical statements, much as the JIC cooperated to produce agreed UK–US intelligence estimates for the Combined Chiefs of Staff. The similarity continued after 1945, when the Government Statistical Service developed as a statistical community with a matrix of central and departmental control. Specialist statistical divisions have for many years been integral parts of government departments, yet owe a parallel professional allegiance to the Head of their Service.

Can a lesson be drawn from this for establishing a Whitehall-wide foreign research profession? The problems of area expertise spring largely from the small size and limited opportunities of the departmental graduate research pools. Government statisticians, economists and others have an interdepartmental identity in government-wide specialist classes. Perhaps the overseas specialists need a similar identity, as a Foreign Research Officer class spanning the present FCO Research Cadre, the DIS, some posts in the Assessments Staff, and perhaps other parts of government – even, just conceivably, some presence in the civilian intelligence agencies. Wizardry in interception and codebreaking and other single-source skills will still be important. But they will increasingly have to be matched by developing all-source area expertise in assessment and interpretation. It is difficult to see how this challenge will be met without something beyond purely departmental responses. For its chosen world role Britain invests in high-quality diplomacy, armed forces and intelligence collection. Is there the right national investment in understanding the foreign areas and situations in which we are prepared to act?

Covert Collection: The Challenge of Satellites

The Intelligence Revolution

These proposals for all-source analysis have minimal financial implications. If cuts are needed in the future – contrary to the present indications of intelligence expenditure on a plateau – they should be directed at collection, not analysis. Some adjustments between different collection agencies might be needed from time to time. The human sources of SIS and the Security Service may have some degree of insulation through their targeting of Irish and other terrorism, international trade involving the proliferation of weapons of mass destruction, and links with organised crime. Sigint as the biggest collector is a target for economies, though there (and elsewhere) technology provides scope for savings in running costs in return for capital investments. However, the dominant issue of future resource allocation concerns satellite imagery, of which Britain has no collection of its own.

Satellite collection, embracing both Sigint and imagery, has indeed been the main area where British policy over the UK–US relationships has been tested.[58] American and Soviet collection of this kind first developed in the early 1960s and subsequently became the most important intelligence development since the introduction of radio interception and aerial photography in the First World War. It revolutionised imagery by providing guaranteed and uncontested observation of foreign territory, initially by traditional photography and latterly with the addition of all-weather radar imagery and other refinements. The imagery results are of particular military importance and are the greatest intelligence contribution to the Revolution in Military Affairs. The effect on the interception of foreign radars and similar electronic emissions (Elint) is almost as great, with similar consequentials for electronic warfare. Media comment suggests that the significance for communications intelligence (Comint) is less all-embracing but is still very great.

In all, the impact of satellites on intelligence can be likened to the effects of radar on war. Their effects have not completely dominated Western operations over Iraq and the former Yugoslavia, since aerial reconnaissance and drones have been able to share the load. But satellites have been major contributors, and remain unmatched where conventional air reconnaissance cannot be guaranteed.[59] The Falklands campaign would have been very different had modern satellite surveillance been available to focus upon it. States with collectors in space have a quite different reach from those without them.

Yet the cost and variety of these systems pose major problems. By and large, intelligence satellites are not multi-purpose and are designed for one kind of collection, and the only safe generalisation on costings is that they are more expensive by several orders of magnitude than any comparable ground-based collection. Unofficial estimates have put the cost of American Keyhole (imagery) satellites as two billion dollars each, but the complete accountancy for satellites, launch costs and ground segments is not available.[60] Any conceivable non-US system can match only a small proportion of these American systems; 'the disparity between the United States and other nations is quite marked. US investment in ISR (intelligence collection, surveillance and reconnaissance) – particularly the high-leverage space-based aspects of this set of systems – exceeds that of all other nations combined.'[61] Costs may now be coming down, and there is talk of lightweight, low-orbit satellites, each costing about US$30–50 million. Additionally, there is the growth of commercially available imagery satellite material which may enable some national requirements to be met by this open source; though questions remain about this material's quality, reliability and speed of response, for example for the targeting of precision weapons.

In fact, a process of specialised intelligence satellite proliferation already involves an increasing group of second-class powers. This collection in the Cold War was the two superpowers' prerogative, perhaps accompanied by some Chinese developments, but subsequently the French Helios system was launched in 1995 (costing the equivalent of £1.5 billion[62]) as part of France's major intelligence expansion after its dependence on American material during the Gulf War.[63] It has some Italian and Spanish support, though German participation in follow-on systems is said to have been cancelled through defence economies. Israel has a programme of some kind, India may have one, and Japan has apparently decided to move into the field.[64]

There have also been ambitious proposals for international projects. International satellite monitoring for arms control and confidence-building was first proposed at the United Nations in 1978 and has subsequently been brought occasionally off the back burner. This has been followed by the more realistic Western European Union (WEU) proposals for a European effort of some kind. A WEU (now EU) interpretation centre has been in operation in Torrejón in Spain since 1991 and now uses a mixture of commercial imagery, French Helios output and some Russian material, and there has been regular pressure to develop it as a basis for a European collection system of some kind. The last ten years have demonstrated Europe's dependence on the US for this material, and there have been hints of problems when it was not forthcoming; it has been claimed that in the period of Western disunity before the mounting of IFOR there was American reluctance to supply imagery bearing on its alleged breaches of the Bosnian arms embargo.[65] According to the WEU Assembly some years ago:

> Both France and Germany are prepared to share their satellite cooperation programme with other WEU member states . . . It will be necessary to quickly acquire an independent space capability to free Europeans from their dependence on the United States for intelligence which may be given or withheld but which in any event is selective and sifted by NATO . . . WEU must acquire an independent satellite data-acquisition system . . . It must at least be a ground segment sharing resources with other national programme users or using them on a cooperative basis.[66]

Europe committed itself at the 1999 Cologne Summit to creating a military capability that will make NATO a more equal US–European partnership, with greater European participation in political and military decisionmaking and an ability to operate if necessary without US participation. There is the familiar argument that Europe, with two-thirds of the US's GNP, could produce a better defence capability through more integration. If this is applicable to defence, why not to intelligence imagery? Despite its sensitivity, it could be an important test case.

British Policy

Britain has been fortunate in receiving the output from the wide variety of American satellite programmes without having any of its own. Its access to these American efforts is not uniformly robust and complete, but the overall relationship with them has indeed continued to be 'special', on a par with the rest of the intelligence relationship. For many years Britain has taken substantial steps to ensure the service in the Sigint part of the field. An ambitious attempt in the 1980s to develop a British Sigint satellite was found to be too costly but was reportedly superseded by 'buying in' in various ways to parts of the American Sigint system to ensure access to the whole. It has been claimed that this is a long-term and recurrent commitment.[67]

By contrast, there has been no similar UK action over imagery. Thanks to an association going back to RAF participation in overflights of the USSR early in the Cold War, Britain has received most of the American satellite material, and has performed its own interpretations of it at JARIC.[68] There has been collaboration in this analysis, but not in the expensive business of collection. The service of this material therefore remains relatively fragile, without any irreplaceable contribution to the US. The material itself is particularly relevant to military operations of all kinds. There is no guarantee that it will be available to meet British needs if British and American priorities differ, or if the US is not involved in joint operations and not necessarily a supporter of them.

With the international move towards satellite collection some greater stake in it now seems a UK necessity. It may well be assumed that the UK–US arrangements are adequate for satellite Sigint, but in imagery it seems contrary to the rest of national policy to be no more than a country member of the growing satellite imagery club. Britain has relied on the US service and trusts that it will continue, but on a longer view there appear to be three options. One would be to have a genuine national imagery programme; a satellite with echoes of Bevin's determination in 1946 to have a nuclear weapon 'with a bloody Union Jack flying on top of it'.[69] Another would be to make a demonstrably important contribution by buying in to the American imagery capability, on the lines reported for Sigint. The third would be to participate in a European project, presumably based on the French Helios satellite and its successors, and the existing Torrejón centre.

The first seems unrealistic in the present climate of cooperative international initiatives. Of the other two, the British instinct would be to take the transatlantic route of an increased contribution to American imagery, though the problems of doing so should not be understated; the culture of sixty years of UK–US Sigint cooperation could not be created easily in this quite separate field. On continental collaboration there would be British resistance to joining as a subordinate in a French-led programme, and there is the deep fear that close Anglo-European collaboration might be seen by the US as a betrayal of American secrets, including technological ones of value to Europe's space industry.[70] On 8 December 1999 a former Defence Secretary joined with a Field Marshal and a retired head of the FCO to warn that in their view the 'unique' UK–US intelligence cooperation would be threatened by the pooling of defence intelligence with the French; 'we will lose a vital pillar of our relationship with the United States, and NATO will be severely undermined'.[71]

Yet the transatlantic and European routes may not be mutually exclusive. Top-level American opinion has always favoured British collaboration with Europe, promoting transatlantic links while increasing Europe's ability to contribute more to NATO. There is no reason why satellite imagery should be regarded as an exception. Indeed, a framework reconciling national, transatlantic and European approaches to intelligence satellites may exist in the proposals by the Brown Commission, presumably reflecting professional US opinion: that there should be a satellite policy of two-tiered international burden-sharing and exchanges of product, with the US providing the more sophisticated systems and its allies contributing to the less costly, bread-and-butter coverage. In this policy,

> The United States would retain in the first tier its own high-end classified systems which involve the most sophisticated technology and techniques and are used to collect against the most critical consumer needs. The second tier would be developed in conjunction with friendly and allied governments and would consist of capable, but technically less sophisticated, reconnaissance systems that would emphasise the application of commercially available technology where possible as well as the application of existing industrial capacity. Foreign partners would be able to build, operate, and control their own satellites and ground stations, which would form part of a larger overall system.[72]

It is implicit, though unstated, that this proposal refers to imagery, and not Sigint. Underlying it in the concept of the 'information umbrella' of US power is the view that security constraints on satellite surveillance should be loosened, and that for international security purposes this intelligence should be seen as 'a public good, but not a free one'; those able to make a contribution should have to do so.[73]

One possible result could be some form of EU–US imagery satellite agreement on these lines, dedicated to the support of international security, with UK participation. An agreement of this kind would be a matter of great complexity. Yet it is a logical development of NATO intelligence and an EU/WEU identity within it. For Britain it is difficult to see any other means of providing an affordable stake in satellite imagery collection, buttressing the transatlantic connection while providing some guarantee of imagery support for deployed British forces and other national needs. In the light of current policy towards the European Strategic Defence initiative, Britain seems bound to move eventually in this direction.

Hence the issue arises of how policy matters of this importance are handled. Mention has already been made of the intelligence community's devolved structure, far removed from the single service originally postulated by Churchill. Satellite policy has implications for the whole community and needs central leadership. It is by no means the only issue of this kind. The remainder of this chapter therefore considers central management and its development.

Management of the National Capability

Responsibilities

Churchill's 1940 minute about the Intelligence Service posed another question: who was the man responsible for it?[74] Despite all the changes, the question remains, sixty years later: who's in charge? The remainder of this chapter discusses the answer. The management forum is usually seen as the JIC and discussion must start with the part it plays.

The Committee evolved at the beginning of the Second World War with two distinct functions, joined almost by accident: the production of agreed national assessments, so that government action 'should be based on the most suitable and carefully coordinated information available'; and intelligence management, or 'the consideration of any further measures which might be thought necessary in order to improve the efficient working of the intelligence organization as a whole'.[75] Setting aside the points made earlier in this chapter about detailed analysis and expertise, the Committee has a distinguished record on the first of these functions. Warts and all, JIC assessment is like democracy: the least bad arrangement yet invented.

Its record on the second function is less impressive. It was effective in the Second World War in sorting out disputes between the three armed services but had limitations where the civilian agencies were engaged. It kept out of disputes between the Security Service and SIS, and (more surprisingly) the management and priorities of wartime Sigint. After 1945 the wartime machinery for the management of Sigint remained (and remains) in use, distinct from the JIC. Nevertheless, the JIC's management got broader, inspired perhaps by a seminal recommendation that the intelligence attack upon the opaque Soviet target should be mounted and coordinated as a campaign. It developed a network of subcommittees to coordinate and stimulate collection and analysis (for example a Scientific and Technical Intelligence Subcommittee and its subordinate Guided Weapons Working Party) and saw itself as a principal management forum. Thus, for over ten years after 1945 it is said to have maintained the Second World War machinery for the provision of pigeons for clandestine wartime communication; as part of the contingency planning of that time for a Soviet occupation of Western Europe this does not deserve the ridicule it might now receive. It illustrates the Committee's continued management role on a wealth of interdepartmental matters, including the activities of the JICs and LICs (Local Intelligence Committees) established where British forces were deployed overseas.

But it was still a coordinating committee, with a neutral Foreign Office chairman holding the ring. It did not – could not – control the ultimate levers of management: money and appointments. And eventually the network of subcommittees atrophied, particularly after the three single-service intelligence departments and the Joint

Intelligence Bureau were subsumed into the DIS. The Committee's original *raison d'être* of knocking military heads together had disappeared, or at least been transferred to the MoD.

This does not mean that the JIC has not been useful for sorting out specific managerial problems. Many of these are best settled by consensus and give and take, and successions of chairmen have brought intellect and impartiality to them. The Committee has always played a part in reviewing formal intelligence requirements and priorities, though arguably the result has been a legitimisation of what is already happening.

However, the emphasis in central management has gradually shifted towards the role of Intelligence Coordinator. The post was originally created in 1968 on a part-time basis, but soon became involved in the managerial issues posed by the Irish situation in 1969. Successive incumbents have expanded its role to include the presentation of the intelligence budget to the PSIS, and other community issues. They have developed considerable managerial clout, not entirely exercised in the JIC forum, and have significant achievements to their credit.

Nevertheless, some features need comment. First, Churchill's question 'Who's in charge?' still has no clear answer. The JIC Chairman has clear responsibility for the Committee's intelligence output, but the post's institutional weight has varied. From 1985 to 1992 it was held by a retired diplomat in combination with the influential role of Prime Minister's Foreign Policy Adviser, but after a brief tenure by his successor it reverted to being the part-time responsibility of a succession of busy FCO officials on secondment as heads of the Cabinet Office's Overseas Secretariat. Intelligence Coordinators have had greater continuity but lower profiles, concentrating on the professional efficiency and priorities of the covert agencies. When next there is an intelligence failure, those conducting the post-mortem may find it hard to allocate responsibility between the JIC's dyarchy.

Second, the Coordinator's own remit is enigmatic in a typically British way. Most Coordinators have been former Heads of Agencies, on retirement from single-agency careers; the British system does not breed multi-agency professionals.[76] Others were appointed in earlier years without professional intelligence experience; not necessarily a handicap. In recent years the professional status of the post has been reduced relative to its Heads of Agency peers. In short, although the post is senior and important it has never been seen as intelligence's national Head of Profession. Finding future Coordinators worked for many years on the principle that it would be all right on the night.

The basis of the post is influence and advice, not executive responsibility. The Coordinator sits as a member of the JIC, and is influenced by the ambience of committees and consensus. The official description of his functions is in terms of advice, coordination and chairing committees; his clearest responsibility is in establishing intelligence requirements and advising on the allocation of resources to meet them.[77] The Coordinator has only a very small staff to help him. It is a very personal job, dependent on his own personal observations, initiatives and relationships. Elsewhere the author has likened the position, not entirely in jest, to a strong-minded Head of an Oxford College: able to achieve a great deal, but dependent on being able to carry colleagues with him.[78] In the collegial ambience of British intelligence it might be slightly more accurate to compare him with a college's much-respected and influential Vice-Principal. Neither analogy is quite accurate. They overlook the Cabinet Secretary's concern for intelligence matters, and the Coordinator's position as the conduit of his power. But they convey something of the way in which central management has evolved on subfusc lines. The Coordinator's reflection of the Cabinet Secretary's authority carries limitations with it, reminiscent of those inherent in the position of the Head of the Civil Service in the old Civil Service Department of the 1970s: dependent on Prime Ministerial interest and backing, and powerless – and abolished by Mrs Thatcher in 1981 – when deprived of this support from above.[79]

Budgets

These untidy features are reproduced and accentuated in the key instrument of policy: budgets. JIC management in the Second World War involved coordination of the three services and the joint-service organisations set up to meet their needs, and the establishment of the DIS lessened the need to bring interservice issues to the JIC table. As part of this trend for MoD to settle its own intelligence affairs, its intelligence budgets are now divorced from the central budget-setting, resource allocation and policy oversight procedure through which the PSIS 'scrutinises the agencies' annual expenditure forecasts, management plans and intelligence requirements, as part of the Public Expenditure Survey arrangements'.[80] Budgets for the DIS and other national-level military intelligence are vested in CDI and determined as part of the Defence Budget. Despite its name, the SIV is not a single intelligence vote, but a single vote for the three covert agencies.

The result is another duality in top-level management and oversight. The whole political and official structure for this purpose – the Coordinator's annual reviews of performance and initial advisory scrutiny of bids and budgets; the PSIS; the Ministerial Committee on Intelligence Services; the Parliamentary Committee – is formally limited to the three agencies. It is not charged with responsibility for the national intelligence capability as a whole; specifically, not the DIS, nor imagery analysis based on JARIC, nor even the JIC's performance. The futures of the DIS and JARIC are determined within MoD, not in the intelligence structure. At the level of budgets, strategy, planning and oversight, it would now be correct to speak of the management not of one intelligence community, but of two: the main community responsible to the Cabinet Office on one side of Whitehall, and CDI's defence intelligence community based on the MoD on the other. The pattern was symbolised in the newly instituted annual House of Commons debate on intelligence in 1998 in which the Foreign Secretary led and the Home Secretary wound up; the Defence Secretary was not involved. To sum up, there is fuzziness about central responsibilities and about the community to which these responsibilities apply.

Case for Central Overview

Too much should not be read into these managerial disjunctions. The Whitehall machinery is flexible and closely knit; in 'the Whitehall village' everyone knows everyone else and values a reputation for interdepartmental cooperation. CDI and the DIS are constant participants in the JIC's assessment process and are in regular contact with the rest of the community, in the

Committee and bilaterally. The JIC's remit 'to give direction to, and keep under review, the organisation and working of British intelligence activity at home and overseas' still provides a setting for coordination extending well beyond the three agencies.[81] The present combination of the JIC forum together with the elastic relationships between the Cabinet Secretary, Coordinator and CDI provide some balance between central influences and devolved responsibilities. The Parliamentary Committee pragmatically stretched its mandate in 1999 by criticising the JIC's performance over Sierra Leone.[82]

Nevertheless, some issues seem too big for a system that depends so much on cooperation, consensus and influence, especially when issues affect community members' own territories and budgets. The centre needs some ability to take a national view that cuts across institutional interests and boundaries, with some supra-agency capacity rather greater than 'coordination'. Intelligence everywhere has this problem; the verdict of the Brown Commission on the US community was that 'the process for allocating resources to intelligence is severely flawed'.[83] Britain is not above such criticism. The present government's concern for achieving 'joined-up government' through an enhanced Cabinet Office role is as relevant to intelligence as to other things

All-source analysis and satellite policy as discussed here illustrate the problems. The present machinery is not called upon to review the balance between collection and analysis, either in quantity or quality, and is not capable of doing so. For the whole of the Cold War everyone grumbled about the DIS, but helping it to pull itself up by its bootstraps was not seen as a national, PSIS-worthy issue; the substantial increases in intelligence budgets under Mrs Thatcher were directed towards the Cabinet Office side of Whitehall, not the MoD. A similar imbalance has applied to satellite collection. Imagery has been regarded as MoD's business, not a matter of intelligence policy. There has been no forum for forming an intelligence satellite policy.

Two other historical examples can be quoted to make the same point. One was the delay in developing a community-wide architecture for information technology, to facilitate a common bank of knowledge, accessible by intelligence and its users.

(The US community has recently stated the objective as developing 'interactive data bases to enable the policy maker to initiate a single request, search all community databases, and receive the requested data'.[84]) There were many difficulties, not least the importance of agencies' individual transatlantic connections. Nevertheless, although the concept of community IT was articulated nearly thirty years ago, its implementation repeatedly ran up against institutional interests. Contributing towards a community system was in no single organisation's immediate interest, and there was rarely sufficient central power to push towards coordinated planning. Some of Scott's findings on intelligence handling can be traced back to this origin.

A second issue needing a community perspective was intelligence on Irish terrorism. Despite major operational successes the effort was replete with organisational problems, and it took twenty years from the first bomb on the mainland to resolve (in 1992) the divided responsibilities of the Security Service and the Metropolitan Police Special Branch for intelligence on IRA threats there.[85] Even after that, a former Prime Minister (Sir Edward Heath) advocated the need for a more centralised effort; 'there is not one EC country that has succeeded in defeating terrorism without first establishing a proper, national central agency'.[6]

Heath's was a simplistic solution for a complex problem. The focal point for operational/tactical intelligence on the IRA had to be Belfast, just as the focal point for operational intelligence on the Desert War was Montgomery's Eighth Army and not the War Office. Yet London also had to cope with the tactical requirements posed by the IRA's campaign on the British mainland and by the search for a political solution, plus the 'foreign intelligence' dimension added by the IRA's sanctuary in the Irish Republic and arms acquisition elsewhere. Britain had a well-established model for intelligence on colonial insurgency; but Northern Ireland is not a colony, and intelligence there did not fit any neat model. Yet this made it all the more necessary to maintain some continuous, central, non-departmental oversight of the system – to search for improvement and conduct intelligence as a campaign, waged in the spirit of Churchill's 'action this day' response to junior staffs' complaint in October 1941 that administrative delays were handicapping the breaking of German ciphers.[87]

Organisational Changes

Even if all these problems have been solved, they illustrate the need for central management. Since the creation of the Coordinator's post its influence has been on an ascending curve, but should be rising further.

The management of defence provides a parallel. Over the last fifty years military power has gradually come to be seen as a unity, rather than independent land, maritime and air elements. British defence policy has moved towards more responsibility for individuals, with rather less reliance on committees. The responsibility and influence of the Chief of Defence Staff (CDS) has grown, at the expense of the Chiefs of Staffs' Committee, and operations have come increasingly under individual Joint Force Commanders. In the 1980s it became accepted that 'CDS was to be the principal military adviser to the Government in his own right, and not just as Chairman of the Chiefs of Staff Committee'.[88] Power shifted from single-service staffs towards his strengthened 'purple-suited' central ones, after decades in which the CDS had only 'a small personal briefing staff of his own, which left him, in effect, with little power and no executive responsibility'.[89] The process has been gradual and partial; centralisation is still set in a framework provided by the three single services. Though CDS 'must rightly have the ultimate responsibility for advising the Government on military policy', he 'is not there to ride roughshod over them [his professional colleagues], but rather to provide the central dynamic'.[90] US military arrangements have evolved in the same direction. Less is now said in both countries about 'coordination' and 'collective advice', and more about personal roles and responsibilities.

In Britain the management of intelligence is moving in the same direction as military power, but some thirty years behind. This points to further evolution, not revolution; but deliberate evolution nonetheless. The present arrangements at the centre are personality driven and workload driven. The roles of the JIC Chairman and the Coordinator are derived from Cabinet Secretaries' special concern for intelligence, an inheritance from Hankey's position as the first holder of the post. But intelligence issues with a political content – intelligence legislation; political oversight; cases of leaks and unauthorised intelligence publications *à la* Peter Wright; intelligence and

291

trade unions – are bound to take priority with busy Cabinet Secretaries over matters of professional organisation and effectiveness, especially if these are long term. Cabinet Secretaries are now additionally Heads of the Civil Service, besides being directly responsible for a clutch of modern Executive Agencies. With such a workload it would be unrealistic to expect holders of the post to reproduce Lord Trend's position as Cabinet Secretary caricatured in his obituary as 'intelligence's chief shop steward'.[91]

Hence the need for some underpinning of the centre vis-à-vis the Heads of Agencies and CDI. Large national and international conglomerates in the private sector take great trouble to avoid over-centralisation and to balance the requirements of corporate strategy and planning against the need to keep operating units' accountability for their own success and failure. But responsibility for performance is vested somewhere at the top of the organisation. British intelligence should move in this direction.

This might be achievable without organisational tinkering. As a practical matter, the Coordinator in his present role may need some small reinforcement of his central staff to match widening responsibilities. Possibly (but more controversially) he might also have some small 'seed corn' budget at his disposal to launch programmes like community-wide IT compatibility that are in no agency's immediate interest and attract no agency sponsorship. Signs, symbols and procedures may be even more significant. If the three Heads of Agencies need their publicly declared right of access to the Prime Minister, the Coordinator should also have it. If the JIC is to keep its dual assessment-producing and managerial roles, the Coordinator should chair it as a managerial forum. His post should be demonstrably the summit of an intelligence career, military or civilian.

Despite the attractions of these modest revisions, it would be braver to make a more substantial change. The dual responsibilities for intelligence assessment and management do not sit easily together, since the first always seems more urgent than the second. Yet the US Director of Central Intelligence has always been both the President's chief intelligence officer and his central intelligence manager, admittedly with major problems of exercising authority over the largely DOD-financed American community. More relevantly, the UK for two years, just after the Falklands War, had the same arrangement, with the Coordinator's post combined with JIC chairmanship and occupied (full time) by an officer with unusual energy and ability.[92] The experiment was a great success. Having found a winning formula once, it seems perverse not to seek to repeat it. It is defeatist to assume that Britain cannot find a successor for the combined Chairman-Coordinator role, with appropriate support.[93] By comparison, responsibility for the collection and analysis of national statistics (plus headship of the Government Statistical Service) were combined in 1996 in a new, single post, the Director of the Office for National Statistics. If this can be done for statistics, why not for intelligence?[94] It has been convenient to write here of intelligence's management. But what perhaps is even more important is leadership.

Irrespective of the central management post, there should be some means of reviewing the national capability as a whole. The 'policy' and budgeting responsibilities of the Ministerial Committee and PSIS should be broadened to include the defence intelligence component, and the same should apply to the Parliamentary Committee. MoD intelligence funding should remain part of the Defence Budget, with defence intelligence competing there with other military requirements. But it should also be considered by the PSIS-Ministerial machinery, to optimise the balance between it and the single-agency investments. Other parts of the Defence Budget (for example the Meteorological Office, and air-sea rescue) are influenced by more than strictly military considerations, and there is no intrinsic reason why this should not apply to MoD intelligence. Despite all the problems, US intelligence has a genuine national intelligence budget, and there is no reason why the UK on its smaller scale should not follow suit.

Community Mindedness

Structure is linked with community culture. Since 1945 most civilian intelligence practitioners have spent their careers in their own, single organisations. There are indeed exceptions. GCHQ has recently had three Directors in succession brought in from outside intelligence; most of the intelligence organisations provide some staff with non-intelligence exposure; the few available secondments

293

to the Assessments Staff and other JIC machinery also widen experience. Intelligence is now quite good at promoting knowledge of the 'outside world'. It has been less good at exchanges within the community itself. There has been no system for 'broadening' postings for promising officers between the agencies and the DIS, or between the agencies themselves. Half a century of professional intelligence in peacetime produced sets of leaders without inside knowledge of each other's professional disciplines, or the community-mindedness that springs from it.

Here again something can be learned from armed forces' experience of modifying single-service tribalism by interservice training and postings. Since 1945 there have been consistent attempts to encourage interservice 'jointery', as in the foundation of the Joint Services Staff College 'to nourish and to disseminate among the higher commanders of all Services and their staffs that mutual understanding and Inter-Service comradeship in arms which, in war, were the very basis of our success'.[95] Single-service cultures are deeply embedded, and the Canadian attempt at a unified defence service was not a success. But it is recognised everywhere that armed forces' senior commanders need to shed single-service blinkers. Experience in joint staffs or with another service has become required for the CV of an ambitious officer. Intelligence is too small to have a joint staff college on military lines. Nevertheless, it could introduce community-oriented training and 'broadening' postings as part of career development. (It is interesting that for the US the Brown Commission came to the conclusion that 'intelligence agencies should function more closely as a "community"',[96] and recommended rotation between agencies and the creation of a common list of senior posts.) A British initiative in this direction would need a push from the centre. In this, as in other things, someone needs to take a view of the national capability as a whole.

Summary

British intelligence has a unique 'upper second class' status in world terms. This status underpins the transatlantic relationship and a service from it of almost the total US product. From its national effort plus the US relationship, HMG receives a quasi-superpower level of intelligence support. Factors governing the value of this support include:

- The continuing need for covert collection, despite the world's generally increased openness and the growth of other information sources; and the increasing technical scope for this covert collection in the modern electronic world.
- The direct value of some of this single-source covert material, particularly in providing 'diplomatic support' for HMG's overseas relationships.
- The critical importance, nevertheless, of the relatively small effort in all-source analysis and assessment, integrating both covert and overt material as inputs to high-level policy and decisions; and of the rather larger military intelligence effort needed for peace-making, peace support and other use of military forces.

These reinforce long-standing British expectations of intelligence and public assumptions about the high-profile foreign policy world and the defence roles set out in the 1998 Strategic Defence Review.

The intelligence community is well managed by world standards, but its devolved and pragmatic style runs the risk of being driven by events. Three issues merit attention. One is the balance of investment between single-source collection/exploitation, about 90 per cent of the total, and the remainder in detailed, all-source analysis. More emphasis should be given to the latter by a variety of managerial and administrative measures. Their costs would be trivial compared with total intelligence budgets, but the measures would reflect the increasing importance of the all-source effort.

Another is the challenge posed by the development of intelligence satellites, at a time when a group of second-class intelligence powers are moving into what is now no longer a superpower preserve. The UK receives the product of many American satellite programmes. Among these it is reported to be contributing on Sigint to an extent sufficient to assure continued UK access. But it makes a less self-evident input on imagery, and there is no guarantee that this American material will continue to be available in all circumstances, such as any EU operations taking place without

US participation. Britain should play an active part in this modern spacefaring. A concept put forward by the American Brown Commission in 1996 of overseas partnerships and load-sharing on satellite imagery provides the possibility of US–European collaboration in which the UK could join at affordable cost, reconciling its transatlantic and European imperatives.[97]

The third is the need for more powerful, less lopsided central management – or, rather, leadership. The JIC is a forum without managerial teeth. The Intelligence Coordinator has influence rather than responsibility. The formal structure of official, Ministerial and Parliamentary oversight is geared only to the three civilian agencies, not the wider community. Hence:

- Under existing arrangements the Coordinator should have the status of intelligence's professional head; but an effort should be made to repeat the successful experiment of the 1980s of combining this post with chairmanship of the JIC.
- The strategic-level elements of the 'defence intelligence community' should be clearly recognised as an element in the national community, subject to some degree of national resource allocation and planning.
- The remits of the Ministerial Committee on Intelligence and the PSIS should be amended accordingly, to provide oversight of the national intelligence capability as a whole. The statutory status of the Parliamentary Intelligence and Security Committee should at some stage be modified in the same way.
- With the same objective of viewing intelligence as a national entity, 'broadening' postings among the agencies and the DIS should be planned as normal forms of career progression.

Notes

1. Originally published as *British Intelligence Towards the Millennium: Issues and Opportunities* (London: Brassey's for the Centre for Defence Studies King's College London, 1997) and reprinted as 'British Intelligence in the New Century: Issues and Opportunities', in Herman, M., *Intelligence Services in the Information Age: Theory and Practice* (London: Frank Cass, 2001), pp. 67–111.

2. Hinsley, F. H. with E. E. Thomas, C. F. G. Ransom and R. C. Knight, *British Intelligence in the Second World War: Vol. I* (London: HMSO, 1979), p. 291.
3. As set out in *Central Intelligence Machinery* (London: HMSO, 1996). Note that a later version is *National Intelligence Machinery* (Norwich: The Stationery Office, 2000).
4. It is not clear how the collective label 'intelligence and security' came to be used. 'Security' relates to the Security Service's roles in security intelligence and in defensive security measures; but it could also cover GCHQ's role in supporting communications and other electronic security.
5. *Central Intelligence Machinery*, p. 23.
6. For a discussion of these subjects see Herman, M., *Intelligence Power in Peace and War* (Cambridge: Cambridge University Press/RIIA, 1996), chapter 7. The author's conclusion is that the core of all-source intelligence is likely to remain 'national security' subjects (including warning, threats, foreign forces and armaments) plus foreign affairs with elements of instability, violence, obscurity or concealment. It is less often seen as the authority on close allies or more open aspects of world international affairs.
7. *Central Intelligence Machinery*, p. 24. Sec the previous note for the emphasis in practice. A popular Whitehall perception is that the JIC 'puts covert intelligence into context and assesses it', but this is too limited.
8. *Central Intelligence Machinery*, p. 11.
9. Ibid, p. 23.
10. JARIC is now a devolved agency with its own published *Framework Document* (London: HMSO, 1996). There is an (mainly MoD) Advisory Board, a Chief Executive, Customer Agreements and a Business Plan, but 'the Secretary of State for Defence has ultimate responsibility for determining the policy, financial framework, delegations and freedoms within which the Agency operates' (para 1.2).
11. For the definitions of 'strategic' and 'tactical' intelligence and electronic warfare, see Herman, *Intelligence Power*, chapters 5 and 7.
12. Ibid., pp. 37, 38, for indications of the reductions in this period.
13. *Treasury Supply Estimates 1999/2000*, Cm 4221. Slightly lower figures appear in all cases in the 1998–9 *Annual Report of the Parliamentary Intelligence and Security Committee* (Cm 4532, 1999), with some technical deductions; the trend is however the same. Figures given from 1997/98 onwards are (in millions) £703.3, £695.4, £742.9, £744.8 and £746.7 (2001/2002).

14. See JARIC document at fn. 10 above.

15. *Military Survey Defence Agency Annual Report and Accounts 1997/98* (London: HMSO, 1999).

16. For indications of Special Branch totals see Herman, *Intelligence Power*, p. 12. The wide variety of Special Branches' law-enforcement and public order commitments must be emphasised.

17. Figures for 1999/2000 are £765 million on diplomacy, £1,794 million as the total budget of the Department for International Development, and £22 billion for defence; see *Treasury Supply Estimates, 1999*.

18. Cohen, E., 'A Revolution in Warfare', *Foreign Affairs*, 75, no. 2, 1996: 46.

19. For the scope for terrorists see Welch, J., 'The International Money Market: A Weapon in Waiting?', *The RUSI Journal*, 141, no. 2, 1996: 34–40.

20. Quoted by Nye, J., 'Redefining the National Interest', *Foreign Affairs*, 78, no. 4, 1999: 26.

21. Gillmore, D., 'Representing Britain Overseas', *The RUSI Journal*, 138, no. 6, 1993: 14.

22. Cohen, 'A Revolution in Warfare', p. 40.

23. Accounting for 6 per cent of world output in 1990, according to Michael Clarke in 'Constraints on United Kingdom Foreign and Defence Policy', in B. Bond and M. Melvin (eds), *The Nature of Future Conflict: Implications for Force Development* (Sandhurst: Strategic and Combat Studies Institute, Occasional Paper no. 38, 1998), p. 45.

24. Cohen, 'A Revolution in Warfare', pp. 44–5.

25. Hibbert, R., 'Intelligence and Policy', *Intelligence and National Security*, 5, no. 1, 1990: 112. His generalisation was probably intended to exclude military details.

26. Rimington, S., *Security and Democracy – Is There a Conflict?*, Richard Dimbleby Lecture 1994 (London: BBC Educational Developments, 1994), p. 9.

27. Tugendhat, C. and W. Wallace, *Options for British Foreign Policy in the 1990s* (London: RIIA/Routledge, 1988), p. 118.

28. Clarke, 'Constraints on United Kingdom Foreign and Defence Policy', p. 50.

29. Lord Hurd, 'British Foreign Policy in the Aftermath of the Cold War', *The RUSI Journal*, 143, no. 6, 1998: 10.

30. *NATO Strategic Concept*, 23–24 April 1999, para. 53d.

31. As put for example by Sir Percy Cradock, BBC TV programme, *Panorama*, 22 November 1993.

32. It has been suggested that the Cabinet's Overseas and Defence (OD) Committee really needs an OD (Resources) subcommittee to consider these complementary but competing investments.

33. Urban, M., *UK Eyes Alpha: The Inside Story of British Intelligence* (London: Faber and Faber, 1996), pp. 239, 103.

34. Andrew, C., 'Churchill and Intelligence', in M. I. Handel (ed.), *Leaders and Intelligence* (London: Cass, 1989), pp. 190, 191.

35. Hinsley et al., *British Intelligence in the Second World War: Vol. II*, p. 16.

36. General Strong wrote in 1970 that the JIC was 'still a long way from the ideal of an interdepartmental committee to control intelligence, with an independent chairman divorced from any department and responsible directly to the Prime Minister'; see Strong, K., *Men of Intelligence* (London: Cassel, 1970), p. 150.

37. For the rationale and the Gulf War influence see Defence Committee Session 1993–4, Fifth Report, *Implementation of Lessons Learned from Operation Granby* (London: HMSO, 1994), evidence of 24 November 1993, questions 23–37.

38. But see Jones, R. V., *Most Secret War: British Scientific Intelligence 1939–1945* (London: Hamish Hamilton, 1978); McLachlan, D., *Room 39: Naval Intelligence in Action 1938–1945* (London: Weidenfeld and Nicolson, 1968); and Annan, N., *Changing Enemies: The Defeat and Regeneration of Germany* (London: HarperCollins, 1995).

39. Lord Hunt, quoted by Hennessy, P., *Whitehall* (London: Fontana, 1990), p. 227.

40. McLennan, A. D., 'National Intelligence Assessment: Australia's Experience', in D. A. Charters, S. Farson and G. P. Hastedt (eds), *Intelligence Analysis and Assessment* (London: Cass, 1996), p. 84.

41. Tomkys, R., 'The Financial Management Initiative in the FCO', *Public Administration*, 69, no. 2, 1991: 263.

42. Scott, R., *Report of the Inquiry into the Export of Defence Equipment and Dual-Use Goods to Iraq and Related Prosecutions: Vol. II* (London: HMSO, 1996), D8.11, p. 814.

43. Cabinet Office press release, 15 February 1996. Some improvements in Cabinet Office communications were however included, and the DIS was said to be conducting 'co-ordinated assessments of proliferation in particular regions and countries'.

44. Urban, *UK Eyes Alpha*, p. 6.

45. *Report of the Commission on Roles and Capabilities of the United States Intelligence Community (the Brown Commission), Preparing*

for the 21st Century (Washington, DC: US GPO, 1996), Executive Summary, p. 5.

46. Urban, *UK Eyes Alpha*, p. 262.
47. Dedijer, S. and N. Jequier, 'Information, Knowledge and Intelligence', in *Intelligence for Economic Development: An Enquiry into the Role of the Knowledge Industry* (Deddington: Berg, 1987), pp. 18–19, quoted by Sigurdson, J. and P. Nelson, 'Intelligence Gathering and Japan: The Elusive Role of Grey Intelligence', *International Journal of Intelligence and CounterIntelligence*, 5, no. 1, 1991: 21.
48. Herman, *Intelligence Power*, chapter 14.
49. Smith, M., 'Sir Edgar Ludlow-Hewitt and the Expansion of Bomber Command', *The RUSI Journal*, 126, no. 1, 1981: 55.
50. For example, 'the CIA as a whole adopted a hands-off attitude towards the concept of joining in the organised support given combat commanders. It refused to join the Joint Intelligence Center (JIC) located in the Pentagon . . . Agency officials asserted that . . . they needed to remain outside the JIC so they could provide independent assessments for senior policy makers' (Committee on Armed Services, House of Representatives, *Intelligence Successes and Failures in Operations Desert Shield/Storm* (Washington, DC: US GPO, 1993), p. 6).
51. Jenkins, S. and A. Sloman, *With Respect, Ambassador* (London: BBC, 1985), pp. 49–50.
52. Foreign and Commonwealth Office Scrutiny, *The Need to Know: Research and Analysis Department and Library and Records Department* (FCO Report), p. 27.
53. Quoted at the Council for Arms Control seminar on the Scott Report, 28 March 1996.
54. For the earlier investigations see note 52, Annexe C.
55. Herman, *Intelligence Power*, chapter 15.
56. All-source intelligence analysis 'had a major impact on the shape of scholarship in American universities in the first two decades after World War II'; see Winks, R., *Cloak and Gown: Scholars in the Secret War, 1939–1961* (London: Collins, 1987), pp. 114–15. See also the review by Bradley Smith in *Intelligence and National Security*, 6, no. 2, 1991: 498–9, of Katz, R. M., *Foreign Intelligence: Research and Analysis in the Office of Strategic Services* (Cambridge, MA: Harvard University Press, 1989): 'Katz makes a strong case for the view that the R and A [Research and Analysis Department of the wartime OSS] experience exerted a profound influence on aspects of US post-war academic life'.
57. Taylor, A. J. P., *English History, 1914–1945* (London: Penguin, 1970), p. 409.

58. Using satellites to 'see' terrestrial targets, literally or for electronic interception; not to be confused with the ground-based interception of communications relayed from communications satellites. It is the difference between looking down and looking up.

59. For the British lessons drawn from the importance of imagery (in all its forms, including infra-red and radar images) in the Gulf War, see the official evidence in House of Commons Defence Committee, *Implementation of Lessons Learned from Operation Granby* (London: HMSO, 1994), evidence of 24 November 1993, questions 19–22.

60. *New Statesman*, Supplement, 4 November 1995, p. 12.

61. Nye, J. S. and W. A. Owens, 'America's Information Edge', *Foreign Affairs*, 75, no. 2. 1996: 28.

62. Hayward, K., *British Military Space Programmes* (London: RUSI, 1996), p. 60.

63. After the humiliation of depending on American intelligence in 1990–1, the French volte-face over intelligence produced a 1996 'prevention' sector of the Defence Budget (covering intelligence, space and communications) of 23.1 billion francs, claimed to provide for 57,555 staff, at 12.2 per cent of the defence total; plus expansions of the French equivalents of the British Agencies. The intelligence elements are not clear in all the French figures, and international comparisons are in any case confusing; nevertheless, the figures give some impression of a modern continental scale; see Western European Union Assembly Defence Committee Report, *A European Intelligence Policy* (13 May 1996), p. 5.

64. For Japanese intentions to launch four intelligence satellites see *The Times*, 16 June 1999.

65. Hayward, *British Military Space Programmes*, p. 61.

66. Western European Union Assembly Defence Committee Report, *A European Intelligence Policy*, 13 May 1996, paras 40, 69(iii), 97.

67. Hayward, *British Military Space Programmes*, p. 45. An account (not necessarily authentic) is given in Urban, *UK Eyes Alpha*, chapter 5.

68. Lashmar, P., *Spy Flights of the Cold War* (Stroud: Sutton, 1996).

69. Hennessy, P., *Never Again: Britain 1945–1951* (London: Vintage edition, 1993), p. 268.

70. Though press comment suggested that European collaboration in imagery was under active consideration by the UK in 1995; see *The Times*, 20 September 1995.

71. Correspondence, *The Times*, 8 December 1999.

72. *Brown Commission Report*, chapter 11, pp. 1–2.

73. See Nye and Owens, 'America's Information Edge', particularly p. 35.

74. Hinsley et al., *British Intelligence in the Second World War: Vol. I*, p. 291.

75. Ibid., p. 43.

76. The exception has been Sir Dick White, who was successively Director General of the Security Service, Chief of SIS and Intelligence Coordinator. His appointment to SIS resulted from Prime Ministerial anger over the Agency's unsuccessful operation by Commander Crabb in 1956.

77. *Central Intelligence Machinery*, p. 4.

78. Herman, *Intelligence Power*, p. 309.

79. For a brief account see the obituary of Lord Bancroft, *The Times*, 21 November 1996.

80. *Central Intelligence Machinery*, pp. 11, 12.

81. Ibid., p. 24.

82. Intelligence and Security Committee, *Sierra Leone*, Cm 4309 (London: HMSO, 1999), pp. 3–4.

83. *Brown Commission Report*, Executive Summary, p. 1.

84. *National Security Agency Objectives 1999*, Goal 3.

85. Rimington, *Security and Democracy*, p. 8. It is interesting that in 1966 the Director General of the Security Service, resisting a DIS proposal for a central point to handle IRA intelligence, had maintained that it was a police problem. The JIC agreed. See Aldrich, R. J., *Espionage, Security and Intelligence in Britain 1945–1970* (Manchester: Manchester University Press, 1998), pp. 128–9.

86. Heath, E., 'Outflank the IRA Bombers', *The Times*, 10 June 1993.

87. As described in Milner-Barry, P. S., '"Action This Day": The Letter from Bletchley Park Cryptanalysts to the Prime Minister, 21 October 1941', *Intelligence and National Security*, 1, no. 2, 1986, pp. 272–6.

88. The history of the British evolution is set out in (General) Jackson, W. and Lord Bramall, *The Chiefs* (London: Brassey's, 1992), quotation from p. 400.

89. Ibid., p. 296.

90. Ibid., pp. 447, 449.

91. Obituary, *The Times*, 22 July 1987. A subsequent letter from Lord Hunt of Tanworth and Sir Robert Armstrong (*The Times*, 30 July 1987) criticised this choice of words but affirmed Trend's special concern for intelligence matters.

92. Sir Arthur Antony Duff, 1920–2000. Intelligence Coordinator, 1980–4; Director General of the Security Service, 1985–8; knighted in 1980.

93. There is now no reason why the Chief of the Assessments Staff, since 1983 a full member of the JIC, should not be a formal deputy.
94. This happened in 2000 when it was announced that Michael Pakenham was the holder of both posts (*National Intelligence Machinery*, p. 16). But a Parliamentary Report argues that the post should be associated with greater intelligence background and status; see *Annual Report, 1999–2000* (London: HMSO, 2000), paras 20–7.
95. Chiefs of Staff message on its foundation in 1947, quoted in Jackson and Bramall, *The Chiefs*, p. 462.
96. *Brown Commission Report*, Executive Summary, pp. 1, 6.
97. According to two American writers the idea of transatlantic 'partnering' in the development of 'cheap' satellites was also put forward by John Deutch as US Director of Intelligence at the same time; see Gormley, D. M. and D. M. Hart, 'Extending Network-Centric Warfare', *The RUSI Journal*, 145, no. 2, 2000: 68.

13 Evidence to Butler

[This is a transcript of Michael's testimony to the Review of Intelligence on Weapons of Mass Destruction (known as the 'Butler Review' after its Chairman) on 7 May 2004]

LORD BUTLER: Thank you very much for coming. It's very useful for us to be able to draw on your experience and your expertise and your ideas. Just to say this is on the record, in other words there will be a transcript of it but it's private to the Committee, though you will be very welcome to see the transcript of it in case there is anything you want to correct or add. But really it's your ideas we want to draw on, and you will have seen that you have had an extra sale. I do not know whether that's the book of yours you would recommend . . .?

MICHAEL HERMAN: So I see. There is a more recent one actually.

LORD BUTLER: That's *Intelligence Services in the Information Age* is it?

MICHAEL HERMAN: Yes.

LORD BUTLER: I have taken particular notes of your chapter on accuracy in that book – and you say in your, I think it was RUSI wasn't it, your RUSI address . . .?

MICHAEL HERMAN: Yes.

LORD BUTLER: . . . that intelligence has turned out to be a disaster. The disaster, I expect you would say, is the fact that the intelligence so far appears to be wrong?

304

MICHAEL HERMAN: Yes.

LORD BUTLER: I think we have got to take a provisional view about that, because we do not know quite how wrong it is – some of it was right. Now, drawing on what you say about the reasons why intelligence can be inaccurate – have you got a view of why in this case the intelligence – if wrong – has turned out to be wrong?

MICHAEL HERMAN: Well, that's correct. I have only seen what the ISC has said about the reports, so it is a pretty provisional judgement. But I suppose my judgement, well my diagnosis, is the familiar one that it was too difficult for people to get, as it were, outside the box of the thinking that they themselves had got locked into. I put a couple of quotes into this paper, which seemed to apply really to all intelligence failures. Why did they go wrong? If they did, my guess (and it can only be a guess) would be, they were too close to policy, and not able to stand back and be critical of their own assumptions. Why does that happen in intelligence organisations? It happens of course in all organisations, all walks of life, but that drove me to this very tricky question of the make-up of the Assessments Staff, which I think would be my point of entry. And that drove me back to the papers of the 1960s, which I happened to be working on, to Burke Trend's proposals for the 1968 reforms which created the Assessments Staff. It's very interesting how explicit he was that he was aiming at a professional staff, and I have got the recommendations here if anyone wants to look at them. A professional staff, people who are going to be long term in post; perhaps I could read you just two or three lines of what Burke Trend wrote to Wilson – this was '67:

> First, we should need to recruit the staff of the JIC on a longer-term basis than at present, and to transform the existing collection of temporarily seconded individuals into a permanent entity whose members would have time and scope to immerse themselves in problems, which often develop over long periods, and to develop a distinctly professional technique for dealing with them.

305

LORD BUTLER: Well now there are one or two aspects I want to ask you about, but let us go in there, to that expertise. Let's start with that expertise as you have stated it. I have been asking myself this question: if you have the greatest expert in BW that's available to your government, would you put them in the DIS where they are dealing with the way in which troops in war would cope with the threat, or would you put them in the Assessments Staff? My feeling is that if I had that choice I would put them in the DIS. Would you share that view?

MICHAEL HERMAN: I think I would, but again going back to the texts of the 1960s, as you may recall, part of the idea behind the creation of the Assessments Staff was for the JIC to be much more economic-literate and scientific and technically-literate. So in fact the original Trend proposals were for three JICs. The main JIC, the economic one which actually happened . . .

LORD BUTLER: JIC (A) *[the main one]*

MICHAEL HERMAN: . . . and the scientific JIC, which never happened.

LORD BUTLER: And of course the economic one *[JIC (B)]* did not last for very long.

MICHAEL HERMAN: Quite. And part of that package was that in the Assessments Staff there should be scientific and technical qualifications – interesting, which almost happened but never quite.

So the original concept was that there should be people in the Assessments Staff who could have as it were intelligent and informed conversations with experts qualified to meet them to some extent on their own ground. It's a very interesting speculation. I phoned Brian Jones (whom I hardly know, I have just met recently)[1] and I asked him the question: 'Would he have welcomed someone more technically, scientifically literate in the Assessments Staff, to understand what he was saying at CIGs?' I think his answer was yes, though I am not sure.

LORD BUTLER: Yes that's a very interesting point. What you're suggesting is somebody who can speak the language – not necessarily putting your greatest expert in the centre, but having somebody who can speak the language and who has then close contacts with your biggest experts who are in the DIS. Would that be the sort of structure you are you have in mind?

MICHAEL HERMAN: I think so, yes. I think, and I have always argued, that it's a pity that part of the original concept did not actually happen. Can I just give you a quotation on this? From John Thomson, first Chief of the Assessments Staff, in '71. They were reviewing it, and John put the requirement as: 'People on the Assessments Staff, scientific and technically who need sufficient knowledge to maintain quote sensible dialogues unquote with desk officers and experts.'

LORD INGE: Can I ask two questions first? Do you think people really understand the difference between policy, analysis and assessment? I don't mean people like yourself, I mean enough people who are going to be handling information. And secondly: are you saying – I understand why you need experts, but you also need (and I suppose I am a prisoner again of my past, because I was dealing with operations then), but you need people who understand the importance of intelligence but at the same time challenge it, because they are not dealing with it all the time. Now how do you get that balance right?

MICHAEL HERMAN: Can I step back slightly to the first question, and say I am certainly not one of the people whom you sometimes find in the intelligence services who say, 'you know, if they only left it to us professionals and kept the Foreign Office out of it all would be well'. I have never taken that view. The great strength of the Assessments Staff since it was created in '68 was that the Foreign Office took it over, more or less, and posted a lot of their best people to it – very good, with all sorts of talents needed for good assessment. But I think the case I am putting to you, for you to shoot down if you like, is that the people in the Foreign Office are very good at policy: they've got lots of gifts, and lots and lots of them are transferable to the assessment process. And as you say assessment has to be very close to policy, you can't have a Chinese wall between them. But the gifts to do it well aren't quite the same, aren't quite the same, as the man who is very good at deciding: 'in this bloody mess, what do we actually decide to do?!' Whereas the assessors have to have just a slightly different caste of mind, a slightly awkward caste of mind – saying 'no, look, look, I must go back to the evidence: have we really taken into account of this that and the other?' Tedious people, sometimes!

LORD BUTLER: Did you know Frank Panton in the Cabinet Office?

MICHAEL HERMAN: No, I don't think I did.

LORD BUTLER: He worked there during my time. The Cabinet Office did have a Nuclear Adviser, Frank Panton, who was available to the Assessments Staff, but I think you are thinking of someone a little more embedded aren't you in the . . .

MICHAEL HERMAN: No I am simply thinking of the right mixture in the Assessments Staff. I am certainly not trying to professionalise the whole thing. Did you know Harry Burke?[2]

LORD BUTLER: No.

MICHAEL HERMAN: Well he was in the Assessments Staff about the time you became Cabinet Secretary. He was a GCHQ colleague of mine and when I was running the Soviet effort at GCHQ he was my Deputy Head of the Soviet Effort at GCHQ, in effect the chief analyst of the Soviet Division at Cheltenham, presenting the GCHQ view, forming it, coming up to CIGs, so on and so forth. He had a high reputation as an analyst. And after the Falklands, when Tony Duff[3] was keen to do something about the Assessments Staff, he put in a very firm bid to get him to the Assessments Staff.

And it was put to him, rightly or wrongly, by the management of the day that 'well, you're not a manager, we do not see you as a chap to run a big Division, you know. You're a jolly good analyst. Go to the Cabinet Office.'

He was a howling success there, and he achieved one important breakthrough that I don't think the UK or the US communities would ever have made without him: realising that the Russians were absolutely scared stiff of a pre-emptive American strike, around the time of the Able Archer exercise in Autumn '83. Bits of the evidence came from Gordievsky, and some from Sigint, but Burke put it together in a way no one else had done, and fought against almost everyone in London to get his conclusion accepted. One result was that the JIC produced a report in early 1984 on the Soviet alert; and also another report, which I don't think they ever did at any other time, on 'How do the Russians see us?', in 1984. I understood at the time that that had got to Thatcher, went over to Reagan, and may have played some part in Reagan's change of tack in the 1984 Presidential campaign: from the Evil Empire to a slightly different slant. Now could some other chap in the Assessments Staff have done that? Could some very bright Foreign Office person brought in new to intelligence analysis, would he have spotted that? Perhaps, but I think not. I think you want a presence of people like my colleague like that in the Assessments Staff, if you can get them.

LORD BUTLER: Would you also stick to your point that they should be there on a longer-term basis?

MICHAEL HERMAN: Yes, I think so.

SIR JOHN CHILCOT: It's very interesting listening to you, as well as reading your paper. If you are going to protect the intelligence community for intelligence-based, analytically evaluated and properly assessed reporting from political and policy-makers' pressure, do you look first to the personality of the leadership of the intelligence community or do you look to the structures in which they have to work? Where is the balance to be found?

MICHAEL HERMAN: A case in point. Tony Duff had deliberately expanded the JIC after the Falklands War. I think it was after

Franks '83. And his view was very interesting: 'I want a wider view, I want a wider representation of Whitehall views, than I have previously had.' So he brought in the DUS(P) (as it was then) in MoD and the Prime Minister's policy adviser was brought in, and one or two other things like that. Was it a good thing or a bad thing? I can't find it in me to say 'I think it's a bad thing', because these are very able people with a lot to contribute. But I do think you should balance it somehow, and my suggestion which I made in that paper is 'try and find a jolly good academic, as the Americans do for their National Intelligence Council, and give him a seat on the JIC'.

LORD BUTLER: But that was what you meant by the non-Whitehall element?

MICHAEL HERMAN: Yes that's right. Since you mention a name, I would appoint someone of Adam Roberts's calibre.[4] Or, additionally, find some good younger academics and give them contracts in the Assessments Staff.

LORD INGE: And how long do you see them having to stay there to develop this?

LORD BUTLER: Very good question.

MICHAEL HERMAN: You'd have to have a sort of hire-and-fire clause, wouldn't you? After a year so the agreement can be broken on either side. But I think you would have to aim at five years.

ANN TAYLOR: And where would they go afterwards?

MICHAEL HERMAN: Yes well the academics would go back to academia.

ANN TAYLOR: Yes they would: but other people?

MICHAEL HERMAN: Well I think . . .

SIR JOHN CHILCOT: And lose their analytical career?

MICHAEL HERMAN: And that's Mrs Taylor's point I think. Well, I can offer various ideas. One of the things which strikes me, because I do see quite a bit of international relations students now, postgraduate students – I have talked to them and got some idea what they go into. I am struck by the fact that analysis is a burgeoning modern profession, in all walks of life.

SIR JOHN CHILCOT: Sorry to interrupt you, but it may be at twenty-five or even thirty, but what happens when they get to forty-five and fifty, who would know where to go?

MICHAEL HERMAN: I suspect there's a career. You take a postgraduate degree somewhere, you go and work for Oxford Analytica – an interesting organisation: their morning meetings are like those of the JIC. A chap I am thinking of worked there for five years, married a girl in London, works now for the Economist Intelligence Unit. Wrote his thesis on the Baltic States. He's the sort of person who might well come to the Assessments Staff on a five-year contract. And then after that it would be up to him to decide what he was going to do! But he would probably pick up a Chair somewhere . . .

LORD BUTLER: Do you think it could . . .?

ANN TAYLOR: In one sense, I see what you are saying from the expertise point of view. But you don't want a group of people who are outwith the realities; I mean, in trying to protect people from too much influence from policy-makers, you don't want to fall into the trap of having two separate worlds. They have got to be real worlds. So from your point of view you want people who can come out of the mainstream to be trained as analysts, or from academia to be trained as analysts. But you need a re-entry into the mainstream for them to have an ongoing role and interaction with policy-makers, and you want the people who are in policy to have an understanding of how the analysis has taken place in the assessments and things. Isn't the danger of what you are suggesting that you have twin tracks and too great a separation, and therefore analysis and policy becomes, well, a bit too academic?

MICHAEL HERMAN: That would be an absolute disaster in this place. I cannot see it happening somehow. I go back to my point. I am still thinking of the right sort of mix. Keep the good Foreign Office people coming into the Assessments Staff, you do want them. It's simply a question of adding a mix to it. But perhaps the other question which you really were putting to me was, 'is there a career inside government for people who come in late and decide to stay?' It's always a problem with small specialist classes, for instance in the Defence Intelligence Staff (DIS). I am sure it's improving – at least I hope it's improving – but in my day they had difficulty in recruiting and keeping really good people because it was fairly small professional group; it hadn't much of a pyramid. It had pretty rotten pay. One of the oddities of the 1945 post-war settlement is that GCHQ people like myself were far better paid than the people who formed the original Joint Intelligence Bureau and then became the DIS. So the bigger you can make your speciality, the better it is for all sorts of things. My model is perhaps the Government Statistical Service, who staff that central department [*the Office for National Statistics*] but are also brigaded with other departments' statisticians, and with a Government Chief Statistician still keeping some idea of the whole thing.

Now this is very visionary and it might not be on, but if you ask me I would look at the DIS, the research and analysis people in the Foreign Office, and look around a bit elsewhere, and see whether you could create a specialist class of Foreign Analysts. That's not a good name, you'll have to find a better name for it, but something of that sort. In other words people whose *métier* was looking at foreign things, but not to be policy-makers or executives.

SIR JOHN CHILCOT: Could I just ask you about that? You said 'foreign' – why 'foreign'? What you are seeing in, for example, the National Criminal Service is exactly what you are describing. This is the implication for me: is there actually an intelligent analyst profession coming into being on your model. Why 'foreign'?

MICHAEL HERMAN: I agree. I did not want to shock you by bringing in NCIS! Yes, if NCIS or its successor could in some way weld their careers into this new specialist group, how nice. But of course, in any case people are pretty mobile now, aren't they? Pensions are transferable. If you were advertising for people to join your new research class (let's call it that), you would certainly put adverts at the NCIS people.

LORD BUTLER: I tried to bring more academics into government when I was Head of the Civil Service.

MICHAEL HERMAN: Oh did you?

LORD BUTLER: I had difficulty because I had rather hoped that academics would take the view that it would be wonderful to have a little practical experience of the centre of government to see how the system really worked, and I was disappointed in that. Because they felt actually that it was more important to them to be publishing and continuing their research, so they were not actually terribly interested on the whole about coming in. I just wonder, do you think it would be practicable for these appointments to be part time? In other words perhaps some academics that you called up, rather like Oxford Analytica does, for particular subjects and to attend at the JIC for those purposes, or the CIGs?

MICHAEL HERMAN: Well I am sure you could do that for the JIC meetings, and I am sure you could nominate someone, 'look, he comes to the JIC, he gets all the papers, but combines that with his academic post'. I think that would work.

LORD BUTLER: Professor Adam Roberts type?

MICHAEL HERMAN: Yes. Whereas on the Assessments Staff there are two questions really. Should they be letting more contracts outside, to academics or people like that, and should they have more academics actually in the Assessments Staff? I believe they let some contracts now and that's fine, terribly good. But I think there is something slightly different about having an input from outside, and having someone academically trained, not Whitehall trained, who joins the Assessments Staff full time, contributing to the general collegial views and approaches.

LORD INGE: What's the difference between a Whitehall training and an academic training?

MICHAEL HERMAN: Whitehall people are trained to stop the ship from going on the rocks, aren't they? They are the people whose gift is to keep government going, working out 'what should we actually do? How do we cope with this mess!' Great skills, highest admiration.

LORD INGE: And academics?!

MICHAEL HERMAN: Academics are not terribly well qualified to do that sort of thing, are they?

SIR JOHN CHILCOT: Do you think the answer to Lord Inge's question might be, the difference between writing twenty-four pages and two?

MICHAEL HERMAN: It might well. Fair point, fair point.

LORD BUTLER: Are there any more questions on the JIC staffing? There is just another couple of subjects I'd like to raise. Well there are two other points, which took my eye that you made. One was that the result of the pressure on the JIC is a bit less qualified.

MICHAEL HERMAN: Yes.

LORD BUTLER: And we have been giving a bit of attention to this, because obviously we have been looking at the relationship between the raw intelligence, the assessments and the reports that were put to Ministers. It is the current fashion that has come and gone, that at the end of the day the intelligence community should reach a view. Are you critical of that? Would you prefer to have an arrangement whereby judgements were more qualified, and if so, how would you have them qualified – by degrees of confidence, or what?

MICHAEL HERMAN: And could I add one further question to yours? Of course there's always been the question that the American

NIEs have always had this wonderful Dissenting Note – you know, 'the DIA does not agree with it'. And Tony Duff, I can recall, was very anxious when he was JIC Chairman to get more dissent and to reflect it in that sort of JIC report. Because the whole tendency of Whitehall, rightly, is to try and agree on something. I think the answer is – I have not seen any JIC reports for seventeen years, I am out of touch – that Ministers rightly want bullet points 'we agree this, the implications are so on and so forth'. I am just thinking. The danger I am suggesting is that if you are in that frame of mind, under pressure, how do you step back and say 'we have *got* to say "we don't know"?' If you do, the customers, all of them, will sit back and say 'it's the bloody JIC, it's sitting on the fence again'. But sometimes it should sit on the fence, absolutely.

LORD BUTLER: Yes. So there are times you say, 'this is what we believe, but the evidence is pretty scanty'. Is that the sort of thing, is that the way you'd do it?

MICHAEL HERMAN: Yes; or 'the evidence is too scanty for any real judgement, but if it is any help to you, Ministers, half of us think this and the other half think the other'.

LORD BUTLER: You would really do that? That would not be much help.

MICHAEL HERMAN: It would be better than forcing a synthetic agreement. You would be saying to Ministers: 'Sorry, you can sack us if you like, but it is up to you, Ministers, to decide whether to go to war or not. Bad luck!'

LORD INGE: That's when intelligence is being used for the wrong reasons, to enforce policy?

MICHAEL HERMAN: Yes.

LORD BUTLER: Good. OK. Now one other thing in this area was the point about separating policy from assessment. Do you feel that the JIC has become too policy dominated, and do you think for example that the Chairman of the JIC in the Gulf War, to the extent you could observe it, got too sucked into the Number 10 policy-making? Two aspects to the same question.

MICHAEL HERMAN: Yes. The press are of course saying this and have been awful this morning about John Scarlett's appointment. I don't think the JIC Chairman should be a fief of any particular department. So I was very glad to see the John Scarlett appointment as the first MI6 Chairman of the JIC. But I would rather have read that, after having been an outstandingly successful 'C', he was moving now on promotion, or equal terms, to be Chairman of the JIC. I think the JIC Chairman has to have some considerable presence with his community colleagues. He has to have some presence. In the RUSI paper I put a quote from a 1947 report that the Chairman of the JIC had to be in effect the country's chief intelligence officer.[5] And to do that, to answer your point on policy, your ideal person should be someone who has not got anything else to prove.

SIR JOHN CHILCOT: So it's a last appointment?

MICHAEL HERMAN: Or the Percy Cradock, Tony Duff appointment on retirement – as great Chairmen. I suppose that could be dangerous if the world saw it as a pleasant retirement job. But, yes, something of that sort.

LORD BUTLER: How much should the Chairman of the JIC directly see the Prime Minister do you think? I just wondered if you historically happen to know – the question occurred to me, did Bill Bentick used to see Churchill, directly?

MICHAEL HERMAN: I don't know. Truly don't know.

LORD BUTLER: Have you got a view on that, do you think that in order to keep assessment pure and away from policy that it should not be often that the Chairman of the JIC directly sees the Prime Minister, or attends Cabinet Committee meetings – have you got a view on that?

MICHAEL HERMAN: I do not agree, I am afraid I should say no, he should be in the action. The more he sees the Prime Minister the more I'd be pleased. I rather naughtily said at the RUSI that I can't quite see why the Heads of Agencies have this often repeated right of direct access to the Prime Minister. I think if anyone has a right of direct access it should be the JIC Chairman.

LORD BUTLER: An interesting point. I think he has, actually.

MICHAEL HERMAN: Yes I think he has.

LORD BUTLER: Any other points? Anything else you would like to put in our minds while you are here? Bruce is just pointing out to me that he *does* have direct access to the Prime Minister. Anything else that you think we ought to be paying attention to, either arising out of recent events or . . .?

MICHAEL HERMAN: I think you have covered the Assessments Staff and the quality of research. Of course the position of the DIS has always been fairly important. For about twenty years after 1945 this idea of a central intelligence organisation of some sort was still floating around and it did not happen; it probably could not have happened, but somehow out of that the DIS came to be seen as a rather poor relation in the Whitehall community. This business of what do you do to get good people to join, and stay . . .

I have touched on letting analytic contracts out from the Assessments Staff, which of course the Assessments Staff could not do with its present size. If you are going to let contracts out all over the place, you have to have people to do it. The size of the Assessments Staff is I am sure is something you will want to consider.

Could I roll one particular log at you, if I may? I am now a pseudo-academic or quasi-academic, so I wonder if I could put in a plug about the role of academics in training, starting with the Assessments Staff? I gather that some sort of training has just started for it. I was told that the DIS's training is done largely at Chicksands, which is fine but it's rather military oriented. I think it would be easy to lay on a two-and-a-half-day-long, or weekend, seminar, for people coming in to the Assessments Staff initially, not asking them to reveal any secrets at all, on what the academic world can bring to them. There are no clear lessons from history, we all know that, but just as the military study campaigns, so should some intelligence history be known to intelligence practitioners. It seems absurd to me that an officer is plunged into the Assessments Staff with a week's handover. He has no time or inclination to read all the intelligence literature on warning failures, for example. There is something to be taught. I have just been to an excellent CIA conference which they organised in Rome, on the analytic process. One thought this was going to be a nice jolly, but it was actually surprisingly positive. We had good people from many European nations and elsewhere and did all of the good Civil Service College things: we split up into syndicates. There was a real feeling of professionals discussing professional problems.

So I would start with academics as trainers, and I'll talk flippantly, but not entirely flippantly. If you gave me the money to organise a two-and-a-half-day seminar of this sort, I'd do it for you. I would get the CIA people to come over and help. This looks as though I am . . .

LORD BUTLER: No thank you.

MICHAEL HERMAN: Carrying on on academics. It's not quite the point of your investigation, I know, but there are two questions. Jointery, and the equivalent of staff college training in the intelligence world. I don't mean a permanent college or anything like that, but a week's course, or two weeks' course at late twenties level – first staff college course if you like – and a week's course at forty plus for the flyers. Again, as a joint intelligence course. Intelligence agencies give superb courses to their own people but as far as I know there is nothing joint. Academics could contribute, for example with a view of past intelligence as a whole.

And here is my final plug for academics. You can learn from the past by going back and looking at intelligence over a long period, but it can seem very distant. One of the weaknesses of the British system, and I suspect abroad and probably all systems, is that it just hasn't time to look back critically over recent assessments, say three to five years. There was a very interesting exercise of the JIC in the late seventies–early eighties, the Douglas Nicoll report. Douglas was commissioned on retirement to look at previous JIC practice and he produced his very impressive series of reports. He chose warning failures, he didn't choose the JIC's performance on longer-term issues and perhaps this put him too close to the agencies. I don't see why you shouldn't get together a small academic body looking as objectively as they could at JIC performance two or three years ago and just say, 'well, how does it look now?'

LORD BUTLER: Yes, that is very interesting. Well thank you very much indeed. That is very kind, that is an area that nobody else has covered and you have given us a very good overview we hope. So thank you very much indeed.

Notes

1. Brian Francis Gill Jones, 1944–2012. Defence Intelligence Staff, 1987–2003; author of *Failing Intelligence: The True Story of How We Were Fooled Into Going to War in Iraq* (London: Biteback Publishing, 2010).
2. For more details see Chapter 20 in this collection, 'Harry Burke and Able Archer'.
3. Sir Arthur Antony Duff, 1920–2000.
4. Sir Adam Roberts, 1940–. Montague Burton Professor of International Relations at Oxford University, 1986–2007; President of British Academy 2009–2013.
5. This is the Evill Report. See Chapter 14 in this collection, 'Joint Intelligence and Butler'.

14 Joint Intelligence and Butler[1]

[2004]

As put in an intelligence recruitment brochure, 'government cannot make the right decisions unless it has the full picture'.[2] Britain went to war against Iraq in the belief that intelligence showed that operational Iraqi Weapons of Mass Destruction (WMDs) existed, and it now seems that they did not. Our intelligence community costs upwards of £1.5 billion annually,[3] and prides itself on the top-level assessments of its much-admired Joint Intelligence Committee (JIC), yet something went wrong in this case. The Review of Lord Butler's Committee of Privy Counsellors now casts light upon it.[4] It is the first report of this kind to concentrate on intelligence,[5] and warrants extended study. What follows is a preliminary comment on it.

The JIC's Error and its Results

Though it deals with varied issues, notably the intelligence 'dossier' produced for public consumption, the main focus of the Review is on the JIC's classified reports to government on the Iraqi WMD threat. It is as careful and measured as might be expected from the Privy Counsellors responsible for it and gives credit warmly to the JIC where it is due in this and other, related areas. Nevertheless, it accepts that, on the present evidence, Iraq

> ... did not have significant – if any – stocks of chemical or biological weapons in a state fit for deployment, or developed plans for using them.[6]

320

and it is critical of the JIC's findings to the contrary. Its formal conclusion is limited: 'there was a risk of over-cautious or worst case estimates, shorn of their caveats, becoming the prevailing wisdom'.[7] But its text supports the public impression that the cumulative effect of the JIC reports, plus the many oral briefings that accompanied them, was to create or at least buttress the government belief that Iraqi WMD was a current threat, and not a matter of prediction or possibility. It shows that the JIC was cautious in its drafting and drew attention to the paucity of evidence but tipped towards underscoring the threat. Thus it finds that the key assessments on Iraqi biological and chemical warfare (BW and CW)

> . . . tended to be over-cautious and in some areas worst-case. Where there was a balance of inference to be drawn, it tended to go in the direction of inferring the existence of banned weapons programmes.[8]

The Review strongly implies, though does not conclude explicitly, that the JIC, along with its US, Australian and other counterparts, has to be included in the verdict of Dr Kay, on his retirement as head of the UK–US Survey Group in Iraq in January 2004, that 'we were almost all wrong'. Having got many things right, British intelligence failed – narrowly – over this most important issue, perhaps by not being sufficiently determined in its uncertainty.

Some may say 'Did it matter? Iraq was going to be invaded anyway, irrespective of intelligence.' The Privy Counsellors sensibly do not discuss the effects of intelligence on British, or American, policy. Policy was driven by many other factors, and it will be for historians to consider the might-have-beens if the JIC had assessed roundly at some point that the WMD threat was no more than conjectural.

Nevertheless at a professional level the JIC's performance merits the overused label of intelligence failure. Intelligence cannot guarantee success. Iraq was a difficult target, and when confronted with sophisticated concealment and deception by a secretive target intelligence can only hope to 'win some, lose some'. Yet it was not confronted here by questions at the most testing end of its normal spectrum of difficulty. It was not required to assess the intangibles of Saddam's policy, or forecast future WMDs, but to assess the physical existence and operational status of usable weapons here and now. It was not deceived by a deliberate Iraqi concealment and deception plan, but in a sense it deceived itself. Its failure was in attaching too much weight to relatively few strands of what seemed positive evidence, and not giving sufficient weight to what the other extensive, top-priority and prolonged collection efforts of the UK, the US and their allies had *not* found.

One result has been a blow to the reputation of British intelligence: if this happened over Iraq, what credence can be given to intelligence estimates of the terrorist threat, or anything else? Not much is left of the faith in Britain's role as a good influence on American intelligence assessments. Internationally it marks a setback for the idea that was making slow progress worldwide of 'honest' intelligence as a contribution to good governance and international order. For example, the Department for International Development under left-winger Clare Short had committed to support local intelligence services in the developing world in order to make realistic assessments of security threats.[9] International law was then emphasising the need for 'justifications' on the use of force, justifications which might well turn on the credibility of 'objective' national intelligence. UNSCOM and UNMOVIC, and the national inputs to them, were indeed seen as prototypes for a new, UN-centred intelligence system. But who is now going to take intelligence seriously as an international force for good? Much of the world will be confirmed in its view that it does no more than legitimise what powerful governments have decided to do anyway: in effect, it is the KGB's view of intelligence as a weapon, not a contribution to governmental rationality.

So there is every reason for learning lessons and implementing them. How, then, did it all happen?

Causes

The Review exonerates the JIC and its Chairman from producing 'intelligence to please' or knuckling down under political pressure, and it suggests an explanation in terms of 'groupthink' and 'prevailing wisdom'. Its account reads, indeed, precisely like a case-study from the many academic findings on the effect of groupthink, cognitive rigidity and the like on international relations.[10] Once having formed what we believe to be an objective view, we interpret new evidence to accommodate it and obstinately hold it thereafter. This applies anywhere, but all the more so in closed groups like intelligence and a professional Civil Service. British government depends on the consensus of the closely-knit 'Whitehall village', with intelligence as part of the consensus. Intelligence itself is partly a warning mechanism and is bound to give particular attention to bad news and worst cases; as Sir Percy Cradock said about the JIC's preoccupations, these are with 'the hard world of shocks and accidents, threats and crises . . . the dark side of the moon'.[11] To this has been added over the last twenty-five years the pressure of British governments of both parties upon civil servants to become more purposive, less analytical, better as 'can-do' people. Intelligence is always sensitive to the charge of sitting on the fence, and it is not surprising that over this period JIC assessments have become 'starker', emphasising key judgements, with less scope for qualifying them or expressing degrees of confidence. With this mixture of permanent and transitory influences intelligence was indeed vulnerable to being carried away in a Whitehall consensus, losing its ability to go back and reassess the evidence from scratch.

Vulnerability of this cognitive kind is a factor in most intelligence failures, but there are always specific reasons that bring it into play. Here again the Review provides the answer, though it has attracted less attention than it deserves. The JIC's judgements about Iraqi BW/CW capability owed a great deal to apparently authentic Secret Intelligence Service (SIS) reports from three human sources. The JIC was advised to take them seriously. Its misfortune was that they have subsequently been judged unreliable: for the SIS, on the face of it, a professional failure of the first order. The Report largely attributes this to recent managerial changes within SIS, and concludes that

> Part of the reason for the serious doubt being cast over a high proportion of human intelligence reports on Iraq arises from weaknesses in the effective application by SIS of its validation procedures and in their proper resourcing. Our Review has shown the vital importance

323

of effective scrutiny and validation of human intelligence sources and of their reporting to the preparation of accurate JIC assessments and high-quality advice to Ministers.[12]

It can be inferred that the pressure to produce positive results on this highest priority issue overrode the normal checks and balances. The Review concludes in unequivocal terms that the SIS should put its house in order. This will no doubt be done and needs no further discussion here.

Cognitive Risk: Balancing Empathy and Independence

So the JIC was more sinned against than sinning. Rare and apparently reliable confirmation of the threat at crucial periods could not be ignored. Nevertheless its experience rubs home old lessons. Single-source reports may be worth their weight in gold but must always be subject to all-source assessment. Those 'owning' (and, necessarily, 'selling') any one line of material – be it Humint, Sigint, imagery, or diplomatic reporting – can get carried away by it; they must never have the last word about its significance. A strength of the JIC system is its duty to evaluate everything in an all-source context: to be, if necessary, a constructive sceptic.

But there are no 'rules' here. Covert Humint over-emphasised the threat in this case; yet similar intelligence before the Falklands invasion pointed in the opposite direction, and deflected attention from warning indicators in diplomatic and open source material;[13] while the lesson of an important official study of earlier failures was just the opposite, that secret reports had been given too little weight compared with diplomatic appreciations. The only 'lesson' is that assessment at this level is intensely difficult. It needs experience in judging different kinds of material and those who provide it, but also – ideally – a quasi-academic detachment, free of government's preconceptions and responsibilities.

This detachment is something intelligence can never have. It *has* to be close to policy. The JIC Chairman *has* to be close to No. 10; the Committee *has* to be sensitive to government's needs, policies and preconceptions. It exists to make judgements, not to pass the buck. Nevertheless, as an American put it many years ago:

> Men who have participated in a decision develop a stake in that decision. As they participate in further, related decisions, their stake increases.[14]

They can never go back to square one and start again. Writing about the Iraq war, Matthew Parris described the effect of policy commitment as follows:

> Spies and their political masters will have tried to push it [the secret evidence] further than they should . . . And so from the accretion of slight miscalculations and minor errors of judgement and emphasis, a large untruth will have been floated upon a pontoon of small exaggerations.[15]

Intelligence needs some insulation from this risk. It contributes to policy but does not have a stake in it. Its relationship with policy-makers needs a sensitive balance between empathy and intellectual independence. Sir Roderic Braithwaite as a former JIC Chairman has argued recently for a Chinese wall between intelligence and policy, but I prefer his predecessor Sir Percy Cradock's image for preventing analysts from becoming courtiers: intelligence and policy should be in separate rooms but with an open door between them.[16] How then should the JIC system be fine-tuned to be closer to the Cradock image?

Quality in Analysis and Assessment

Criticism has centred on the JIC Committee itself, but a merit of the Butler Review is that it devotes considerable attention to the analysis below it. The quality of the Committee's output depends on the Assessments Staff that serves it, and on the Current Intelligence Groups at which the staff draws on the community's information, analysis and interpretations, particularly those of the Defence Intelligence Staff (the DIS). The original JIC of 1939 and 1940 was ineffective until it developed its Joint Intelligence Staff with the talent and independence to do its thinking and drafting for it, and a peacetime version of it, staffed by short-term secondments, then continued after 1945. In a set of JIC reforms in 1968 – the largest at the time in the Committee's history – this was replaced by the more powerful Assessments Staff. Fine-tuning can logically start there.

This Staff has won golden opinions, but the Butler Review draws attention to two of its features. One is that it is still about the same size as when created thirty-five years earlier, and is small compared with its equivalents overseas. The other is that we have never had what was originally intended. The objective in 1968 was to make the JIC's assessments more 'professional', and it was envisaged that the new staff would be established as a 'permanent entity', staffed on a long-term basis and not by temporary secondments. The specification was for first-class people with varied backgrounds, including qualifications for scientific and technical assessment. It was recognised that special appointments might be needed, some perhaps from outside the public service. The vision at that time was explicitly of creating CIA-style expertise within the very different British system.[17]

This has never happened, and the Staff has continued to be manned in the main by normal secondments from elsewhere in the public service, including policy departments with a strong Foreign Office element among those seconded. Good people have been chosen. The strength of the system has been in the talent of these secondees, but – with some notable exceptions – not in the development of any long-term professionalism within it.

This should not lead to a sterile argument about the relative merits of Gentlemen and Players. Good intelligence judgement is not a product of any particular discipline, and by no means follows from a specialised intelligence career. Nevertheless, the limited experience that the system has had of the professionalism envisaged in 1968 shows that, when continuity in post can be combined with a 'green fingers' aptitude in assessment, something distinctive is added to the team. The requirement is not for wholesale change, but for some adjustment of the blend of qualities within the Assessments Staff.

The Privy Counsellors have taken the point. They recommend a review of the Assessments Staff's own size and skills, but go much further. More 'professionalism' in JIC assessment, and the crucial community support given to it, cannot be guaranteed without doing something about the place of analysis in the British system as a whole. The 1968 vision for the Assessments Staff was a touch unworldly: where were these assessment professionals to come from, and go to? Answers to these questions are still unclear. After the end of the Second World War Britain provided quite well for covert collection, including the creation of GCHQ, plus the continuation of the JIC, but made little provision for all-source analysts to bridge the two. This analysis had no constituency except in the small, newly created and unloved Joint Intelligence Bureau. This was in time incorporated in 1964 into the new DIS, but this has itself remained substantially geared to defence requirements rather than wider ones. A bright student can go to his or her university careers office and find attractive recruitment literature about worthwhile careers in GCHQ and the Security Service, but he or she will find fewer inducements to become a central analyst.

Much of this follows from the British rejection in 1945 of proposals for a single analysis agency. There have been subsequent flirtations with the idea, but it is probably now too late to redesign the intelligence community from scratch. Nevertheless the Review grasps the interlocking organisational and personnel issues of trying to improve analysis. It has considered but rejected giving the DIS a new, non-departmental status, but it recommends marking its position as a national asset through a much closer association with the rest of the intelligence community, an association that would be reflected in budgetary arrangements and an obligation to respond to the JIC's national intelligence requirements. It notes that both the DIS's two top posts have recently been filled by non-professionals from outside the DIS and hopes this need not continue. It then goes further and recommends consideration for an improved career structure for analysts.[18]

In financial terms this would all cost no more than peanuts and has implications extending well beyond intelligence. Professional analysis has become a feature of the information world, and arguably Britain's global outlook needs more systematic support from it – inside intelligence and outside it – than it has had. These are important proposals and need support if they are not to be kicked into touch.

The JIC Itself

John Scarlett's Chairmanship and his appointment as Chief of SIS have been matters of political controversy, and here as elsewhere the Privy Counsellors take a positive line. They decline to make him a scapegoat for what was largely a failure of an agency not under his command at the time, with effects compounded by the less-than-ideal features of the JIC system that had been accepted without question for the previous thirty-five years. Albeit in the limited context of the public 'dossier', the Review reminds its readers of the Committee's collective responsibility.

Nevertheless, it points to the varied arrangements for the Chairmanship that followed the post's tenure by a single full-time occupant throughout the war. The Chairman's post-war importance was recognised in a 1947 recommendation that it should have the 'the added authority that is needed to give more forcefulness and influence to our intelligence organization as a whole'. Ministers should have 'a single individual to whom they could refer any general issue ... and who would equally give to intelligence as a whole a spokesman well placed to voice its possibilities and its needs'.[19] It was recommended that the post should be filled from the new MoD or the Foreign Office, and the verdict was for the latter. It remained there until the Franks Committee proposed after the Falklands War that it should be a full-time Prime Ministerial appointment. This was substantially (though not completely) implemented for ten years but not thereafter, until Scarlett was appointed in 2001.

Iraq now has confirmed the Franks instinct that, despite the JIC's collegiality in many matters, its Chairman has to act in some respects as government's chief intelligence officer, and to be seen as such. The Prime Minister and other Ministers may need to see single-source material and discuss it with heads of the covert agencies, but the JIC's all-source assessments and advice must remain the principal and authoritative basis of intelligence support. The Review therefore draws attention to the anomalous situation in which the Chairman has recently been substantially outranked on his Committee, and it concludes that the post should be filled by someone with top-level experience, demonstrably beyond influence, and probably in their last post. Reasonably long tenure might also have been specified as a requirement, but in other respects there will now be no argument about the need to return to the 1947 view of its status. Care will no doubt be taken in selecting the next incumbent. The test of Butler's impact will be the amount of thought and planning that goes into subsequent successions to the post when the Iraq war has faded into history.

The Privy Counsellors have also considered the JIC's own composition. Foreigners are always astonished when they learn that, in a sense, it is not an intelligence committee at all. It brings together all relevant government knowledge and interpretation – not just intelligence – in a forum of mixed intelligence chiefs and senior policy people, acting in an intelligence mode. The Review notes that JIC membership now contains 'more policy heavyweights than in the past', including 'two of the leading policy advisers'.[20] It considers whether the Committee's policy-free objectivity has been compromised thereby, but in this instance finds rather surprisingly for the status quo. (It suggests having a part-time senior scientist as an adviser, but for a different reason.) Perhaps the Privy Counsellors met closed ranks inside the system:

> We have been assured by all witnesses that the tradition of the JIC has prevented policy objectives from dominating objective assessment in the JIC's deliberations[21]

There is little question that, odd as it appears, the inclusion of policy advisers in the JIC process contributes to the quality of its product and its credibility with Ministers. Intelligence is not so well endowed that it can dispense with Whitehall's best brains in their key policy positions.

On the other hand the JIC's composition would still seem purpose-designed to promote groupthink and reinforce prevailing wisdom. So it is a pity that the Review has not considered whether new challenges can be encouraged by bringing 'outsiders' into the system. The Washington example of appointing distinguished academics to its National Intelligence Council provides a pointer. So too is the possibility of recruiting suitable international relations experts by contract, to work in an expanded Assessments Staff. Indeed if any criticism can be made of the Review it is that, at a time when academic contacts with government are increasing elsewhere, it still sees intelligence assessment as essentially the business of career 'insiders', without much reference to what 'outsiders' might bring to the table.

Perhaps the Privy Counsellors thought that there were limits to the amount of shaking Whitehall could stand. Nevertheless there is at least a hint of drawing on the non-official world in their suggestions that there should be 'occasional external peer review' of JIC assessments,[22] and that there might be scope for formal techniques of challenge 'for major issues when the "prevailing wisdom" risks becoming too conventional'.[23] So perhaps they give the idea of drawing on outsiders some subfusc currency. Surely its time will come.

The Future

The Committee's Review has made the important and constructive recommendations discussed here, covering SIS's professional procedures, the chairmanship of the JIC, the 'professional' staffing of the Assessments Staff, the integration of the DIS within the intelligence community, and a better career structure and room for advancement for those whose *métier* is all-source analysis rather than agency specialisation. It is in effect an audit of intelligence for top government, or substantial parts of it: an unprecedented contribution on this subject often regarded as too esoteric and sensitive for investigation. It should be read as a classic of good sense and intelligence's demystification.

That is not all. It also comments on assessment technique and the drafting of JIC judgements: apparently small matters for its high-powered authors, but actually crucial in successfully telling truth to power. It additionally goes further and asks whether the Assessments Staff has the resources needed for 'thinking radically'.[24]

It points out that the Staff's cost is minimal in relation to the cost of intelligence collection: '[i]t is false economy to skimp on the machinery through which expensively-collected intelligence passes to decision-makers'.[25] Quality depends partly on doing the small things well, and properly funding them.

No doubt these points will all be taken seriously and acted upon. But along with the main recommendations they suggest another conclusion which the Privy Counsellors might have drawn – but did not. For the single issue of Iraqi WMD they were able to freeze-dry the assessment process and evaluate its performance, with the findings they have set out. But why did it need an intelligence failure of this significance to bring out the scope for improvement? Even if the lessons are learned in the short term, who will be charged thereafter with keeping the machinery fine-tuned to the changing challenges it faces? 'Maintaining our Intelligence Organisations at a high standard of efficiency' was specified by the Chiefs of Staffs in 1947 as one of the 'fundamentals' of defence policy,[26] and no one would now disagree. But the Butler Committee cannot remain in permanent session to do it.

On some things the Review proposes where action might lie – with the Parliamentary Intelligence and Security Committee, the Security and Intelligence Coordinator in the Cabinet Office, and in one case the JIC itself, which is encouraged to conduct regular lessons-learned processes.[27] But it does not discuss overall intelligence responsibilities; it does not tackle Winston Churchill's unanswered question in 1940: 'Who's in charge?'[28] Neither does this article. But the most important lesson of the Review might be that the effectiveness of the machinery of joint assessment cannot be left entirely to the secondees who are fully stretched in doing it under day-to-day pressures.

We have a good system but have been too satisfied with it. As Peter Hennessy has put it, quoting Kipling on the Boer War,

> Let us admit it fairly, as a business people should,
> We have had no end of a lesson: it will do us no end of good.[29]

For the spirit this requires I revert to the reforms of 1968 from which the present assessment system came. I recently asked a former colleague how it was that the Cabinet Secretary of the time, Lord (then

Sir Burke) Trend, came to be the prime mover in them. In reply he reminded me that Trend's characteristic approach to anything was 'Can we do it better?' I hope that the lasting legacy of Iraq will be to encourage, perhaps institutionalise, that positive spirit of 1968, determined to do things better.

Notes

1. Originally published as 'Intelligence and the Iraqi Threat: British Joint Intelligence after Butler', *The RUSI Journal*, 149, no. 4, 2004: 18–24. Copyright © *RUSI Journal*, reprinted by permission of Taylor & Francis Ltd on behalf of *RUSI Journal*: http://www.tandfonline.com
2. GCHQ graduate careers brochure 1996.
3. There is no British intelligence budget. The published Single Intelligence Vote for GCHQ, SIS and the Security Service does not include the cost of Defence Intelligence and other MoD-funded intelligence, or of other small parts of the national intelligence effort.
4. *Review of Intelligence on Weapons of Mass Destruction: Report of a Committee of Privy Counsellors* (London: HMSO, 2004).
5. The Franks Report of 1983 dealt with intelligence performance up to the invasion of the Falklands, but only as a small part of the much larger picture of British policy.
6. *Review of Intelligence on Weapons of Mass Destruction*, para. 41, pp. 155–6.
7. Ibid., para. 28, p. 153.
8. Ibid., para. 454, p. 111.
9. Department for International Development, *Policy Statement, Poverty and the Security Sector*, 1999, pp. 4, 6, the basis of an address by Ms Short, then Secretary of State DFID, at the Centre for Defence Studies, King's College London, 9 March 1999.
10. The classic statement is Janis, I., *Victims of Groupthink: A Psychological Study of Foreign Policy Decisions and Fiascos* (Boston, MA: Houghton Mifflin, 1972).
11. Cradock, P., *In Pursuit of British Interests: Reflections on Foreign Policy under Margaret Thatcher and John Major* (London: Murray, 1997), p. 37.
12. *Review of Intelligence on Weapons of Mass Destruction*, para. 19, p. 152.
13. *Falklands Islands Review: Report of a Committee of Privy Counsellors* (London: HMSO, 1983), para. 316, p. 85.

14. Quoted by Johnson, L., *Secret Agencies: U.S. Intelligence in a Hostile World* (New Haven, CT: Yale University Press, 1996), p. 28, from Thomson, J. C., 'How Could Vietnam Happen', *Atlantic Monthly*, 221 (April 1968).

15. *The Times*, 7 February 2004.

16. As put orally many years ago. In his recent publication Sir Percy has preferred 'intelligence and policy in separate but adjoining rooms, with communicating doors and thin partition walls, as in cheap hotels'. See Cradock, P., *Know your Enemy: How the Joint Intelligence Committee Saw the World* (London: Murray, 2002), p. 296.

17. See submissions from the Cabinet Secretary to the Prime Minister published with commentary by Professor John Young, 'The Wilson Government's Reform of Intelligence Coordination, 1967–68', *Intelligence and National Security*, 16, no. 2, 2001: 133–51. Documents are in the UK National Archives (TNA) PREM 13/2688 and elsewhere.

18. For analysis see *Review of Intelligence on Weapons of Mass Destruction*, paras 446–59, pp. 109–12, and paras 586–605, pp. 142–6.

19. *Review of Intelligence Organisation 1947*, by Air Chief Marshal Sir Douglas Evill, 6 November 1947, CAB 163/7, TNA.

20. *Review of Intelligence on Weapons of Mass Destruction*, para. 592, p. 143.

21. Ibid., para. 596, p. 144.

22. Ibid., para. 605(g), p. 146.

23. Ibid., para. 599, p. 144.

24. Ibid., para. 600, p. 145.

25. Ibid., para. 600, pp. 44–5.

26. *Future Defence Policy: Report by the Chiefs of Staff*, 22 May 1947, reproduced in Dockrill, M., *British Defence since 1945* (London: Blackwell, 1988), appendix I.

27. *Review of Intelligence on Weapons of Mass Destruction*, para. 605(g), p. 146.

28. Hinsley, F. H. and E. E. Thomas, C. Ransom and R. C. Knight, *British Intelligence in the Second World War: Vol. I* (London: HMSO, 1979), p. 291.

29. Hennessy, P., 'The Lightning Flash on the Road to Baghdad: Issues of Evidence', in W. G. Runciman (ed.), *Hutton and Butler: Lifting the Lid on the Workings of Power* (Oxford: The British Academy and Oxford University Press, 2004), p. 64.

15 Butler Reviewed[1]

[2014]

The Butler committee was the first critical consideration of intelligence's service of assessment to top government since the changes of the 1960s. I had been publishing proposals for reform for some time before 2004 and had the luck to be able to put them to Lord Butler's committee. I was later sent a copy of the transcript and it is reprinted in this collection, along with my RUSI article on the committee's report which was published shortly afterwards.[2] Here I offer my reflections ten years later, with an impression of the changes that followed Butler's recommendations.

Like everyone else I had judged after the Iraq War that the Joint Intelligence Committee (JIC) might have done better over Saddam's Weapons of Mass Destruction (WMD).[3] For intelligence as a whole it was a disturbing failure, the more so since its task of estimating what weapons a secretive regime possessed, and informing government reactions, was more of a throw-back to the Cold War than a novel, twenty-first-century problem. The basic challenge for assessment on Iraq was drawing conclusions from the relative absence of evidence, and of this there had been ample Cold War experience. I was vividly reminded of the debates in the late 1950s and early 1960s about the Soviet missile threat, when analysts struggled to determine whether there were hundreds of operational Soviet ICBMs or none at all.[4] Intelligence officials were uncertain on the key aspects of Iraq's WMD, but they were not determined enough in their uncertainty.

This may have been influenced by pressure on the JIC for some years to provide positive 'key judgements' instead of sitting on the fence. I judged that intelligence on Iraq was caught up in the assumptions and excitement of the day and had slipped into the role of government's counsel for the prosecution rather than its judge of evidence, or in this case the absence of evidence. There is an open academic question of whether intelligence is ever capable of questioning conventional wisdom in circumstances of political importance and stress. Sir Lawrence Freedman observed more than thirty years previously that intelligence analysts are 'socialised into a particular world-view which is shared by the main consumers of their work'.[5] On this view the JIC's performance over Iraq might have led us to scale down our expectation of analysts getting politically difficult questions right, and of government's willingness to be guided by them. Indeed a body of writing at the time encouraged scepticism about policy-neutral assessment: two influential Americans wrote in 2000 that '"Objectivity" in intelligence is no longer good enough . . . The best truth is one that is delivered in a way that meets the needs of the individual users.'[6] Robert Gates had also enjoined CIA analysts to be 'down in the trenches' with policy-makers.[7] It should not be forgotten how difficult top-level intelligence assessment can be: a high-wire act, like trying to write history before it happens, with a narrow margin between success and failure. One reaction was to simply not depend on intelligence for politically contentious, top-level issues of state.

But this was not the reaction of Butler's committee, and on this I strongly supported it. Democratic officials are expected to look at facts and not preconceptions, and this must apply even more to intelligence. Britain had developed a good assessment system in the JIC, and the main problem in my view has been a degree of complacency within it. British officials had spent more effort commending the JIC model to other nations than on working to keep improving it. The Butler report was the first external review of it since 1947,[8] and for the ideal of objective analysis to be maintained someone was needed who was close enough to the system to exercise responsibility for its standards without being too involved in day-to-day management. It needed a conscious striving for excellence, rather like the coach of a national sports team seeking to increase the chance of success. The post of Intelligence Coordinator was originally intended in 1968 to have a responsibility of this kind for the Assessments Staff, but the new organisation never developed in quite that way.

These were my concerns when I was invited to give evidence to Butler's committee. My starting point was that the Assessments Staff had been created in 1968 to provide more central support for the JIC with 'a distinctly professional technique'.[9] It replaced what was then the Joint Intelligence Staff, and the intention was that it would be made up of able people with varied backgrounds who would be appointed on a long-term basis. It was not clear at the time whether the required professionalism was in analytic skills, expertise in subject matter, or just long periods in post, or a mixture of the three; but whatever was intended, it never really happened. This was basically because the peacetime intelligence machinery created in 1945 had catered better for the collectors than those performing all-source analysis and assessment. The Assessments Staff at the time of the Iraq War was thus still quite small, about thirty strong, smaller than the comparable units in Canada and Australia. I suggested that Lord Butler should concentrate his inquiry on this staff and the Current Intelligence Groups which it used to draft the JIC's reports, rather than the Committee itself.

I see from the transcript that I made a dozen proposals and was treated with patience and indulgence. I argued for improved all-source analysis across the intelligence community, with better training and improved recruitment, status and careers. My thinking was that the Defence Intelligence Staff (DIS; subsequently Defence Intelligence (DI)) should cease to be a purely departmental resource, as should the FCO's Research Officers, and the status of the JIC Chairman should be enhanced. This was not a bid for a complete intelligence takeover at the expense of the FCO and MoD, nor for professionals against amateurs. It was trying instead to get a new blend of skills in the centre that would be less influenced by Whitehall's policy consensus. I rested part of my case on the story of the Soviet Union's alert of November 1983 and its detection by Harry Burke, a GCHQ professional posted to the Assessments Staff the previous year to improve its 'warning' performance.[10] An increased professional element of this kind would improve the JIC's performance on threats, but this meant taking all-source analysis more seriously, on the analogy

of the Government Statistical Service as a central body of expertise. On the same lines I suggested having some contract appointments in the Assessments Staff of specialists from academia and
the private sector: I recalled some good appointments of this kind
in the early 1970s. I also suggested the use of external contracts
to draft some JIC papers, and the appointment of a part-time
academic to the JIC itself, following the example of Washington's
National Intelligence Council.

Lord Butler's committee supported the main lines of these suggestions, though not the recruitment of outsiders. His committee made sensible recommendations on the themes of intellectual
independence and analytic quality. On the first of these it recommended that the JIC Chairman should no longer be outranked
by other members of his committee (as had been the case with
John Scarlett over Iraqi WMD), and should be someone 'with
experience of dealing with Ministers in a very senior role, and
who is demonstrably beyond influence, and thus probably in his
last post'.[11] As a result of the report the government appointed
someone of this kind, though he had no previous experience of
intelligence work. This seniority was a welcome recognition of
the post's importance, although it is to be hoped the government
in the future will plan well in advance about the selection and
career development for this post, and not trust that it will be
all right on the day.[12] It is heartening that a recent Chief of the
Assessments Staff had an intelligence background, and that he
subsequently became the deputy head of DI in 2014, an MoD
post that the intelligence analysts should never have lost earlier.[13]
Apart from this consideration of the JIC's chairmanship, the committee strongly endorsed the recommendation of serious training
for assessment posts, and this turned out to be one of Butler's
most successful recommendations.

On the other hand, Butler did not recommend giving the JIC
as a body any additional insulation from policy-making. In fact
the committee has never been a pure intelligence body. It has
always had strong representation from the FCO, traditionally
including the chairmanship, and has continued with the mixture
of intelligence chiefs and what Butler called Whitehall's 'policy
heavyweights'.[14] This is the Whitehall consensus incarnate. The

non-intelligence representation had been increased after the Falkl-ands War under the influence of Sir Antony Duff (JIC Chairman and Coordinator at various times and for one period both).[15] It was a pity that Butler's committee did not recommend some non-government membership to introduce different perspectives. It did however suggest making improvements to the career prospects of intelligence analysts. This was needed for the Assessments Staff, but also for the DIS as the principal centre of all-source expertise.

In response, the government created a new post of Professional Head of Intelligence Analysis (PHIA) in the Cabinet Office to advise on analyst capabilities, recruitment, career structures, interchanges within and beyond government, methodology and training.[16] By 2014 a lot had been done about training in intelligence analysis, arguably one of the most successful of Butler's recommendations (and incidentally one of mine to his committee).[17] While it is perhaps too early to judge the long-term impact of these changes, training will hopefully become something like the naval officer's watchkeeping certificate, attesting that a graduate will have some competence if he or she finds themself in charge.

Within the Assessments Staff there are experienced analysts, but some will only be familiar with intelligence product without having experience producing it, while others may be entirely new to the process. Training will mean there is less need for these people to learn on the job and should act as a safeguard against basic errors, but it is unclear how much PHIA alone can strengthen the core of professional excellence in the centre of government. The craft of analysis is not just a set of basic skills to be learned quickly, at least not at the national assessment level. Everyone there has native ability and knowledge of rules and conventions is easily learned. So is the knack of intelligence writing, though some do it better than others. In my experience the most capable analysts are like historians but working inside out: not on a vanished past, but on an opaque present and uncertain future. We are not sure how to produce successful historians, and something of this uncertainty applies to top-level analysis, even though training can improve general standards over time.

There is also the question of the continuing reliance on seconded policy officials. The JIC has operated largely on a basis of convention and assumptions. Relatively little is laid down – that, for example, it does not 'do' policy; is more 'foreign' than 'domestic'; does not 'do' the US or the EU; and so on. There are questions of process and methodology for all-source analysis which can benefit from a more searching reflection than what would be imparted in training. For instance, should the JIC on its own initiative tackle subjects about which government does not want to hear? When tackling an uncertain issue, where does 'forming a view' and avoiding fence-sitting stop, and the need to reflect differing views and uncertainty start? Another issue is intelligence's priority: is it being right, or is it getting its message across to government; or perhaps some combination of the two?[18]

There is thus ample justification for a wider analytical education to debate and criticise intelligence's conventions. A post-Butler initiative in this direction is the education programme sponsored by PHIA and delivered at King's College London. This course introduces the concepts, issues and debates from scholarship to career analysts across government, not just those in the Cabinet Office. Its historical case studies and hypothetical problems explore the challenges analysts typically face under pressure, the role of other intelligence organisations in the analytical process, and the mindset of policy users who consume their product.[19] Over time this may help to develop a common frame of reference for governmental analysts. It also delivers on a key aspect of professionalisation, which is for practitioners to reflect on the purpose and scope of analytical judgement. At the very least, there may be some analysts who, encouraged by deeper study in combination with training, have more opportunity to hone innate ability into professional flair.

A decade later it may be that Butler's most practical legacy is from this training and education. This provides an element of the professionalism intended in 1968. I wonder, however, if the JIC itself is still operating in its pre-Butler mode: good at producing assessment well aligned to government, but not the optimum arrangement for avoiding nasty surprises. Do we yet have a JIC that is at times *not* helpful to government; a Committee that recognises the need to produce assessments which the government may not want to hear. Does the standing of career intelligence analysts across Whitehall reflect this requirement? Nothing much appears to have happened to the status of DI since the Butler report, and I hear the weight of responsibility in the Assessments Staff still tends to fall on policy officials on secondment. Is it still a feature of our system that no one (except Sir Percy Cradock) has ever been the JIC Chairman after earlier experience as Chief of the Assessments Staff or its other senior posts? Is it a general rule that people are not seconded to senior assessment more than once, however good they are at it? Are we still suffering from the failure after 1968 to build more professional analysis at the centre of government?

Notes

1. Adapted from a presentation to the conference 'The Butler Report: 10 Years On' hosted by King's College London and the Ministry of Defence, 1 December 2014.
2. Chapter 14 in this collection, 'Joint Intelligence and Butler'.
3. For an excellent overview of British intelligence on Iraq and its post-mortems, see Aldrich, R. J., 'Whitehall and the Iraq War: The UK's Four Intelligence Enquiries', *Irish Studies in International Affairs*, 16, 2005: 73–88.
4. Dylan, H., 'Britain and the Missile Gap: British Estimates on the Soviet Ballistic Missile Threat, 1957–61', *Intelligence and National Security*, 23, no. 6, 2008: 777–806.
5. Freedman, L., *US Intelligence and the Soviet Strategic Threat*, 2nd edition (London: Macmillan, 1986), p. 186.
6. Berkowitz, B. D. and A. E. Goodman, *Best Truth: Intelligence in the Information Age* (London: Yale University Press, 2000), p. xi.
7. Godson, R. (ed.), *Intelligence Requirements for the 1990s: Collection, Analysis, Counterintelligence, Covert Action* (Washington, DC: Lexington Books, 1989), p. 111.
8. *Review of Intelligence Organisation*, by Air Chief Marshal Sir Douglas Evill, 6 November 1947, CAB 163/7, the UK National Archives. The major reorganisation of 1968 came from in-house discussions at Permanent Secretary level in Whitehall; see Davies, P. H. J., *Intelligence and Government in Britain and the United States: A Comparative Perspective* (Oxford: Praeger, 2012), pp. 206–7.
9. Young, J. W., 'The Wilson Government's Reform of Intelligence Co-ordination, 1967–68', *Intelligence and National Security*, 16, no. 2, 2001: 137–49.

10. See Chapter 20 in this collection, 'Harry Burke and Able Archer'.
11. *Review of Intelligence on Weapons of Mass Destruction: Report of a Committee of Privy Counsellors* (London: HMSO, 2004), para. 63, p. 159.
12. The positions of the JIC and its Chairman changed again more recently, in some ways following the Butler recommendations but not in others. An unexpected development was the creation of the Prime Minister's National Security Council in 2010, and the direct involvement of the individual heads of the intelligence and security agencies in it. This changes the role of the JIC's assessments and meetings and its Chairman's status. Rather earlier the JIC's collective managerial responsibilities for the intelligence community were also formally reduced.
13. Paul Rimmer, now retired after basically an intelligence career interleaved with mainline policy appointments in MoD.
14. *Review of Intelligence on Weapons of Mass Destruction*, para. 592, p. 143.
15. This representation was variable but for some periods included the senor policy staff of the MoD.
16. Secretary of State for Foreign and Commonwealth Affairs, *Review of Intelligence on Weapons of Mass Destruction: Implementation of its Conclusions* (London: HMSO, 2005), para. 26, p. 9.
17. There are now a number of courses run by other Whitehall departments following PHIA's lead, with formal accreditation for participants, although this raises questions about standardisation of effort. See Devanny, J. and R. Dover, M. Goodman and D. Omand, 'Why the British Government Must Invest in the Next Generation of Intelligence Analysts', *The RUSI Journal*, 163, no. 6, 2018: 82.
18. Of the two greatest JIC Chairmen of my time, it has been said of Sir Percy Cradock that his greatest concern was 'what exactly are we trying to say'; while for Sir Antony Duff it was 'how exactly are we going to put it to government?'.
19. Goodman, M. and D. Omand, 'What Analysts Need to Understand: The King's Intelligence Studies Program', *Studies in Intelligence*, 52, no. 4, 2008: 1–12.

PART 4

Personalities in British Intelligence

16 Recruitment in 1945 and 'Peculiar Personal Characteristics'[1]

[2019]

In the last months of 1945 two senior British civil servants corresponded about the size, structure and pay of the post-war Sigint organisation that was to become GCHQ, the continuation of the pre-war Government Code and Cypher School (GC&CS) and its greatly expanded wartime version at Bletchley Park. One of the officials, J. I. C. Crombie, was the Foreign Office's Principal Establishment and Finance Officer with the grade of Assistant Under-Secretary of State, the antique title of Chief Clerk, and an annual salary of £1,700. In considering Bletchley's post-war resources he was continuing the Foreign Office's pre-war sponsorship of GC&CS, though unusually for its Chief Clerk he was a home civil servant with a Treasury background and not from the diplomatic service.[2] The other civil servant, A. J. D. Winnifrith, was younger though still quite senior: an Assistant Secretary in the Treasury, on a scale of £1,150–£1,500, who exercised the Treasury's responsibility for controlling Civil Service costs and numbers.[3] They had been to Cambridge and Oxford and had joined the Civil Service through what was then its annual academic competitions, and were fliers rising to the top. Sir James Crombie retired in 1962 after eight years as Chairman of the Board of Customs and Excise; Sir John Winnifrith was Permanent Secretary of the Ministry of Agriculture, Fisheries and Food from 1959 to 1967 before taking a clutch of post-retirement appointments.

Thus, in their careers they were exemplars of the subsequently maligned mandarins or 'gifted Oxbridge amateurs' of the British

345

administrative class, at the top of the Civil Service tree,[4] and were creating a virtually new peacetime organisation in 1945 at a time of extreme national stringency. Bletchley's post-war bid was for 260 'officer grade' staff to replace the 1939 complement of 35, and 750 subordinates replacing 133. (Bletchley's maximum official wartime complement was quoted as 8,902 civilians and military.)[5] The country was economically and financially ruined, with rescue from Marshall Aid not yet on the horizon: food rationing was to continue well into the next decade. The historian coming to this correspondence might therefore expect these standard-issue mandarins to greet Bletchley's proposal with disdain and questioning, penny-pinching and cutting everything by half; but this view could not be more wrong. At the outset, Winnifrith expressed his support for Bletchley's substantial post-war bid: 'the scope of the School's [GC&CS's] activities has enormously increased, and we cannot afford to starve them'.[6] What followed, in the usual Whitehall style of personal letters addressed by surnames, was in effect a teach-in between the two officials, with Bletchley interventions, on the requirements of a viable peacetime Sigint organisation. It ranged widely, but a central point was that Bletchley's successes sprang from the special talent deployed there: how then was this talent to be recruited and nurtured in peacetime? Winnifrith wrote that the pre-war pay and careers at GC&CS had been a muddle (through no proper planning of recruitment, age structures and promotion) and something better was needed. It was probably the first time a new intelligence organisation had been conceived by administrators in quite this way. British public administration for most of its functions was still wedded to the hierarchy of the three main 'generalist' Civil Service classes with entrance by examination, though there was another class for scientists, as well as some specialist functions like statisticians and tax inspectors with their own pay and structures. There was thus a range of career models to follow, but where were GCHQ's key elements to be fitted among them? This chapter outlines the arrangements agreed in 1945 to recruit for GCHQ's long-term skills and abilities, and their subsequent modification.

The Treasury's starting point was to accept that, as before the war, 'the staff of the School will have to continue to be specialists, not interchangeable with the rest of the Government Service'.[7] It recognised that 'persons entering the School must regard this as their life [sic] work', and hence 'the prospects must be sufficient to attract candidates of the same calibre as would be recruited for the Administrative and Technical Classes'.[8] It wrote of the organisation's people that 'their work is of an exhausting and highly intellectual character' for which they would need 'considerable academic qualifications',[9] and it concluded that 'neither the Administrative nor the Scientific examinations would produce the right type of candidate who has to have peculiar personal characteristics to make him suitable for the work of the School'.[10] (Women were not mentioned, except for a reminder that by the Civil Service rules of the time they would be paid less.) Special ability or flair (the 'peculiar personal characteristics') was a prime concern. It was not defined in these exchanges, but the requirement was based on the wartime achievements of the mathematicians and chess players in breaking German machine ciphers, developed from the School's pre-war model of diplomatic code-breaking and linguistics. This flair was discussed as an individual quality, though it had often been harnessed at Bletchley in teams, and had also had the wider role of technical leadership. Of Hugh Alexander, a leading Bletchley cryptanalyst and head of GCHQ's post-war cryptanalytic division for twenty-one and a half years,[11] his successor wrote of his wartime and post-war career that

> On the technical side Hugh put in more individual work than any head of division has a right to; but his most important contribution was by encouragement and suggestion, by clear-cut views which simplified the problem, by going around sections, looking over people's shoulders, asking questions, having ideas; and more than anything else by sheer infectious enthusiasm.[12]

This cryptanalytic flair and its wider effects was one component of the wartime successes, but Bletchley also recognised that its wartime codebreaking had been matched by an effective production and distribution system that was geared to the scale and speed of decryption and gave it much of its operational value. A senior cryptanalyst, Gordon Welchman,[13] had not only contributed to codebreaking but had also emerged as the leader of the mechanisation that enabled Bletchley by the end of 1942 to be reading some 4,000 high-grade German signals *a day*, with slightly smaller numbers of Italian and Japanese, and managing a worldwide intelligence production line from them.[14] Equally important, the post-war proposals also recognised Bletchley's development of the other areas of signals analysis and exploitation that had been part of its evolution from a pre-war codebreaking organisation into a broader signals exploitation centre. Of this one example was given not long ago in Sir Arthur Bonsall's published account of the wartime exploitation of 'low-grade' German Air Force (GAF) codes:[15] the success in exploiting apparently unprofitable material that was often repeated in later years against Cold War targets. Flair ranged widely: Bonsall described Josh Cooper, a long-serving Sigint polymath with a personal technical influence akin to Alexander's, but not just in codebreaking. As Bonsall put it, 'with his wide-ranging knowledge, he [Cooper] was eminently suited to guide and inspire his young and individualistic staff, encouraging and assisting them to devise solutions to what were entirely novel problems'.[16] Flair for Sigint exploitation merged in turn into the skills of intelligence officers and then into the qualities of direction and policy-making: Bonsall as a young man at Bletchley became an expert on GAF codes, but also rose to run his section, and in later life became GCHQ's Director. Cooper was similarly influential in its post-war Directorate. In 1945 the civil servants accepted Bletchley's contentions that the new Sigint centre would need people with a puzzle-solving flair, wider than cryptanalysis though related to it, but also that running it would need people 'as good as those whom it is desired to attract to the Administrative and Scientific Grades [of the main civil service]'.[17]

This was a source of disagreement with Bletchley's initial proposals in 1945 that the 260 'officer class' posts would all belong to a single recruitment and grading system. The Treasury and Foreign Office insisted to the contrary on distinguishing between those with the policy and managerial qualities of the administrative class and those with the technical flair of the Sigint profession, and Bletchley accordingly accepted that their originally proposed officer-level posts, apart from being reduced in total, would not be in one class but would instead be divided into two separate ones, A and B. There would be fifty-nine As with pay and careers close to those of Whitehall's main administrative class to ensure that, in the Treasury's words, the School had 'the required number of first class brains' for which 'they must look for candidates of the same intellectual qualifications possessed by candidates for the Administrative Grade of the Home Civil Service'.[18] The other 104 posts would be in the B class and would have 'good intellectual qualifications possessed by university entrants who, whilst unsuitable for the administrative grade, might have made a successful career in, say, education':[19] their pay scale would be rather less. There would be a linkage between the two through a common cadet grade for recruitment. Recruits would all be Junior Assistants (JAs, the title of the pre-war entry grade for GC&CS), and some would become As, though most would become Bs, with conditions comparable with those of the Civil Service's specialists. Below them the intelligence production machine would be supported by a C class and clericals, with conditions based on those of the Civil Service's main executive and clerical classes, but also with some provision for graduate entry.

In these arrangements it is surprising that the Treasury's rather unenthusiastic description of the B class ('might have made a successful career in education') was not contested more vigorously. GCHQ had argued that these people needed academic qualifications very little below those of Class A; but it perhaps accepted the A and B package as offered, in order to secure good Bletchley people who were contemplating staying in the post-war organisation but would not wait very long for offers. It was common ground that GCHQ would need some 'absolute flyers',[20] but neither party pushed the question whether a hypothetical applicant with the 'absolute flyer' potential of another Turing (great technical brilliance, complete disinterest in management) would be offered a career as an A or as a B. Over the roles of the As and Bs this subsequently became a running controversy, but with this exception these arrangements at the end of 1945 provided GCHQ with a stable senior structure for the Cold War. Along with the other features agreed at this stage they established GCHQ as part of the national Civil Service, albeit a specialised one, with many of the service-wide features, such as recruitment by open competition supervised by the Civil Service Commission, and the encouragement of national staff associations – something that led eventually to government's controversial 'de-unionisation' of GCHQ in 1984 and its restoration in 1997.

In this setting GCHQ's post-war management worked hard and successfully for the next forty years to gain a Whitehall reputation as a well-run department, run as far as possible on normal Civil Service lines. In some ways it was a strange aim for an organisation whose work was still unacknowledged before 1983, but a sensible one for the conditions of the time, and one that distinguished it from its smaller sister agencies the Security Service and Secret Intelligence Service, which remained (and perhaps remain) crown servants but technically not part of the Civil Service, and free on this account from some of the pressures for conformity. Though not part of the senior structure discussed here, it should be mentioned in passing that the large Civil Service classes established in 1945 for GCHQ's non-graduate and clerical entry probably brought a bigger share of flair and weight to post-war Sigint production than was foreseen when their supporting role was planned. Throughout the Cold War there were significant contributions from non-graduates who had left school at eighteen, in some cases earlier; but the input of the highest fliers was still essential.

To return to the A and B classes and their creation in 1945 to meet GCHQ's peacetime requirements for both flair and management: at the beginning of the 1950s there was an important lurch in the recruitment agreed for them. It was decided then that, though the recruitment of JAs was producing enough B class specialists, it was not providing enough potential policy-makers and managers, and the Treasury was persuaded to replace the single cadet grade by separate A and B streams (A4s and B4s) with separate recruitment competitions, pay scales and prospects. It would need research to determine exactly how this was decided, and by whom, but one can guess that it reflected the influence of Eric Jones (later Sir Eric) who was to become GCHQ's Director in 1952. Before the war he had left school at fifteen, joined the family textile firm, then formed his own company; and as a wartime RAF officer he was drafted to Bletchley and made an outstanding contribution there in running the assessment and reporting machine for the German army and air force decrypts. In this key operation he had resolved what had been endemic interservice conflicts with firmness and common sense, and no claims to the special skill and knowledge of those he was supervising. He stayed with Bletchley in 1945 and after an important year as GCHQ's first liaison officer in Washington he returned and in 1950 became Deputy Director.[21] It would have been consistent with his attitude throughout his career for him to be influential in this period towards recruiting more potential managers.

However it was brought about, JA recruitment was replaced by the separate A and B cadets, and one JA of outstanding ability (Tovey, a future Director)[22] was regraded as the first A4. The first public competition to recruit 'managerial types' to this grade was held in 1952. In the two annual competitions that followed a total of six A4s were recruited up to the mid-1950s, four with degrees in history, one in English and one in Oxford 'greats' (classical languages and history with philosophy). Two had trained as Russian linguists during their military conscription. Of the six, one (a bizarre selection) resigned and another was regraded; the other four eventually rose to senior positions, two at Directorate level. All had been trained as generalists, with an emphasis on the output end of the production line as well as introductions to management and policy issues.[23] More A4 recruitment followed, but the focus on these new 'managerial types' remained controversial and associated with more typecasting into the two classes – the As as 'managers' and the Bs as 'researchers': distinctions that caused debate over individual posts and upset people in both streams. At one stage the senior staff association, the GCHQ branch of the Civil Service's First Division Association, took issue with the distinction, with a climax in a packed meeting in the mid-1950s – probably the biggest and most heated meeting that unspectacular body ever had in its life – at which it was forcibly argued that GCHQ's success depended on flair, and those who had it would provide all the management talent needed. A more extreme position, though not without some wartime justification, was that educational qualifications of any kind were poor predictors of Sigint ability, and everyone should start at the bottom.

This blew over: memories faded of Bletchley's wartime informality and rise by technical merit, and the separate cadet streams became accepted. But official positions also softened, as eventually did Whitehall's attachment to different pay and structures for specific skills. GCHQ devised its own tests of potential Sigint abilities for the B4s' selection, and someone sensibly suggested that they should also be taken by the A4 candidates. The two competitions then coalesced, and candidates were considered for both streams, and eventually the two classes of cadets were merged again into one, as in 1945, though under a new title. In the 1980s Treasury control over gradings weakened, and the three main Civil Service classes were rebranded into a common structure with more scope for departmental variations within them. GCHQ's A and B posts became assimilated to these new gradings, and the distinctive labels disappeared. The internal debates continued about Sigint flair and its importance, but now in the context of individuals' recruitment and careers, rather than posts and structures, and by the end of the Cold War the department was offering more varied careers, to general satisfaction. Nevertheless the earlier conformity to Civil Service orthodoxy had served a purpose. GCHQ had become recognised as a fully-fledged government department responsible to a Secretary of State (the Foreign Secretary), its Director a full member of the Joint Intelligence Committee, and no longer in its predecessor's pre-war position as a satellite of the SIS and the Foreign Office.

This was only a tiny part of GCHQ's history, and everything about it is now greatly changed. But one guesses that it still needs people with the qualities demonstrated by Alexander and Cooper at Bletchley and afterwards and discussed by Crombie and Winnifrith in 1945: the 'absolute flyers' with the flair embraced within Winnifrith's 'peculiar personal characteristics'. Other intelligence agencies probably identify and seek their own distinctive kinds of flair. Those seeking to understand intelligence in all its aspects should give attention to flair, and the prosaic arrangements on which its recruitment depends. They can make the difference between intelligence's success and failure, and sometimes, for those whose work it supports, between life and death.

Notes

1. Originally published as 'Intelligence Recruitment in 1945 and "Peculiar Personal Characteristics"' in Gearon, L. F. (ed.), *The Routledge International Handbook of Universities, Security and Intelligence Studies* (London: Routledge, 2019), pp. 362–7. Copyright © 2019 Routledge. Reproduced by permission of Taylor & Francis Group.
2. Sir James Crombie, 1902–69. Home Civil Service, 1926–62 (War Office, Treasury, Ministry of Food, Foreign Office, Customs and Excise).
3. Sir John Winnifrith, 1908–93. Home Civil Service, 1932–67 (Board of Trade, Treasury and War Cabinet, Agriculture Fisheries and Food).
4. Crombie had a Scottish education which included a degree at Aberdeen before a year at Cambridge. Success for Scottish students in the Civil Service examination was not unusual.
5. Winnifrith to Crombie, 13 October 1945 (date emended and unclear, probably 15), attachment page 1, FO 366/1518, UK National Archives (TNA). All archival references hereafter refer to TNA records. The expression 'officer grade' was not used elsewhere in the correspondence and was perhaps a pre-war usage. It survived for many years afterwards in one of the other agencies.
6. Winnifrith to Crombie, 13 October 1945, attachment page 2, FO 366/1518.
7. Ibid., attachment page 3.
8. Winnifrith to Crombie, 29 October 1945, attachment page 4, FO 366/1518.
9. Winnifrith to Crombie, 13 October 1945, attachment page 4, ibid.
10. Ibid.
11. Conel Hugh O'Donel Alexander, 1909–74. GC&CS/GCHQ, 1940–71.
12. Denham, H., 'In Memoriam: Conel Hugh O'Donel Alexander', *Cryptologic Spectrum*, 4, no. 3, 1974: 31. Accessed on 29 June 2017 at: https://www.nsa.gov/Portals/70/documents/news-features/declassified-documents/cryptologic-spectrum/in_memoriam.pdf
13. William Gordon Welchman, 1906–85.
14. Hinsley, F. H. and A. Stripp (eds), *Codebreakers: The Inside Story of Bletchley Park* (Oxford: Oxford University Press, 1993), preface page v.
15. Bonsall, A., *Another Bit of Bletchley* (Bletchley Park Trust 2009), pp. 6–14. Arthur Wilfred ('Bill') Bonsall, 1917–2014. GC&CS/GCHQ, 1940–78 (Director 1973–8).
16. Ibid., p. 39. Joshua Edward Synge Cooper, 1901–81. GC&CS/GCHQ, 1925–61.

17. Winnifrith to Crombie, 13 October 1945, attachment page 1, FO 366/1518.
18. Winnifrith to Crombie, 31 December 1945, ibid.
19. Ibid., attachment page 2.
20. Winnifrith to Crombie, 29 October 1945, attachment page 4, FO 366/1518.
21. Sir Eric Malcolm Jones, 1907–86. RAF, 1940–3; GC&CS/GCHQ, 1943–60 (Director 1952–60). See also Chapter 19 in this collection, 'GCHQ Directors'.
22. Sir Brian John Maynard Tovey, 1926–2015. GCHQ, 1950–83 (Director 1978–83).
23. Personal recollections. This apparent preference for 'arts' over science degrees remained a feature of this recruitment through the Cold War, though not consistently so.

17 Up from the Country: Cabinet Office Impressions 1972–5[1]

[1997]

I was once a modern Dick Whittington, travelling to London to explore its mysteries – though without a black cat, and not on foot. I was summoned from my provincial Civil Service department to be the Secretary of the Joint Intelligence Committee (JIC) in the Cabinet Office from 1972 to 1975. My contacts there with the heart of government were intermittent and tenuous; in the cricketing metaphor, I was lucky to get a touch. Yet, like Dick Whittington, I was an impressionable innocent. Recollections of the milieu may be of interest.

Impressions

The Cabinet Office was still relatively young. Sir Burke Trend, the Cabinet Secretary, was only the fourth holder of the post. But the Office was already much more than the War Secretariat which evolved from the pre-1914 Committee of Imperial Defence to provide minutes of War Cabinet and Cabinet meetings from 1917 onwards. Even since the end of the Second World War it had expanded. The JIC had become a Cabinet Office committee when it was transferred from the Chiefs of Staff in 1957 after the Suez fiasco.[2] The Central Statistical Office had subsequently become nominally part of it, and in 1970 Heath's Central Policy Review Staff had been based within its building and administered by it.

Nevertheless, the Cabinet Office's role was relatively clear and unencumbered. Trend's predecessors' competing responsibilities for the Treasury and as Head of the Civil Service had been eliminated, and the Cabinet Secretary was free to focus on making Cabinet government work. Throughout the Office there was the understated, subfusc but secretly intoxicating sense of being at the centre of power.

The first few weeks brought a kaleidoscope of impressions. One was given a cordial welcome and a folder of useful information, including the history of the building (which I fear I never read). But the institution remained opaque and slightly mysterious, in some ways like the Kremlin. It was a world of common understandings and unspoken agreements. Everything was implicit, nuanced, understated; not exactly secret, but not conveyed by announcements and explanations. I was reminded of my Oxford college just after the war, in which I had lived for five terms before I found that there was a seamstress who would sew on one's buttons. Useful people find out what they need to know; if they do not, they are not useful enough to be worth telling.

This applied to one's duties. Like my confrères in the Ministry of Defence (MoD) on the other side of Whitehall, I had been brought up to think of well-defined responsibilities and clear chains of command. After the handover week in the Cabinet Office I confessed to my predecessor that I still had no idea who was my boss. A naive question. He explained to me, as to a yokel, that I would work nominally for three masters, but should not make too much of subordination and chains of command. One was there to get useful things done.

Such was the introduction to the Whitehall policy-making village, in which everyone in the Administrative Class knew everyone else and had probably been at Oxford or Cambridge together. One of the institutions was the Cabinet Office Mess on the top floor. Originally the Mess used by the War Secretariat, it was by then a modest annex to the canteen, with a waitress service, a bar and a few easy chairs. As befitted the Cabinet Office, it was not a grand organisation: two-star, compared with the rival and plusher four-star MoD Mess on the opposite side of Whitehall. It was usually in financial trouble with the Treasury. Subsequently I heard that it was being closed down, after successions of senior civil servants had had to worry about its viability.

It was an exclusive club, used by the senior Cabinet Office officials and Administrative Class people from other Departments, plus a handful of MoD generals; in the Whitehall village it was the saloon bar, not the lowerclass public bar. Its barriers were typically implicit rather than articulated – except for a rule that politicians were not admitted as guests. (I understand that some years earlier there had been difficulties over the membership of a senior Cabinet Office lady; gender prejudice had still ruled). It was an important institution for exchanging information, organising business and building up the Whitehall consensus. Security was regarded as a matter of good sense, on Whitehall's 'good chap' principle; I was (yet again) gauche in asking whether the Mess was formally cleared for classified talk, and at what level. Tables were not reserved, except for the corner table at which the Cabinet Secretary sat with his Private Secretary; one wondered what they talked about. There was usually sufficient pressure on places to fill tables where conversations had begun *à deux*. It is a commonplace of modern management theory that efficiency depends on horizontal information flows across vertical organisational boundaries. Encapsulating the Administrative Class's combination of hierarchy and equality, the Mess helped to make government work in this way.

It was also a pleasant haven, retaining some shreds of its wartime origins. Though it was a lunchtime club, the bar when I first arrived was still specially opened on Thursday evenings by the ex-Royal Marine barman who had survived from the war, since this was the day the JIC met and its minutes and weekly papers (including the 'Red Book' summary of intelligence) were issued. After the week's output had been put safely to bed, my Colonel deputy and I would repair upstairs to drink red wine and dissect the day's performance of the JIC's Heads of Agencies. We were keen students of form. The military were particularly unpredictable runners, and we would mark the Chairman for the style and dispatch he had shown in controlling them that morning. Much fortified by appraising our betters, I would repair to my flat; my friend would face the weary Underground journey to his distant military quarters. It was a pleasant life, much different from the provinces.

Other Cabinet Office practices also seemed new and intriguing. The material received on joining included a paper setting out the canons of Cabinet Committeemanship. Secretariats were managers of business, not just scribes. Meetings took papers; never problems *sans* papers circulated beforehand. Minutes were issued within twenty-four hours, and not cleared with chairmen and participants. They were records of decisions, reasons for them and the main points of argument; never of statements 'for the record'. The classic formulation was the notional chairman's introduction (actually the minute-writer's recapitulation of the paper circulated beforehand); the impersonal summary of the main arguments, in which attributions to individuals were exceptional and discouraged; and the (crucial) chairman's summing-up followed by agreed decisions and assigned actions.

Writing these minutes was an art form of seductive elegance and attraction never forgotten, like riding a bicycle. In the JIC Secretariat we took a pride in crafting precise conclusions, recording worthy points made in discussion and eliminating what we judged to be irrelevancies. We saw ourselves as jockeys paid to keep our expensive but mettlesome horses on tight reins; we censored from the record the Committee's occasional end to its meetings with what the Colonel condemned as 'the port and nuts stage' of unprogrammed discussion. I never reconciled myself in later life to minutes that did not meet the Cabinet Office criteria of brevity, impersonality, focus on decisions and immediate issue.

These details are part of the warp and woof of Cabinet government, but encapsulate its nature in two words. Decisions are *agreed* by the meeting, not taken by individuals; and Departments are *invited* to take action, not instructed. Decisions are collective, not personal; the system depends on seeking consensus, not staking out individual positions; decisions must be seen to proceed from discussion and reason, not intuition or conviction. In one of his rare public utterances after retirement, Trend set out the Cabinet Office doctrine that 'There has to be one centre round which the rest of the official machine can come together', but that the Cabinet Secretary had to arrange it 'to deal with that endless upward surge of business, driving it downward as much as he can'.[3] The forms of minutes are part of the organising and disciplining process.

Another impression of the Cabinet Office was as a microcosm of the wider Civil Service distinction between policy and execution. The Office's role at the senior, 'policy' level needed support from its paper-handling and other apparently mechanical services. Peter Hennessy has referred to some of them as follows:

> So long as Cabinet government survives, the minutes will be taken, typed and distributed, prodding the rest of Whitehall into action after every Cabinet and Cabinet Committee meeting. At eight, one and five precisely, the brown vans will go out carrying the green boxes. Whatever the circumstances, like Wells Fargo, they will always get through.[4]

There was quite a sharp distinction between the policy-related officials and the operators of these supporting services. The so-called 'administrators' of the Administrative Class were birds of passage, on two- or three-year secondments from their own departments, birds being groomed to fly higher; the only non-migratory bird was the Cabinet Secretary himself. By contrast the Executives and other supporting Classes were permanencies. The difference emphasised the distinction made in the Old Civil Service between the clever and the practical. To use a shorthand which I shall later reject, the transient administrators and the permanent regulars had the relative status of officers and troops, or Gentlemen and Players.

Consistent with this was a certain Cabinet Office conservatism. Documents were produced by the typing pool on the wax stencils now long forgotten. Cabinet minutes in a special typeface looked quite presentable, but the product of official bodies like the JIC resembled leaflets produced on a clandestine printing press in Occupied Europe. There were regular complaints from seconded Foreign Office officials that the impact of their high-quality analysis was lost through this sub-standard presentation. I suspect that our American allies were rather attached to it, as an example of British quaintness. An offset litho machine had been tried out in the 1960s, found wanting one evening and removed by fiat from Trend; modern technology must not be allowed to wreck the serious business of government.

The Office also seemed old-fashioned in other ways. The Cabinet Secretary had a handsome room, accurately reproduced in the *Yes, Prime Minister* television series, and there were some grand conference rooms. But the building as a whole was shabby. Clerical staff worked in unattractive conditions. There was a certain vagueness about things like job enrichment, staff appraisals, career planning and training that were then becoming *de rigueur*. Welfare services and fire precautions seemed sketchy. Lectures to junior staff in the JIC were a bizarre innovation. The Cabinet Office did not concede much to fashion.

Yet my recollection is of the high efficiency of all this supporting machinery. The quite small body of regulars was astonishingly flexible and Whitehall-wise. Accommodation and support services for Ministerial reorganisations were fixed at the drop of a hat. One became accustomed to the speed and reliability of the day-to-day services that summoned meetings, organised conference rooms, and carried out the typing, checking, production and distribution of papers and minutes. They were the foundations for the Rolls-Royce machine. And it goes without saying that, in those days, it never occurred to us that the Civil Service could leak. These were my impressions of the policy-related and supporting levels. Four portraits may help to clarify them.

Burke Trend

Sir Burke Trend was in many ways the quintessential top civil servant. He had joined the Civil Service in 1936 with first class Oxford honours in Mods and Greats and rose quickly in the Treasury. He became Secretary of the Cabinet in 1963 and retired in autumn 1973 to become Rector of Lincoln College Oxford. He died in 1987 as a peer and Privy Counsellor. The memorial service in Westminster Abbey was a moving occasion, a rollcall of the highest national leadership; mere KCMGs got no further than the North Transept.

He was a prodigious worker, and tough, keeping up with the pressure of government year after year; in appearance carrying unobtrusiveness almost to shabbiness, with a glint of natural authority behind the spectacles. Incisive summaries of complex subjects were dictated without a pause. One's own submissions were returned with gentle, understated manuscript notes in a neat hand. On one imbroglio that I referred to him for immediate solution he wrote 'I could have borne with rather more notice of this problem', but then noted how he had solved it in three or four deft telephone calls. He worked with a small outer office of a young Principal and two young Executives.

But nothing of this was remarkable. Permanent Secretaries do not bark like Generals, or have the same retinue. Indeed, his obituary in *The Times* gave a rather colourless impression.[5] Yet there was more to him than that. I admire him more than any other public servant I encountered.

My 'joining interview' with him in January 1972 set the pattern. In reply to the conventional enquiry about what I had been doing, I mentioned a particular project on which I had spent some years, before its cancellation.[6] 'We should have carried on with it', Trend said decisively; he had apparently backed it in Whitehall. I countered that it had been an unrealistic idea from the start. A brisk viva voce followed, and we passed on to other things. But the exchange had made its mark. One's opinion was genuinely worth seeking, not a formality to be endured. I doubt whether over the next eighteen months I was alone with him more than half a dozen times, but my memory is of an inspirational quality; the ability of some first-class people to inspire second-class people to raise their sights and perform better.

This was not 'people management' in any modern way. Trend never 'visited the troops', and did not give routine praise and thanks. He was a civil servant of his time, a slightly preoccupied and austere figure, tending to take the Office's supporting machinery for granted. Yet he left a trail behind him of a humanity outside a stock mandarin mould. The Cabinet Office had a twenty-four-hour intelligence watch, shared in those days between five elderly retired military officers. Every Christmas Day the Duty Officer was telephoned by Trend with seasonal greetings, plus the news that one of his wife's cakes was on its way from Blackheath via the official driver. And at his crowded farewell party the customary speeches and presentations had an unusual finale – a bouquet for

Lady Trend from an embarrassed, inarticulate office messenger 'for being so kind to us when you used to come to collect him'.

There were other not entirely standard dimensions. There was a hint of the philosopher-turned-administrator about him. The record of his evidence to Lord Franks's review of the Official Secrets Act in 1972 reads like an oral examination in political philosophy, the candidate passing with flying colours.[7] There was also a streak of romanticism and enthusiasm.[8] And what most sticks in the memory is 'spin' in the sense originally coined by C. P. Snow: not exactly unconventionality or eccentricity, but an element of the intriguing and unexpected.

Thus stories about Trend tend to be slightly off-centre. In one, Cabinet Office legend maintained that he had wrestled personally with that first offending offset litho machine on that late evening in the 1960s, before consigning it to outer darkness. In another, an SIS (MI6) acquaintance told me many years later that, on delivering a paper after working on it all the previous night, he was invited to take a nap on Trend's office sofa before the meeting to consider it. No doubt both tales have gained in the telling, but they would not be told about all Cabinet Secretaries.

A third, authentic anecdote comes from one who was then a middlegrade military officer dealing with nuclear policy. Some issue had arisen which kept him late with Trend and others. By two in the morning the problems had been settled, the telegrams dispatched and cars summoned for transport home. At his normal time the next morning the officer met Trend as they walked from Waterloo station. (Why, he asked himself, was Trend mysteriously using the train and not the official car?) The night's events were not mentioned. Conversation developed on some recondite subject, perhaps tribal customs in Borneo. Trend sought information with increasing intensity as they walked up Whitehall. He worried at the subject as a dog worries a bone, and his companion found himself more or less shanghaied into the Cabinet Secretary's office before they went their separate ways. Recounting this episode fifteen years later my informant, by then a retired General, still wondered about Trend. 'Did this mean something? Had his curiosity simply been caught by tribal habits in Borneo? Or was it a coded signal to this officer new to Whitehall, that one must never pick

over the previous day's events; a new day brings new challenges?'
One never knew, but remembered.

His conduct of affairs was notably direct, but he could be unexpected. My JIC deputy was once summoned in my absence on leave to be the secretary at a meeting of high-level, civilian officials about a proposed new Cabinet Office committee on internal threats. Things did not go well; there were predictable departmental objections. Trend suddenly announced that the meeting needed the Colonel's opinion; for that subject and forum, it was as surprising as asking a member of a Covent Garden audience to step up and sing an aria. 'Just the answer to our problem' announced Trend after my friend extemporised. The meeting acquiesced, demoralised by the flank attack; another piece of interdepartmental machinery was created.

These stories are trivial. Yet they convey the style of someone who, for all his studied anonymity, was far more than a standard-issue bureaucrat. Someone should attempt his biography.

The Executives

As in a set of Russian dolls, the Civil Service's policy-executive division was reproduced not only in the Cabinet Office but also in the JIC Secretariat within it. The Secretariat was housed in a suite of offices linked by an internal corridor. One end was 'policy'; the other execution. The physical divisions mirrored those of an old-fashioned boarding school. The Secretary's office at one end was the headmaster's sanctum. The large, battered, scruffy room at the other end – staffed entirely by young, male clerical officers, among furniture that could have been of First World War vintage – was like the lower school's classroom. (I never thought to ask why there were no women there; perhaps in those days it was thought that women should not be asked to make their way home after late evening working.) Linking the two ends were the offices of the Secretariat's own small hierarchy: the temporarily seconded Deputy and Assistant Secretaries towards one end, the senior regulars towards the other. The clerical officers at their end were the JIC infrastructure of checking, security classification, proof-reading, collation, publication and distribution of draft and 'final' papers: in effect the publishing house for the JIC and its numerous Current Intelligence Groups. The Secretary from his end was not supposed to interfere. On the school analogy, he dealt with the masters and hobnobbed with the prefects, but had no part in the classroom. If he appeared there it was regarded as an amiable eccentricity, rather out of the mould. I can hardly exaggerate the scale and intricacy of the routine work of the clerical officers; the complexity of the various security regulations to be implemented; the procedural variations from document to document, and recipient to recipient; the scope for damaging errors, like sending 'UK Eyes Only' documents to foreign allies; the meticulousness needed, day after day and year after year, in emergencies and late evenings as well as normal hours. I found it a marvel that the system responded so well to the demands placed upon it. I cannot recall a serious mistake, nor a misprint that seriously distorted intelligence on an important issue. Where was the credit due?

A trio of regulars were in charge: Betty Green, Reg Pullen and Mervyn-Smith, all now long retired. Betty joined the Office in 1938 when Hankey was still in post as the Cabinet Secretary. She was a London graduate, recruited as a lady typist – an illustration of women graduates' careers at that time. In the Second World War she became General Ismay's secretary, travelled with him to the big wartime conferences, supported him again when he became NATO's Secretary-General, then joined the JIC Secretariat and remained there for the rest of her career. She had to be coaxed to produce wartime reminiscences, but recalled that Churchill remarked to her after the war that she must have many secrets locked in her bosom. Reg was a cheerful, rubicund figure who had become a Post Office messenger-boy at the age of fourteen, and came to the Cabinet Office shortly after wartime military service. Both were Higher Executive Officers who would probably have gone further in most other Departments. I never asked them if they had tried to move. Both received MBEs, and I always think of them when people now advocate fewer honours for civil servants and more for footballers. They were in one sense the archetypal Executive Class officers who knew the precedents and rule books; but they also ran a complex production machine with initiative, sensitivity and commonsense.

Under them came Mervyn-Smith, who directly supervised the clerical officers and was more of a mystery than the others. He had held a post-war army commission, and rumour had it that he had once passed the Administrative Class entry competition. I never knew how he came to be where he was, as an Executive Officer in late middle age; but he was there, owlishly supervising the young clerical officers from the top corner of the old fashioned, big room. A wing collar and a high desk would have completed the Dickensian impression he gave. He was a silent man of considerable intelligence, *mutatis mutandis* as enigmatic as Burke Trend himself.

I never knew at first why the clerical officers stuck at their intricate and boring jobs so willingly. The trio's management style was parental rather than populist; but the swinging 1960s had brought no sign of restlessness, no demands to wear jeans. (Though there was one such sign of the times. At the JIC's weekly meeting a clerical officer was always on duty among the Secretariat for various fetching and carrying purposes. For the newly joined, gentle Gary this posed a problem. He did not possess a tie, and could not see his way to buying one expressly for this purpose. What would now cause a great furore was handled otherwise. The Colonel's successor, a Group Captain, brought a tie and handed it over when required on Thursday mornings, rather like a head waiter in a good restaurant supplying suitable neckwear for an improperly dressed client.) There were probably some material incentives in the overtime and 'unsocial hours' payments that the job involved; in those distant days such financial matters were left to the regulars to sort out, not something for the senior birds-of-passage. Perhaps working in the JIC Secretariat also had an element of status and mystique about it. But I realised quite soon that the motivation came from the influence of the management trio, and the examples they set.

They were not pushovers: Betty, the most correct of civil servants, once met the demand from a young diplomat for a special messenger to carry a document to the Foreign Office a hundred yards away, by remarking gently that he could always carry it himself. But the ethic was of service. I earlier likened the two separate elements of the Cabinet Office to officers and men, and Gentlemen and Players; but the analogies are unfair. If informationhandling and communication are central to the battle for effective government, the trio were the front-line company commanders in it; we

365

others were the red-tabbed staff officers back at base. The front line could be relied upon; it would not break.

One incident sums it up. The JIC at one of its weekly meetings had an unexpected policy issue on its hands. It broke up at about 12.30, decreeing (unusually) that I was to write a paper to be available at a reconvened meeting at 17.00. My first step was to ask about the latest possible deadline for reproduction, checking and collation. Reg replied with a time which seemed to cut things fine. As the deadline approached he hovered with mild anxiety symptoms, then made off at speed with the completed draft. In due course the great and good of the JIC began to assemble for 17.00. By 16.58 a certain restlessness began to manifest itself around the table. Generals prepared to bark; diplomats to assume expressions of hauteur; intelligence Heads of Agencies to mark the Secretary's professional card.

The outcome hardly needs to be recorded. At 16.59 Reg entered the conference room, pink-faced, bearing the stack of papers; recovering his breath, he distributed them with butler-like aplomb, and proceedings commenced. There is only one significant thing about this recollection. Normally it is prudent to assume that if things can go wrong they will. Yet I had absolute confidence, in that place and with those people, that I would not be let down.

Implications

These are elderly recollections of middle-aged salad days in Whitehall. I went to London expecting to scorn. In the event I was fascinated, indeed bowled over, by the Cabinet Office and its insight into Whitehall. Like Dick Whittington after his London fling, I never saw things in the provinces in quite the same light again. These impressions are tainted by this nostalgia. Nevertheless, they lead me to two reflections on British public administration. The first is on the influence of civil servants, specifically the extent to which those in the Cabinet Office influence politicians' decisions. The literature emphasises the lines drawn between officials' recommendations and Ministers' responsibilities. Anthony Seldon's account of the Cabinet Office in later years, under the first two Thatcher governments, concludes that its marks on the substance of decisions were confined to a relatively small number of episodes; the main satisfaction of most Cabinet Office officials was that

> they had done their work expeditiously, invited the right people to committee meetings, briefed the chairmen correctly, ensured that papers were circulated in good time, that decisions were taken in the light of the fullest information available at the time, and that clear instructions following meetings were sent to the relevant people in Whitehall.[9]

In his view this was nothing new; apart from some structural changes, 1979–87 'in many other ways will be seen as an unexceptional period during which the [Cabinet Office] machine operated along lines already established'.[10]

For the earlier period about which I write, Trend's usefulness to Prime Ministers of both parties is not in question. A JIC Chairman commented to me that he had made himself quite indispensable, in overseas as well as domestic matters.[11] Kissinger while in power in Washington regularly visited him en route to senior Ministers and No. 10, and Kissinger was not one to waste his time. A Private Secretary captured Trend's relationship with the Prime Minister in describing how, at the Commonwealth Conference in Canada in 1973, he and Heath would meet after the long evening's proceedings and discuss outstanding London business; Trend would then dictate telegrams into the small hours, in a sense covering for the Prime Minister's absence. At home, his weekly meetings on Thursday afternoons organised Cabinet and Cabinet Committee business for the next week, squeezing quarts out of the pint pots of Cabinet and Prime Ministerial time, seeking always for the proper handling of issues (What preparation, in what forum? Who needs to comment beforehand? How long should they be given to see the papers? What position on the agenda?). The meeting's tone had the senior civil servant's brevity and lightness of touch; the language was allusive, incomprehensible to the neophyte. But clearly this was the engine room that kept central government moving.

But was it also one of the rudders that steered? No doubt the wording of Cabinet Minutes has always helped Prime Ministers to get their own way; but has the Cabinet Office itself influenced decisions in particular directions? Perhaps this can only be known when its Steering Briefs become available in the Public Record Office.[12] I can offer only one minuscule bit of evidence from my sole foray through the connecting door into No. 10. It was to do the record of a small 'meeting of ministers' in the Cabinet Room. Some legislation then in hand raised quite incidentally an issue of national security and intelligence. My recollection is that discussion ran into the sand, with an ambiguous summing-up from the Prime Minister, less through Ministerial disagreement than because all sensed that it fell into a 'too tricky' category. It was a complex but unspectacular issue, taken on a hot afternoon; I have no reason to think the meeting was typical of that government's style.

Nevertheless, what followed has the vividness of unrepeated experience. On the way out of the Cabinet Room Trend said to me 'I want a conclusion in favour of intelligence'; no more. I retired bemused; but then realised that a logical progression could be constructed by standing the order of the subjects on its head and selecting a suitable sequence of discussion, summing-up and conclusions. The record was dictated, and ready to go out that evening. For the Cabinet Office this was run-of-the-mill stuff. But it raises the question of the official imprint on policy. Did Trend know the Prime Minister's mind, or was he himself tilting the decision? All I can say with confidence is that historians using my record will have a distinctly synthetic view of the decision process.

I am inclined to think that this particular case illustrated a special role for the Cabinet Secretary on some matters. Hennessy described how Trend felt he had to use his own initiative as 'custodian of Cabinet confidentiality' over Sir Anthony Nutting's book about the Suez Crisis, in a way compared by Crossman with the position of the monarch as arbiter 100 years earlier.[13] My record was written to favour intelligence as directed. Trend consistently took a special interest in the intelligence and security services, including the protection of their information and sources.[14] In the incident I describe he may have felt it right to influence the outcome in their favour: not to disregard Ministers, but to give national security the benefit of the doubt in a situation of Ministerial ambiguity – rather as a cricket umpire favours the batsman in doubtful cases.

Perhaps things are different now. Personally I hope that this official influence still exists, derived as it is from Hankey's orientation towards security and defence issues and Cabinet Secretaries' subsequent role as chairmen of the Permanent Secretaries' Committee on the Intelligence Services.[15] Attlee's explanation of not involving the Cabinet in the decision to develop nuclear weapons – that he 'thought that some of them were not fitted to be trusted with secrets of that kind'[16] – showed an admirable and not yet outdated realism. Politicians and their associates do not change. Many years later, intelligence professionals were shocked by a former Minister's revelation in Parliament, on the day after the Falklands invasion, that Argentine ciphers had been readable under the previous government.[17] I have no problem with seeing the Cabinet Secretary as a constitutional check-and-balance on certain national security subjects.

Whether or in what degree this influence has extended further I am not qualified to say. But I wonder if some features of the available evidence do not weigh the conclusions drawn from it. Most Ministers write their memoirs or publish their diaries; few civil servants do. Ministers seek to register their mark on history; while, even in confidential recollections, officials are influenced by their lifetime style of understatement and reticence. It is now unfashionable for politicians to blame civil servants for past failures, and arguably the two have a common interest in buttressing the received view of the master-and-servant relationship between them. Perhaps these factors lead historians marginally to underrate Cabinet Office influence on specific decisions, and perhaps the effects of senior civil servants as a whole.

My second, less tentative reflection is about the significance of the Cabinet Office's supporting services and those who provide them. Cabinet government would be impossible without this support. Despite its efficiency, reliability and importance, this part of the machine has never attracted the interest or got the credit it deserves. Those writing about government have neglected it, rather as historians of war tend to overlook logistics. To pursue the military analogy: if government is a continuous battle for coherence against cock-up, chaos and the unforeseen, then masses of paper are like the food and ammunition on which armies depend. War depends on supply systems; the quality of government is set by the paperwork and how it is handled. The JIC section I have described reflected the standards of the Cabinet Office machine to which it belonged, and depended, like it, on Old Civil Service virtues.

This has implications for one's view of the restructuring over the last ten years of the New Public Management.[18] The three Executives I have described had not been specially selected as fliers, in the way that the Administrative Class people were chosen for their Cabinet Office tours. The trio embodied the role and qualities of the Executive Class in the stratified Civil Service that then existed. Subsequently, the Fulton reforms of the 1970s moved a little way towards bridging the grading system's institutionalised gulf between policy and execution. Now we have gone back to an even greater separation, between the policy-making centre and the devolved executive agencies of Next Steps – but with a deliberate attempt to produce a new kind of civil servant (or short-term employee) and destroy the old system.

This is not the place to discuss these changes. But my strongest memory of the Cabinet Office regulars is of their idea of service at the core of government. Institutions have to develop, and information technology is now the catalyst for massive changes. It is to be hoped that the Cabinet Office's Wells Fargo-like system is being electronically transformed. But the system will still be needed in some form, and will still depend on the values held by those operating it. All good organisations have their values, but they are not identical, transferable or creatable in short order. The spirit of the Old Civil Service was not the same as that of other excellent but different organisations. Yet it was there, as the underpinning. I hope my pen-pictures have hinted at its nature. I am saddened that it is now so little esteemed. Modern public service slogans such as IiP ('Investment in People') are praiseworthy if seeking to build on the best elements of tradition; catchpennies if waved as banners for a state of permanent revolution.

Notes

1. Originally published in *Contemporary British History*, 11, no. 1, 1997: 83–97 and reprinted in Herman, M., *Intelligence Services in the Information Age: Theory and Practice* (London: Frank Cass, 2001), pp. 164–79. Reprinted by permission of Taylor & Francis Ltd, http://www.tandfonline.com.

2. The JIC Secretariat and the Joint Intelligence Staff had been part of the Cabinet Office (which included the Office of the Minister of Defence) in the Second World War. I have been assured that the small permanent civilian staff described in this chapter remained titularly within the Cabinet Office in the reorganisation of 1945–6, even though the central defence committee structure was then deemed to be part of the new MoD; JIC reports were issued as MoD documents. See General Jackson, W. and L. Bramall, *The Chiefs* (London: Brassey's, 1992), pp. 192, 268. After the major change of 1957 in which the JIC in all its aspects became a Cabinet Office and not a Chiefs of Staff committee there was still a nod towards its COS origins in its terms of reference, whereby 'special assessments requested by the Chiefs of Staff shall be directly submitted to them in the first instance'. This still stands and is quoted in the official terms of reference, now *National Intelligence Machinery* (London: The Stationery Office, 2000), p. 20. It is a touching bit of British traditionalism, of no significance whatever.

3. Hennessy, P., *Cabinet* (Oxford: Blackwell, 1986), p. 20.

4. Ibid., p. 15.

5. *The Times*, 22 July 1987.

6. Some details are in Aldrich, R. J., *GCHQ: The Uncensored Story of Britain's Most Secret Intelligence Agency* (London: Harper Press, 2010), pp. 259–64.

7. *Departmental Committee on Section 2 of the Official Secrets Act 1911,* Cmnd 5104 (London: HMSO, 1972), vol. 3, p. 316 onwards. It must be a matter of historical regret that Lord Franks – the examiner *par excellence* – was (unusually) absent from Trend's session.

8. As described in Hennessy, P., *Whitehall* (London: Fontana, 1990), pp. 214–17, with reference to Trend's special concern for the Commonwealth and US relationships.

9. Seldon, A., 'The Cabinet Office and Coordination', *Public Administration*, 68, no. 1, 1990: 120–1.

10. Ibid., p. 120.

11. Compare with Crossman's hostile diary notes that Wilson was 'really fond of Burke Trend and sees him as a close personal friend and confidant', and that government had become 'a Wilson-Burke Trend axis' (quoted by Hennessy, *Whitehall*, pp. 217, 218).

12. For the Cabinet Office briefs, and Trend's attitude to them, see Hennessy, *Cabinet*, p. 79. I recall that at one Thursday afternoon meeting Trend reported a complaint from the Prime Minister that the briefs asked too many questions and gave too few recommendations. He had characteristically argued in reply that policy emerged best from the Socratic method but had not converted the Prime Minister. Trend enigmatically ended the Thursday meeting with the guidance, 'Well, we must do our best.'

13. Because the government of the day could not have access to the earlier papers of the other side. See Hennessy, *Whitehall*, p. 214.

14. Thus, Trend in the late 1960s had been exercised by the question when and how the codebreaking successes of the Second World War should be revealed, and was engaged in prolonged correspondence with Sir John Masterman over his intentions to publish what eventually became Masterman's *The Double Cross System in the War of 1939–45* (New Haven, CT: Yale University Press, 1972). For the description of him in his obituary as intelligence's 'shop steward' see note 5 above, and subsequent comment in a letter to *The Times* from Lord Hunt of Tanworth and Sir Robert Armstrong on 30 July 1987. If there is any truth in pictures in the 1960s of struggles within No. 10 between Trend and Marcia Williams, later Lady Falkender, the issue was probably access to classified information, rather than influence on policy.

15. *National Intelligence Machinery*, p. 12. Sir Robert (later Lord) Armstrong's role in the Peter Wright affair was consistent with this special concern for the protection of intelligence.

16. Quoted in Hennessy, *Cabinet*, p. 131.

17. E. Rowlands (Hansard, 3 April 1982, col. 650). The claim that this revelation was without effect – made by Urban, M., *UK Eyes Alpha: The Inside Story of British Intelligence* (London: Faber and Faber, 1996), p. 68 – should be treated with reserve.

18. For the term and its scope see, for example, Rhodes, R. A. W. (ed.), 'The New Public Management', *Public Administration*, 69, no. 1, 1991.

18 The Joint Intelligence Committee 1972–5[1]

[Since this paper was given in 2009 there have been major changes in the Committee's intelligence routine and managerial responsibilities]

I have written separately about my reactions to being plucked out of the provinces to be the JIC's Secretary in London from 1972 to 1975.[2] I offer here some additional impressions of the Committee. As I have said, I was thrilled by the whole thing: I became an admirer of the senior Civil Service which politicians and commentators have tried to wreck for the last fifty years. I also came to respect the JIC system. Like democracy, it is the least bad arrangement on offer.

I was told before I went there that I would not be producing intelligence: the Secretary's main job was to sort out intelligence problems. I was in fact secretary not only of what was then called the JIC (A) – really the old Committee – but also the new JIC (B), the economic JIC established as part of the 1968 reorganisation. The JIC (B) had a talented group in the Assessments Staff (including a future Cabinet Secretary, Richard Wilson) but it never seemed to hit the button with economic policy-makers, and it was abolished in an economy cut some years later.[3] Perhaps the prominence of Britain's economic problems in the 1960s and 1970s made people concentrate on seeking intelligence for strategic economic issues rather than improved tactical applications in international negotiations. I was also secretary of two related bodies, one connected with covert action and the other with domestic intelligence, and at the end of my time I also became secretary of the Permanent Secretaries' Committee which met annually to consider intelligence budgets.

As Secretary I was responsible for the mechanical part of the JIC machinery, which was virtually a publishing house for drafts and product, plus the role of the Duty Intelligence Officers and their twenty-four-hour watch. But much of the mechanics were in the hands of the Cabinet Office regulars to whom I have already paid my tribute. In the senior part of the Secretariat (myself, a Deputy Secretary and two Assistants)[4] we did the minutes of meetings by Cabinet Office rules: always issued before the close of play; never submitted for agreement by participants, and never contested by them; pruned to be the record of decisions taken and reasons for them; and no statements just for the record. We flattered ourselves that we made order out of confusion. It had the mild intoxication of unseen power, but for me it was really only a small though enjoyable part of the working week.

If anyone was the head of the intelligence community in 1972–3 it was Sir Burke Trend, the Cabinet Secretary when I arrived. His successor in October 1973, John Hunt, had been a JIC Secretary in his youth, but was less interested and supportive, as was hardly surprising with the crises of the winter of 1973–4 that hit him.

My JIC (B) Chairmen were FCO and Treasury officials. My first Chairman of the main JIC (A) was Sir Stewart Crawford.[5] He was of a high calibre, a stickler for detail, a precise chairman, though as Secretary I found him discouraging. He was deputy head of the Foreign Office, having started his career as wartime secretary to Air Ministers. I soon realised that the chairmanship was a part-time job for a busy person. It now seems surprising that the JIC routine never required me to consult the Chairman over the make-up of the weekly agenda. (I recall with shame that I once agreed to arrange that the draft of the JIC's important paper on the Soviet threat would be taken when Crawford was on leave, as he was said to be 'awkward' about it.) He was a professional, perhaps pedantic, drafter of JIC assessments, but on matters of management he dealt with them as they came up but did not go further into them. He was himself about to retire, and by that stage the Coordinator had become the management post, as I will describe.

First, however, a word on Sir Geoffrey Arthur,[6] Crawford's very different Foreign Office successor. A distinguished Arabist who had retained his Derbyshire accent, he was brilliant when he set his mind to it, and erratic, disorganised and loquacious when he didn't. He had not wanted the JIC job, and brought a maverick attitude to it. He was soon to retire to be the Master of an Oxford College, where some found him as disturbing as he had been in the JIC. His chairmanship of the JIC drove the Committee members mad. I personally found him kind and considerate, and enjoyed working for him.

The Coordinator's post in the Cabinet Office had been created as part of the 1968 changes. Originally it was to oversee the two wings of the new Assessments Staff – one on the traditional JIC subjects and the other on economic matters, each with its own head – and John Thomson was appointed to run the traditional JIC wing, but he was promoted in the Foreign Office before he arrived and therefore became head of both wings. The Coordinator took on mainly community managerial matters, previously the role of the JIC Secretaries (though White and his successor Hooper still felt some responsibility for supervising the 1968 arrangements, a feeling emphatically not shared at the time by the Chiefs of the Assessments Staff). So as Secretary I was largely the Coordinator's right-hand man. For the three years before my arrival there had been an effective team of Sir Dick White as part-time Coordinator and my predecessor Brian Stewart as JIC Secretary,[7] dealing *inter alia* with the intelligence challenges of Irish terrorism; and they had Trend's backing. White then retired and was succeeded part-time by Sir Peter Wilkinson, who had just retired as Ambassador to Vienna after a distinguished war in the Special Operations Executive,[8] but with no direct peacetime intelligence experience, and a sick man with a sick wife.[9] He was often absent and was effectively a non-player: an unfortunate appointment.

He was succeeded full-time in October 1973 by Sir Leonard Hooper, who came with the highest reputation as a long-time GCHQ Director and stayed in post until 1978. Perhaps not surprisingly, his advisory role as Coordinator was a disappointment to him after this hyperactive worldwide leadership. He set what became the future pattern of the Coordinator's job: influential, and doing useful things, but only up to a point.[10] I had been Hooper's protégé at GCHQ and had everything to thank him for, but I found him surprisingly diffident outside the Sigint field where he had spent his whole professional life. It probably went against the grain for a former baron to trespass on others' baronies, except perhaps his own former area. It is a pity he did not have Trend's spur and authority behind him. In my experience, up to my retirement in 1987 only Sir Antony Duff – with his background as a decorated wartime submarine commander before becoming a diplomat – exercised real authority in the community as Coordinator and Chairman (and at one time both),[11] until Sir David Omand did so subsequently, exceptionally, and at the higher, top Civil Service grade.

Of the Heads of the three Agencies on the Committee I will make only one comment. The received view of the JIC was that it led in assessments and gave government a distinctive input from its world of secret sources. I was struck instead by its relative reticence in much of the discussion of the assessment drafts that made up the main part of most committee meetings. The Committee offered judgements about its own material but on the whole left the nuances of intelligence conclusions for the Chairman, the DIS representatives, the Foreign Office and the Assessments Staff to argue about. This may have been an untypical period for the Committee, but it casts a light on the JIC's balance in this period between 'intelligence-led' subjects and those relying mainly on diplomatic and overt material.

As for the Assessments Staff, Percy Cradock – later the distinguished JIC Chairman for seven years after 1985, and the only official ever to do both jobs – had just taken over from John Thomson when I arrived. Both were powerful operators who consolidated what was in effect – though probably not deliberately – the Foreign Office takeover of the central assessment machinery established in 1968. A feature of the British intelligence system has been the extent to which the Foreign Office had kept it under its thumb since 1939, perhaps until recently with counterterrorism. It has sent and continues to send its able people, and the original idea of having a long-serving 'professional' Assessments Staff was never realised, probably because it was not obvious where they would come from.

The Staff as established in 1968 also felt some degree of independence from the JIC itself. Thomson minuted my predecessor that it should not be called the *JIC* Assessments Staff, and Cradock had a similarly robust attitude. At that time the Committee minutes would record that the Chief of the Assessments Staff was *instructed* to take particular action: in later years he became a full member of the Committee and henceforth was *invited*. In my time in London the Assessments Staff produced some reports outside the JIC system – and still does – and it also had considerable freedom in the selection of the JIC's topics, apart from the routine summaries of Soviet military strength produced by the DIS. To some extent the Assessments Staff at that time drove the JIC, with Cradock's meetings on Monday mornings as the engine of the Committee's short-and-medium-term production. I have a recollection that this relative independence lasted until after the Falklands War when the programme became much more tightly controlled by the Committee.

This was all intuitive, rather the Cabinet Office style, the opposite of the service ideal of a highly organised tight ship. It was effective with small numbers of able people but it could be found wanting, as with the Yom Kippur War of October 1973. An Egyptian attack on Israel had seemed likely in the early summer but we now know that it was postponed.[12] The JIC reported the evidence at that time but had been cautious, partly because its two strongest members – Geoffrey Arthur the Arabist and General Willison for the DIS – were convinced that Arab states would never risk an attack.[13] When evidence of it reappeared in the autumn, people had perhaps got blasé about it, and the JIC's Current Intelligence Group (CIG) was not called until Friday morning on 5 October, and produced an assessment at the end of the afternoon that reached the main London customers that evening but got its judgement wrong about the probability of an attack. War started around midday the following day (Saturday), and the CIG met and issued an assessment late that night. Geoffrey Arthur, the JIC Chairman, happened to be the senior Foreign Office official on call that weekend, and claimed later that he had spent the whole of the Saturday in his office working on his in-tray before going to the opera in the evening, and was never told by anyone that a war had started. That morning Willison was getting his yacht out of the water for the winter on the south coast and was reluctant to be called to London. In all it was not the system's happiest moment. In its worldwide consequences the UKUSA communities' failure to alert Henry Kissinger earlier that week was arguably the most serious warning failure of the post-1945 years.[14]

The Committee was then two different things: a means of providing assessed intelligence for top government, and a management body for intelligence as a whole. On the first, as the producer, it is always assumed that its assessment is objective and policy free, yet this has never appeared in its official terms of reference. Similarly, there had been no official definition, as far as I know, of the subjects that JIC reports were supposed to cover, or not cover. The terms of reference were so wide that they covered almost anything. After the 1968 reorganisation and creation of the Assessments Staff the Committee's product had perhaps rather more emphasis than formerly on open and diplomatic sources. I recall a JIC forecast of the result of the impending French election, though to my knowledge this experiment in psephology was not repeated.

I can offer only one other comment on the JIC's intelligence production in my time. Having spent much of my professional life engaged with the Soviet target, I was surprised that this seemed to be a relatively small part of the JIC's assessment output. There were of course some major papers on Soviet matters, and when there was a fear of possible Soviet action it became the top priority. But there was little in London of the strife that wracked the American community about reading the Soviet mind and the significance of its weaponry. Soviet military matters were not normally for JIC attention. My recollection is that the JIC's week-by-week emphasis was on trouble spots in the rest of the world, particularly the Middle East, rather than the politics of the Soviet Union and Warsaw Pact. The Cold War was the top intelligence priority, but was a 'given', something to be lived with, not questioned except in the periodic reviews of the Soviet threat. Cabinets decided on the defence budget, and the use of intelligence in the armed forces' infighting for resources usually took place inside the MoD without coming to the JIC.

Of the Committee's two roles, management was subsidiary. At a quiet time the JIC weekly meeting in those days would start at 11.00 on Thursdays, clear intelligence product by perhaps 12.00, and would cope with a couple of management items for half an hour or less afterwards: all in good time for lunch. Yet there was still a flattering assumption that the JIC Secretary would know everything that was going on at the top level: perhaps a relic originally of the status of my wartime predecessor, in office throughout the whole war and influential not only in intelligence.[15] This was not the case. GCHQ and SIS had their close links with the Foreign Office, as they still have. The Security Service had similar connections with the Home Office. When sensitive issues came to the Cabinet Office they would be settled in the Cabinet Secretary's office without necessarily coming anywhere near the JIC Secretary, though they might. Trend would quite often have me at his meetings; Hunt less often.

Historically this goes back to the JIC's Second World War origins, when the secret agencies avoided being sucked too far into the JIC's supervision, especially with the uncertainty about its writ in home affairs, with counterespionage and subversion normally outside its purview. As far as I can tell, the report-producing and management roles came together in 1939 without any particular thought.[16] Should they be in this one body? When the Irish 'Troubles' began in 1969 the JIC was active in many ways, led by White and Stewart.[17] Its involvement later became shallower. It continued a monthly review of the Irish situation, but the Security Service's Director General grumbled to me once that these reviews were 'just theatre', and I was inclined to agree with him. This raises the question of the JIC's role in domestic affairs. Part of the difficulty in my time was that the Security Service felt a special responsibility for the covert, domestic threats, and its instinct was that it was a security organisation and not an intelligence-producing one. It was never entirely easy with the JIC and its foreign orientation, or with the role of an intelligence producer.[18] It was convinced that it had a direct responsibility for national security though it was never explicit what this was.

It is worth remembering that the British intelligence community is a loosely knit one. The JIC originally existed to bring the intelligence directorates of the three armed services together, and not to supplant the shadowy Secret Service committee that had occasionally been convened to consider the secret agencies between the two wars. The involvement of the secret agencies in the Second World War was perhaps patchier than the received view of the JIC suggests. It is interesting that Sigint – the most important intelligence activity – was not within the Committee's regular wartime purview.[19]

Despite these limitations, handling things in the JIC was usually an effective way of doing business and encouraged everyone to think in community terms. Foreign countries find it hard to understand why British agencies are not always at each other's throats, and the historic collegiality of JIC meetings is part of the explanation. The JIC is partly for bonding: it had no standing over the agency budgets which really determined policy change. There was little strategic thinking in my time about the community as a whole. No one had the clout to carry community plans through at the expense of individual agencies, for instance by developing a community IT system.[20] It was apparent even then that over this issue there was an opportunity for national excellence, and a JIC subcommittee had already been established to explore the possibility. But progress over the years remained ineffective. I have a recollection of Duff at one stage putting his foot down and demanding that a particular line of IT service be provided for the Cabinet Office irrespective of departmental objections; but that sticks in the memory because it was unusual (and admirable). At a much later date Sir David Omand as Coordinator with other responsibilities, and Permanent Secretary status, saw himself as responsible for 'the professional health of the community as a whole', but this is not something said previously or, I suspect, since.[21] Running the community should not be left entirely to the barons.

I offer some final conclusions from this view of the JIC system long ago. I thought it was admirable, but in my time it had a degree of complacency about it. People were busy running it, not looking ahead enough to make it better, or in place long enough to do so. It could have done with clearer central leadership. The other conclusion was the significance of individual strengths and weaknesses. Individual impact was important and varied, perhaps more than is recognised. Getting a system that earmarked and trained people for the key jobs in the future was probably more important than worrying about organisation. But, oddly enough, over the years it has seemed strangely difficult to organise.

Notes

1. Adapted from a presentation delivered to the fourth biennial Centre for Intelligence and International Security Studies (CIISS) conference at Gregynog Hall, Wales, UK, 30 April–2 May 2009.
2. Chapter 17 in this collection, 'Up from the Country: Cabinet Office Impressions 1972–5'.
3. Davies, P. H. J., *Intelligence and Government in Britain and the United States: A Comparative Perspective, Volume 2: Evolution of the UK Intelligence Community* (Santa Barbara, CA: Praeger, 2012), pp. 221–3.
4. One service officer at full Colonel level, one a rank lower, one civilian of equivalent grade from the DIS. The uniformed posts rotated between the three services.
5. Sir Robert Stewart Crawford, 1913–2002. Political Resident in the Persian Gulf, 1966–70; Deputy Under-Secretary of State (FCO), 1970–3.
6. Sir Geoffrey George Arthur, 1920–84. Political Resident in the Persian Gulf, 1970–1; Deputy Under-Secretary of State (FCO), 1973–5; Pembroke College Oxford Master, 1975–84.
7. Stewart told me much later that he persuaded White to move to part-time work as there was not enough work for two of them (private letter). I never heard this from anyone else.
8. His account of this experience was later published as *Foreign Fields: The Story of an SOE Operative* (London: I. B. Tauris, 1997).
9. Sir Peter Allix Wilkinson, 1914–2000. Ambassador to South Vietnam, 1966–7; Ambassador to Austria, 1970–1; Intelligence Coordinator, 1972–3.
10. Aldrich, R. J., 'Counting the Cost of Intelligence: The Treasury, National Service and GCHQ', *The English Historical Review*, 128, no. 532, 2013: 626.
11. Sir Arthur Antony Duff, 1920–2000. Intelligence Coordinator, 1980–4; Director General of the Security Service, 1985–8.
12. Bar-Joseph, U., *The Watchman Fell Asleep: The Surprise of Yom Kippur and its Sources* (Albany: State University of New York Press, 2005), pp. 34, 50.
13. In a recent interview, John Davies from the Assessments Staff recalled that his warnings of an impending Egyptian attack were torn 'to shreds' by Willison during one JIC meeting in spring 1973. See Rezk, D., 'Re-evaluating the Yom Kippur "Intelligence Failure":

The Cultural Lens in Crisis', *The International History Review*, 39, no. 3, 2017: 187.

14. Kissinger, H. *Years of Upheaval* (Boston: Little, Brown and Co., 1982), p.465. See also Kissinger quoted in Shlaim, A. 'Failures in National Intelligence Estimates: The Case of the Yom Kippur War', *World Politics*, 28: 3, 1976, p.361.

15. Denis Capel-Dunn, who was also responsible for the Joint Staff Secretariat in the Cabinet Office, which saw him attend wartime conferences in Moscow and Yalta. Capel-Dunn was presumed dead after his plane went missing in July 1945. He was returning from San Francisco where he had attended the signing of the UN Charter as a member of the British delegation. See chapter 11 in this collection, '1945 Organisation'.

16. The Official History records that the JIC's management role developed in January 1939 after several members noticed there was no clear division of responsibility for intelligence on air defences in Spain and China; in response, the full Committee began to decide which service was responsible for collecting and collating the different types of information. See Goodman, M. *The Official History of the Joint Intelligence Committee* (Abingdon: Routledge, 2014), p.41.

17. O'Halpin, E. '"A poor thing but our own": The Joint Intelligence Committee and Ireland, 1965-72', *Intelligence and National Security*, 23: 5, 2008, pp.667-75.

18. Aldrich, R. J. and R. Cormac, *The Black Door: Spies, Secret Intelligence and British Prime Ministers* (London: William Collins, 2016), p.304.

19. Goodman, *The Official History of the Joint Intelligence Committee*, p.168.

20. As Coordinator White had advocated greater use of computer technology, a point which was repeated by his successors in the mid-late 1970s. See Aldrich, R. J. 'GCHQ and UK Computer Policy', in Murfett, M. (ed.) *Shaping British Foreign and Defence Policy in the Twentieth Century: A Tough Ask in Turbulent Times* (Basingstroke: Palgrave Macmillan, 2014), pp.242-4.

21. Omand was the first Security and Intelligence Coordinator, a senior permanent secretary position established after the September 11 attacks to assume the Cabinet Secretary's responsibility for the intelligence services, in addition to the traditional functions of the Coordinator. This has not been repeated. See Van Puyvelde, D. 'Profiles in Intelligence: an interview with Sir David Omand', *Intelligence and National Security*, 35: 2, 2020, p.173.

19 GCHQ Directors

An earlier chapter in this collection described how careers were determined for the top echelon of GCHQ as the organisation was being created in 1945.[1] Whitehall officials tried hard to get the right recruitment strategy, and historians will judge the results. For them I offer some memories of the GCHQ Directors in the period when I was in relatively junior positions, from my joining the organisation in 1952 to the mid-1970s. The three Directors were Eric Jones (1952–60), Leonard 'Joe' Hooper (1965–73) and more briefly Clive Loehnis who held office between them (1960–4). I introduce them with some additional impressions of GCHQ's management in these early Cold War years.

This treatment omits Edward Travis, effectively Bletchley's Director in the second part of the war and with full responsibility during 1945–52.[2] Travis had retired just before I joined, and I subsequently heard little about him. There is an intriguing description of him as 'gruff, rough and burley', who 'won little love but muted respect'; and also that he was a bridge player of international standard, perhaps reflecting a professional flair for codes and ciphers.[3] One would like to know more about him and his influence, but there is still no substantial account of his career, and I do not offer it here.[4]

Post-war Management as a Whole

My recollection is that GCHQ's Directorate up to the mid-1970s usually comprised the Director, a Deputy (not always nominated as such) and two Assistant Directors, plus a Chief Scientist dating from the early 1960s. As might be expected, most of them were recruited in 1945 after wartime experience at Bletchley. Travis as the first post-war Director was also a link with the pre-war code-breaking of the Government Code and Cypher School (GC&CS), as was 'Josh' Cooper, the Sigint polymath whose career there went back to 1925.[5] When I joined in October 1952 Jones had recently become Director, at what was a time of incipient change. GCHQ's move from Ruislip to its permanent accommodation in Chelten-ham was about to take place over the next three years, and its main production areas were reorganised just afterwards into the form they would take for the rest of the Cold War.

One memory of my first year is of the interest taken at the top level in the recruitment and training of the two new potential 'generalist' managers, of which I was one: more interest than we deserved, and far more than would be accorded to our succes-sors. I also soon became conscious that GCHQ's staff took a spe-cial pride in belonging to their virtually new organisation with its major wartime achievements: 'we are not part of the normal Civil Service' was a common conversational introduction. Memories of Bletchley redounded, with much less recollection of the relatively small, pre-war GC&CS. A related feature of this institutional cul-ture was the belief in GCHQ's newly acquired independence as an intelligence-producing Sigint centre, no longer just a codebreak-ing agency producing decodes. This was formed mainly from the Bletchley experience but was then strengthened by the move from London and GCHQ's developing place in the intelligence war, par-ticularly its key role in warning of a potential Soviet attack.

These were dominant features of the organisation, but one other influence in senior management should be mentioned. GC&CS had always had an ex-naval flavour in its leadership from Denniston and Travis, but this was intensified with the recruit-ment of the distinctive group of four naval officers who changed careers to join GCHQ at senior levels after 1945 without having belonged to wartime Bletchley. Of this group Loehnis was older than the others and had been close to Bletchley in wartime naval intelligence before joining GCHQ at the end of the war, so was not really a newcomer. The other three came from wartime service at sea, two of them as sons of distinguished wartime admirals. The third (Poulden) came to GCHQ through Sigint responsibilities in the Far East.[6] As naval officers they had all qualified as signals officers and brought a familiarity with radio to their Sigint work. They followed Loehnis into senior posts in the 1950s and in subsequent promotion to Directorate level. I am inclined to think this group had a distinctive impact on GCHQ's management, adding a naval stiffening to what was otherwise a rather looser style inherited from Bletchley. They were part of the culture on which Jones and Hooper made their own major impact.

Eric Jones[7]

Jones was not a graduate, which he was said to have much regretted. He attended Kings School Macclesfield from the age of thirteen and left at fifteen to go into the family firm of textile manufacturers. At eighteen he set up on his own and built a large textile agency which he handed over to a manager when he joined the RAF in 1940. From 1942 onwards he had important success in bringing order to Hut 3 at Bletchley in its key role of analysing enigma decrypts and signalling reports to operational commanders. He was made a Group Captain and stayed with GCHQ after the war. He spent 1945–6 in Washington negotiating the postwar Sigint agreements, becoming Deputy Director in 1950 and Director in 1952.[8] He took early retirement on health grounds in 1960, and subsequently accepted a number of non-executive directorships in industry. It was rumoured at the time of his retirement that he had upset Whitehall with an uncompromising bid for GCHQ's expansion to cope with the increasing Soviet target and was not offered another post after eight years as Director. It was put to me much later by one of his former Assistant Directors that 'the job killed him: he was in awe of those clever people around him and never comfortable with them'.[9]

Jones was dignified, rather ponderous, with an air of great rectitude. His prose style was covertly ridiculed, but he was deeply respected: in a later account, Douglas Nicoll recalled that 'it was said of him that corruption was unthinkable in his presence'.[10] This was combined with a determination to be the best at anything he attempted. I was told that as an amateur golfer he had competed in the Open,[11] and in his fifties he made himself into an expert skier. To his posting in Washington in 1945–6 he brought his classic Bentley sports car in its British racing green. It now seems surprising that he had his car shipped to the USA for this short posting so soon after the war. (It had been sold to him by Colonel Sayer who was active in post-war Sigint; Sayer told me that, alas, the Bentley was dropped from the crane unloading it at the American port and was never the same car again.) He probably appealed to the Americans as an archetypal English gentleman. His ambition was to have GCHQ recognised as an independent and well-managed department, and a full member of the JIC.

My contact with Jones was accidental. My belief now is that GCHQ's plans to recruit more 'management-type' cadets and not just potential Sigint specialists reflected his conviction about what the organisation needed. I was one of the two recruits in 1952 to the new programme for potential managers, which was aborted six months later after our criticism of it. We were eventually summoned to see Jones, for which we were driven 100 miles from Cheltenham to his office, still in Ruislip, to receive his apologies. It was a gesture from a Director to a new entrant that seems more remarkable to me now than it did then.

My subsequent memories of Jones are mainly of small things that stick. I remember reading the record of a Directorate meeting on the forthcoming move to Cheltenham which among other things had to decide GCHQ's future office hours there. There were then relatively few private cars, and many staff would use the public bus service. This was fully occupied at morning school times, and GCHQ's starting time therefore had to be either earlier or later. Jones opted for the earlier time to encourage people to play a full part in the evening life of Cheltenham, as well as to avoid any public image of GCHQ as 'ten o'clock starters'; long the image of the Foreign Office in London. It was a small matter but showed a concern for public relations not normal for the head of secret agencies.

Jones was also fond of messages to all staff in his personal style, sometimes unexpected ones. I recall that he once issued a general notice about the importance of delegation: a theme of the management courses that had recently started, though it hardly fitted the style of Bletchley's wartime achievements. But why had it become a subject of top-level exhortation? In another episode, after a Christmas celebration, Jones banned all alcohol at office parties, in an announcement I remember for its dramatic opening that 'Events took place on our official premises recently that were a disgrace to the public service.'[12] I still wonder what actually happened. On a more serious matter he announced in the late 1950s that he was moving Hooper, the rising star, from his over-sight of production to a new appointment supervising all admin-istration, but instead of an administrative notice Jones issued a lengthy explanation to everyone of his reason for giving Hooper this wider experience. It was indeed a message of confidence, but not usually the stuff of routine announcements. It must be added that, to no one's surprise, Hooper threw himself into administra-tion for several years, and later had GCHQ commended by the Treasury as a well-managed department.

It might be thought from such examples that Jones was a man-ager without much sensitivity, but this was not so. At the end of the war a member of Hut 3 wrote to ask him for a job recommen-dation, and the reply came as an eight-page letter in Jones's own hand with four typed copies. The recipient wrote that he counted it as his war medal.[13]

Clive Loehnis[14]

Loehnis succeeded Jones in 1960 and was in office until 1964. He was spoken of at the time as a safe pair of hands between the powerful but distant regime of Jones and the inexhaustible concentration and energy of Hooper. This may not be completely fair. He was deft in his relationships with the London authorities, particularly the armed forces, and in directing the interception effort including what were formerly the naval stations with which he had been familiar. He deputised successfully for Jones in his sickness toward the end of the latter's career.

Loehnis had joined the navy as a cadet in 1915 and retired in 1935 to go into film production, but he was recalled in 1938. He had private means and was said to have raced cars at pre-war Brooklands. In the war he worked in the Admiralty's operational intelligence centre and became its liaison officer with Bletchley, and in early 1945 he was involved in high-level Anglo-American planning for the Far East and post-war Sigint arrangements. He joined GCHQ on demobilisation and was promoted to the Directorate in 1951, assuming the Deputy post in 1954.[15]

Loehnis always kept his family home in Belgravia, and when he became Director he drove to Cheltenham twice a week, returning to London mid-week for the JIC meetings. He would drive his powerful Jaguar in the early Friday morning and, as appropriate for a former racing driver, was said by the office drivers to hold the record for the journey's time.[16] When questioned about it he would claim his record was for the slowest journey: ninety days, after a heavy crash from skidding on ice. Continuing the idioms, he was not just a former naval officer turned civil servant but also something of a 'card': a wise old bird as well as a safe pair of hands.

'Joe' Hooper[17]

Hooper was quite unlike Jones and was privately critical of him: there was no affection on his side of the relationship. Yet the two of them were complementary influences in Sigint's evolution. He was born in London in 1914, the only child of elderly parents. From Alleyn's School in Dulwich he went to Worcester College Oxford and got a half-blue in cross-country running and a first class degree in history. He then started a doctorate on seventeenth- and eighteenth-century English Jesuits but did not complete it. He was recruited via the Air Ministry for GC&CS in 1938. He had a good war at Bletchley, initially working on Italian and then Japanese Air Force traffic, and later orchestrating efforts that spanned the UK, the US and the Far East. As an organiser and manager he emerged as the outstanding member of the younger people who stayed at GCHQ after the war, and his talent was recognised by Jones. He attended the Imperial Defence College in 1953–4, and became an Assistant Director in 1954, Deputy in 1960 and Director from 1965 to 1973.[18] He then moved to become Intelligence Coordinator in the Cabinet Office until 1978.

I was closer to Hooper than might be expected from the difference in our ages and positions. He interviewed me for my recruitment in the civilised surroundings of my Oxford college's senior common room, and he was among those who persuaded me to stay at GCHQ after the unsatisfactory introduction. He supported the office rugby club and would drink beer with us afterwards. His second wife (he married three times) became a friend after I helped her with the scripts for the GCHQ revues that were staged publicly in those terrorist-free days of the 1950s. When Hooper moved to the Cabinet Office I was the JIC Secretary and effectively became his staff officer. I was his protégé and owed much of my career to him.

Hooper was clever and energetic, with great stamina. Work was his passion. One of his Assistant Directors commented that his idea of a nice weekend was dealing with a pile of files in his office and reading and annotating them from beginning to end. His other interests were limited, mainly sport, though in later life he accepted school governorships and typically took on wide responsibilities for them. He was lucky that under Jones and Loehnis he was given wide responsibility in establishing his way to the top of GCHQ. His style was informal, gregarious, warm-hearted and enthusiastic, and he was widely known throughout GCHQ's diverse organisation. He was no delegator; Jones's message about delegation would have bounced off him without touching. He was friendly with junior staff, though with the seniors who worked directly to him he could be brusque and authoritative, not easily persuaded, much respected, but sometimes emotional: there was a pressure-cooker underneath the professional persona which needed careful handling.[19] He was highly competent at anything, but after a lifetime of Sigint responsibility he was frustrated in his advisory role as Coordinator in Whitehall, yet was reluctant to seek matters outside his background. His instinct was probably for the intelligence community to operate as a loose federation.[20] He would have been an admirable Head of British Intelligence if the authorities had wanted one and planned his career accordingly.

So much of post-war Sigint bore Hooper's imprint that it is difficult to identify him with particular achievements. Having started at a desk he had a professional empathy with analysis and production that did not desert him. He was the architect of the 1954 reorganisation of GCHQ's production that lasted until after the end of the Cold War, and little happened that did not have his imprimatur.[21] Among the department's external connections he paid particular attention to those with the US and Old Commonwealth. The warmth of his transatlantic relationships with the NSA's military Directors and senior civilians was of special importance, and in some cases these became genuine friendships.[22] It was in this way that the UK eventually learned the details of Henry Kissinger's attempt to bring political pressure on the UK through interrupting the service of American raw material in summer 1973.[23] Perhaps his most significant transatlantic achievement was towards the end of his command, in developing the connection with the important new American field of satellite interception.

By contrast Hooper was a reluctant European and had no enthusiasm for expanding continental connections along the lines of transatlantic and Commonwealth ones. On these, and particularly the joint UK–US relationship with West Germany, it was left to others to make the running. Domestically Hooper also devoted much time and energy to GCHQ's relationships with the British armed forces in what were still the important committees for Sigint direction. The forces were suppliers of manpower and money as well as being intelligence consumers, and Hooper took great trouble to respect and steer this double stake in the Sigint effort.

Perhaps Hooper's most lasting though least spectacular achievement was in following Jones's lead by developing GCHQ as far as possible along the lines of a normal Civil Service department. After government criticism of GCHQ's financial control he made substantial changes in the 1960s to tighten its technical equipment procurement, and at the same time he established a central staff: the most important changes since the 1954 reorganisation. On management issues Hooper supported such Civil Service practices as staff inspections, the grading of posts by Civil Service standards, and the recognition of staff associations. Most of us attended the standard courses at the government's Civil

Service College. I even found myself responsible at one stage for running a Whitehall-model staff suggestions scheme, in which I took some pleasure in making awards for (anonymous) technical suggestions from someone with whom I played cricket. On a more serious matter, GCHQ pay became increasingly settled by alignments with standard Civil Service rates through accepted negotiating procedures with the unions. Jones had established the strategic objective of developing GCHQ as a well-regarded department, and Hooper embraced it with his typical thoroughness and drive. All this became taken for granted yet it was a striking feature of GCHQ at the time, and it was much influenced by having these two early Directors, so different in character and outlook but agreed on objectives. While having little else in common they shared in their different ways an overriding professional intensity.

To these impressions a note should be added on what was perhaps Hooper's most controversial contribution to GCHQ's history: his reaction to the unions' industrial action that eventually led to government's de-unionisation measure. This action began in 1969 when two unions sought arbitration on a routine pay claim for radio operators, did not accept a disappointing result, and declared a 'work to rule' in response.[24] Hooper as Director took personal charge of the negotiations and secured a fresh arbitration with a more generous result. He told me that this was finally accepted by the unions at a Sunday meeting in his London flat for which he cooked lunch. There was then a decade of strained relations with this group of staff, which merged into national actions by unions against the pay awards under Mrs Thatcher's government.[25] It could be argued that Hooper sold the pass in 1969, leaving John Somerville, his newly appointed Director of Administration and Finance, to contain the consequences (with constant effort and some success) for the next ten years in what Somerville described late in life as his personal Golgotha.[26] On the other hand, the Labour government was in no state in 1969 to fight Civil Service unions over an intelligence issue; it was hardly an option in the spirit of the time. Settling in 1969 was perhaps Hooper's most controversial decision, and we await more analysis of the circumstances in which it was taken.

Notes

1. Chapter 16 in this collection, 'Recruitment in 1945 and "Peculiar Personal Characteristics"'
2. Sir Edward Travis, 1888–1956. KCMG, CBE, recipient of First World War French and Italian honours and Second World War American Medal for Merit.
3. Nicoll, D. R., 'Sir Edward Wilfrid Harry Travis', *Oxford Dictionary of National Biography*, online edition (Oxford: Oxford University Press, 2004).
4. There are scattered references in the authorised history of GCHQ to his early career as a naval paymaster, his expertise in signals security, and his responsibilities at GC&CS and wartime Bletchley. See Ferris, J., *Behind the Enigma: The Authorised History of GCHQ, Britain's Secret Cyber-Intelligence Agency* (London: Bloomsbury, 2020), especially pp. 98–100, 209–10.
5. See the Bletchley Trust biography of Cooper, accessed on 22 July 2020 at: https://bletchleypark.org.uk/cms/record_attachments/2123.pdf
6. John Burrough, John Somerville and 'Teddy' Poulden. All retired from the Navy as Lieutenant Commanders and eventually received high awards for service at GCHQ. See also Aldrich, R. J., 'GCHQ and UK Computer Policy', in M. Murfett (ed.), *Shaping British Foreign and Defence Policy in the Twentieth Century: A Tough Ask in Turbulent Times* (Basingstroke: Palgrave Macmillan, 2014), p. 242.
7. Sir Eric Jones, 1907–86. KCMG, CB, CBE, recipient of Second World War US Legion of Merit.
8. Ferris, *Behind the Enigma*, pp. 286–7, 340, 343. See also the Bletchley Trust biography of Jones, accessed on 22 July 2020 at: https://bletchleypark.org.uk/cms/record_attachments/1860.pdf
9. Private conversation.
10. Nicoll, D. R., 'Sir Eric Malcolm Jones', *Oxford Dictionary of National Biography*, online edition (Oxford: Oxford University Press, 2004).
11. The leading international golf tournament in Britain annually, for which a few amateurs qualify. I have not been able to confirm that Jones actually competed.
12. Personal recollection.
13. Calvocoressi, P., *Threading My Way* (London: Duckworth, 1994), p. 119.
14. Sir Clive Loehnis, 1902–92. KCMG.
15. Ferris, *Behind the Enigma*, p. 294.
16. Prescott Currier, a member of the American codebreaking mission to Bletchley in January 1941, recalled Loehnis's passion for motoring.

In his words, Loehnis 'drove what was called a flying bedpan and he offered me a lift down to Winchester to see the intercept station and I was strongly advised by several other people in NSD9, don't take him up on it. Make your own way. Which we did.' See Currier, P., 'My 'Purple' Trip to England in 1941', *Cryptologia*, 20, no. 3, 1996: 198.

17. Sir Leonard James Hooper, 1914–94. KCMG, CMG, CBE. See also Herman, M., 'Sir Leonard James [Joe] Hooper', *Oxford Dictionary of National Biography*, online edition (Oxford: Oxford University Press, 2004).

18. Ferris, *Behind the Enigma*, pp. 294–5.

19. Arguably Hooper became too attached for too long to the Sigint ship project, after it became clear that the Navy was unenthusiastic about it. Some details are given in Aldrich, R. J., *GCHQ: The Uncensored Story of Britain's Most Secret Intelligence Agency* (London: Harper Press, 2010), pp. 260–4. For a subsequent comment by the Cabinet Secretary, see Chapter 17 in this collection, 'Up from the Country: Cabinet Office Impressions 1972–5'.

20. Chapter 18 in this collection, 'The Joint Intelligence Committee 1972–5'.

21. Ferris, *Behind the Enigma*, pp. 398–9.

22. See for example the warm sentiments expressed in Hooper's correspondence with Marshall Carter, Director of NSA (1965–9) which were later published in Bamford, J., *The Puzzle Palace: A Report on America's Most Secret Agency* (Boston, MA: Houghton Mifflin, 1982), p. 337. Carter was embarrassed that Hooper's private letters were exposed in this way; see the declassified NSA Oral History transcript, 'Interview with L. General Marshall S. Carter', 3 October 1988, NSA OH-15-88, pp. 281–2, accessed on 22 July 2020 at: https://www.nsa.gov/Portals/70/documents/news-features/declassified-documents/oral-history-interviews/NSA-OH-15-88-Carter.pdf

23. Aldrich, *GCHQ*, pp. 289–90.

24. Chapter 9 in this collection, 'Manual Morse and the Intelligence Gold Standard'.

25. Ferris, *Behind the Enigma*, pp. 469–72; Aldrich, *GCHQ*, pp. 419–22.

26. Somerville's obituary noted that he steered GCHQ through 'the choppy waters of the Cold War'; see 'John Somerville, 1917–2005', *The Times*, 1 December 2005. He was originally intended to move in the normal course of events to one of the operational Directorships but was asked to forego this in order to cope with the continued threat of union problems.

20 Harry Burke and Able Archer

In an earlier chapter I described the massive, multinational, near real-time coverage of Soviet military activity as a defining characteristic of the intelligence war.[1] NATO's credible military posture came to depend on warning of Soviet attack, and American influence made this surveillance a prime Sigint objective. The cost of this arrangement was essentially doing things the American way, harnessing technology for twenty-four-hour operations. At GCHQ we contributed to this transatlantic effort while also seeking to present objective British assessment in Whitehall. We ran an efficient production machine to meet the needs of our customers quickly, but did I sufficiently encourage the kind of analytical breakthroughs which allowed for deeper knowledge of the Soviet target? At times I worried about this balance, but I am reassured by the memory of Harry Burke, my deputy at GCHQ who led the British reassessment of the 1983 Able Archer crisis. My recollection of this episode has been briefly summarised by Len Scott,[2] but I offer an expanded account here to underline the importance of recruiting and deploying the right people in intelligence analysis.

It was perhaps remarkable that the leaders of GCHQ – a secret organisation, its role undeclared until 1983 – took pride in cultivating the reputation of a well-managed government department, yet this was the case throughout my career. Wartime Bletchley had been the model when GCHQ's post-war structure was drawn up in 1945, and officials sought to recruit successors to the mathematicians who achieved codebreaking triumphs.[3] Among the new recruits, it was hoped that at least some would combine a personal flair for cryptanalysis with the ability to provide technical leadership for the organisation. Bletchley's output of decrypted Enigma messages had risen from 39,000 monthly at the beginning of 1943 to 90,000 from the end of that year; this was mass intelligence production, on a scale that needed high-quality management to direct it to best effect.[4] The initial position in 1945 was that GCHQ would have a single senior graduate entry, but GCHQ soon took the view that more people were needed than they were getting for a general managerial role. Whitehall was persuaded to move to separate lines of entry for specialists and generalists. I believe this initiative came from the Director-designate, (Sir) Eric Jones, who had run a textile firm before successfully organising and managing a key area of intelligence production at Bletchley; far from the model of top civil servants or mathematicians.[5]

While the distinction between generalists and specialists softened over the decades, Jones's belief in management was a lasting influence on GCHQ. This was reflected in the constant pull on resources between the organisation's dual roles of research and production machine. For instance, while running GCHQ's worldwide effort against Soviet and Warsaw Pact targets in the 1970s–1980s I encountered this managerial challenge in trying to decide where to deploy our most able people. Western governments required skilled analysis of Soviet capabilities to assess the military threat, and yet there was also the need to follow and, where possible, predict Soviet military action on something close to a twenty-four-hour basis. Sigint could beef up its contribution to current assessments of Soviet behaviour, but there was always the risk of becoming too absorbed in the transatlantic effort. Alternatively, we could deploy people on new lines of research for a better understanding of our target, although these might not turn out to be profitable.

The contribution of Harry Burke to Western understanding of Soviet attitudes in the early 1980s was an example of the benefits that could be gained from in-depth research. Harry's family – then Burkovitch – had come to Britain before the war as Jewish émigrés from what was then Yugoslavia. He went to a good London school, served in the RAF at the end of the war, and read Serbo-Croat and Russian at Cambridge. He joined GCHQ as an analyst in the early 1950s and had a successful career, mainly though not entirely on Soviet targets. He had considerable presence, in a British public school-cum-Oxbridge style, allied with a determined and disputatious temperament; he was not easily put down. He had worked for me in the past, and I eventually managed to get him made my deputy in GCHQ, effectively as the chief Soviet analyst. He was a great strength in the period 1980–1, observing the Soviet and Warsaw Pact preparations for the military move against Poland that was eventually abandoned in favour of Polish martial law.[6]

In 1982 Harry was transferred to London to the JIC's Assessments Staff, and it was in this role that he in a sense 'discovered' the whole Able Archer crisis in 1983. I had moved to do something else by then, so my knowledge of this period is second-hand, based entirely on conversations with Harry before he died. In 1982 the JIC had considered the Nicoll Report, with its criticisms of the Committee's earlier warning record, plus the lessons of the Falklands invasion.[7] Sir Antony Duff, at various times JIC Chairman and Intelligence Coordinator and at one time both, reacted by getting Harry appointed to the Assessments Staff, with a special responsibility for warning. After NATO's Able Archer exercise in November 1983, it was Harry who detected the signs of military alerts on the Soviet side. This finding, along with other intelligence, led the JIC eventually to report that there had been defensive Soviet fears of an American strike under the cover of a military exercise. Over time this view helped to modify British and American policy at the highest level, recognising the extent of Soviet insecurity.[8]

The Soviet response to Able Archer has been explored by historians, who tend to focus on the KGB material supplied by Oleg Gordievsky for British assessment.[9] While Harry was aware of Gordievsky's reports on the KGB alert, the moving force as he explained it to me was the unusual Soviet military communications described in some of the Sigint reports during the exercise,[10] though apparently these had not been highlighted by the Sigint agencies. He put them together with Gordievsky's intelligence to argue for the evidence of genuine Soviet fears of Able Archer. He then fought single-handed in the winter of 1983–4 against almost everyone to get this view set out as a JIC report. If my memory is correct Harry also told me that the JIC also contributed to another more general paper on Soviet fears of the West, and that these two papers went on to Washington. On his final visit to Washington in 1990 Harry was invited to discuss Able Archer with the President's Foreign Intelligence Advisory Board (PFIAB) in connection with the Board's re-examination of the incident, and its eventual conclusion that intelligence's previous confidence about the Soviet posture had been misplaced.[11]

I have only limited evidence for this story. Some years later, in the early 2000s, the then GCHQ historian showed me a redacted copy of the JIC's Able Archer report. My recollection now is that it was much more tentative than I expected from Harry's explanation; but the weakness was actually consistent with his account of the scepticism within the Committee, presumably leading to its tentative wording about the Soviet alert. I have since tried to get a sight of this under the Freedom of Information Act but failed. The few Whitehall records which have been released point to several re-drafts of the first JIC report, and a renewed interest in confidence-building diplomacy prompted by its findings.[12] Without offering more detail, Professor Ferris's history also notes in passing that 'GCHQ's analysis of Soviet reactions to NATO's Able Archer exercise of 1983 drove Britain's road out of the Cold War'.[13]

The most surprising thing about this episode was that Harry, usually the arch-hawk in all his Soviet judgements, was arguing for Soviet fears. There are morals here for the staffing of top-level assessment units. With his personal background it is not surprising that Harry was always suspicious of Soviet motives. In the JIC's reaction to Gorbachev he was a strong supporter of the Chairman, Sir Percy Cradock, in his scepticism about changes in Soviet policy and objectives.[14] Harry's analysis of Able Archer was thus a striking example of professional conscience overriding policy preconceptions. Its impact was all the more significant because UK analysis of the Soviet Union had got into something of a rut at the time. The JIC machinery had only one long-term Soviet expert,[15] and it may have been too preoccupied with the Soviet position in Afghanistan and Poland. It is surprising that Gordievsky's evidence of RYaN (the recently instituted alert system), plus the Soviet speeches from 1981 onwards, did not lead to an earlier assessment of Soviet fears. Another likely weakness was that UK assessors were probably not aware of the full extent of US confrontation and provocation to the Soviet Union in Reagan's first administration.[16] In hindsight, it is not surprising that the Soviet leaders felt threatened.

Until all the evidence is declassified historians cannot judge the seriousness of the Able Archer crisis.[17] Robert Gates, then Deputy Director for Intelligence in the CIA, lists an impressive number of military actions by the Warsaw Pact;[18] but in reviewing Cold War crises there is always a risk of sweeping quite unconnected activities into the military picture. On the other hand, the patterns of warning indicators for Soviet military activity could have a patchiness about them. I recall a complete stand-down in Soviet flying in August 1969 that was part of genuine preparations for military action against China, though no other valid indicators were then detected. Perhaps the Soviet military system was less closely orchestrated than we sometimes think; or maybe our coverage of Soviet indicators was less complete than we thought.[19]

This brings me back to the challenge of managing Sigint resources and intelligence expertise. Harry's understanding of the Able Archer crisis was a singular achievement by an intelligence professional discerning Soviet policy thinking at the height of East–West tension in the early 1980s, which has mostly gone unnoticed in Cold War histories. But this individual contribution relied on the wider surveillance of Soviet military behaviour that provided Western leaders with valuable reassurance they were not about to fall victim to a surprise attack. Both intelligence tasks needed constant fine-tuning against a large and complex target. Defining and recruiting the right people like Harry for the appropriate levels, and judging how they should focus their careers, was an essential part of our business. It is well worth the historian's attention.

Notes

1. Chapter 7 in this collection, 'The Intelligence War: Reflections on Sigint'.
2. Scott, L., 'Intelligence and the Risk of Nuclear War: Able Archer-83 Revisited', in M. Herman and G. Hughes (eds), *Intelligence in the Cold War: What Difference Did It Make?* (Abingdon and New York: Routledge, 2013), pp. 18–19.
3. Chapter 16 in this collection, 'Recruitment in 1945 and "Peculiar Personal Characteristics"'.

4. Hinsley, F. H. and A. Stripp, *Codebreakers: The Inside Story of Bletchley Park* (Oxford: Oxford University Press, 1993), p. 144.

5. Ferris, J., *Behind the Enigma: The Authorised History of GCHQ, Britain's Secret Cyber-Intelligence Agency* (London: Bloomsbury, 2020), pp. 286–8.

6. Ibid., pp. 548–9.

7. Goodman, M., 'The Dog That Didn't Bark: The Joint Intelligence Committee and Warning of Aggression', *Cold War History*, 7, no. 4, 2007: 529–51.

8. For some relevant US intelligence files see 'The 1983 War Scare: The "Last Paroxysm" of the Cold War, Part 3', National Security Archive Electronic Briefing Book No. 428, May 2013.

9. Miles, S., 'The War Scare That Wasn't: Able Archer 83 and the Myths of the Second Cold War', *Journal of Cold War Studies*, 22, no. 3, 2020: 86–118.

10. Some of the unusual Soviet activities during the exercise, subsequently declassified by US authorities, are summarised in Barrass, G., 'Able Archer 83: What Were the Soviets Thinking?', *Survival*, 58, no. 6, 2016: 19–20.

11. President's Foreign Intelligence Advisory Board (PFIAB), 'The Soviet "War Scare"', 15 February 1990. This report was declassified in 2015 and is available at the National Security Archive at GWU. Accessed on 12 April 2020 at: https://nsarchive2.gwu.edu/nukevault/ebb533-The-Able-Archer-War-Scare-Declassified-PFIAB-Report-Released/2012-0238-MR.pdf

12. Ten files were obtained by Peter Burt of the Nuclear Information Service and are available at the National Security Archive at GWU. See the minutes regarding 'Soviet Concern about a Surprise Attack' dated 10 April 1984 and 4 May 1984. Accessed on 12 April 2020 at: https://unredacted.com/2013/11/04/british-documents-confirm-uk-alerted-us-to-danger-of-able-archer-83/

13. Ferris, *Behind the Enigma*, p. 321.

14. Urban, M., *UK Eyes Alpha: The Inside Story of British Intelligence* (London: Faber and Faber, 1996), p. 30.

15. Malcolm Mackintosh who was in post from the creation of the Assessments Staff until his retirement in 1987 but became much involved in the support of Britain's diplomatic position on the USSR in NATO and other fora.

16. This was also a challenge for the US analysts who drafted the National Intelligence Council Estimate 'Recent Soviet Military-Political Activities' in May 1984. According to Fischer, '[t]he principal drafter knew

that the Pentagon had engaged in some unusual activities aimed at impressing the Soviets with US military prowess but little more. Those activities were highly classified and in some cases were conducted on the basis of oral, not written, authorization from the White House.' See Fischer, B., 'Anglo-American Intelligence and the Soviet War Scare: The Untold Story', *Intelligence and National Security*, 27, no. 1, 2012: 88.

17. For a recent overview of the scholarship see Scott, L., 'November 1983: The Most Dangerous Moment of the Cold War?', *Intelligence and National Security*, 35, no. 1, 2020: 131–48.

18. Gates, R., *From the Shadows: The Ultimate Insider's Story of Five Presidents and How They Won the Cold War* (New York: Simon and Schuster, 1996), pp. 270–3.

19. This concern was also raised by the PFIAB report; see PFIAB, 'Soviet "War Scare"', p. 76.

21 A Special London Contribution[1]

[1998]

I have argued in this collection that when Britain established the post-war intelligence machine in 1945 it under-invested in the professional skills of analysis, assessment and reporting. This is the business of assembling and examining information as well as conveying conclusions, if necessary mixed with persuasion; most of all, it means judging likely outcomes in difficult situations. The post-war Joint Intelligence Bureau (JIB) met part of this requirement, but it was explicitly created to meet the military needs for intelligence in economic, geographic and other supporting fields. JIB and its successor the Defence Intelligence Staff (DIS)[2] only offered limited careers to attract the potential 'intelligence professionals' who were then assumed to be available for the new Assessments Staff when it was created in 1968.

This criticism may not do full justice to the solid contributions by retired service officers in the DIS throughout the Cold War, who faced a range of complex questions about a secretive target.[3] Nevertheless the relative weakness in defence and military assessment remains my considered criticism, if only because of the exceptional impression left by the more capable officers provided by the Ministry of Defence (MoD) for intelligence duties. I revive here an older account of a British naval officer who made an outstanding personal contribution to assessment as head of the DIS's naval section. This is quite the reverse of the general DIS style I have depicted and is a reminder that personal impact on the quality of intelligence was certainly possible within the organisation; just rarely so.

The officer was Michael (Mike) MccGwire,[4] who became a friend while serving at GCHQ after I joined the organisation in 1952. He was born in India in 1924, and after the family moved to Britain he was educated at Dartmouth and had a war at sea from 1942 onwards. He continued with normal naval appointments after the war but these included learning Russian at Cambridge and studying Soviet naval building programmes at GCHQ in 1952–4. (He said in later life that his time in GCHQ introduced him to the standard of rigorous scholarship.) He became Assistant Naval Attaché in Moscow for two years from mid-1956, and after a tour with NATO and other appointments he moved to Whitehall in the naval rank of commander to run the DIS's Russian naval section from 1965 to 1967. At the end of this appointment, despite the award of an OBE and the prospect of further promotion, he stuck to his intention of retiring from the Navy to take a degree and pursue a different career.

The DIS section under MccGwire's leadership was the authority for information and operational assessment about the Soviet Navy, and this in turn was an important part of the lens through which the West saw the Soviet Union. It was fed by massive data flows from the various kinds of covert collection activity, particularly from American sources, and was the thinking body which transmuted this information into usable intelligence. Few naval officers at that time sought jobs in the DIS since they did nothing for promotion, so there had been a regular pattern of naval officers learning intelligence as they went along, with no previous experience to guide them.

MccGwire was the first holder of this appointment to bring anything like his experience of the Soviet Union, including proficiency in the Russian language. He joined knowing the subject from his time at GCHQ and in Moscow, and knowing what he planned to do about it. In his two years there he had an impact on the way the intelligence-led naval lens was focused and how the Soviet Navy was presented in assessment. Partly this was due to his personal leadership, which was long remembered by colleagues; as when all the officers in his section 'volunteered' to join him in working nights as well as days to bring the essential index properly up to date. His was an inspirational style of management, of which I had a foretaste at GCHQ where he captained the office rugby team and raised it from the disorder of moving from London to become an efficient local side. Professionally, his personal qualities gave him a wide range of NATO intelligence contacts, particularly in North America. His impact in these years on the international conference machinery on Soviet naval power was also a sign of the charisma and influence that marked his later academic life.[5]

This style served a method and a cause. For some years the nature of the Soviet military threat was felt to be well established, and naval intelligence had coasted along, keeping track of Soviet numbers, equipment and tactics and supplying naval commanders with other information they would need for a potential war. By the mid-1960s US satellites were also beginning to provide detailed photographs of Soviet vessels and equipment, and NATO-wide tracking systems gave a reasonably good account of their movements at sea. Threats to the West's Atlantic communications and aims of worldwide politico-military 'power projection' were assumed to be the Soviet naval aims. Details of naval construction and maritime research were accepted without much curiosity about the difference from Western equivalents and explanations that 'the Russians do things differently'. To draw on an academic debate about historical writing, naval intelligence (like much other military assessment) was like old-fashioned 'scissors-and-paste' history, fitting incoming evidence uncritically into an established conceptual framework.[6]

MccGwire approached the job with a conviction that the available data could answer more searching questions about what the Soviet Navy was designed for. A prerequisite was the reorganisation of data handling and indexing described above. Also important was his use of those Soviet military books and journals which were officially produced but managed to find their way into Western hands and appeared as open sources.[7] Although heavily censored these presented serious discussions of doctrine and issues.[8] The in-depth study of this material in Britain began in the middle of the Cold War at the Soviet Studies Research Centre which pioneered this open source analysis in old huts at Sandhurst, financed by the Army Directorate of Training and Doctrine. This centre would go on to produce work of the highest class, particularly on issues of army interest,[9] but when MccGwire was at DIS this exploitation was still in its early stages, and he was virtually on his own in studying the Soviet and Warsaw Pact naval periodicals in the UK, though not in the US where the CIA consulted these sources (in addition to a classified, top-level Soviet military journal acquired by the SIS/CIA agent Oleg Penkovsky in the early 1960s).[10] Using open sources alongside secret material is standard practice for assessment today, but it was an important departure for naval intelligence under MccGwire.

The result was a two-year crusade at the DIS, of which one member of the staff concluded, 'It is my sincere belief that he has succeeded in contributing something tangible to the security of the country and to the stability of the world in a way that is not given to many of us to do.'[11] Drawing on all the intelligence at its disposal, MccGwire's section first tested the conceptual framework of naval assessment and began to rebuild some of its guiding assumptions. An early influence on his thinking had been information from Yugoslav delegates at the British naval staff college in 1959 that Soviet staff exercises at the Frunze Military Academy in 1945–8 were focused on defending their homeland against a Western, Normandy-type assault. With this in mind, he worked from Soviet naval requirements to explore the wider assumptions, interests and intentions at play in Soviet policy. Over time his effect was to get the official British estimates rewritten, with a new picture of Soviet objectives, in which naval expansion was seen as a move forward in strategic defence, supporting the traditional naval mission of defending the homeland against Western attacks from the sea. The seemingly threatening presence of Soviet ships in the Eastern Mediterranean and South Norwegian Sea, for example, were interpreted as a peacetime counter to the capability of US carriers and submarines to launch nuclear strikes against the Soviet industrial heartland.

This had some long-lasting effects on British naval intelligence. Late in my career it seemed to me that in its research of Soviet thinking the naval part of DIS incidentally still had one of the best databases to draw on. But British policy-makers concerned with the size of the Navy never completely accepted MccGwire's conclusions. By 1970 these assessments sat uncomfortably with a US Navy that faced budget cuts in the wake of Vietnam. Both the British and US naval lobbies had a strong interest in fostering the image of a Soviet fleet bent on worldwide power projection and challenging Western naval supremacy. Three years after he left the DIS the British naval hierarchy issued what amounted to an anathema against the 'MccGwire thesis'. Nevertheless, his reappraisal had opened up threat interpretations for debate. During the Middle East wars of 1967 and 1973 there was probably less Anglo-American anxiety about the Soviet naval presence in the Mediterranean – 'marking' the US Sixth Fleet and its part in plans for an American strike on the Soviet Union – than if it had been accepted as evidence of Soviet ambitions to take over Egypt.

MccGwire's work in the 1960s was also the foundation for his own later contribution as an academic in understanding the subsequent Soviet naval role of defending the northern waters as 'bastions' – the description he coined – for their ballistic missile submarines. This in turn led to later work on Soviet military power as a whole. I remember that for me at GCHQ his early book drafts in the 1980s on this subject convinced me for the first time that intelligence might fit into a more complex Soviet objective than just an 'inexorable' pursuit of military superiority. For all this, MccGwire's naval role in 1965–7 had been seminal.

As with much else in Cold War intelligence, it is still too early to know how far the Soviet archives will confirm MccGwire's interpretation of Soviet capabilities and doctrine. A recent history of British naval intelligence notes a subsequent evolution in American thinking at odds with the British position of the post-MccGwire years. By the early 1980s US intelligence assessed that the wartime Soviet navy would be largely occupied with defensive operations closer to home waters instead of threatening NATO supply lines in the Atlantic, apparently reflecting new intelligence partly from American tapping of Soviet undersea cables.[12] This revised assessment might be taken as a vindication for MccGwire, or it could be that his views were not justified by the information available at the time, however prescient they might later seem. Whatever the final judgement, MccGwire's contribution at DIS does not depend on his assessments being uniformly right. British defence intelligence on the USSR was not on the whole staffed by ideologues;

nevertheless, it was wedded to a set, two-dimensional view of the target that subconsciously underwrote the bipolar world of the Cold War. MccGwire's work thus set an early precedent for digging deeper and assessing the place of fear alongside ambition in Soviet policy, even if his conclusions are still disputed.

Are there lessons for historians in this example? It is a reminder of the particular problems of military customers and their receptivity to intelligence.[13] Writing on the British Joint Intelligence Staff in the Second World War, Donald McLachlan recorded that it:

> set out consistently and stubbornly to see the various problems put before it exclusively from the enemy's point of view ... The value of this way of looking at the facts and prospects of war was considerable; not so much for its positive grasp of the enemy point of view – though this was the main business of intelligence – as for its critical influence on the concourse of facts, ideas, political and personal influences pressing on the conduct of the war in London and Washington. 'But this is how the enemy may, or must, see it; these are his resources, his positions, the distances he has to cover, the principles of strategy he has so far followed. He is probably capable of this but he is certainly not capable of that'; this kind of staunch reminder, from a small body of men who gradually achieved a collective intellectual integrity which no amount of ministerial cajolery could shake, was salutary.[14]

In my experience, Mike MccGwire had a rare impetus among staff officers of the Cold War DIS to apply these principles to defence intelligence in peacetime. Taking evidence in context, with sensitivity to potential inferences and an empathy with the target, were hallmarks of the intelligence professionalism he practised. Though now distant in time, they are still an example of the standard which should be developed across the British assessment system as a whole, not just among a few long-term civilian experts. I have been sceptical of the MoD's ability to get inside the head of an adversary when 'threat assessments' are the principal weapon in its fight with Treasuries. As MccGwire showed, a professional defence intelligence effort can contribute to a safer world, but this is dependent on attracting enough people of vision and stature into the process.

Notes

1. Revised version of the chapter extract 'Naval Intelligence' published in Booth, K., 'A Cold War Life, and Beyond', in K. Booth (ed.), *Statecraft and Security: The Cold War and Beyond* (Cambridge: Cambridge University Press, 1998), pp. 93–8. Copyright © 1998, Cambridge University Press. Reproduced with permission of Cambridge University Press through PLSclear.

2. Davies, P., 'Estimating Soviet Power: The Creation of Britain's Defence Intelligence Staff 1960–65', in M. Herman and G. Hughes (eds), *Intelligence in the Cold War: What Difference Did it Make?* (Abingdon and New York: Routledge, 2013), pp. 64–87.

3. For an overview of Cold War intelligence from a DIS insider's perspective see Morrison, J., 'Intelligence in the Cold War', *Cold War History*, 14, no. 4, 2014: 575–91. For a pen-portrait of a desk-level analyst on whose reliability the JIC depended see Herman, M., *Intelligence Power in Peace and War* (Cambridge: Cambridge University Press/RIIA, 1996), pp. 249–50.

4. Michael Kane MccGwire, 1924–2016. Dalhousie University, Professor 1970–9; Brookings Institution, Senior Fellow 1979–90; Cambridge University, Visiting Professor 1990–3.

5. His two principal publications on the Soviet Union were *Military Objectives in Soviet Foreign Policy* (Washington: Brookings Institution Press, 1987) and *Perestroika and Soviet Military Policy* (Washington: Brookings Institution Press, 1991). A discussion of MccGwire's research and impact can be found in his obituary by Professor Ken Booth accessed on 22 July 2020 at: https://www.aber.ac.uk/en/development/alumni/ obituaries/obituary-profiles/michael-mccgwire/

6. For a readable introduction to issues of historical objectivity, see Collingwood, R. G., *An Autobiography* (London: Oxford University Press), pp. 77–8.

7. For an account of the periodicals in the late 1970s, and a cross-section of their contents, see Erickson, J., 'The Soviet Military Press 1978', *Strategic Review*, 7, 1979: 83–96. The value of this 'open' material for assessment was one of the subjects discussed in my first publication after retirement from GCHQ; see Herman, M., 'Reflections on the Study of Soviet Military Literature', *RUSI Journal*, 133, no. 2, 1988: 79–84.

8. In MccGwire's words, '[d]espite being a partly closed society, the Soviet Union produces a vast amount of evidence and is unusual

in the way it publicly articulates ideology, doctrine and plans'. See MccGwire, *Military Objectives in Soviet Foreign Policy*, p. 1.

9. For example Sherr, J., *NATO's Emerging Technology Initiatives and New Operational Concepts: The Assessment of the Soviet Press* (Camberley: Soviet Studies Research Centre, 1987).

10. *Soviet Navy: Intelligence and Analysis during the Cold War* (CIA-US Navy Booklet, 2017), pp. 14–16.

11. Private communication (July 1967).

12. Boyd, A., *British Naval Intelligence through the Twentieth Century* (Barnsley: Seaforth Publishing, 2020), pp. 643–6.

13. Rietjens, S., 'Intelligence in Defence Organizations: A Tour de Force', *Intelligence and National Security*, 35, no. 5, 2020: 719–20.

14. McLachlan, D., *Room 39: Naval Intelligence in Action 1939–45* (London: Weidenfeld and Nicolson, 1968), pp. 241, 251.

Index

CPSIA information can be obtained
at www.ICGtesting.com
Printed in the USA
BVHW011723180422
634623BV00002B/28